Talking to Terrorists

How to End Armed Conflicts

JONATHAN POWELL

THE BODLEY HEAD
LONDON

Published by The Bodley Head 2014

2 4 6 8 10 9 7 5 3 1

First published in Great Britain in 2014 by
The Bodley Head
20 Vauxhall Bridge Road,
London SW1V 2SA

www.bodleyhead.co.uk
www.vintage-books.co.uk

A Penguin Random House Company

Penguin
Random House
UK

global.penguinrandomhouse.com
A CIP catalogue record for this book
is available from the British Library

ISBN 9781847922298 (Hardback)
ISBN 9781847922304 (Trade Paperback)

Penguin Random House supports the Forest Stewardship Council®
(FSC®), the leading international forest-certification organisation. Our books
carrying the FSC label are printed on FSC®-certified paper. FSC is the only
forest-certification scheme supported by the leading environmental organisations,
including Greenpeace. Our paper procurement policy can be found at
www.randomhouse.co.uk/environment

MIX
Paper from
responsible sources
FSC® C016897

Typeset in Sabon LT Std by Palimpsest Book Production Limited,
Falkirk, Stirlingshire
Printed and bound in Great Britain by
Clays Ltd, St Ives plc

To all the victims of terrorism, in the hope there will be fewer of them in the future if we learn the lessons of the past

Contents

INTRODUCTION

Peace hath her victories
No less renown'd than war.
  John Milton, Sonnet XVI, 'To the Lord General Cromwell'

'All terrorists, at the invitation of the government, end up with drinks in the Dorchester,' said Hugh Gaitskell, the former leader of the Labour Party. What he meant was that governments of all political colours and in all countries repeatedly say they will never talk to terrorist groups and yet they nearly always do so eventually, and in the end usually treat their leaders as statesmen. The British government called Menachem Begin a terrorist and tried to kill him, they described Jomo Kenyatta as a terrorist and imprisoned him, and they labelled Archbishop Makarios a terrorist and exiled him to the Seychelles – and yet later welcomed all three to London as distinguished leaders of their countries.

From 1997 to 2007 I was the chief British negotiator on Northern Ireland. On the basis of that experience, when I left Downing Street in 2007 I proposed publicly that we should talk to the Taliban, to Hamas, and even to al-Qaeda. A Foreign Office spokesman said: 'It is inconceivable that Her Majesty's Government would ever seek to reach a mutually acceptable accommodation with a terrorist organisation like al-Qaeda.' Only a few years later, NATO countries are now talking to the Taliban, and the US and Israel have talked to Hamas, at least indirectly. And in her excellent 2011 Reith Lectures, Eliza

Manningham-Buller, the former head of MI5, called on governments to talk to al-Qaeda.

I don't mind the hypocrisy of governments on the subject –
that is part and parcel of politics – but I do mind the fact that
they never seem to learn from past experiences, often with
devastating consequences. Each time we meet a new terrorist
group we start again from scratch, partly because governments
change so regularly while the leaders of the terrorist groups
tend to stay in place far longer. Gerry Adams and Martin
McGuinness have seen eight British prime ministers come and
go while they have been in the leadership of the Republican
movement. One of those involved in the disastrous 1998–2002
negotiations with the Colombian terrorist group FARC said
'One gets the impression sometimes that the guerrillas think
that every four years a new group is going to arrive [in govern-
ment], to try the same thing over again.'

As a result, when governments do engage with terrorists
they almost always leave it far too late. General David Petraeus
admits that in Iraq the US government delayed too long before
talking to those 'with American blood on their hands'. In the
case of the Taliban, despite a long mating ritual, a sustained
peace process with the US has still not begun, even though
NATO forces will leave Afghanistan in the course of 2014.
The process of engaging with these groups and winning their
trust takes a lot longer than people realise. They need time to
adjust to the outside world and grasp what might be a realistic
demand and what is not. When we do eventually engage, we
forget the techniques and skills we learned last time. Terje
Roed-Larsen, the Norwegian facilitator of the Israeli–Palestinian
talks in Oslo, says 'what is truly shocking to me is that it
seems as if every new set of negotiators . . . [is] trying to
reinvent the wheel once again as they make exactly the same
mistakes'. Even if individual governments do not stay in power
long enough to learn these lessons, surely we can do so
collectively.

By happenstance I have spent the last seventeen years of my

life talking to terrorists of different sorts. I have not always been in favour of such dialogue. The first time I met a terrorist, I did so reluctantly. My father had been hit by an IRA bullet in an ambush in 1940, and my eldest brother was on an IRA death list for eight years while he worked for Margaret Thatcher. When I met Gerry Adams and Martin McGuinness in 1997, I declined to shake their hands – a petty gesture I now regret, but interestingly one that recurs again and again in the stories in this book. Tony Blair was more sensible and shook hands normally as if he were meeting any other human being. Immediately after the meeting we went on a walkabout in a shopping centre in Protestant East Belfast. It started off calmly enough but after a few moments we were mobbed by a crowd of old ladies waving their fists and who then started throwing rubber gloves at Tony. He was puzzled and asked me what it was about, half wondering if it was a protest about washing-up. I had to explain they were suggesting he should have worn gloves if he was going to shake hands with murderers.

My experiences have, however, changed my mind and convinced me that talking is the right thing to do. A few days after the meeting I got a call from Martin McGuinness asking me to come and meet him in Derry, incognito. He asked me not to tell the 'securocrats' and to come alone. I flew to Aldegrove, took a taxi to Derry and stood on a street corner feeling mildly foolish. After ten minutes or so, two men with shaved heads approached me saying 'Martin sent us' and pushed me into the back of a taxi. They drove me round in circles for an hour until I was completely lost and then ejected me when we arrived in front of a neat modern house on a small estate. I knocked on the door and Martin McGuinness opened it on crutches, making a not very funny joke about kneecapping, the IRA's favoured method of punishment. I spent three hours with him in front of an open fire with tea and sandwiches left by the considerate owner of the house. We didn't make any breakthroughs, but it set a pattern and I spent a good part of the next ten years flying across the Irish Sea to meet Adams and McGuinness in safe houses in West Belfast, Derry and Dublin, going on to their turf rather than demanding they come to grand government buildings. These encounters weren't really dangerous. In fact the only time I was under any threat was once on the Falls Road, hanging around on the street waiting for a Sinn Féin office to open. Republican leaders worried we might become targets for dissident Republicans and made sure it didn't happen again. But it was the shared risks that helped establish a relationship of trust where progress could be made. Something that holds true of most of the stories in this book.

The Northern Ireland negotiations were the most frustrating and most difficult challenge I faced in my life, but also, at least in retrospect, my most important and most satisfying achievement. Since leaving government I have continued working to try to end conflicts between governments and armed groups, first with the Geneva-based Centre for Humanitarian Dialogue, also known as the Henry Dunant Centre (HDC), and later founding Inter Mediate, a London-based NGO which aims to open up contacts between governments and armed groups where they do not exist and, where possible, to turn those contacts and channels into negotiations.

My experience in Northern Ireland convinced me that no conflict – however bloody, ancient or difficult – is insoluble. With attention, patience and above all political leadership, they can be solved, even if previous attempts at making peace have failed repeatedly. In her Reith Lectures, Eliza Manningham-Buller said some of the lessons we learned from Northern Ireland 'are relevant to thinking about the very different threat from al-Qaeda. One is the belief that the divisions in Northern Ireland society, manifested in terrorism, could not be solved militarily. Nor could intelligence and police work, however successful in preventing attacks and informing government, resolve those divisions, although that work could buy time for a political process. Intelligence was critical in helping ministers manage that process, the aim of which was to reach long-term political resolutions with those who had prosecuted the terrorist campaign. These lessons apply elsewhere as well.' I am not suggesting that there is a Northern Ireland 'model' that can be deployed elsewhere unaltered – that would be ludicrous: each conflict has different causes and will have different solutions – but it would equally be nonsense to suggest that none of the lessons we learned in the negotiations in Northern Ireland, from our successes and our failures, could be applied elsewhere. If people are going to make mistakes negotiating with terrorists, they should at least make their own, new, mistakes rather than repeating those already made by others.

I was curious to know which of the lessons we learned in Northern Ireland had also applied in peacemaking efforts elsewhere in the world. I am a practitioner, not a theorist or academic, and while there are plenty of books on the theory of negotiation and even more on the theory of dealing with terrorists, there are precious few on the practice of negotiating with terrorists. This book is designed to fill that gap.

For obvious reasons I cannot write about live negotiations in which I am involved – if I did, no one would ever talk to me again. Instead, this book is based on the experiences of government figures, leaders of armed groups and intermediaries who have been involved in talks to end armed conflicts around the world over the last two decades or so. It tries to establish why some succeeded (including in El Salvador, South Africa, the Oslo talks on the Middle East, Mozambique, and Aceh in Indonesia), and why some have failed (including in Sri Lanka, Colombia and Angola), as well as looking at those that are somewhere in between (such as ETA in Spain and the Maoists in Nepal). All these experiences show that there is a remarkable pattern to what works and what does not.

Terrorism is not a new phenomenon, even if we treat it as such. Most histories of terrorism try to take the story back to the 'Sicarii' in first-century Judea, who used their small daggers or *sicae* to attack Romans, and 'the Assassins' in medieval Persia who murdered religious rivals in the certain knowledge they themselves would be killed. While it is true that political and religious violence is as old as man, it is stretching the meaning of the expression to suggest it goes back that far. The term 'Terror' in this context was first coined in the French Revolution, where it was used to describe the government's campaign to protect the revolution and had a thoroughly positive connotation for those using it (although Edmund Burke at the time attacked the Jacobins as 'Hell hounds called Terrorists'). Probably the first use of the term 'terrorist' was to describe the men who attacked Napoleon's coach on Christmas Eve 1800 in the 'Infernal Machine' plot (named after an earlier bomb attack in Flanders during the sixteenth-century revolt against the Spanish).

The first armed group that we might consider terrorists in our terms were the Fenians in the nineteenth century, who grew out of an ancient tradition of insurrection in Ireland. Their most ambitious attempted attack was in Chester in February 1867, where they planned to seize 30,000 rifles which were to be shipped to Holyhead by train and then on to Ireland. The attack was to be mounted by Irish American veterans of the Civil War, together with several hundred Irishmen from Liverpool. The plot was easily frustrated by the police who had penetrated the movement. The American veterans fled to a heroes' welcome in the US, while those captured in Britain were imprisoned. *The Times* thundered that '"Terrorism" must be repelled by harsh terms.' Friedrich Engels, whose wife was a Fenian, wrote perceptively that 'The only thing the Fenians lacked were martyrs. They have been provided with these.' By locking them up, treating them as political prisoners and hanging their leaders, the government gave them a cause.

There is something familiar about the Fenians' approach. Their objective was to spread fear and panic in order to sap the morale of the 'imperial enemy'. Because there was insufficient support for an uprising in Ireland itself, they had to resort to terrorism on the mainland led by an 'enlightened vanguard'. They brought in their weapons and bombs from

the US and set up assassination units to kill agents and inform-
ants. Their targets were familiar too, including government
buildings in Parliament Street, the gasworks in Glasgow and,
in 1883, the District Line in the first London Underground
bombing at the same station targeted by one of the 7/7 bombs
nearly 125 years later. Like later terrorists their methods were
driven in part by developing technology. In December 1867
they used gunpowder in a thirty-six-gallon beer cask to try to
blow down the walls of Clerkenwell prison to release their
comrades; but they had to relight the fuse three times and then
take the bomb home on a trolley when it didn't explode. They
came back the next day, and when it did finally go off, the
direction of the blast went the wrong way and destroyed a
series of tenements, killing civilians including a small child.

The arrival of nitroglycerine – dynamite – gave the Fenians
a great boost, just as the arrival of Semtex did to their successors, the Provisional IRA, a century later. It was small, safe and
could do great damage. They set up bomb factories and one of
their leaders, Jeremiah O'Donovan Rossa, became known as
'O'Dynamite' because of his repeated use of the explosive to
mount a mainland campaign in the 1880s. The Fenians, and
their successors, used dynamite in part for its psychological
impact so that the killings would not be interpreted as mere
ordinary murder. The Fenians disappeared when Parliament
started discussing the Home Rule Bill for Ireland in 1886, and
the issue at the heart of their campaign looked as if it would
be resolved politically; but the movement was reborn as the
Irish Republican Brotherhood a couple of decades later when
those hopes were frustrated by political impasse in Westminster.

Another early group we would recognise as terrorists were
the nineteenth-century anarchists and nihilists, who coined the
expression 'propaganda of the deed' which has been the inspir-
ation of all subsequent terrorists – to win attention for their
cause by acts of wanton violence. Louise Richardson, a leading
author on terrorism, says 'The whole point is for the psychological impact to be greater than the actual physical act.' The

first suicide bombing was carried out in March 1881 by a Russian nihilist who assassinated the tsar. An officer who survived the attack said 'Through the snow, debris, and blood you could see fragments of clothing, epaulets, sabres and bloody chunks of human flesh.' The violence of the nihilists and anarchists provoked harsh government repression, but this crackdown was exactly what the terrorists wanted. The anarchist in Joseph Conrad's *The Secret Agent* says: 'Nothing would please me more than to see Inspector Heat and his like take to shooting us down in broad daylight with the approval of the public. Half our battle would be won then; the disintegration of the old morality would have set in.'

The parallels with modern terrorism are striking: the nihilists fantasised about getting their hands on weapons of mass destruction so they could kill and maim ever larger groups of people; they used suicide bombers; they engaged in robberies to fund their activities; their threat appeared to be global rather than confined to one country. They even dug a tunnel from a cheese shop under a street in St Petersburg and filled it with explosives with the aim of killing the tsar when he drove by, just as ETA dug a tunnel under a road in Madrid and filled it with explosives to kill Franco's prime minister a century later.

Terrorist groups have always been keen to learn from each other. The Fenians studied the techniques of the nihilists, and the original IRA studied the Boers in South Africa. According to the historian Rory Miller, the Jewish terror groups Irgun and the Stern Gang in Palestine in the 1930s and 40s 'viewed the Irish precedent as an important historical model, not least because it provided evidence that it was possible to force the British to enter into negotiations with those responsible for violent insurrection'. Avraham Stern, the leader of the Stern Gang, adopted the name 'Yair', after the leader of the ancient Sicarii. Menachem Begin, the leader of the Irgun in the 1940s, studied both the IRA campaign of 1919–21 and the campaigns of the Russian anarchists. His memoir *The Revolt* was in turn found in an al-Qaeda training camp in Afghanistan. Louise Richardson quotes Osama Bin Laden as saying 'Happy is he who learns from others' mistakes.'

In modern times the expression 'terrorist' has been so over-used as to lose virtually all its meaning. The Nazis described partisan groups in Europe during the Second World War as terrorists. Bernard Ingham, Mrs Thatcher's spokesman, described the ANC as terrorists in 1987, according to Thabo Mbeki. In 2000 Nelson Mandela said on *Larry King Live*, 'I was called a terrorist yesterday, but when I came out of jail, many people embraced me, including my enemies.' Addressing the UN General Assembly in 1974, Yasser Arafat said 'The difference between the revolutionary and the terrorist lies in the reason for which each fights. For whoever stands by a just cause and fights for the freedom and liberation of his land from the invaders, the settlers and the colonialists, cannot possibly be called terrorist.'

The question of who is a terrorist and who is a freedom fighter has bothered commentators for decades, but the world can't agree on a definition of terrorism. The UN requires states to 'take the necessary steps to prevent the commission of terrorist acts' but there is no international consensus on what constitutes terrorism. Diplomats have been trying to draft a comprehensive Convention on Terrorism since 1996, without success. International jurisprudence has been no more successful in finding an agreed definition. Official definitions in Russia and China are very broad indeed and hard to distinguish from enemies of the state. President Assad's definition is certainly not the same as ours. The official British version has three parts: serious violence against a person or serious damage to property; designed to influence a government or an international organisation or to intimidate the public or a section of the public; with the aim of advancing a political, religious, racial or ideological cause. But it is not accepted by others and it is highly unlikely we will resolve the debate any time soon. Professor Lawrence Freedman rightly concludes that 'The question of how to define terrorism has become familiar to the point of tedium.'

Even if there were a commonly agreed definition, it still wouldn't make 'terrorist' a useful term to define a group. Terror is a tool used by governments to instil fear at home or support the enemies of their enemies abroad, and by insurgent and separatist groups to attract attention when they are ignored or see no peaceful political route to achieving their objectives, or to scare a government into giving in to the demands of a minority. Academics David Martin Jones and M. L. R. Smith say that 'For a strategic theorist the notion of terrorism does not exist as an independent phenomenon. It is an abstract noun. More precisely, it is merely a tactic – the creation of fear for political ends – that can be employed by any social actor, be it state or non-state, in any context, without any necessary moral value being involved.' Indeed the word 'terrorist' is usually deployed as a calculated pejorative term, a way of demonising the enemy. The main impact of labelling a group as 'terrorist' is simply to make it harder to talk to them. The Maoists in Nepal, for example, were added to the US list of terrorist organisations in 2003, making it impossible for any American organisation to engage with them. (It didn't, however, prevent them ending up in government in 2008.)

Sometimes the discussion gets side-tracked into the distinction between insurgents or guerrillas and terrorists. Bruce Hoffman of Georgetown University believes terrorism is 'often confused or equated with, or treated as synonymous with, guerrilla warfare' but there are 'fundamental differences between the two. "Guerrilla" . . . is taken to refer to a numerically larger group of armed individuals, who operate as a military unit, attack enemy military forces, and seize and hold territory . . . Terrorists, however, do not function in the open as armed units, generally do not attempt to seize or hold territory, deliberately avoid engaging military forces in combat and rarely exercise any direct control or sovereignty either over territory or population.' On the other hand, David Kilcullen, an Australian soldier and terrorism expert who advised General Petraeus, concludes

'Terrorism is a component in virtually all insurgencies, and insurgent objectives (that is, a desire to change the status quo through subversion and violence) lie behind almost all terrorism.' ISIS in Syria and Iraq, for example, is clearly a terrorist organisation but is also operating informed units and taking and holding territory as if it were a guerilla force.

Nonetheless, while the academic debate continues, the word 'terrorist' is in common currency and there is no point in pussy-footing around it. In this book when I talk about 'terrorists' I use the word to mean non-state armed groups that enjoy significant political support and which deliberately use the tactic of terror by attacking civilian as well as military targets to advance their political aims. Writing about it like this does not mean I excuse in any way the use of terrorism by any group. The acts of mass murder of innocent people that were carried out by many of the groups described here were horrific, and familiarity with them over time does not make them any more acceptable or justifiable than current attacks. As Rudy Giuliani, the ex-mayor of New York, puts it: 'Let those who say we must understand the reasons for terrorism explain those insane, maniacal reasons to the children who will grow up without fathers and mothers!'

The most familiar prism through which government officials look at the issue is counter-terrorism or counter-insurgency. Counter-insurgency is an old discipline. Colonel Sir Charles Callwell wrote the definitive book on the subject in 1896, *Small Wars: Their Principles and Practice*, drawing on nineteenth-century campaigns in India, Upper Burma, Afghanistan and South Africa. He says that unlike conventional warfare, these battles 'stand on a very different footing. They are necessarily internal not external campaigns. They involve struggles against guerrillas and banditti. The regular army has to cope not with determinate but with indeterminate forces. The crushing of a populace in arms and the stamping out of widespread dis-affection by military methods, is a harassing form of warfare even in a civilised country with a settled social system; in remote regions peopled by half-civilised races or wholly savage tribes, such campaigns are most difficult to bring to a satisfactory conclusion, and are always most trying to the troops.' This is true today, except that in a good part of the world crushing armed groups in this way is no longer acceptable within our norms of democracy and human rights.

Governments, like terrorists, have tried to learn from past experience in adapting their counter-terrorism or counter-insurgency strategies. The campaign in Malaya in the 1950s was regarded as a breakthrough by the British military. They had armed and trained the Malayan Communist Party to fight the Japanese, but after the war the Communists turned on the British. In 1948 a state of emergency was declared and at first the army struggled to cope with the threat, but under the leadership of Field Marshal Gerald Templer and General Harry Briggs, they realised the answer lay 'not in pouring more troops into the jungle but in the hearts and minds of the people'. They set about driving a wedge between insurgents and the broader population with the aim not of solving but of reducing violence. In this they were learning Chairman Mao's lesson, who wrote that 'The guerrilla fighter, like a fish out of water, gasps helplessly until he dies' if he is separated from the local population, the water they swim in. The British resettled rural inhabitants in new villages to keep them from infiltration by the guerrillas, and opted for intelligence-led rather than large-scale military operations against the guerrilla groups. The counter-insurgency strategy handbook Templer and Briggs wrote, *The Conduct of Anti-Terrorist Operations in Malaya*, is still drawn on by the British military.

The revision of the *US Army Marine Corps Manual on Counter-Insurgency*, or *COIN*, led by General Petraeus in 2006 followed this approach. It concludes that insurgencies cannot be defeated by military means alone and argues that, as in Malaya, the military needs to focus on removing the grievances that build support for the insurgents and splitting off individuals or groups through 'reconciliation' and 'rehabilitation'. Richardson writes that 'Successful counter-terrorism almost invariably requires a combination of coercive and conciliatory policies. It is imperative for success to ensure that these policies do not undermine one another by being used against the wrong audiences. Coercive policies should be restricted to the few actual perpetrators of the violence, while conciliatory policies ought to be focused on their potential recruits.'

While this is a useful advance, it is not enough. In my view there needs to be a third strand to *COIN* in addition to the security response and the 'hearts and minds' campaign, and that is talking to the armed groups. The argument of this book is that each time we meet a new terrorist group we say they are different and that we are never going to talk to them. But if they have significant political support, we end up doing so – usually too late. As a result a large number of people die unnecessarily and we forget how we went about it last time.

I am categorically not saying that security measures are unnecessary in tackling terrorism. Unless the position of the armed group is rendered uncomfortable there is no reason for them to talk, especially if they still think they can win. Equally, security measures are not enough by themselves. If there is only military pressure and no political way out other than surrender, the armed group will resist to the death. If you accept that you cannot kill them all – and that in attempting to do so you will create martyrs and more recruits for the cause – then, at some stage, you will have to talk, and however long you continue fighting you always arrive back, sooner or later, at that same point.

While I believe in talking to terrorists, I am an unlikely peacenik. I grew up in a military family and was involved in the decisions on all of Tony Blair's wars. I do not think that wars are always wrong. Sometimes they are necessary to stop a dictator or prevent massive human-rights abuses or to expel an invader. But I also observe that in the modern world civil wars are the greatest threat to humanitarian security. If you want to fight starvation, or mass rape or the spread of disease, or to help suffering children, whether child soldiers or the victims of war, then the most important thing you can do is to help stop armed conflict, which is why I have decided to dedicate the rest of my life to that aim. My NGO, Inter Mediate, aims to spread the lessons that have been learned in resolving other conflicts so that governments and armed groups don't make the same mistakes over and over again.

This book tries to draw some common lessons from failures and successes in negotiations around the world to end conflicts with armed groups in the last couple of decades, and then looks back at earlier experiences to see if the same lessons applied then too. For the leader of a government or an armed group, it is all too easy to focus exclusively on the all-consuming minutiae of your own conflict and to insist that it is special, uniquely difficult and no one else can understand it. If you are going to succeed, however, it is important to lift your head and look around at the lessons from the past and from conflicts elsewhere. If this book contributes in even a small way to people learning from previous experiences in talking to terrorists, and as a result lives are saved, I will be immeasurably satisfied.

Talking to terrorists will always be practically difficult and morally hazardous, but I firmly believe it is the right thing to do. President Franklin Roosevelt justified Allied relations with Stalin during the Second World War by reference to his favourite Balkan proverb: 'It is permitted you in times of grave danger to walk with the Devil until you have crossed the bridge.' The same is true of talking to terrorists.

CHAPTER ONE

Why We Must Talk to Terrorists

Let us never negotiate out of fear, but let us never fear to negotiate.

John F. Kennedy

In the aftermath of the 9/11 terrorist attacks, President George W. Bush said 'No nation can negotiate with terrorists, for there is no way to make peace with those whose only goal is death.' His vice president, Dick Cheney, put it more pithily, saying 'We don't negotiate with evil; we defeat it.' These few words capture the essence of the question. Is it moral to talk to terrorists? Is it effective to do so? And, in the end, is there any alternative?

Of course it is not just Bush and Cheney who have taken this uncompromising line. In 1901 Teddy Roosevelt called for a crusade to exterminate terrorism everywhere after President McKinley was assassinated by an anarchist. In 1985 President Reagan insisted 'America will never make concessions to terrorists. To do so would only invite more terrorism . . . Once we head down that path there would be no end to it, no end to the suffering of innocent people, no end to the bloody ransom all civilised nations must pay.' More recently President Obama's National Security Adviser, Susan Rice, said 'we don't negotiate with terrorists, that's the policy of the United States'. It is not just American presidents but French, Colombian, Sri Lankan, British, Spanish, Israeli, Turkish and pretty much all other world leaders who have repeated, time after time, that they will never negotiate with terrorists.

At an emotional level the refusal to have any dealings with people who are prepared to engage in barbarous acts is understandable. It seems obvious that the only answer is to respond with force and to suppress the perpetrators of terrorism. No politician hoping for re-election would ever contemplate proposing anything else. Michael Burleigh, the author of a racy history of terrorism, says 'The milieu of terrorists is invariably morally squalid, when it is not merely criminal . . . If you imagine that Osama Bin Laden is going to evolve into Nelson Mandela, you need a psychiatrist rather than a historian.' This emotional response extends elsewhere. The play *Talking to Terrorists* by Robin Soans, which suggests that countering terrorism through force alone will only lead to more violence in the future, was opening in London when the 7/7 Tube bombings occurred. The *Telegraph* theatre reviewer, Dominic Cavendish, wrote the day after, 'when the threat of a terrorist strike seems only a remote possibility, it's easy to admire . . . these two hours of theatre', but 'the implacable, hate-filled face of terrorism has announced its arrival on these shores again – and I don't think it's asking for a conversation'.

Former soldier James Wither sums up the moral arguments against engagement: 'Talking to terrorists represents a betrayal of fundamental values and principles as it appears to legitimise illegal violence and promote discourse with individuals who have rejected the rules and norms of international society'. American lawyer and controversialist Alan Dershowitz takes an even more uncompromising approach: 'Never negotiate. By listening to terrorists you are fulfilling their aims, and encouraging them . . . The reason terrorism works . . . is precisely because its perpetrators believe that by murdering innocent civilians they will succeed in attracting the attention of the world to their perceived grievances . . . We must commit ourselves never to try to understand or eliminate its alleged root causes, but rather to place it beyond the pale of dialogue and negotiation. Our message must be this: even if you have legitimate grievances, if you resort to terrorism as a means toward eliminating them we will simply not listen to you, we will not try to understand you, and we will never change any of our policies toward you. Instead, we will hunt you down and destroy your capacity to engage in terror.'

Such views are often based on a gut reaction to the horrors of terrorism. The American academic Audrey Cronin says the debate on talking to terrorists 'produces plenty of heat but scarce light, having more to do with the emotional aftermath of an attack' than the practical questions of what to do to prevent further attacks. But it is too easy to dismiss such responses as purely emotional. The arguments against talking to terrorists deserve to be considered one by one.

The first argument put forward is that talking to terrorists is to give in to blackmail and simply encourages others to take up arms to achieve their aims. Democratic governments cannot allow terrorism to be seen to work. The leading academic in the field of conflict resolution, William Zartman, summarises this argument: 'negotiation actually encourages terrorism. President Richard Nixon's statement on hostage negotiations that "saving one life endangers hundreds" can be expanded by orders of magnitude in regard to negotiations with political terrorist organisations. It is irresponsible to let terrorists shoot their way through civilian casualties into policy decisions; rewarding their blackmail only encourages others to do the same.' Politicians go as far as to suggest that talking to terrorists is tantamount to appeasement. Speaking to the Israeli Knesset in 2008, George W. Bush said: 'Some seem to believe we should negotiate with terrorists and radicals', yet 'We have heard this foolish delusion before. As Nazi tanks crossed into Poland in 1939 . . . [We] have an obligation to call this what it is – the false comfort of appeasement.'

This represents a complete misunderstanding of appeasement. The issue in 1938 was not that Neville Chamberlain went to Munich to talk to Hitler – talking was a sensible attempt to avoid another apocalyptic world war – but in thinking that Hitler could be bought off with a large chunk of Czechoslovakia.

The problem is not talking to terrorists, it is giving in to them. They are not the same thing. Talking would indeed be to reward blackmail if it consisted of conceding to all of the terrorists' demands, but no democratic government would survive if it were to do so. The British government talked to Irish Republicans but never gave in to their demand for a united Ireland at the barrel of a gun. Zartman concludes 'it is not the act of negotiating that encourages or discourages further terrorist blackmail; it is the terms of the negotiated agreement. If the terrorists win their goals in the negotiation process and give the state little or nothing beyond the end of conflict in exchange, others will indeed be encouraged to follow the same course.' Nick Burns, a former senior American diplomat, adds 'Talking to our adversaries is no one's idea of fun, and it is not a sure prescription for success in every crisis. But it is crude, simplistic and wrong to charge that negotiations reflect weakness or appeasement. More often than not, they are evidence of a strong and self-confident country.'

The next argument is that terrorists are psychopaths and talking to them is pointless as well as wrong. There are indeed psychopaths in the ranks of terrorist groups, but Louise Richardson says 'terrorists, by and large, are not insane at all. Their primary shared characteristic is their normalcy, in so far as we understand them. Psychological studies of terrorism are virtually unanimous on this point.' Marc Sageman, a psychiatrist, found little evidence of personal pathologies in the backgrounds of the 172 mujahedin he studied, and Martha Crenshaw of Stanford University states bluntly that 'the idea of terrorism as the product of mental disorder or psychopathy has been discredited'. Richardson sums it up: 'terrorists are neither crazy nor amoral but rather are rationally seeking to achieve a set of objectives'. Terrorist groups have their own rationality, just one that we don't always understand immediately. It takes time and effort to talk to them to try and understand what has driven them to take up arms and what they really want to achieve. It is impossible to untangle their rationale without talking to them.

Thirdly there is the argument that talking to terrorists is immoral and that by engaging with them we reward their behaviour. As they are both unrepresentative and illegitimate they should not succeed by breaking the rules of society. Zartman and his French colleague Guy Faure put forward the argument that 'On the moral level, the terrorists' choice of means – violence against civilians – makes engagement and negotiation unethical. The very act of dealing with terrorists, particularly given the status and equality that engagement and negotiation imply, tarnishes the state, since the state is supposed to represent the highest values of legality and legitimacy.' Yet we are ready to talk to governments that use violence, even horrific violence, against their own people, so it is perverse to suggest we should refuse to talk to non-state armed groups that do the same. Furthermore we would never in our daily lives, at least not amongst grown-ups, use talking to someone as a reward and refusing to talk to them as a punishment. As the Saudi foreign minister Saud Bin Faisal pointedly asked when making the case for engaging with Hamas, 'If we don't talk to them, how do we convince them they should change their attitudes towards peace?' In the play *Talking to Terrorists* the 'ex-Secretary of State' character based on Mo Mowlam says 'talking to terrorists is the only way to beat them . . . If you want to change their minds, you have to talk to them.' From a more theoretical point of view, Robert Mnookin, the head of the Program on Negotiation at Harvard, argues in his book *Bargaining with the Devil* that our ingrained biases often lead us to reject negotiation prematurely, and we should therefore establish a rebuttable presumption in favour of negotiating even with those who are evil.

The absolute moral arguments against talking to terrorists don't really stand up, and they certainly fall away in the face of the practical, if distasteful, need to talk to terrorists if we are to stop them killing. Even the toughest of American generals in the 'war on terror' accepts that we cannot kill all the terrorists, and that for each one we kill we probably create two more, so in the end we will have to talk to them and it is a question of when and how, not whether. General Petraeus recalls that central to the strategy in Iraq was that 'we would not be able to kill or capture our way out of the industrial-strength insurgency that was tearing apart the very fabric of Iraqi society'. A 'key element' of the strategy was an 'explicit decision to aggressively support reconciliation with Sunni insurgents who were willing to become part of the solution in Iraq rather than remain a continuing part of the problem – and, later, to do the same with Shia militia fighters'.

An unlikely ally for the moral case for talking to terrorists is Ami Ayalon, the former head of the Israeli internal security agency Shin Bet, who says 'anything you can do to shorten war is ethical'. The Israeli ex-foreign minister Abba Eban went further. He believed that negotiation is not an arbitrary option, but an unconditional duty: 'The issue is how to quench the fires, not to hold interminable debate about who kindled them . . . Negotiating with terrorists is not a question of forgiving or forgetting the past, but holding a pragmatic position about the future. It is an ethical perspective that is based on humanistic precepts that place the saving of lives and the cessation of bloodshed as the highest priority.'

This is not to say that it is morally comfortable talking to people who have committed unspeakable acts of murder. Governments walk a thin moral line when they engage with terrorist groups. When we in the British government engaged with Irish Republicans we were very conscious of this narrow ground. On the one hand we did not want to tip the IRA into another Canary Wharf bomb by mistake, as John Major had done; but nor did we want to find ourselves negotiating under the threat of violence and allowing ourselves to be influenced by that threat, which would have been both immoral and extremely bad practice. Governments need to be conscious of the moral peril they run in talking to terrorists, while recognising that doing so is often the only way to spare lives. Antonia Potter, a humanitarian expert, says that mediators 'must be willing to live with what might kindly be described as moral ambiguity. They must be prepared to talk to and even befriend those whose hands may be stained with blood.' Martti Ahtisaari, the former Finnish president and a successful mediator, said in his Nobel Peace Prize acceptance speech, 'I have made my career by talking to people that have at some point been branded as terrorists. For me, this is the only way to have a successful peace mediation process. Reaching a solution that ends a conflict means talking to all those who are parties to the conflict.'

Although many academics and diplomats concede that despite the moral hazards it can sometimes be acceptable to talk to terrorists, there is an increasing genre of academic and political writing which argues that doing so can be counter-productive or wrong in practical rather than moral terms. One of its proponents, Mitchell Reiss, a former Northern Ireland envoy for President George W. Bush, discovered to his cost how controversial even such a moderated approach can be. His book *Negotiating with Evil: When to Talk to Terrorists* was dragged into the presidential campaign in 2012. Reiss was a foreign-policy adviser to Mitt Romney and had argued in his book that although it was often a mistake to talk to terror-ists, in the case of the Taliban it might be worth considering. During the TV debates between the Republican candidates, one of Romney's rivals raised the issue and demanded to know if he agreed. Romney immediately distanced himself from both the argument and his adviser, and said no negotiations should take place with the Taliban while they were fighting American soldiers. Alan Dershowitz, who belongs to this school, believes that talking to terrorists is nearly always a bad idea, and should only be considered when the terrorists are on the verge of giving up, at which point the government might as well finish them off militarily rather than talking to them. He claims the West has built up terrorism, especially Palestinian terrorism, by pandering to it instead of defeating it. This is a variant of the 'one last heave' argument that was common during British decolonisation and is heard sometimes about Northern Ireland, in retrospect at least, running as follows: the terrorist group is deeply penetrated and on its last legs as a result of security force successes; if the politicians would just stand back and let the military, police and intelligence finish the job without their hands being tied behind their backs by political considerations like respect for human rights, the terrorist group would be finished off without any need to negotiate with them. The politicians who try to talk to the terrorists are, in the idiom of the COMINTERN, 'useful idiots' who, although well meaning, play into the hands of terrorists and rescue them from defeat.

The former conservative Spanish prime minister, José María Aznar, takes this line: 'My personal approach is that any policy is appeasement if it means negotiating'; the government should enter negotiations 'only if a terrorist group is in failure'. In 1996 he said that 'the policy of a frontal battle against terrorism that we are leading gives good results, and that there is no other way. My responsibility is to hit at ETA as hard as possible, and that is what I'll do . . . There is no negotiation possible between the government and ETA.' Aznar's security adviser, Javier Zarzalejos, argued that in 2004 'We were very close to putting an end to ETA.' In his view the socialist government of Prime Minister José Luis Zapatero that succeeded Aznar saved ETA from defeat by agreeing to talk to them. ETA was on the back foot, under pressure from the French and Spanish police and intelligence, successive leaderships had been arrested (three groups in one year), and they would have been wrapped up entirely if the police had been left to do their job. 'Zapatero restored ETA when they were down,' says Teo Uriarte, a Basque politician.

There is, however, precious little empirical evidence to support this 'one last heave' argument. In Northern Ireland it is true the IRA were heavily penetrated by British intelligence in the 1980s and 90s and this made it harder for them to launch successful attacks. It is also true that they were tired and were being driven to resort to increasingly desperate tactics. But, as the leaders of the British army and police conceded, they were not going to be defeated by military means alone. The same is true of ETA. The 'one last heave' approach is a delusion.

The ideological opposition to talking to terrorists runs deep. Neocons David Frum and Richard Perle write 'Terrorism remains the great evil of our time, and the war against this evil, our generation's great cause. We do not believe that Americans are fighting this evil to minimise it or manage it . . . There is no middle way for Americans: it is victory or holocaust.' Fellow ideologue Irving Kristol has criticised 'peace processes', whether in the Middle East or Northern Ireland, as '"doing something nice" without really doing anything'; it is 'hard to find a peace process that has accomplished anything, anywhere' based on the belief 'that if only we can get the parties in conflict to talk to one another, the level of "mistrust" will decline and mutual understanding increase, until at some point the conflict itself will subside'. Kristol argues that the Middle East peace process is an 'appeasement process, whereby Israel makes concessions and Arabs simply demand more'. The reason peace processes fail is because, in his view, 'no mediator can envisage an end situation satisfactory to both parties. An expert in conflict resolution can easily and always envisage a radical reformation of feelings, attitudes and sentiments in the populations involved, so that the problem, as it were, resolves itself. Unfortunately, he is not in possession of a therapy to create such a miracle.' These arguments, however, depend more on assertion than on reasoning.

Three academics, John Bew, Martyn Frampton and Inigo Gurruchaga, have tried to develop a more subtle revisionist case in their book on the Basque Country and Northern Ireland. They do not try to argue against ever negotiating with terrorists, as they take it as a given that governments have done so in the past and will do so again, but they think that talking in the wrong context can make matters worse. Furthermore they do not accept that negotiations were the primary factor in ending either the Northern Irish or Basque conflicts, but rather that military and intelligence successes made a defeat of the armed groups possible. Bew writes 'the assumption that "talking to terrorists" provided the key variable in the search for peace in Northern Ireland simplifies the history of the conflict there beyond recognition . . . First, the British state had tried to talk to the IRA at various intervals, starting as early as 1972. The offer of dialogue was on the table more than it was off it. At various points, this encouraged the terrorists that momentum was on their side and coincided with a surge in expectations and in violence.' He quotes former Irish prime minister Garret FitzGerald as saying that the government should only have talked to the IRA once it was 'prepared to consider throwing in the towel'.

Bew's co-author Inigo Gurruchaga argues that the killings of suspected ETA members in France by GAL, the Spanish government-sponsored death squad, altered the equation in the Basque conflict by persuading the French of the need for closer security co-operation with the Spanish. It may well be true that the fear of the Spaniards taking the law into their own hands influenced French policy, but it is a dangerous suggestion to argue that dirty wars can succeed in the long term, akin to believing Loyalist revenge killings of innocent Catholics in Northern Ireland helped persuade the IRA to end the conflict, rather than prolonging and complicating the violence (which they did). Gurruchaga goes on to suggest that it became 'possible to raise the prospect that ETA might actually be defeated by security measures alone'. This assertion illustrates the danger of elaborating theories on the basis of a snapshot of what is happening in a conflict at any given moment. When the book was published in 2009 it did indeed look as if the Spanish government had opted for a purely security approach but, unbeknownst to the author, secret discussions were going on that led ETA to announce that it was ending the armed struggle for good in 2011.

The trio conclude on the basis of their reading of these two conflicts that talking to terrorists is not always right: 'There is a crucial qualitative difference between talking to terrorists who are on the crest of a wave – in terms of propaganda, confidence and momentum – and talking to terrorists who have been made to realise – by hard power as well as soft power – that their aims are unattainable by violent means.' They are of course right to argue that hard power has an important role to play, but the notion that you should only talk to terrorists once they are losing assumes the terrorists share your perception that they are indeed on the back foot. And the trouble for the wider revisionist argument is that both the Northern Irish and the Basque conflicts were ended by peace processes, and there is absolutely no evidence that either group could have been wiped out by purely military and intelligence means. As Martin van Creveld argues in *The Transformation of War,* 'from the failure of the French in Algeria and Indochina, the British in India, Palestine, Kenya, Cyprus and Aden, the Soviets in Afghanistan, the Belgians in Congo, the Dutch in Indonesia, the Portuguese in Angola and Mozambique, and, not least, the Americans in Vietnam, conventional forces have been unable to wage asymmetrical "low intensity conflict" successfully against a technologically, financially and organizationally inferior opposition'. Even more pointedly Hugh Orde, the former chief constable in Northern Ireland who presided over the end of the Troubles, said there is 'No example that I know of, of terrorism being policed out' or fully defeated by physical force anywhere in the world. In Northern Ireland the state had had to bring the IRA to a place where they had to negotiate by policing and military pressure, but he believes we were never going to defeat the IRA by police, military or intelligence methods alone.

The revisionists put forward a series of practical arguments to suggest that talking to armed groups can, in certain cases and at certain times, be counterproductive. The first is that the offer of talks may make the terrorists believe that the government is weak and that if they escalate the violence they can succeed. Conservative Cabinet minister Willie Whitelaw's ill-fated 1972 meeting with the IRA in the Cheyne Walk home of the Northern Ireland minister, Paul Channon, is quoted as an example of this mistake, followed as it was by Bloody Friday, the IRA's most spectacular series of attacks with twenty-six bombs in Belfast in the space of just eighty minutes, killing eleven and injuring 130. While it was certainly a mistake to allow the meeting to become public, thus alarming the Unionists, it is not obvious that the meeting itself provoked the renewed IRA campaign by indicating weakness. In fact the attacks were probably triggered by Whitelaw's tough line in making it clear that the IRA's demands were completely unacceptable.

The next argument is that by talking to terrorists the government gives their organisations the legitimacy and publicity they crave. Zartman sets out the case: 'engagement and negotiation carry with them the recognition of the terrorist organization . . . [which] confers a degree of legitimacy and status, and an implication that the party speaks for the client population it claims to represent. Since terrorist groups, like any other rebel group, seek, above all, status and representational recognition, engagement carries them a long way toward their goal.' Daniel Byman of the Brookings Institution in Washington says 'Most terrorist groups crave legitimacy, as their very tactics rightly lead them to be shunned by the world and by many would-be constituents. Even if talks involve no concessions on the part of a government, by recognising terrorists as worthy interlocutors they have gained a victory with potential followers and other states.' The journalist Daud Khattak has looked at the impact of the Pakistani government's peace talks with the Pakistani Taliban and concludes that they have bolstered militants: 'From the Taliban's perspective, by levelling demands at the government and then entering into negotiations, it demonstrates to civilians in the tribal areas that militant leaders are strong enough to sit at the same table as the country's top military officials. This solidifies support for the Taliban among their followers, and suppresses the voices of resistance from civilian populations living under their authority.'

While it is certainly true that the craving for legitimacy and publicity draws armed groups into talks, it is not obvious that they benefit from that legitimacy once talks have broken down. When the Aceh talks broke down in 2002 the GAM rebels in Indonesia lost legitimacy, which they were desperate to recapture, and the FARC in Colombia were seen as even less legitimate after the charade of the talks in Caguán from 1998 to 2002 than they were before. The public and the international community judged them to have rejected a generous peace offer from the government and they were thereafter marginalised as 'narco-terrorists'. Bestowing temporary legitimacy on armed groups is not necessarily too high a price to pay for a peace process, and it usually proves to be entirely temporary if the talks break down, especially if the breakdown is seen to be the fault of the terrorists. What a government absolutely cannot do of course is recognise the armed group as the 'sole legitimate representative' of their people, which is often what they demand, because to do so is to deny a role to other groups who may well have more support in the community than the terrorists do.

Thirdly it is argued that by dealing only with the terrorists, the government undermines moderates, who also become nervous that the government is doing a secret deal behind their backs. This was the argument that Seamus Mallon, the leader of the moderate Catholic SDLP in Northern Ireland, used to make. He complained that the British government was talking to Sinn Féin rather than to them because the Republicans had guns. That was exactly right. If you want to stop violence then you have to talk to the men with guns, rather than only to those who act purely politically. It is not, however, correct to suggest that we sacrificed the moderates. Our first and preferred option had been to build from the centre with the moderate Ulster Unionists and the SDLP, but the SDLP made it clear to us they could not move forward without the Republicans and, since we had to have a Catholic partner, we were left with no option but to negotiate with Sinn Féin. In a sense the SDLP sacrificed their political future for the cause of peace. Avoiding undermining moderates should of course be an important aim for any negotiator when engaging with terrorists.

Fourthly it is suggested that talking to terrorists risks bringing down the government and even destabilising the political system. Michael Ignatieff, the former Canadian Liberal Party leader, says: 'There are good reasons never to negotiate with terrorist groups . . . terrorism is a form of politics that aims at the death of politics.' It is certainly true that by talking, a government opens itself up to political attack for jeopardising national security and sacrificing victims. If a leader appears desperate for peace at any price he can fatally undermine himself politically, as President Pastrana of Colombia did in the Caguán talks with the FARC. Once engaged in talks it is often difficult for the government to pull out without looking unreasonable, and they are generally condemned to continue until the armed group breaks off contact. Although there are clearly political risks it is, however, possible to guard against these dangers by proper preparation. If it is clear that the government is approaching the process seriously and for selfless motives, the public are likely to give them the benefit of the doubt. And refusing to enter into talks just because of political risk would be an abnegation of responsibility.

Fifthly there is the danger of harming relations with allies and undermining international efforts to fight terrorism – when, for example, one country insists on paying a ransom for its hostages, thereby encouraging more hostage-taking. Mitchell Reiss suggests meeting terrorists 'may demoralise foreign allies who have taken risks, committed resources, and lost people in counterterrorism efforts' only to have you legitimise the terrorists. Byman says 'Talks with terrorists may also diminish the stigma of the Foreign Terrorist Organisation designation . . . US exceptions to its own list may weaken the moral sanction of any listing and encourage other states to offer similar exceptions, hindering co-operation.' Normally, however, allies will understand why a peace process makes sense and will want to help and support, as the Obama administration has done with President Santos's talks with the FARC in Colombia.

Sixthly it is argued that talking gives terrorists a chance to rest and gather strength. Dutch terrorism experts Isabelle Duyvesteyn and Bart Schuurman conclude that 'opportunities for dialogue can be misappropriated by irregular opponents in order to bide time for a renewed offensive. The past few decades have offered plentiful examples of parties who found themselves in dire straits and displayed a willingness to talk merely as a ruse in order to gain time to recover from recent losses or to prepare new offensives.' There is, however, something slightly paradoxical in looking at a ceasefire as a threat to a government or society. It is governments that demand an end to the violence, and terrorists who fear the effect of a ceasefire on their morale and on their ability to restart the fighting. The longer the ceasefire goes on, the harder it is to go back to killing. And a ceasefire makes life better for the population, while also allowing economic improvements. Political negotiations are much easier if they are not held against a background of continuing violence. As long as the armed group is not handed unreasonable advantages which strengthen it in the long term, ceasefires are on the whole to the advantage of the government.

Lastly, and perhaps most important, is the curse of unintended consequences. Opening negotiations can lead to a spike in violence. One of the worst ever ETA bombings took place during the secret talks with the Gonzalez government in Spain when they detonated a bomb in a Barcelona supermarket car park in June 1987, killing twenty-one people. The government carried on talking and ETA bombed the Civil Guard barracks in Zaragoza that December because they wanted to be 'negotiating from strength'. Even more gruesomely, 'Marc', the chief ETA negotiator, threatened at the key secret meeting with the Spanish government in Lausanne in September 2006 that he would pile 'bodies on the negotiating table' to increase his leverage. It is therefore essential to be very clear about the signals you send in these circumstances. In opposition we had severe doubts about the signal that John Major sent when he indicated he was still prepared to talk to the IRA even after they had blown up Canary Wharf, although given our commitment to bipartisanship over Northern Ireland, we kept these doubts to ourselves. During our early months in government in 1997 Tony Blair made it absolutely clear to the IRA after they killed a policeman that if they ever went back to violence he would not be talking to them again, and that he intended to be in power for a very long time. Governments need to be careful to avoid creating perverse incentives that encourage more violence rather than help to end it.

Although there is something to each one of these practical points, they are not arguments against talking per se. They are all in the end tactical, about ensuring that you go about the talks in a sensible and thought-through way. Of course it is possible to mishandle a peace process just like any other political act, but that is no reason for not having a peace process. Writing in the context of hostage-taking, Guy Faure concludes that 'The point would not be to negotiate or not to negotiate, but rather to negotiate properly.'

The revisionists go on to argue that you should never enter into a negotiation unless you know the other side is sincere. Mnookin thinks it makes no sense to negotiate if one 'believes the other party would never uphold its end of the bargain and there is no effective mechanism for enforcing the negotiated deal'. American analyst John Arquilla writes 'The key is to be able to discern the difference between situations in which the terrorists are simply manipulating the negotiation process to play for time or score propaganda points, and those in which there is real hope for peaceful progress.' This is of course true, but at the same time it is impossible to know whether the other side is sincere or not until you try talking to them. If they act in bad faith once you have begun, then you can always break the talks off and expose their insincerity.

The security forces are naturally the most sceptical about the good faith of the armed group. They are often reading what the terrorists are saying to each other, and the terrorist leaders will be keen to convince their followers in private that they are hard-nosed, not patsies. Alfredo Rubalcaba, the Spanish interior minister, says he was pessimistic about the peace process with ETA in 2005 because, through intelligence, he saw them planning for attacks, and stealing cars and explosives in France while they were engaged in talks. It may well be, however, that the terrorist group carries on such activities to maintain the support of hardliners while simultaneously engaging in peace talks. All that the intelligence is telling you is that the leaders of armed groups are saying one thing to their supporters and another in public. It is not unknown for governments to do the same. The real intentions of the armed group are unknowable and they may not even know themselves. Again, the only way to find out is to start talking to them and establish whether they are serious or not.

Reiss divides terrorists into irreconcilables, reconcilables and those somewhere in between. He says ETA should be seen as irreconcilables unless they give up the claim for an independent Basque homeland. In fact ETA dropped the demand for independence several decades ago, asking instead for the right of self-determination – and this brings us to a central issue: groups can change their position when confronted with hard reality, and talking to them helps to change their minds. The point is that you can't know who is irreconcilable and who is reconcilable until you have talked to them. As we will see in the course of this book, from Aceh to Mozambique to Northern Ireland, the position of an armed group can shift in the course of a negotiation just as governments and other parties shift. No group is irreconcilable forever.

The practical arguments against talking to terrorists are therefore no more categoric than the moral arguments, so is there any alternative to doing so? Bertram Spector of the Center for Negotiation Analysis argues that 'Despite the risks inherent in negotiating with terrorists, the risks of following a no-negotiation policy are likely to be more deadly . . . If not negotiation, then what? Interaction can become a deadly tit-for-tat, escalating the conflict with no apparent way out other than capitulation or retreat by one side.' Byman agrees, writing 'there are risks of not negotiating. Terrorism is not static: a refusal to engage in talks may strengthen extremists by showing that non-violent means offer no hope. Hamas and other Islamists, for example, historically gained more support when peace talks were foundering.' Zartman, having put forward all the arguments against talking, concludes that 'negotiation may be a necessity, the only alternative to defeat or endless, costly conflict. Holding out may be a way to avoid giving in, but the holdout must weigh the cost of such a policy.' Audrey Cronin concludes that 'Time and again, governments and their populations face the unpalatable reality that groups engaging in violent attacks against innocent civilians may be stopped no other way . . . In short, if the goal is to end terrorist attacks, history demonstrates these are situations where they may be no viable alternative to entering talks.'

There is a whole academic canon on the different ways in which terrorism ends in practice. A much-quoted RAND Corporation study from 2008, *How Terrorist Groups End* by Seth Jones and Martin Libicki, looks at 648 terrorist groups since 1968 and concludes that 43 per cent of them ended in a transition to a political process, 40 per cent ended as a result of policing, 10 per cent ended with victory for the terrorists and only 7 per cent ended as a result of military success. The authors were, correctly, trying to demonstrate that George W. Bush's 'war on terror' was not likely to succeed because military defeat of terrorists is very rare. But the numbers they produce give a completely misleading impression of how armed conflicts really end. (And of the 648 groups they list, 244 are still going and 136 have splintered into other groups, so in fact less than half have ended at all.)

The biggest trap they and other academics have fallen into

is to treat tiny groups like the Baader–Meinhof Gang in Germany, the Brigate Rosse in Italy, the Affiche Rouge in France or the Symbionese Liberation Army in the US as if they are in some way comparable with the far more substantial Tamil Tigers, ANC or IRA. The first four are of a type that does not have a serious political base and can either be wrapped up by police work or fizzle out as the activists get too old for conflict or as fashion changes. The latter three had substantial support and represent a political tendency that will have to be dealt with at some stage, regardless of the fact they resort to terrorist methods. The reason we were talking to Sinn Féin was not just because they had guns but because they had real political support. Even at the height of the Troubles they enjoyed a third of the Catholic vote in Northern Ireland. The fact that both they and the Baader–Meinhof Gang used terrorist attacks to draw attention to their cause doesn't really help in working out how to end their very different campaigns. Markus Woolf, the former East German spymaster and godfather of terrorism, dismisses these fractional groups as made up of 'spoiled, hysterical children of mainly middle- and upper-class background'. This book is looking only at armed groups that enjoy significant political support, which while different from each other in many ways, do make up a coherent group.

A rather more considered approach is that of Audrey Cronin in *How Terrorism Ends*. She argues that all terrorist groups end in one of six ways: negotiation, success, failure, reorientation (usually into crime), decapitation or repression. But again if you look at the detail none of the categories except for negotiation seems to work in the end for significant terrorist movements. The first category is success. It is true that a number of armed groups succeeded in expelling their occupiers during the period of decolonisation, although usually the departure of the colonial power was negotiated. In the period of the Cold War, armed groups like the Viet Cong and the Sandinistas succeeded in overthrowing governments in Vietnam and Nicaragua (although usually with outside help); but in modern times such out-and-out victories are pretty rare or non-existent. The second category, failure, does not apply to major groups like the Farabundo Martí National Liberation Front (FMLN) in El Salvador, the Moro Islamic Liberation Front (MILF) in the Philippines, or the IRA. They do not just implode or find themselves being policed out. Some of the groups Cronin lists as having failed either negotiated peace, as the M-19 did in Colombia, or continue to exist like the UVF and UDA, and all of the others are small groups with no real political support. The next category, reorientation into crime, is a distraction. Most groups combine terrorism and crime, not least to fund their armed campaign. A terrorist group like the FARC can put greater emphasis on the drug trade, which provides its funding, but that does not mean it will give up its ideological campaign or its political ambitions.

The penultimate category Cronin suggests – decapitation of an armed group by killing or capturing the leader – is an interesting one. The examples she quotes are, however, problematic (ignoring religious cults like Aum Shinrikyo, which are a different category). She suggests the arrest of Abdullah Ocalan brought about the end of the Kurdish PKK in Turkey. While it was true that the snatch of the movement's charismatic leader in Kenya in 1999 did lead to a temporary reduction in violence, it certainly didn't end the armed conflict. PKK guerrillas actually stepped up the campaign and the conflict is only now being brought to an end by a negotiation centring on Ocalan in his cell on Imrali Island in the Bosporus. Likewise Hamas did not die after the assassination of Sheikh Yassin. On the contrary, it went on to become more violent and popular, and the attempted poisoning of another leader, Khaled Mishal, boosted it still further.

The one group that appears to be the exception is the Sendero Luminoso, or Shining Path, in Peru. The Maoist group was formed by the charismatic philosophy lecturer Abimael Guzmán – Comrade Gonzalo as he called himself – in the late 1960s, and its twenty-year violent campaign resulted in the deaths of some 69,000 people. It started with an attack on a polling station during the 1980 election just as Peru was emerging from a decade of military dictatorship, and developed into a nationwide guerrilla campaign, symbolically blacking out the capital Lima by repeatedly blowing up transmission towers. By 1991 it controlled much of the countryside. The government of Alberto Fujimori responded by suspending constitutional rights and deploying the army and security forces in a ruthless campaign of suppression. When Guzmán was captured in 1992, along with most of the rest of the top leadership in an apartment above a dance studio in Lima, and once he had appeared on television in a cage recanting and calling on his followers to lay down their arms, violence fell by 50 per cent in the following year. It has never recovered to the same level.

There are, however, reasons for thinking that this model of decapitation is not generally applicable. Firstly, Shining Path was based on an extraordinary cult of personality around Guzmán. It is unusual to find terrorist organisations based so completely on just one person. Every time an ETA collective leadership is arrested, for instance, it is simply replaced. And it is questionable how much political support Shining Path enjoyed in the country, given that it based its activities on fear, coercion and blackmail. Secondly, the methods used to repress Shining Path were extreme, with villages laid waste and frequent massacres by the army. A third of those who died did so at the hands of the army and more at the hands of the militias they established. These methods would not be available to a government in a Western democracy, and President Fujimori now languishes in jail as the result of resorting to these methods. Lastly, Shining Path is still not over. A low-level guerrilla campaign continues in two provinces of Peru, and bizarrely Comrade Gonzalo is now seeking negotiations with the government from his prison cell. Most recent academic work suggests that 'decapitation' does not work and at the most creates a temporary setback for the group in question.

Despite the near-impossibility of defeating terrorist groups by purely military means, there are still some people who champion Cronin's final category: no-holds-barred repression. The poster child for this approach is Sri Lanka, and indeed the Rajapaksa government actively promotes their success against the Liberation Tigers of Tamil Eelam (LTTE) in 2009 as demonstrating that there is a military answer to the problem.

The Sri Lankan government had an earlier opportunity to finish off the LTTE in 1987. The army drove the Tigers out of their base in the Vanni and into the Jaffna peninsula. It looked as if defeat was imminent but the bombing of Jaffna and the killing of civilians by the government triggered outrage in Tamil Nadu across the straits in India. The Indian government responded by airdropping supplies into Jaffna and applying political pressure, which led to the Indian–Sri Lankan agreement and the occupation of part of Sri Lanka by an Indian peacekeeping force.

Gotabaya Rajapaksa commanded a battalion in the siege of Jaffna and experienced first-hand the humiliation of Indian intervention robbing the Sri Lankan army of its almost-victory. He was nearly killed in one battle with the Tigers, retired as lieutenant colonel in 1992 and moved to California where he retrained as a computer engineer. When his brother, Mahinda, became president in 2005, he was summoned back to become defence minister. Rajapaksa gave the army a new sense of purpose and appointed his military college classmate, Sarath Fonseka, as commander. They recruited 75,000 new men, instituted a massive training programme, re-equipped the armed forces, including the purchase of drones, and set up Special Infantry Operations teams. India and the US provided intelligence support which enabled them to sink eight Sea Tiger ships, one of them close to Australia 1,700 miles away, and thereby cut off the LTTE's supply lines. He firmly believed the army had been consistently betrayed in the field by weak political leadership and that its hands had been tied behind its back. He invented the 'Rajapaksa Model' which required: unwavering political will; disregard for international opinion; no negotiations; control information; absence of political intervention; complete operational freedom for the security forces; and an accent on young commanders. Most of all he accepted there would be civilian casualties as a result of the army's actions and made it clear he was personally ready to take the blame, which gave the army new confidence.

The majority of analysts considered the war unwinnable and Norwegian diplomats reported that 'all observers think that this is a conflict that cannot be won by military means and most believe that the government cannot beat the LTTE militarily'. They expected stalemate to reappear, either because the Tigers would revert to guerrilla warfare or because they would roll back the army front line as they had in the past. But by 2008 the momentum was with the government. Observers kept waiting for a counterstroke by Velupillai Prabhakaran, the LTTE leader, but it never came. As they were driven back into a small, marshy area of coast, the LTTE used hundreds of thousands of Tamil civilians as human shields. The government declared a 'No Fire Zone' and asked civilians to move there for safety. The Tigers wouldn't let them and the army fired anyway. Tens of thousands died. Even at the last moment the LTTE expected a miracle in the form of an international intervention. Prabhakaran, however, rejected all proposals that would have saved the lives of the top leaders and the civilians. The government sealed the area off and brutally finished the job at Nandikadal Lagoon. There were no CNN or BBC reports from the front line as there were in Syria or Libya, and the political support of China in the UN Security Council meant that the government could escape any effective criticism of their actions.

In the view of Erik Solheim, the Norwegian negotiator in Sri Lanka, the government won so comprehensively because it was able to use methods that would not be regarded as acceptable in other parts of the world, and because Prabhakaran had turned from 'a military genius into a military fool'. Had

Prabhakaran gone back to guerrilla warfare he could have kept going indefinitely. But the LTTE had evolved from a classic guerrilla force into a conventional combat force capable of holding and defending territory, which had taken on and defeated the might of the Indian army. Prabhakaran was suffering from hubris. In 1990 he had warned of 'overconfidence', but by 2006 he believed his own propaganda that the Tamils were a de facto state and impossible to defeat on the battlefield. Since the death of Anton Balasingham, his political comrade, he had become out of touch with the rest of the world. The Tamil diaspora leaders told him to hold on and that international pressure would stop the Sri Lankan army as it had in the 1980s. They were wrong.

The Rajapaksa approach does not therefore provide a viable alternative that can be used elsewhere. In Solheim's words, you can't always count on a guerrilla army trying to fight a conventional war and you can't always count on the international community turning a blind eye to extreme measures. And you can't always count on an out-of-touch leader who hasn't left his area for thirty years fighting to the death with all his comrades in a hopeless war.

More important even than that is the fact that the conflict is not over in Sri Lanka, even if the fighting is (at least temporarily). The grievances that gave rise to the Tigers' campaign did not disappear at Nandikadal Lagoon. If the Rajapaksa government had offered the Tamils some political way forward through devolution or federalism after the defeat of the Tigers they may have been able to resolve the problem for good. But they did not, and the Tamil issue remains unresolved and it is unlikely Tamils will accept being second-class citizens indefinitely. Discontent is bubbling again in neighbouring Tamil Nadu and while there is, thank goodness, no sign at the moment of renewed Tamil terrorism, it is hard to believe it won't reappear if the political problem is not addressed. The Rajapaksa solution would only stand a chance of succeeding if it were matched by political concessions; in other words, combining security pressure downwards with an offer to the Tamils of a political way forward.

While the methods used by the Rajapaksas are not available in a conventional democracy, it is of course possible for an autocracy to defeat an armed group by extreme violence and the suppression of all rights, at least temporarily. Stalin had no difficulty in doing so, nor Suharto in Indonesia. Armed groups can be wiped out, as the Tupamaros were in Uruguay or the Montoneros in Argentina by military dictatorships, through mass arrest, disappearances and murder. As in the battle against Islamic extremists in Chechnya or Algeria, if you adopt a no-holds-barred military approach, have no concerns about human-rights abuses or the rule of law, and the media can be kept out, then it can be done. All it does, however – as Russia discovered when the Soviet Union crumbled – is stick the underlying problems in the deep freeze, and they reappear once the repression is reduced. In 1982 Hafez al-Assad suppressed a Sunni uprising in Hama in Syria with extreme violence, killing between 10,000 and 40,000. It was seen at the time as a success, but some thirty years later the rebellion reappeared. Unless you solve the underlying problem, it is always likely to do so.

None of this is to say that terrorism can be dealt with in the absence of firm security policies and effective intelligence. Without the police successes against ETA, without the infiltration of the IRA by the intelligence agencies, and without the military campaign against the GAM, the conflicts in the Basque Country, Northern Ireland and Aceh would not be over. But there needs to be more than just tough security measures. It was the realisation of this that led to the *COIN* manual being revised under the auspices of General Petraeus, adding the need to win over the communities on which the armed groups depend, as the British discovered in Malaya in the 1950s.

COIN however requires a third instrument: the need to talk to terrorists. Given that armed groups will almost never surrender, applying military pressure by itself leads only to a fight to the death. President Kennedy captured the conundrum well: 'A willingness to resist force, unaccompanied by a willingness to talk, could provoke belligerence – while a willingness to talk, unaccompanied by a willingness to resist force, could invite disaster.' If you offer the terrorists a political way out, then the military pressure can have the desired effect, especially if combined with a sustained effort to address the grievances that underlie the conflict. So the successful equation in dealing with serious terrorist groups is to combine military pressure down with the offer of a political way out through talks which can, over time, lead to an end to the armed conflict. Zartman suggests dealing with terrorism requires three tools: 'keeping its violent means in check, transforming its ends from destruction to participation, and undercutting the grievances on which it rides'.

If we conclude that the moral arguments against talking to terrorists do not outweigh the ethical imperative of saving lives, and if we think the utilitarian arguments against talking boil down to reasons to be careful about how you approach armed groups, rather than being arguments against doing so at all, then the question is whether there is any alternative to talking. Looking at the evidence on how terrorism ends suggests that, while it may be possible to out-police or outwait small groups like Baader–Meinhof and the Brigate Rosse, the alternatives to talking do not provide lasting answers for serious armed groups that enjoy substantial political support. In democracies we cannot kill all the terrorists, so we will have to talk to them at some stage.

That does not mean to say that it is sensible to plunge into a full-blown negotiation straight away with every group that takes up arms. Rather it means that we should try to learn from past experience how best to make contact with such groups, how to build trust, how to combine force and talking, how to use third parties, how and when to turn the contacts into negotiations, how to bring those negotiations to a successful conclusion, and how to ensure the resulting agreement is implemented, so that we don't keep on making the same mistakes. The conclusion from the conflicts covered in this book is that it is always right to talk to terrorists, even if it may not always be the right moment to embark on a negotiation. And if the armed group enjoys significant political support, it is very unlikely to be possible to end a conflict without a negotiation. In her Reith Lectures, Eliza Manningham-Buller said about 9/11, 'Despite talk of military action, there was one thing we all agreed on: terrorism is resolved through politics and economics, not through arms and intelligence, however important a role these play.'

So the question this book looks at is not whether to talk to terrorists, but when and, particularly, how.

CHAPTER TWO

Making Contact with the Enemy

During the American Civil War, Abraham Lincoln made a speech in which he referred sympathetically to the Southern rebels. An elderly lady, a staunch Unionist, upbraided him for speaking kindly of his enemies when he ought to be thinking of destroying them. His response was . . . 'Why, madam, do I not destroy my enemies when I make them my friends?'

Scott Atran, *Talking to the Enemy*

It is by definition difficult and dangerous to make contact with a clandestine armed group. They deliberately operate in a covert manner, often based on a cell structure, and don't advertise headquarters where you can drop by and introduce yourself. Finding them, persuading them to meet you, and then doing so safely requires skill, courage and luck.

Manuel Marulanda, the leader of the FARC, one of the most vicious and intransigent armed groups in the world, was by 2000 an almost legendary figure. Pedro Antonio Marín had taken the *nom de guerre* 'Marulanda' in honour of a murdered trade-union leader but he was more often known to his supporters by his nickname 'Tirofijo' or 'Sureshot'. Marulanda had become a guerrilla at the age of eighteen as part of the peasant self-defence forces formed in Colombia in the 1940s and 50s, founded the FARC in 1963 and had survived in the jungle fighting the Colombian army ever since.

James LeMoyne and Jan Egeland, two special representatives of the UN Secretary General, had been waiting to meet him for months. LeMoyne was a youthful-looking former Rhodes Scholar and *New York Times* journalist who had become an expert on Latin American guerrilla movements, and Egeland was a Norwegian politician and diplomat who as a young man had been a church volunteer in Colombia. He had already played a key role in the Oslo talks between the Palestinians and Israelis.

They had requested the help of the Colombian president Andrés Pastrana, who was poised to start peace talks with the guerrillas, but he had said he could not impose the UN on the FARC. Marulanda would have to ask to see them himself. In the end LeMoyne and Egeland had to arrange the meeting themselves with the help of Raul Reyes, the deputy commander of the FARC and the head of its political operation, whom LeMoyne knew.

Marulanda was a deeply suspicious man. Wherever he went he had six to ten rings of security surrounding him, stretching out sixty miles from where he was based. The two UN officials flew to San Vicente del Caguán, a small town on the edge of the Amazonian jungle, a huge trackless wilderness stretching south towards Brazil. They were driven ten miles out of town by a local employee of the UN and at an agreed point met a jeep full of uniformed FARC guerrillas waiting for them by the edge of the road. The guerrillas loaded them into the back of the jeep and drove them south for four hours along back-breaking dirt tracks to the tiny village of La Sombra, or The Shadow. There they were greeted by about 200 more armed guerrillas, including commanders and sub-commanders, and taken into a large courtyard of thatched huts where Marulanda was waiting for them. He did not shake the UN envoys by the hand but waved at them from his seat at a long, rough-hewn wooden trestle table with wooden benches around it in the middle of the courtyard. Marulanda sat at one end and gestured to the two foreigners to sit at the other, twenty feet away from him. The table between them was lined by forty men with guns, and two FARC guerrillas stood with the muzzles of their AK-47s pointing at the temples of each of the diplomats as they sat for the full two hours of the meeting. To make a gesture in order to emphasise what he was saying LeMoyne at one stage had to push the gun barrel away with his hands, saying 'Excuse me, but can I make a point'. LeMoyne described the encounter as like being 'in a scene from a movie'. The armed men were there because Marulanda had never met international officials before and was taking precautions. Colombia was a member of the UN, and the US controlled the UN Security Council, so it stood to reason that these two men should not be trusted easily.

LeMoyne noted that each FARC commander had their own separate security force. Later, when he attended a meeting of field commanders at a farmhouse in a remote spot in the mountains, he noticed that Raul Reyes, later killed by the Colombian army, sent his bodyguards off on arrival to one corner of the yard, promising that food would be sent out to them. There they remained throughout the meeting without mingling with the guards of the other commanders. Reyes later told him that the organisation had a firm rule that the body-guards of each commander should have no contact with each other in order to reduce the chances of subversion.

Marulanda began the meeting with the UN envoys formally, welcoming the distinguished visitors. It was the first time the FARC had officially received international diplomatic repre-sentatives. Bottles of vodka and glasses were brought out and they downed shots in the blazing sun. Later Marulanda told LeMoyne proudly how Jacobo Arenas, the left-wing ideologue who helped found the movement, had taught him to be a Communist. The FARC was born out of the long civil war in Colombia between the Liberals and the Conservatives known as 'La Violencia' in the 1940s and 50s. Marulanda had been a young Liberal peasant fighter. As the civil war wound down in the early 1960s some peasants kept their weapons and preserved their self-defence forces, and the Communist Party started to recruit them as a peasant revolutionary army. The FARC was formed out of one such group. Its ideology was imparted by the charismatic commissar, Arenas. In the following fifty years as many as 250,000 people are estimated to have died in the violence.

LeMoyne realised that Marulanda had invited so many commanders to be present at the meeting in part to demonstrate to the organisation's leadership that the FARC was being taken seriously. Even the UN was coming to see them. And he wanted to send out a message that there would be no secret meetings or under-the-table deals.

Marulanda said, 'You are the first gringo I have met.' LeMoyne thought he would try to break the ice and replied, 'Well, at least the first who survived,' thinking of the at least six Americans who had fallen into the FARC's hands and were never seen again. There was dead silence, then Marulanda looked at his watch and said, 'But the day is young,' and laughed. The commanders, sub-commanders and guerrillas began to laugh too.

The FARC were embarking on their fourth peace process with the Colombian government. Other Colombian armed groups had already reached deals but they were the largest and most intractable guerrilla movement. The government wanted inter-national involvement in the process and the UN was willing to help, but the guerrillas were suspicious of the organisation and preferred to negotiate direct with the government. LeMoyne and Egeland told Marulanda that it was of course up to him whether he wanted UN participation. Marulanda asked them to tell the Secretary General that the FARC was willing to try for peace. LeMoyne says that in answer to all their questions he said 'Si, si, si,' while his eyes said 'No, no, no.' In the event, the FARC and the Colombian government wouldn't allow the UN to get fully involved until the Caguán peace process was already collapsing some two years later, when it was too late to help.

LeMoyne met Marulanda with large groups of FARC guer-rillas several times more in the course of the next year before he was allowed to meet him alone or to shake his hand. El Mono Jojoy, the FARC military commander, was just as wary. LeMoyne asked him why he and Marulanda were so reluctant to greet him in the traditional fashion and Mono Jojoy replied, 'Because you might have poison on your hands.' LeMoyne told him, 'You are incredibly paranoid,' and Mono Jojoy answered, 'Yes, but I am alive.' Mono Jojoy employed a young female guerrilla to taste his food before he ate. LeMoyne commented that it reminded him of the Borgias. Mono Jojoy, without missing a beat, asked, 'Are they alive?'

It is only by taking this sort of risk that it is possible to start to build trust with an armed group. It is too dangerous for them to come into the open and you have to travel into their territory and put your life in their hands to make a meeting possible. That act of confidence makes them feel that you trust them. This is something primeval in the human spirit. Lawrence Freedman quotes a study by Frans de Waal, an expert on primate behaviour, which demonstrates that chimpanzees behave in the same way. They show vulnerability in order to indicate trust in another chimpanzee and can understand the need for mediation and reconciliation between individuals, in a way that other animals cannot.

According to the UN rules, LeMoyne and Egeland should have been wearing bulletproof vests and travelling in an armoured car accompanied by a UN bodyguard. But as LeMoyne says, the only way to be secure was to put themselves totally in the hands of the FARC. Prior to the meeting LeMoyne had told Reyes that they were trusting the FARC, and Reyes had replied, 'You will be the safest men in Colombia.'

It is not, however, always possible for government negotiators to go on to the terrorists' turf. First conversations between leaders of insurgent groups and government representatives often happen in prison because that is the one safe place the government side knows it can find them. But if being in prison makes it easier to find the armed groups' leaders, it doesn't necessarily make the meeting easier in political terms.

Persuading P. W. Botha, the conservative South African president, to secretly meet the imprisoned Nelson Mandela in 1989 was a tough job. Niel Barnard, the head of the South African National Intelligence Service (NIS), who succeeded in doing so, put the meeting in context fifteen years afterwards: 'Let me

suggest a comparison . . . The state of national security at that
time in South Africa made it as likely for P. W. Botha to talk
to Mandela as it would be now for President George W. Bush
to invite Osama Bin Laden to the White House.'

The first official contacts with Mandela in prison which led
up to this encounter started by happenstance. The minister of
justice, Kobie Coetsee, had a farm near the small town of
Brandfort in the Orange Free State where his old university
friend and former tennis partner, Piet de Waal, also lived and
practised law. Brandfort was chosen as the site for Winnie
Mandela's banishment in 1977 in the aftermath of the Soweto
riots, and as the only lawyer in town, de Waal became, by
default, her representative. In November 1985 she was allowed
to fly down to visit her husband who had been hospitalised in
Cape Town. By coincidence she was in the same plane as
Coetsee and marched up to the first-class compartment to
tackle him on her husband's conditions, trading on their mutual
friend in Brandfort. In doing so she gave Coetsee the idea of
visiting Mandela in hospital. The next week Coetsee went to
see him unannounced on the third floor in the Volks Hospital
in Cape Town. The floor had been sealed off by security, and
prisoner 466/64, dressed in a blue checked gown, was the only
patient. Mandela thought that Coetsee was different from his
overbearing predecessor, Kruger. The two talked about mundane
things but they hit it off on a personal level. Coetsee's visit
had only been a goodwill gesture born out of curiosity, but
Mandela had long been seeking a meeting with a government
minister to discuss peace, and indeed had twice written to
Coetsee himself without receiving a response.

Once back in Pollsmoor Prison, to which he had been transferred from Robben Island, Mandela now demanded to see
ministers. Coetsee agreed to meet again, this time in his official
residence, Savernake, a Cape Dutch mansion in Cape Town.
He offered Mandela a glass of sherry, his first drink in twenty-
two years. The two continued to meet during the next three
years and gradually built up a personal bond of trust. Van der

Merwe, the director general of the Prisons Department, says 'Coetsee went to see PW and said to us we can talk to Mandela. This had to be done in secret. If government was seen to be talking to the enemy, there would be great political problems.'

The contact developed into a strategic approach once Niel Barnard became involved. He was a former lecturer in political science at the University of the Orange Free State who had been appointed by Botha at the age of just thirty to reorganise the South African intelligence service after scandal killed off its notorious predecessor, BOSS. His first meeting with Mandela took place in May 1988. He had been authorised by Botha to try to find out if a peaceful settlement was possible, and to ascertain Mandela's views on Communism and the role of the South African Communist Party, an obsession of Botha's. Barnard says he wanted to explore 'What was Mandela's stance on violence, and how could we understand whether he was prepared to reject violence? Would the ANC use the Communist revolutionary approach if there was to be a negotiated transfer of state power?' Mandela was used to his chats with Coetsee and was suspicious of Barnard. He said later 'It was like asking [Soviet dissident] Andrei Sakharov to talk to the head of the KGB.' They met in the office of the commanding officer at Pollsmoor, Mandela wearing overalls and work boots. The intelligence chief and the iconic political prisoner engaged in small talk, with Barnard occasionally speaking in Afrikaans and Mandela speaking in English. They agreed to meet again to set out an agenda. Barnard says he arranged for Mandela to be properly clothed at future sessions, so they would meet as equals. He considered respect essential.

At the beginning of 1989 Botha suffered a stroke and resigned as leader of the National Party, but remained as president. Barnard tried to persuade 'The Great Crocodile', as he was affectionately known by his supporters, that he could go down in history as the man who had started the peace process if he met Mandela. In Barnard's calculations, it would confront his successor with a political fait accompli. He told Botha that even if it went wrong he would be remembered as the man who had at least tried to make progress. Botha agreed to meet.

Mandela, who was now in Victor Verster Prison, was well dressed for the secret encounter on 5 July 1989. His measurements had been taken and the prison tailor put to work and the NIS had used its covert funds to buy him a suit, shirt and tie. Mandela had been told to be ready at 5.30 a.m. for the journey from his prison to Cape Town. Strict security measures were taken, and even the policeman guarding his house at Victor Verster had to be avoided. The NIS were trying to ensure that Mandela remained safe, but they were even keener to ensure that Magnus Malan's Military Intelligence and the South African Security Police, whom they regarded as the enemy, did not learn of the meeting. Mandela says he prepared thoroughly, writing notes, reading as much news as he could, anticipating Botha's potential lines of argument and formulating responses.

The convoy of five cars swept past the front gate of Tuynhuys, the official residence of the president, the guards having been told that the cars contained 'a politician from an African state'. Even Botha's close personal staff had not been informed of the meeting. Mandela was taken up in a lift from the underground car park to the private quarters. On the way down the corridor to Botha's office Mandela's shoelaces came undone. Barnard noticed and knelt down to retie them. Mandela was expecting a fight when he met the president, but Botha came forward with arms outstretched and shook him warmly by the hand, offering him a cup of tea. They were obstinate and proud men, but they both believed in old-fashioned courtesy.

Mandela had been demanding to see Botha for years and had prepared a memorandum before the meeting making the case for a negotiated settlement, but the two men hardly discussed politics. Instead they talked about their families, and even about the Boer War. Barnard described it as like watching two heavyweight boxers circling each other in the ring, and it was only towards the end of the hour-long meeting that

Mandela asked Botha to release his old friend Walter Sisulu on humanitarian grounds. (Botha said Barnard should attend to it, but Barnard had to explain later in the car that it was just not possible to do so at that stage. Mandela flew into one of his towering rages in response.)

At the end of the tea party they posed for a photograph. That evening, at a game reserve in the north of the country, Botha told a group of friends that he had something in his pocket that would astonish them, and pulled out the photograph. The people who saw it were shocked. One of them later told Willie Esterhuyse, an Afrikaner professor, that 'while we were fighting the terrorists, Botha was chatting quite cosily to their leader'. Botha was worried what 'his people' would think if the meeting became public and had insisted that Barnard record it, Nixon-style, so he could protect himself from attack if necessary. Barnard had not told Mandela about this recording and subsequently destroyed it without informing anyone else. (This led to a bitter dispute later between Botha and his successor F. W. de Klerk. Botha objected violently to de Klerk's claim that he was simply continuing to pursue Botha's policy of making peace, and insisted that he had used his meeting to warn Mandela against Communism. He claimed the secret tapes would prove him right. Only then did Barnard reveal that he had personally decided to destroy them.)

Even before the meeting with Botha the South African government side had established a committee of ministers and senior officials to manage the private talks with Mandela, and they held forty-eight sessions in all. Professor Mnookin says Mandela tried to establish a personal link with each member of the committee, one of whom, Fanie van der Merwe, was 'surprised and flattered that Mandela remembered him from some thirty years before, when they had argued opposite sides of a case. The trust Mandela earned with these simple gestures counted for far more than Mandela's policy position on any issue.'

The ANC's position was that it was for the government to

initiate talks rather than them. Mandela, however, had long
sought dialogue with the government, even writing to the
president a number of times and sending him proposals. Later
Mandela said 'I chose to tell no one what I was about to do.
Not my colleagues upstairs [in prison] or those in Lusaka [ANC
headquarters]. There are times when a leader must move out
ahead of his flock, go off in a new direction, confident that he
is leading his people the right way.' His seclusion in prison
allowed him to keep the contact with the government secret
from the public and, largely, from his own side. Rather than
wallowing in resentment about the appalling way he had been
treated, he concluded that 'If you want to make peace with
your enemy, you have to work with your enemy. Then he
becomes your partner.' He set about convincing the white rulers
of South Africa that peace was possible with the ANC. In the
words of the National Party minister Gerrit Viljoen, in
Mandela's conversations with the government committee 'the
ANC's reasonableness and lack of bitterness came across. It
was clear that their priority was not to destroy their opponent.'
The discussions between Mandela and the government in prison
were the first steps in a negotiation that led to the end of
apartheid and the creation of a democratic South Africa.

If the leader of the armed group is hard to reach, a government may rely on an intermediary to make the first contact.
In 1999, Velupillai Prabhakaran, the leader of the Tamil Tigers,
faced a 200-year sentence for the bombing of the central bank
in Colombo, and was wanted for the murder of President
Premadasa of Sri Lanka and of Indian prime minister Rajiv
Gandhi, as well as numerous other crimes.

Erik Solheim, a former Norwegian politician, travelled north
from Colombo by Sri Lankan army helicopter to meet him.
No foreigner had seen the Tigers' leader since the late 1980s.
The helicopter flew low to avoid radar. Only President
Kumaratunga and the foreign minister knew of his visit. The
president had not even told the prime minister, who was furious
when he found out. Nor could the Tamil Tiger forces be told

of the secret visit, so there was a real risk the helicopter would be shot down by the guerrillas. When it landed at the front line between the rebel forces and the army, Solheim was met by a Norwegian Embassy car driven by a Muslim. The Norwegians were worried that any Tamil would come under irresistible pressure to reveal what was said in the back of the car, while it would not be safe for a Sinhalese to drive into the Tiger-held area. The car took him into the no-man's-land between the front lines and he was dropped at a little Catholic church just inside LTTE territory. There he was picked up by the Tamil Tigers and driven on side roads through the Vanni, the area of the island which formed their stronghold, to avoid being bombed by the Sri Lankan air force. Once he arrived at the Tiger headquarters in Mallavi he was put up in a little bungalow. The next day Prabhakaran appeared with a huge entourage of bodyguards. Solheim noted he had more security than the Indian prime minister, and wore a glass vial of cyanide round his neck in the fashion of the Tigers.

The Tamil Tigers were perhaps the most dangerous armed group in the world in their time. Indeed it was the Tigers that really developed the tactic of suicide bombing with their first attack in 1987 followed by 272 more, as many as fifty of them carried out by women, before the violence stopped. One of the most chilling was an attack in 2006 by a young Tamil woman, Anoja Kugenthirarasah, who reportedly became pregnant by a young soldier and used the relationship to gain access to the military base that contained the office of the commander of the army, to attend the maternity clinic there. She positioned herself inside the camp gates and blew herself and her unborn baby to smithereens as General Fonseka's convoy passed. She failed to kill Fonseka, only badly wounding him, but she did manage to kill nine other people.

A group of a few dozen youths formed the Tamil New Tigers in 1972 and chose the emblem of the ancient Tamil Chola empire, a tiger on a blood-red background, as their symbol. The first known killing by Prabhakaran was at dawn on

27 July 1975. He left a friend's house in Jaffna and went to a nearby temple where he fired a volley of homemade bullets from a rusty revolver, killing the mayor of Jaffna who was bent in prayer. There were some thirty Tamil radical groups in the 1970s and 80s but Prabhakaran managed to wipe out his rivals and merge all the groups into one by the late 1980s. The Tamil rebellion moved from the fringes to become a genuinely popular movement after the 'Black July riots' in 1983 in which Tamils were dragged from their houses and cars and massacred mercilessly by Sinhalese mobs. The sectarian outrage stimulated Indian support for the Tamils, and RAW, the Indian secret service, trained some 15,000 Tamil militants in jungle warfare, explosives and sabotage. A hundred Tigers were also trained by the PLO in Beirut. Their enemy were the young, poorly paid Sinhalese soldiers policing Tamil areas who found themselves in alien surroundings, unable to speak the language. They reacted to their comrades' deaths by burning villages and raping and killing civilians, and reprisal built on reprisal until the country was in the grip of a major civil war in which more than 100,000 people died.

In 1997, Erik Solheim resigned after ten years as the Socialist Left Party's leader in Norway, and spent January and February 1998 in Sri Lanka writing his memoirs. He stayed in the house of Arne Fjørtoft, a long-time resident in Sri Lanka and former chairman of the Liberal Party who had competed with Solheim for the 'green' vote in Norway but was now his friend. Political curiosity led Solheim to meet politicians from across the spectrum while he was there. When he returned to Norway he was approached by representatives of the Tamil community, who asked to see him in October 1998. There are more than a million Tamils living around the world and this diaspora was a key pillar of LTTE support.

(Diasporas are often the 'front door' to the armed groups, and can even have a role of their own in a peace process – as in the case of the PKK, where the leadership of the Kurdish diaspora in Europe has had separate negotiations with the

Turkish government. In the case of Northern Ireland, the substantial Irish American community had an important influence both on the course of the conflict and on the peace process, with leaders of the IRA's former support network in the US helping to urge Sinn Féin leaders into an agreement. The trick for a negotiator is to get past the diaspora and make contact with the real leaders of the armed group. Diasporas often become harder line than the terrorist group they support, opposing compromise even when the people living through the conflict day to day want to reach a settlement.)

The Tamils in Oslo told Solheim they had been to the Norwegian foreign ministry to ask for their help in getting Anton Balasingham, the political leader of the Tigers, out of Sri Lanka for an operation. Like many Tamils, Balasingham suffered from diabetes and needed a new kidney. Solheim telephoned the foreign minister, who put his deputy on the case.

Balasingham had started his career as a translator at the British High Commission in Colombo and then become a journalist. He first met Prabhakaran in Madras in 1979 when both were on the run from the Sri Lankan authorities, and they forged a lasting partnership. Solheim described the two as like 'an old couple'. They were inseparable – although sometimes they would not speak to each other for months on end – and Prabhakaran depended on Balasingham for a political ideology to complement his armed rebellion. Unlike Prabhakaran, Balasingham had seen the world and could understand the international political scene. Prabhakaran could have smuggled dialysis equipment into Tamil-held territory to help treat his old friend, but felt he could not justify to the rest of his supporters spending so much money on just one individual.

The Norwegian government told the Tamils they were ready to assist if the idea proved acceptable to the government in Colombo. While they were not persuaded on humanitarian grounds, the Sri Lankan government wanted to get the peace process going and understood that Balasingham was key. They got as far as negotiating a plan to exfiltrate him by helicopter and ship, but government worries about the political costs if they were found out, and in particular what the opposition UNP would do, overcame their enthusiasm. They imposed a large number of conditions that were simply unacceptable to the LTTE. In the end the Tigers took Balasingham out by their own means. He spent three months in Thailand recovering and then continued on to Britain where, as a UK citizen, he could settle. Solheim visited him in July 1999 in his house in a run-down area of South London. He was still on dialysis, and could only work a few hours a day. Solheim arranged for him to be brought to Oslo for the kidney transplant in March 2000, bringing with him his own organ donor who he claimed was a relative, and this built a lasting relationship of trust between them.

The Norwegian foreign ministry felt they could not talk directly to the Tamil Tigers without destroying their relationship with the Sri Lankan government, so they made Solheim the point man with the LTTE, and the Norwegian ambassador in Colombo built up a similar relationship with the Sri Lankan government. Balasingham formally asked Solheim to become the facilitator between the group and the Sri Lankan government. Solheim continued to travel to London to meet him and the meetings always took the same form. They were joined by Balasingham's wife, Adele, a working-class Australian woman from near Melbourne who had met him on her first visit to Europe working as a student nurse in London. They were very close, literally as well as figuratively, and she would never be more than ten feet from his side. She was his lover, nurse, secretary and adviser all in one. While no intellectual, she had real influence on him. They would usually adjourn to a nearby restaurant for very hot Indian or Chinese food and Balasingham would have a bottle of white wine, which he loved, despite the LTTE ban on alcohol. There he would regale them with tales from his younger days about how attractive he had been to girls (stories that did not always amuse his wife). Solheim listened to his presentation of the Tamil account of Sri Lankan history for hundreds of hours, while Balasingham ate with his hands in the traditional Tamil fashion. At the end of the meal a local London Tamil would come and pay the bill. The hours of listening and the respect he showed paid off for Solheim, and he became so trusted by Balasingham that when a centrist government took over from the socialists in Norway in 2001, Vidar Helgesen, the new state secretary for foreign affairs, came to London to tell Balasingham that the government would keep Solheim in place, although they reserved the right to change their negotiator at any point.

Solheim's 1999 meeting with Prabhakaran was set up by Balasingham, who was the only member of the organisation who could talk to the leader as an equal. They met at a table in the open air in Mallavi. Prabhakaran had by this time become an almost mythical figure, regarded as the devil by the Sinhalese and as a demi-god by many Tamils. Solheim's first impression, however, was a disappointing one. A small man with a weak handshake, Prabhakaran seemed more like a village schoolmaster than a feared terrorist leader. He was shy and reserved and did not speak English. President Kumaratunga, only half joking, later asked Solheim how he knew that it was really Prabhakaran – no one had seen him for so long that he would be hard to identify in a crowd. At the meeting Prabhakaran demanded that the government de-proscribe the Tigers as a terrorist organisation. He would not open talks until that was done.

Two years later, after the ceasefire, Vidar Helgesen travelled with Solheim to meet Prabhakaran. Again they flew by helicopter from Colombo and landed on a cricket pitch, this time in the Tiger-held area. They were left to wait in the compound and then ushered in to the headquarters to meet Prabhakaran and his advisers, where they were served tea and fresh fruit by white-gloved waiters. Helgesen's first impression, like Solheim's, was of an underwhelming character. Prabhakaran had no charisma, a soft voice and damp hands. In negotiations he was stubborn on certain issues, with a singular focus on the implementation of the ceasefire agreement. He wanted a return of normality for Tiger-controlled areas, the embargo lifted and the A9, the main road north, reopened. The Norwegians wanted to talk about getting into the political negotiations, but he was not interested. He just wanted to focus on implementation.

Over the next five years the Norwegians met Prabhakaran fifteen times, more often than any other non-Tamil. They would be served excellent seafood lunches and talk 'about cooking and the films he liked' and about history. According to his biographer, Prabhakaran was obsessed with westerns: 'He would take slow steps with a revolver stuck into his shirt, make a sudden turn, whip out the revolver and fire at an imaginary enemy. He never got tired of it.' The Norwegians found he would stick to his word, and when later he promised to stop the killings, he did so. Balasingham too would never lie. When questioned about terrorist attacks he would give an explanation of why Prabhakaran had ordered them, whereas S. P. Tamilselvan, the head of the LTTE political department, was less straightforward and would give a propaganda answer, claiming implausibly that they had been carried out by the army in order to blame the LTTE.

Solheim and Helgesen demonstrated how a third party can make the difficult first contact between an armed group and a government possible. By building trust over a long period of time, by being prepared to listen to their grievances and show respect, they won over the Tigers and made themselves indispensable to both sides.

In recent years the role of intermediary has increasingly been taken on by individuals and NGOs rather than the UN or governments. For them to be taken seriously by an armed group, rather than mistaken for an approach by an intelligence agency, it is crucial that they are introduced to the group by someone they trust.

Euskadi Ta Askatasuna, or ETA, is best known for the videos of its leaders dressed in white silk hoods, black robes and Basque berets, punching the air with their left fists as they make an announcement. Behind them on the wall is pinned an ETA flag and their symbol, a snake entwining an axe, representing politics and violence, and '*Bietan jarrai*' in Basque, 'Keep up with both'. ETA was established in 1959 in resistance to Franco. When their violence continued and even increased after Spain's transition to democracy in 1974, their campaign became less and less comprehensible to ordinary Spaniards. ETA for their part felt betrayed by the democratic transition since they had expected to achieve self-determination through it. The movement split a number of times, but the violence carried on for four decades, in the course of which more than 800 people died.

ETA survived more than fifty years, despite the best efforts of the Spanish and French police and intelligence services, by always observing strict operational security. So when in 2003 Nancy Soderberg, Bill Clinton's former deputy National Security Adviser, suggested to Martin Griffiths, the twinkly-eyed founder of the Henry Dunant Centre in Geneva, that he make contact with them, he had no idea how to go about it. As Teresa Whitfield records in *Endgame for ETA: Elusive Peace in the Basque Country*, 'he searched the internet and found Bill Douglass, an academic expert on ETA', who had recently retired as director of the Center of Basque Studies in Reno, Nevada, and persuaded him to come to Geneva. Once there, Griffiths and his colleagues pumped Douglass for information, and then asked him to go to the Basque region to talk to his contacts. Douglass says, 'I expressed concern over what might happen to me if I was apprehended in the attempt by the Spanish authorities. Contacting ETA was illegal under Spain's counterterrorism laws and, for that matter, US ones as well. There was a bit of a jocular banter back and forth regarding my being left out in the cold. Depending upon unspecified circumstances the Centre might be able to help, but we would have to see how it all played out on the ground. In short, I would be pretty much on my own.'

Douglass had participated in a previous failed attempt at

mediation with ETA organised by the Carter Center in the mid-1990s, but this time he came back from Spain saying negotiations might be possible. Griffiths persuaded him to return to explore the possibility of the HDC playing the role of mediator. Douglass contacted a trade unionist close to ETA and

> checked into a hotel that is in the R&D industrial park of Zamudio near the Bilbao airport. I did so because I was unknown to its management and on a given night half or more of the guests were likely to be foreigners. I would therefore not draw attention there. I was to return to my room to await news . . . Several hours later I received a call that informed me of the next morning's appointment in my room with the possible emissary of ETA. The wait seemed interminable since I was expecting a stranger who might turn out to be a policeman or worse. My baroque worry fed on the knowledge that ETA was a far from monolithic organisation, with hardliners disposed to pursue the violent campaign at any cost – and therefore possibly ill-disposed toward a messenger of my ilk. The knock at my door was that of my intended contact, an intense man who immediately engaged me in a conversation regarding Basque–Spanish politics. When I informed him of the Centre's position, he was most sceptical. Why should ETA entertain a negotiation that would be tantamount to surrender – even rejection of its own history and abandonment of its longstanding goals? He agreed, however, to pass on the proposal and promised to deliver a reply in person the next day. ETA's response clearly surprised him. There was interest, but no one was about to take some academic's representation of HDC's offer. ETA wanted a letter from Martin specifying details and outlining the Centre's commitment.

In January 2004, Griffiths and one of his Spanish-speaking female colleagues flew to Bilbao with her teenage son. They thought that travelling as a family would make them seem less suspicious to the security authorities. There they met a trade-union official in the same hotel and handed him a letter explaining the role they thought they could play.

This all took place while conservative José María Aznar was still prime minister of Spain and the chances of successful talks had never looked bleaker. Unbeknownst to Griffiths, however, ETA was in the market for a reliable go-between with the Spanish government to begin yet another attempt at negotiation. The HDC just happened to be the right people at the right time in the right place. When a new socialist government was elected later in the year, ETA put a choice of intermediaries to the new administration, including the HDC and the University of Uppsala in Sweden. The HDC was chosen.

Before that could happen, however, there had to be a vetting process. It became clear later that ETA had undertaken detailed research into the HDC to make sure it was not a front organisation. They even knew exactly who on the staff spoke Spanish. In the spring two Basques turned up unannounced at the lakeside villa that served as its headquarters claiming to be from a human-rights organisation. They handed over a response to Griffiths' letter bearing the official ETA stamp at the bottom. Griffiths' deputy, Andrew Marshall, described it as 'a very heavy letter to carry'. Griffiths wrote to a disappointed Bill Douglass to tell him that the HDC had decided not to engage in the Basque conflict as their plate was just too full elsewhere. His white lie was essential to maintain the confidentiality of the channel, but contact had been established and a meeting was set up between the two sides. The arrangements for the HD Centre's first meeting with ETA were set by a man who turned up unannounced at their office in Geneva with precise instructions. The representatives of the Centre should appear on a particular day in front of a particular church in a particular village in France. He should wear a red scarf and carry a blue notebook, and use a key phrase like someone in a spy novel. If no one appeared he should come back in one hour, in six hours, in twenty-four hours and one week later. The first time they drove up no one appeared, but ETA were watching them. A week later they pulled up at the appointed time and a man jumped into the car. No one was sure what to do next, so Andrew Marshall suggested having a meal in a nearby town. Martin Griffiths asked the ETA representative what his name was and he said 'It's up to you.' Griffiths gave him the code name 'George'. They had a lengthy lunch and spent some six hours together. George set out what the organisation wanted and the representative of the Centre set out what they planned to do to prepare the dialogue. Of course complicated arrangements like these can go wrong. On one occasion the liaison was set for 2 January, the first day back at work, and it had snowed heavily. Everything was closed in Geneva, so the HDC representatives decided not to drive to France until the weather cleared. They discovered later that a highly irritated George had been waiting for them for three days in the snow before eventually giving up.

The newly elected socialist prime minister, José Luis Zapatero, authorised the dialogue and he chose Jesús Eguiguren to represent the 'party in government'. Eguiguren, a Falstaffian figure who had long been involved in trying to make peace, had no government position but was president of the Socialist Party in the Basque Country. He had plenty of reasons to hate ETA. He had been a pall-bearer for too many of his friends assassinated by the organisation, starting with his colleague Germán Rodríguez, murdered in 1978. He says 'I know all the churches in the Basque Country because no one has been to as many funerals as me.' He himself at times had to have bodyguards to protect him from a potential ETA attack. But he knew the conflict could not 'be solved by elimination: what we call the patriotic left is not going to disappear'.

In December 2004 Eguiguren was on holiday in Badajoz when he was told a message had arrived from ETA. He drove 800 kilometres to collect it from a friend in France, who in turn had been given it by a French Basque priest. He drove back into Spain to deliver the message to Alfredo Rubalcaba, the parliamentary spokesman of the socialist government, who was in Santander. He in turn passed it on to Zapatero. The letter was just three lines long with the stamp of ETA at the bottom, proposing the organisation and the government start a dialogue to resolve the conflict.

A second letter arrived in February 2005 by the same channel saying that ETA wanted the meeting to take place under the auspices of an international organisation. A third letter was much delayed for logistical reasons – correspondence with a terrorist group is not always straightforward. It proposed a meeting in Geneva and asked the government to confirm to the director of the HDC that the government was content. When he didn't hear from the government, Eguiguren assumed he was no longer part of the exercise and was surprised when he was told by Rubalcaba to go ahead with the meeting on the day proposed by ETA and that he should be the representative. As he put it, 'the postman had become the interlocutor'.

On 21 June 2005 Eguiguren made his way to Geneva for his first meeting with ETA accompanied by his old friend Pello Rubio. Eguiguren knew the city because thirty years earlier he had worked in the kitchen of a restaurant on the edge of the lake. He had been told to report at ten in the morning to the reception of the Hotel Président Wilson. Someone from the HDC calling themselves Mr Scott would present himself and ask for Mr Felipe Martínez. Mr Scott would take him to the meeting place. If no one showed up he should come back an hour later. If again no one came he should come back a day later.

Eguiguren sat in the reception and dozed off. No one came to ask for Martínez so he decided to phone the HDC. They explained that the other side had not arrived, probably for reasons of security. He told them he would have to return to the Basque Country the following day to vote for the new chief minister in the Basque Parliament. His friend Patxi López, the socialist candidate, had told him he would shoot him if he lost to the nationalist PNV party because of his absence. The HDC immediately rearranged the meeting, not in the Wilson, but in the Hotel Beau-Rivage down the road, the doyen of Geneva's lakeside hotels with the office of Sotheby's in the basement, where the world's most expensive watches are sold.

Sometimes the first meeting between two enemy organisations turns out to be between people who already know each other. Neither ETA nor the government had known in advance who would be representing the other side at the meeting in Geneva. When they sat down in a room in the Beau-Rivage, Griffiths introduced Eguiguren, by the code name 'Miguel', to 'George', whom Eguiguren recognised immediately as the two of them had been in the Basque Parliament together. The ETA representative was in fact José Antonio Urrutikoetxea, known as Josu Ternera, one of the historic leaders of the group. Ternera had reputedly participated in ETA's most famous attack, the assassination of Franco's prime minister, Admiral Carrero Blanco, in 1973. The ETA team dug a tunnel across a Madrid street and placed a huge amount of explosives in it. As the admiral drove by on his way back from Mass they detonated it, catapulting his car through the air over a five-storey building and into the courtyard of a Jesuit college, killing both Blanco and his driver and bodyguard. Ternera had served time in jail and disappeared in 2002 after appearing before the National Court charged with involvement in an attack on the Civil Guard base in Zaragoza in 1987 in which eleven people were killed, including five children. He was now fifty-four and Eguiguren felt that the years in jail hung on him and he wanted to end the conflict. George was accompanied by 'Robert' (Jon Yurrebaso), a nervous fifty-year-old ETA veteran who had been released from jail in 1991 and who had trained in a PFLP (Popular Front for the Liberation of Palestine) camp in South Yemen. Robert never spoke in the negotiations. He took notes, typed on his laptop and occasionally whispered in George's ear.

The first meeting was a little stiff and formal. Eguiguren

announced that he had to return to Vitoria in the Basque Country to vote, which was taken amiss by George, who was expecting to get on with intensive negotiations. The meeting lasted no more than a couple of hours, ending at 8 p.m., but it had at least broken the ice. Eguiguren drove through the night and got home at five in the morning. He slept for three hours, then voted in Vitoria, and drove straight back to Geneva.

George proposed they meet every other day in the morning or afternoon, but not all day. ETA wanted time to write up their notes of the meetings and consult. Eguiguren accepted the proposal but had no intention of consulting or taking notes himself. 'I had everything in my head,' he said. He had no instructions or advisers from Madrid, or even a laptop. He did not find Geneva the most exciting city in the world and he spent the summer wandering the streets, going to the cinema, and occasionally his wife visited. He didn't have much money and was told not to use his credit cards so he lived off snacks from Turkish restaurants. Madrid gave him a special mobile to call them on, but he lost it almost at once by leaving it on a bench. He hadn't brought enough clothes and he soon began to look crumpled.

The two sides would meet daily, changing hotels for each meeting, with witnesses from the HDC also attending. The ETA representatives had no guarantees they wouldn't be arrested and so the meetings had to be conducted stealthily. George was very conscious of security. He instructed Griffiths in the proper sequence: who should arrive first, who should leave first, who should know the location of the meeting ahead of time, and so on. It was not for nothing that George had remained on the run for fifteen years, and still remains at liberty despite the best efforts of the French and Spanish police.

NGOs like the HDC can operate under the radar, unlike big-name mediators, and can make contact with covert armed groups and facilitate quiet discussions in a way the UN or a government cannot. In managing the talks with ETA, Griffiths

was building on an earlier success in making contact with
Gerakan Aceh Merdeka (GAM), the rebel movement in Aceh
in Indonesia, where he had arranged the first talks between
the organisation and the Indonesian government.

The leadership of GAM, including their supreme leader
Hasan di Tiro, had lived in exile in Stockholm since 1976.
Their first meeting with representatives of the Indonesian
government took place on 27 January 2000 in a château in
Bavois, north of Lausanne. It was the home of Thierry Lombard,
the eponymous senior partner of Lombard Odier, one of
Switzerland's oldest private banks and a trustee of the newly
established HDC. The Indonesian government was represented
by Hassan Wirajuda, the ambassador to the UN in Geneva,
later to become the Indonesian foreign minister. Wirajuda had
witnessed the talks between the Philippines government and
the rebel Moro National Liberation Front in the 1990s, and
was possessed of a good deal of self-confidence. The HDC had
asked for the approval of the Indonesian Cabinet before going
ahead with the meeting, but that was not forthcoming and
Wirajuda had said 'Let's just do it.'

Aceh, at the north-western tip of Sumatra, Indonesia's largest
island, had been an independent sultanate in colonial times,
and in the nineteenth century resisted the Dutch masters longer
than any of the other parts of the archipelago. At the time of
independence the Acehnese had played a particularly valiant
role in kicking the Dutch out. They were not, however, rewarded
with the independence they had been promised, but instead
faced military occupation, and the initial autonomy statute
granted to them was revoked in 1956. Hasan di Tiro, the
descendant of a famous *ulema* who in the nineteenth century
had led the resistance to the Dutch, declared independence in
1976 and led an uprising with the formation of GAM. The
rebellion was bloodily suppressed by the military dictatorship,
and di Tiro sought sanctuary with some of his supporters in
Sweden. In the following thirty years more than 33,000 people
were killed. The group was nearly wiped out in 1979 but the

brutal behaviour of government forces and the supply of money and training from Libya and Iran in the late 1980s led to a renewed guerrilla campaign. The area was declared an 'area of special military operations' in 1989, and Indonesian forces committed appalling human-rights abuses in attempting to suppress the rebellion.

When the Indonesian military dictatorship finally came to an end with the fall of Suharto in 1998, a new opportunity appeared to resolve the conflict peacefully. The interim president B. J. Habibie publicly apologised for the military campaign and lifted the special military regime in Aceh. Griffiths sent a young Chinese-American researcher to East Timor, which was on its way to independence from Indonesia. There she was told that the conflict was already oversubscribed with organisations offering help and she should go to Aceh. She met and recruited a young Belgian in Jakarta who had recently published a book on Islam which had come to the attention of the new president, Abdurrahman Wahid (known familiarly as Gus Dur), a revered religious leader who had studied at the Al-Azhar University in Cairo and suffered several strokes, leaving him almost blind. (When Griffiths later visited him in the presidential palace he was amazed by the state of his office. There was a bicycle propped up against the wall behind his desk, which was itself piled high with cassettes of classical music, while dry-cleaning lay draped over a chair.) Gus Dur asked to see the researcher, who had already made contact with one of the president's daughters and one of his close advisers. In November they met the president and invited him to visit the HDC in Geneva.

Unbeknownst to Griffiths, the president had already tried to reach out to GAM leaders in Stockholm but his advances had come to naught. He wanted to hold a referendum in Aceh but the Indonesian elite were opposed. The approach from the HDC presented him with a new opportunity to end the violence, despite opposition from within his own Cabinet. On his way to the annual Davos conference in January 2000, he diverted to Geneva and insisted on visiting the HDC to make a speech in support of the peace process. He told Griffiths, sitting in his office with its view of Mont Blanc, that he had come to make a political point, to show the world and particularly the Cabinet members he had brought with him that he supported the HDC. He later confided in Griffiths that one of his heroes was Florence Nightingale, and another was Henry Dunant, the founder of the Red Cross, which was why he had chosen the HDC. In front of surprised Indonesian officials he used his speech to charge the centre with creating a channel to resolve the conflict. Armed with this presidential mandate they were in a position to approach the GAM leadership.

Griffiths didn't have an immediate way of reaching Hasan di Tiro, but he knew he lived in Stockholm. He simply went through the Stockholm telephone directory and started calling everyone with that surname. In the end he got the right person and asked to come and see him. To his surprise he was welcomed by di Tiro. Armed groups can be unexpectedly welcoming as a result of their craving for legitimacy and recognition. Most of all they want someone to listen to them. Griffiths then met Malik Mahmud, the group's chief negotiator, in a Singapore hotel. Mahmud was being followed by incompetent Indonesian secret service agents and Griffiths and his deputy Marshall were being tailed by the far more competent Singaporeans, with lots of darting in and out of revolving doors. Griffiths had deliberately decided to hold the meeting in public, since he had already informed the Indonesians he was going to meet GAM.

Mahmud told him that he was the first person in an international organisation to express any interest in their plight or to make contact with them in two decades of fighting. He explained to Griffiths that GAM were not Islamic extremists. It was their policy not to meet the government but they were prepared to meet intermediaries. Griffiths stressed his UN background and his interest in the humanitarian aspects of the conflict. GAM had long been keen to internationalise their claim in the hope the US and EU would put pressure on the Indonesian government to end the human-rights abuses that were taking place in Aceh. They wanted to take their case to the UN Security Council as the sole legitimate representative of the Acehnese people. Ideally they would have chosen the UN itself or a state as the intermediary, but no state was willing to take on the role, and the HDC appeared to them to be staffed by people who had been in the UN and were well connected.

Griffiths met another GAM leader in Singapore who claimed to be the authoritative voice of the movement. Later it became clear that he headed a breakaway faction, the MP-GAM, known as the Malaysian GAM. The leaders of both groups were based in Sweden. Although they never talked to each other they sometimes ran into each other in the same supermarket aisle in suburban Stockholm. Griffiths' first steps revealed a problem that would-be intermediaries face everywhere. How do you know you are talking to the right people? In the chaos of war people come forward claiming to speak for the armed group from a mixture of motives, ranging from money to a grab for power. Demonstrating beyond doubt to the government side that they are the real leaders of the group can be challenging. Nigel Quinney and Heather Coyne write about one extreme case in Iraq where US military negotiators 'had to determine whether the voice on the other end of the telephone really was the spokesperson for an insurgent group. They tested this by saying "shoot a rocket now". If a rocket was fired they knew it was the right group.'

Griffiths invited the MP-GAM to Geneva as well, so there were in fact two meetings in the château at Bavois on successive days in 2000. Both days went more or less according to plan. Hassan Wirajuda had run across the GAM leaders before at public events in Europe, but this time he adopted an emollient tone and apologised for the excesses of the Indonesian military in Aceh over the previous twenty-five years. He called GAM his brothers. GAM of course talked about their historic struggle, but both GAM delegations were affected by the ambassador's conciliatory approach. Given that GAM's firm policy was not to meet the Indonesian government, the fact that there were meetings at all was an achievement.

Griffiths opened proceedings by congratulating both sides on their courage in making the meeting happen. He stressed that it was confidential and only about humanitarian matters. Both sides nodded politely but then proceeded to talk about politics rather than humanitarian issues, and agreed a joint public statement. In the aftermath, the GAM faction led by Hasan di Tiro made it clear they would not continue with the process unless the Indonesians stopped their engagement with the Malaysian GAM. Wirajuda asked Griffiths for his view on the difference between the two, and Griffiths said that since di Tiro's group seemed to have more influence over the fighters in Aceh, it made more sense to go on with them. Only a few months later Wirajuda met again with the di Tiro GAM in Bavois at an emotional session to agree a humanitarian pause in the fighting, and to start on a peace process.

First meetings are of course more poignant if they are between people who have been engaged in direct conflict with each other, particularly if both sides are prepared at least to forgive (if not forget). The first ever meeting between the leadership of the Irish Republican movement and the leaders of the Northern Ireland police took place at 10 Downing Street in 2004. I asked the chief constable, Hugh Orde, to come, and he in turn called Peter Sheridan, the assistant chief constable and the most senior Catholic in the police service. Sheridan had grown up and served as a police officer in Derry. His car had been blown up by the IRA twice, on each occasion killing all the other occupants. He and his family had been forced to move house three times in the face of IRA threats. Martin McGuinness had been the commander of the IRA in Derry at the time, and yet Sheridan was willing to come to Downing Street, shake him by the hand and demonstrate remarkable magnanimity.

The day before he received the call from Orde, Sheridan had been meeting in Derry with the journalist Nell McCafferty, who had given him a bowl of soup. After he had finished, she asked him to guess who had made it. When he gave up, she said, 'Peggy.' 'Peggy who?' he asked. 'Martin McGuinness's mother,' she said. He made a joke about her trying to poison him, and wrote on a card 'Thanks for the wonderful soup' and gave it to Nell to pass on to Peggy. When the meeting in the Cabinet Room at Downing Street was over, Sheridan stood by the door to shake hands with Gerry Kelly, Gerry Adams and Martin McGuinness. McGuinness was the last to leave and Sheridan held on to his hand and said, 'Your mother makes wonderful soup. I had a bowl of it on Saturday.' 'Where did you get a bowl of my mother's soup?' McGuinness asked in surprise. 'Make sure you come back for another meeting, I'll tell you then,' Sheridan said.

Arriving at such a momentous meeting when two enemies shake hands can take years of preparation, often far longer than outside observers realise. When the extraordinary outcome of the secret talks in Oslo between the PLO and the Israeli government burst on the world in 1993, it was assumed the contacts between the Israelis and the Palestinians had only begun in 1992. After all, Prime Minister Yitzhak Rabin had said 'We will never negotiate with the so-called PLO.' In fact the trail went back far further, based on years of building relationships.

Yair Hirschfeld, the man who made the first contact with the PLO, is a bear of a man, described by his colleague Uri Savir as looking like 'a typical Viennese intellectual of the 1920s . . . with his wild brown beard, untamed hair, and bemused expression'. He is in fact a sensitive and kind professor at the University of Haifa in Israel, who had long been a close adviser to the Israeli Labour Party, and it was he who represented Israel at the secret Oslo talks. He traces the path back to 1979 after he had appeared on Austrian television commenting on Ayatollah Khomeini's takeover in Iran. The Austrian chancellor Bruno Kreisky, known for his close relationships in the Arab world, asked him to come in and see him to discuss Israeli–Palestinian relations. Hirschfeld suggested that the Austrians give economic assistance to Gaza and the West Bank, and speak to Yasser Arafat, to persuade him to give a mandate to Palestinian leaders in the occupied territories to talk to the Israelis. Kreisky did as he suggested, and in the following years Shimon Peres and his deputy Yossi Beilin asked Hirschfeld to begin developing contacts with the two most prominent internal leaders, Hanan Ashrawi and Faisal Husseini.

The Israelis first tried a bottom-up approach, building economic capacity, and even considered elections to endow the leadership with greater credibility. The internal Palestinian leadership, however, consistently made it clear to the Israelis that they would need to speak to the PLO itself if things were going to advance. In 1991 Hirschfeld gave Hanan Ashrawi a piece of paper torn out of a yellow legal pad with a formula on the West Bank written on it. She changed it by hand. He took the words to Peres who had said yes to them on the spot. But when Hirschfeld went back to Ashrawi she couldn't accept yes for an answer, saying she would have to consult. The Israelis heard nothing for a week, despite Hirschfeld trying to get her on the phone three times a day.

Osama El-Baz, an adviser to President Mubarak in Egypt, then suddenly turned up in Jerusalem with a better offer, and one clearly authorised by Arafat, who wanted to demonstrate that he was in charge and he could present the Israelis with a more attractive deal if they talked to him directly rather than negotiating with the internal leadership. The Israelis finally came to the conclusion that if they didn't talk to the PLO, Arafat would block everything. The answer would be no, even if the inside leadership said yes. It was therefore essential to open up a backchannel to move things along. It had to remain a backchannel because the Israeli government could not recognise the PLO until they knew what they could get in return. Peres said 'the bottom line was Arafat. If we did not make direct contact with Yasser Arafat the negotiations would remain at a standstill.'

Beilin and Hirschfeld had tried backchannels before. In 1989 Hanan Ashrawi suggested they use Max van der Stoel, the former Labour foreign minister in the Netherlands, as a go-between. At his suggestion, Beilin and Hirschfeld held prox-imity talks with the PLO over two days in The Hague. The two delegations sat in different hotels and van der Stoel shut-tled back and forth between them. They did not make a break-through but the process continued with van der Stoel meeting Hirschfeld and Beilin from time to time to keep them briefed. Ashrawi had suggested they use as a cover story that van der Stoel was visiting the Israeli finance minister, since Beilin was at that stage deputy minister of finance. The negotiations never became public but when they were revealed to the Israeli government, one Cabinet minister demanded that Beilin resign immediately. Peres refused to allow it to happen.

Once the official peace process got under way in Washington after the Madrid Conference in 1991, the Israelis started searching in earnest for a backchannel. Terje Roed-Larsen, director of the Norwegian Institute of Applied Social Sciences, who was working on living conditions in Gaza and the West Bank and who had good contacts on the Palestinian side, met Beilin in May 1992 and offered to arrange a meeting with Faisal Husseini, one of the PLO internal leaders. Hirschfeld was dispatched in June 1992 to make it clear to Roed-Larsen that they already had contact with Husseini but he maintained contact with Roed-Larsen, and on the morning of his meeting with the PLO in London in December he decided to take the risk of telling him that on that very day he would be meeting Abu Ala, the PLO minister of the economy. Roed-Larsen offered to host the contacts in Norway and said the new Labour government there would pick up the bill and arrange secure locations for the meetings.

Hirschfeld had decided personally to set up a backchannel without obliging the government. He had identified Abu Ala as his ideal interlocutor after European diplomats had sent him a document that Abu Ala had given them on economic development in the occupied territories. Hirschfeld thought he would have a common language with him on economic and development issues. Their first meeting was in London on 4 December 1992 in the genteel surroundings of the Cavendish Hotel on Jermyn Street. Hirschfeld had wanted to rent a private room for the meeting but he didn't have the money, so they met in public in the coffee shop.

The meeting was illegal under the Israeli law banning contact with the PLO. The Israeli Labour Party had just won the election and had promised to change the law, but because the ban had not yet been lifted, Hirschfeld hadn't been able to ask for the authority to hold a meeting. Ron Pundak, who joined him later, says they didn't tell Beilin 'because we didn't want to embarrass him'. Hirschfeld was very clear with Abu Ala in London and subsequently that he did not represent anyone. The meeting had been arranged by Faisal Husseini and Hanan Ashrawi. Hirschfeld told them he would be at his cousin's house in East Finchley if Abu Ala wanted to meet. Abu Ala must have been keen because he phoned over a dozen times before eventually getting hold of Hirschfeld and agreeing to meet at the Cavendish. Hirschfeld went to the meeting alone but Abu Ala was accompanied by Afif Safieh, the London representative of the PLO. Abu Ala stuck to the usual PLO script which seemed to Hirschfeld to be detached from reality. He said the new Israeli government wanted to move ahead and end the occupation, but to do so they needed an agreed structure.

It was Abu Ala's first meeting with an Israeli and he was impressed, while Afif Safieh, who had attended many such meetings, told him it didn't mean anything and advised him against seeing Hirschfeld again. Hirschfeld's primary objective was to secure agreement to a second meeting; thereafter he could get official backing to move ahead with the process. He knew Beilin, his friend and the new deputy foreign minister, was in London, and as soon as the meeting was over he went to consult him. He got the green light to continue and fixed a second meeting in the Ritz the next day.

What he hadn't realised was that the Ritz held a *thé dansant* every afternoon. He and Abu Ala had to shout at each other to be heard over the orchestra as elderly couples waltzed around them. Hirschfeld revealed that he had the full backing of Beilin, and suggested they enter bilateral negotiations in Norway. The official negotiations in Washington between the Israelis and a Palestinian negotiating team from the West Bank and Gaza could go on for a hundred years without finding a solution, not least since Shamir had vetoed participation by the PLO in the talks, but confidential negotiations might get somewhere. Abu Ala was very much taken with this approach. He handed over a non-paper with thirteen points. Hirschfeld perused it quickly and said he couldn't agree with even one point in it but, he said, self-government was on offer. He wanted an in-depth dialogue. Abu Ala responded, 'Yair, whatever it will take, whatever you demand of us, we will come to an agreement.'

Hirschfeld knew Abu Ala's background, knew he was in charge of multilateral negotiations, and knew he needed to get a green light from Arafat for everything he did. Arafat kept his hands on every detail and officials even had to get his signature to have their flights paid for, so he was certain this dialogue was authorised. Arafat needed the channel. In the first Gulf War he had chosen the wrong side and after Saddam Hussein's defeat he had lost the support of the Arab world. The Saudis had even offered Faisal Husseini a blank cheque to start a rival Palestinian movement, which he rejected. Arafat could not control what was happening at the negotiations in Washington, nor could he afford to leave matters to the internal leadership. The Israelis needed a channel too. It was two years after the 1991 Madrid Conference, and the negotiations in Washington were a mess.

Both Abu Ala and Hirschfeld had spoken to Roed-Larsen

before they met. They both knew he was 'hot' on the subject and was prepared to host meetings in Norway. Hirschfeld also knew the ban on contact with the PLO would be lifted in January by the new government, so they agreed to meet in Norway as soon as the law was changed. The next day Hirschfeld saw Dan Kurtzer, the key US official, in London and briefed him. The Americans supported the backchannel. A couple of days after the meetings in London the negotiations in Washington were broken off after the abduction of an Israeli policeman and after Rabin had dumped 500 Hamas activists in the no-man's-land on the border with Lebanon. Both sides needed a confidential dialogue to get the official talks back on track.

Hirschfeld had no idea that the process he was starting would end in ten months with an agreement signed on the lawn of the White House in the presence of President Clinton, but he already had the impression that Abu Ala would do everything possible to make a deal happen. When they did all meet in Washington after the conclusion of the Oslo Accords, Prime Minister Rabin, one of the most impressive leaders I have ever met, said as he reluctantly shook hands with Arafat, 'You don't make peace with your friends, only with your enemies.' In a speech in 1993, Rabin explained: 'I knew that the hand outstretched to me from the far side of the podium was the same that held the knife, that held the gun, the hand that gave the order to shoot, to kill. Of all the hands in the world, it was not the hand that I wanted or dreamed of touching. I would have liked to sign a peace agreement with Holland, or Luxembourg, or New Zealand. But there was no need to. That is why, on that podium, I stood as the representative of a nation that wants peace with the most bitter and odious of its foes.'

Two years later he was killed for trying. If only all other leaders were as brave and prepared to risk as much as he did to end their armed conflicts.

CHAPTER THREE

Building a Channel

While nothing is easier than to denounce the evildoer, nothing is more difficult than to understand him.

Fyodor Dostoevsky, *The Possessed*

It is neither possible nor sensible to jump straight from introducing yourself to the leader of an armed group into a negotiation. Talking, which is always sensible, is not the same as negotiating. There are a number of stages that must be gone through before a negotiation becomes even conceivable.

F. W. de Klerk identifies three stages to the South African negotiations from the point of view of the government: a first exploratory phase with Nelson Mandela and the ANC in exile; second, informal talks to remove obstacles and prepare for structured negotiations; and lastly, formal and representative negotiations that led to a new constitution. Niel Barnard saw six phases: first, making contact and information-gathering; second, building trust; third, exploring the range of opportunities and options; fourth, transferring the process to a wider base, including the ANC in exile; fifth, the return of exiles and the establishment of a ceasefire; and only then the formal and public negotiations leading to a political settlement.

Yair Hirschfeld set out the different stages to his negotiation with the PLO at their first meeting, when he gave Abu Ala a piece of paper torn from an exercise book with the four phases written out by hand: fact-finding, authorisation for the talks, legitimisation of the channel, and breakthrough from backchannel to official talks on the Israeli side. As the talks went on, every so often Abu Ala would ask Hirschfeld if they were moving from phase 1 to phase 2. The plan created a predictability to the process.

Joaquín Villalobos, one of the key rebel military commanders in the bloody civil war in El Salvador between 1980 and 1992, describes three stages to the El Salvador peace process from the point of view of the armed group: 'First using political negotiation as a device to support the war; second using the war to support the negotiations; and only lastly the negotiations central so that war would no longer be possible.'

There are a different number of phases in different peace processes but there is always a series of distinct stages, and having made contact, the second stage is building a channel through which the two sides can communicate accurately and safely. Colonel Mbaye Faye, a Senegalese officer who worked for ten years on the Burundi conflict, says 'The first victim of a conflict is confidence', and so the primary objective in talks is building trust, understanding the group's real interests and helping them understand their own aims better. American academic Dean Pruitt believes such contacts 'can overcome most of the concerns that make parties (governments or terrorists) reluctant to negotiate openly with each other. They allow low-cost exploration of the other party's flexibility and trustworthiness. If concessions made in backchannels are not reciprocated, they can easily be disavowed and prior positions reasserted . . . Also, because they are not publicised, backchannel talks do not accord legitimacy to the terrorists and their complaints and demands. Furthermore, there is relatively little risk that hawks will find out about them and attempt to discredit a leader who engages in them.'

The establishment of a clandestine channel is often conducted on behalf of the government in the first instance by members of the intelligence agencies. They have the necessary skills to do so safely, and the ability to act deniably. The British government had a secret channel to communicate with the IRA from

1972 onwards, even though the conflict still had twenty-five bloody years to run. Soon after the Troubles broke out, the British government opened an office in a predominantly Protestant, and therefore safe, middle-class suburb of Belfast, and staffed it with British diplomats. Frank Steele, whose previous experience had been in Kenya and elsewhere in the colonies as they moved to independence, arranged the first meeting between the British government and the IRA, represented by Dáithí Ó Conaill, their chief of staff, in a house on the border with Donegal. The IRA delegation included a twenty-three-year-old Gerry Adams who had been let out of the Long Kesh internment camp for the meeting in June 1972. The IRA had bizarrely demanded that the government representatives carry with them signed letters from Willie Whitelaw, then Secretary of State for Northern Ireland, testifying to their identities and their authority to talk, and had even brought along a local solicitor to authenticate the notes. The British side proposed a meeting between the IRA and Whitelaw in return for a ten-day ceasefire, and a telephone hotline was established to avoid misunderstandings. These details out of the way, the discussion moved on to a more normal conversation with the aim of drawing out the IRA representatives, and Steele was surprised to find Adams a 'very personable, intelligent, articulate, and self-disciplined man' who would have chosen to go to university had he not felt the need to get rid of the British first.

There was no meeting of minds at the subsequent encounter with Whitelaw in Paul Channon's house in Cheyne Walk in early July. The IRA demanded that the British leave Ireland by 1975. Whitelaw made it clear that was not going to happen. The IRA subsequently made the encounter public, causing huge alarm in the Unionist community and serious political damage to Whitelaw. The ceasefire collapsed into one of the bloodiest periods of the Troubles, including Bloody Friday two weeks after the meeting, and the reoccupation by the British army of the no-go areas in Belfast and Derry in Operation Motorman, the largest movement of British troops since Suez. Only two months after the ceasefire had collapsed, Frank Steele received an approach from Brendan Duddy, a go-between from Derry and a friend of Ruairí Ó Brádaigh, the president of Republican Sinn Féin, asking to meet him as he had a message from the IRA. Duddy said that there was a split in the IRA between the militants and the political wing, and that contacts with the British would help to strengthen the moderates.

Steele was succeeded by Michael Oatley in April 1973. Oatley started venturing into the IRA strongholds in West Belfast and Derry by himself, taking his life in his hands. He never asked for permission as he knew it would be refused. 'One finds oneself walking around in areas where officials and soldiers went in armoured cars,' he said, 'and I was on my feet hoping I wouldn't attract too much attention. People I wanted to meet, people recommended to me, people who wanted peace but connected to the IRA, wouldn't come out to meet me so I had to go and meet them.' On one occasion, he was 'talking to a close relative of a former chief of staff of the IRA and at the end of the meeting he said to me, "For goodness sake don't tell us when you are coming back, then we can't be blamed when they kill you."'

It was Oatley who realised the potential of Duddy, a successful Derry businessman who was a convinced Republican but opposed to violence, and started to cultivate him. According to Oatley, Duddy was 'worried no one was trying to put an arm round the political thinking of those who engaged in violence. He was looking for a link to the British government.' They would meet in a safe house in the mountains near Derry where each tried to educate the other on their respective political sensitivities.

There was a ban on any contact with the IRA on the British side as a result of the public relations disaster caused by the Cheyne Walk meeting. Duddy told Oatley the IRA were usually good at keeping a secret, and killed people who were not secure. He said they had not understood the need to keep the

Chelsea meeting private, but if they re-engaged they would keep the contact secret. The link was in fact so secret that Duddy's existence was hidden even from the new Secretary of State for Northern Ireland, Merlyn Rees. Oatley went to see Frank Cooper, the permanent secretary in the Northern Ireland Office, and told him he had constructed 'a bamboo pipe' between himself and Ó Bráidaigh. 'The pipe is held by Brendan Duddy. I haven't said anything yet since we are not allowed to talk to the IRA. But if I go puff puff at one end then he can feel me going puff puff and if he goes puff puff back I can feel him, so we know we are there. Now we have this pipe can we start putting bits of information down it to turn it into a relationship or a dialogue?' Cooper secured agreement from the prime minister and they started providing small scraps of information, for example the date of the release of a high-profile IRA detainee, to help the 'doves' in the leadership. They kept it going in this way for a number of months.

Duddy says 'bit by bit Oatley and I got friendly' and as he became the most reliable intermediary, the British government dropped two other existing channels to the IRA and other proposed channels were rejected. While it is sensible to try many different routes to the armed group to start with, to see which works best, it is important that once you have one clear channel working you close down the others in order to avoid interference.

Even after he had left Northern Ireland, Oatley deliberately kept the channel open and would meet Duddy or speak to him on the phone from time to time, despite the injunction from Roy Mason, Merlyn Rees's successor as Northern Ireland Secretary, that all contact, direct or indirect, should cease. Oatley agreed that Duddy should brief the new IRA leadership, including Martin McGuinness, about the existence of the channel and inform him that it could be reopened whenever they wanted and wherever Oatley was in the world. It sprang back to life at the time of the hunger strikes in 1980, when Duddy phoned Oatley in London late at night and said there might be a way of resolving the issue before the first hunger striker died. Oatley went to see the new permanent secretary who in turn sought agreement from Mrs Thatcher. Armed with her permission, Oatley flew to Belfast and met Duddy and Father Meagher, the IRA prisoners' go-between, in a deserted arrivals terminal at Aldegrove airport, and handed them a document listing the concessions the government was prepared to make. As a result, the first hunger strike was called off, although sadly the agreement collapsed and the second hunger strike resulted in a number of deaths and a worsening of the violence. In 1991 the channel sprang to life again, and Oatley met Martin McGuinness just before Oatley retired from the SIS. This encounter began the exchanges with John Major that eventually led to the 1994 IRA ceasefire.

In Northern Ireland the channel was established right at the beginning and remained in place for most of the conflict. More usually the channel takes a long time to develop and there are many slips along the way. In the El Salvador civil war a coalition of five armed groups ranging from Communist to Christian Democrat came together in 1980 at a fortnight-long conference in Managua, Nicaragua. Salvador Cayetano Carpio – leader of the Communist Popular Liberation Forces (FPL) faction, and described by Castro as the 'Ho Chi Minh of Latin America' – was only prepared to accept a merger of the groups if the others agreed to name the new movement after Farabundo Martí, a Communist leader in the 1930s. Carpio had trained in both a seminary and in Moscow under Stalin; not surprisingly, he retained a very black and white view of life.

Joaquín Villalobos was the leader of the People's Revolutionary Army (ERP) faction of the merged Farabundo Martí National Liberation Front (FMLN), a highly determined man full of nervous energy, famous for his military exploits. In 1984 he arranged a trap for Lieutenant Colonel Domingo Monterrosa, the commander of the elite Atlacatl Battalion of the Salvadoran army, who was obsessed with Radio Venceremos, the rebels' pirate radio station. Monterrosa was quoted by colleagues as saying, 'So long as we don't finish off this Radio Venceremos, we'll always have a scorpion up our ass.' Monterrosa was the central figure in several brutal massacres, and Villalobos had noticed he always came himself to inspect articles captured from the guerrillas, including a small-scale model they had used to plan an attack. Villalobos therefore arranged for the original transmitter for Radio Venceremos to be left abandoned near the town where Monterrosa was operating. After his troops found it in a cemetery and excitedly informed him, Monterrosa wanted to film the capture and waited till an army TV crew arrived. This was an enormous propaganda coup, and he prepared to take the trophy back to San Salvador in a recently provided American Huey helicopter. The guerrillas watched from a hill north-west of the town as the helicopter took off. Once it was clear, the guerrillas pointed their remote control device at it and pressed the button. Nothing happened, and they panicked. Then a second helicopter took off and when the button was pressed again, the helicopter turned into a ball of fire. The rebels had planted an explosive device in the transmitter to finish off Monterrosa.

Throughout the early 1980s the issue of whether or not to negotiate was debated by the guerrillas, with Carpio opposing negotiations. The leaders of the different groups that made up the FMLN went to Cuba in 1982 to attempt finally to decide their position. Villalobos describes it as like going to the Vatican to resolve a theological issue: no one could argue with the Pope, in this case Castro. Fifteen FMLN leaders sat on one side of the table in a government building in Havana and on the other side sat Castro and his aides. Castro stood up and read out a document with the text of the position supporting negotiations that he wanted them to adopt. Carpio, whose intention was to go back to El Salvador and launch a violent power struggle inside the FMLN, said he needed to 'consult the base'. Castro demanded that he sign the document immediately. There was huge tension in the room. Carpio said he had to go to the lavatory. Villalobos thought Carpio might even commit suicide. When he came back, Carpio looked very serious and continued to try to resist but Castro insisted that he sign the document there and then. Carpio had no choice but to back down. It was a major humiliation.

Carpio had acquiesced but the argument continued within the FMLN, with his second-in-command, Ana María, opposing his view and supporting negotiations. Ana María's real name was Mélida Anaya Montes and she had been a professor who was arrested and tortured by the security authorities before joining the guerrillas. She was found dead at her home in Managua on 6 April 1983, stabbed eight times with an ice pick. In order to create confusion her murderers had tried to make it look as though the crime had been carried out by Salvadoran special forces and for good measure had left a pair of bloodstained gloves in a house belonging to Villalobos's ERP group in an attempt to implicate them too. Carpio himself had made sure he was out of the country in Libya seeking weapons supplies at the time of the murder to provide an alibi. The Nicaraguans investigated and one of Carpio's group confessed, by which time Carpio had returned. The police surrounded his house in Managua, and Manuel Piñero, Castro's lieutenant in charge of Cuban support for guerrilla movements, went inside to speak to him. After half an hour he left and Carpio reportedly shot himself, although according to other accounts he was executed by the Nicaraguans or other members of the FMLN. He left behind a letter saying the revolution should continue.

Even when the armed group has firmly decided they do want to talk, the usual pattern is for there to be a series of failed efforts to establish a channel which only succeed some time later. From the early 1980s onwards there were numerous attempts to bring the two sides in El Salvador together. Villalobos recalls Hans-Jürgen Wischnewski, a German official close to former chancellor Willy Brandt, who had already mediated with the Red Army Faction in 1977 and was later involved in Nicaragua and Lebanon, starting to shuttle between the two sides on behalf of the Socialist International in 1981.

Carpio 'lost' the key document that Wischnewski had brought to the FMLN and it mysteriously made its way into the hands of the Salvadoran army together with a document by Carpio, on which he had not consulted the other groups, suggesting that the international mediation was nothing more than a tactical manoeuvre. When Wischnewski went back to meet José Napoleón Duarte, at that stage head of state under the military junta, the president had already seen Carpio's document, which had the effect of comprehensively discrediting the German's peace proposals. Duarte told Wischnewski that he was being used by the rebels. The German went from San Salvador straight to Cuba to complain. Fidel Castro demanded to know what had happened and the FMLN leaders apologised and said they had been unaware of Carpio's document, but it was too late to resuscitate the process. In 1984, Archbishop Emilio Lorenzo Stehle from Ecuador travelled to the mountains of El Salvador with a message from Duarte for the guerrilla leaders. He said that the president agreed with their political programme and offered to disband the right-wing death squads and to find a political solution, but the guerrillas doubted that Duarte had the power to rein in the police and the military, and the talks led nowhere.

After his election as president in 1984, Duarte announced that he intended to end the civil war by 'dialogue without arms' and proposed to the rebels that they meet inside the country. The rebels accepted the offer and proposed La Palma, forty-five miles north of the capital in the centre of their operational zone, where no government official travelled without an army escort. Duarte announced he would go unarmed, and walked the last several hundred yards to the church where the meeting took place. As he arrived, three Red Cross vehicles drew up containing the guerrilla leaders wearing military fatigues. Four and a half hours later the two sides reached an agreement and the archbishop read it out. Before the planned follow-up meeting, however, the FPL faction kidnapped the president's daughter Inés, and the negotiations to free her in

return for 126 FMLN prisoners preoccupied him over the
following months. His next attempt at making peace misfired.
Duarte and Villalobos came close to meeting in the town of
Sesori near the border with Honduras, but at the last moment
the army took control of the area to prevent the encounter
taking place. In desperation Duarte took to the short-wave
radio saying he was still ready to meet, but it was too late.

In 1986 a British diplomat based in Mexico City managed to
make contact with the FMLN with the help of the Mexican
intellectual Jorge Castañeda, who introduced him to Salvador
Samayoa, a leading member of the FPL faction, a thoughtful man
in his mid-thirties with a dry sense of humour. Samayoa had
been a philosophy lecturer at the Jesuit Central American
University in San Salvador and briefly minister of education until,
appalled at the murderous intransigence of the far right, he had
joined the rebels. He was now their unofficial foreign minister.

The first meeting between the two men took place in an
open-air café on a sultry evening in Managua. Samayoa was
initially wary of contact with a British official, given Britain's
relationship with the US, but concluded that as direct links
were impossible, there might be some merit in talking to a
government close to Washington. The British diplomat was
taking a risk since he had no official authorisation to meet a
representative of the FMLN, but he wanted to pursue the idea
of a negotiated solution to the conflict. During several months
of meetings, mainly in Mexico City, they agreed to explore the
possibility of the British government hosting peace talks
between the FMLN and the Salvadoran army – 'army to army',
as Samayoa put it – in Belize. Their thinking was that if the
two forces could sit down together it would be difficult for
other actors, such as the right-wing political party ARENA, to
sabotage the talks. After further exchanges the FMLN drafted
a memorandum signed by Schafik Handal, the new leader of
the Communist FPL faction of the FMLN, as the basis for
further discussions. At this point, however, the British Foreign
Office decided not to pursue the initiative on the grounds that

it would be badly received in Washington, which still believed the FMLN could be defeated militarily.

Despite all the misfires, in El Salvador and elsewhere, once you have established contact the first step is to be prepared to listen and treat your interlocutors with respect. As former US Secretary of State Dean Rusk said, 'One of the best ways to persuade others is with your ears – by listening to them.' And there is a lot of listening to do. I used to joke in Northern Ireland that if we cut off a meeting with a party after half an hour we would only have got to 1689, leaving another three centuries of grievances to get through. Uri Savir says that in the Arab–Israel conflict 'each side considered itself a victim' and both want to air their grievances while disregarding totally those of the other side.

Listening was the central point of the informal channel between the ANC in exile and Afrikaner intellectuals set up by Michael Young in 1987. Young was the head of corporate affairs at Consolidated Goldfields, a London-based mining company with huge interests in South Africa, and had been a political adviser to Edward Heath and Alec Douglas-Home, specialising in Southern African issues. After a public meeting he approached the ANC leader Oliver Tambo to ask what British business could do to help resolve the conflict. Tambo took his hand and looked off into the middle distance, before saying 'I want you to help me build a bridge to Pretoria, because when the signals come I don't think I will recognise them. We need to have a channel of communication which is not a microphone or amplified through the media but is as direct and personal as possible.' There had already been a number of high-profile encounters between liberal white anglophone South Africans and the ANC in Dakar and Lusaka in the mid-1980s, but nothing serious with mainstream Afrikaners. Persuading members of the Broederbond, the tightly knit Afrikaner equivalent of the Masons, to meet secretly in England with the ANC in exile for 'talks about talks about talks' was a bold idea.

The first meeting took place incongruously in the basement of the Compleat Angler, a pub in an isolated spot near Marlow on the banks of the Thames, in November 1987. The three academics from Stellenbosch University who made up the Afrikaner delegation stood in the car park waiting for the ANC participants, who arrived in a black chauffeur-driven limousine. As they got out of the car, Aziz Pahad, leader of the delegation, greeted the academics in Afrikaans in an effort to break the ice, asking a question about the South African sun they all missed in the cold and misty English autumn.

Both sides were nervous. The ANC group included Harold Wolpe, a Communist who pulled off a spectacular escape from jail after the Rivonia Trial in the 1960s, and was regarded by the Afrikaners as 'the Devil incarnate'. The formal session started off tentatively with no predetermined agenda, each side hesitant and waiting for the other to say something specific. Vitally there was plenty of time for socialising between sessions and they were able to swap notes about their past lives. Willie Esterhuyse, one of the academics, discovered he and Pahad had acquaintances and experiences in common.

Shortly after agreeing to participate in the dialogue, Esterhuyse had received a call from the NIS in Pretoria asking to see him. When two men came to the door of his house, his wife said 'They look like security policemen. Be careful what you say.' They wanted him to act as their eyes and ears in the dialogue with the ANC. He was given a code name, 'Gert', and told not to breathe a word of his mission even to his closest friends. They trained him in security techniques and conducted all their meetings in safe houses. When he questioned all the security measures, they explained it was not to protect him from the ANC, but from 'the brown shirts' in their own system. He became the NIS's means of communicating with Thabo Mbeki and other ANC leaders in exile.

Although he had not attended the first meeting, Mbeki came to the second at Eastwell Manor, a hotel in Kent, in February 1988. Esterhuyse took the first opportunity when they were alone to tell Mbeki about the role he had been given by the NIS. He hadn't told Michael Young or any of the other participants. Mbeki was naturally suspicious and played for time by filling his pipe, lighting it and puffing away, allowing himself to get his thoughts in order, and asked 'You are aware you are taking a risk by informing me? Why are you doing it?' Esterhuyse explained that he thought not telling him would be a greater risk. It was apparent to him that Mbeki had been looking for a channel to Pretoria for some time, but Mbeki came under criticism from his own side for participating in the sessions. Chris Hani, chief of staff of the ANC's armed wing, Umkhonto We Sizwe (MK), used a meeting of the ANC executive that coincided with the meeting in Kent to attack Mbeki for talking to Afrikaner intellectuals without a mandate or prior consultation. Aziz Pahad says 'There was a feeling by some that those who were talking were being co-opted and were selling out,' but they were protected by Oliver Tambo.

For the third meeting in August 1988, the process moved to its permanent venue at Mells Park, a Lutyens mansion near Bath belonging to Consolidated Goldfields. This time F. W. de Klerk's brother, Wimpie, attended and became the centre of attention for the ANC participants at that and subsequent meetings. Mbeki asked him which way his brother would go once in office. De Klerk took the view that he would be conservative. Later Wimpie described briefing his brother about the contacts with the ANC: 'The essence of my message was "Look boys, everything is OK. We can do business with the ANC. They are not that radical. They are willing to negotiate. They are willing to compromise. They see the Afrikaners as an indigenous part of the South African population. They are not that dangerous."'

Nothing very concrete was achieved at the talks, but that was not their point. The purpose was to build trust and create a channel down which messages could be exchanged between the ANC in exile and the government in Pretoria. The formal sessions were not as important as the gatherings in the evening around the fire in the library. As Michael Young put it, 'From time to time I would leave them with a bottle of Glenfiddich. They didn't do business. What they did do was get to know each other – what their real tolerances were, why this or that was not acceptable.' Esterhuyse had heard the American nego-tiator Chester Crocker say that the human factor had been crucial in the talks on Namibia. The negotiators there had discovered that they could trust each other, and Van-Dúnem, the Angolan justice minister and a former law professor, had talked with his Afrikaner opposite numbers in Dutch. Describing the process later, Niel Barnard said, 'If you're seriously interested in negotiating you start with a private clarification of positions and possible ways to resolve deadlocks and strategic impasses. It's a slow process. Patience is more important than publicity.'

In May 1989 the NIS agents contacted Esterhuyse and asked him to travel to London to meet Mbeki privately. No one else was to know what they discussed. The message he was to carry was that the NIS wanted to start talking officially to the ANC. They wanted a phone number for Mbeki, they said, and the code name of the person calling would be John Campbell. Mbeki's code name was to be John Semelane. Esterhuyse called Michael Young and he arranged to meet Mbeki in the offices at British American Tobacco, where Young now worked. Young greeted them and left them alone in the conference room. Mbeki poured them both a cup of tea and they engaged in small talk. After a while Mbeki became restless. 'Why did you come here?' he asked. 'You're talking about issues we already discussed.' The NIS had told Esterhuyse not to pass on the message in a place that might be bugged, and he had brought along two handwritten notes. One said 'The walls have ears', and the second told Mbeki that a senior person in NIS wanted to make contact to explore the possibility of future talks. 'They need a reliable telephone number for you.' Esterhuyse handed him the notes and went to the lavatory. When he came back they left the BAT building, shook hands and went their separate ways. A little while later they met at the Albert pub, at a corner table. Mbeki gave Esterhuyse his telephone number and asked 'How do I know it is not a trap?' Esterhuyse attempted to reassure him, repeated the code name and said goodbye. That evening he went on to see a play in the West End, *A Walk in the Woods* starring Alec Guinness, about US and Russian negotiators at the SALT talks on nuclear weapons, building trust between themselves as individuals to advance the negotiations. It seemed appropriate.

Esterhuyse says he learned from his experience that 'trust between political enemies is also built as a result of shared risks', and this is true elsewhere. It was this shared risk that bound the two participants in the secret contacts in the Basque Country that led on eventually to the negotiations between the socialist government and ETA in 2004. The Basque socialist politician Jesús Eguiguren is a remarkable man. He is roly-poly, untidy, disorganised, enjoys a drink, is completely opposed to violence and, like the SDLP politician John Hume in Northern Ireland, he reached out to the armed group to try to bring peace to his native region rather than becoming vengeful. In 2001 he started meeting Arnaldo Otegi, leader of Batasuna, the political wing of ETA, secretly in a remote farmhouse up a rough country track from the little village of Elgoibar deep in the Basque countryside. The house belonged to Eguiguren's close friend in the Socialist Party, Pello Rubio. Rubio had been a Trotskyite and a member of the Workers' Committees and had got to know the leaders of Batasuna through that radical past. He brought Eguiguren together with Otegi, both of whom had grown up in these rural valleys. Eguiguren was taking a big risk, both political and physical, by meeting Otegi. ETA was in the middle of a brutal campaign in which forty-six people had already been killed, including one of his socialist colleagues in San Sebastián. Batasuna was banned and the Socialist Party had just concluded an Anti-Terrorist Pact with Aznar's conservative PP (People's Party) government. As Eguiguren put it, 'Otegi could have gone to jail and I could have been killed.'

Extraordinarily, in a small place like the Basque Country they managed to keep their meetings secret by informing almost no one in their respective parties. On one occasion a woman from a neighbouring farmhouse came to tell them that there was someone hiding behind a tree in a nearby wood watching the farmhouse. She said anyone in a wood alone in the cold of winter was up to no good. The two men therefore slipped up the cart track that took them behind the wood and found a car parked with out-of-town plates. They were very pleased with their artisan counter-espionage efforts and decided they needed to move their talks to another location.

They discussed the lessons that could be learned from both the failure of the previous attempts to make peace in the Basque Country, and from the Northern Ireland peace process. Batasuna was always formal and liked to have agreed minutes of the meetings. Eguiguren said that 'Otegi and I knew that we belonged to different worlds, which functioned with different beliefs' – Otegi wanted the right to self-determination, which he said had been offered in Ireland by the Downing Street Declaration, but Eguiguren had to operate within the laws and constitution of Spain, which did not recognise that right. At that time Aznar was still firmly in control and the two men thought they were working up ideas that could be deployed with a conservative government after the election on 14 March 2004. But all that changed on 11 March when Islamic extremists blew up a series of suburban trains in Madrid, killing 191 people and injuring 1,841. Otegi called Eguiguren that day to tell him that it was not ETA. Prime Minister Aznar, however, made the fundamental mistake of publicly insisting that it was ETA and persuading the UN Security Council to pass a resolution condemning them for the attack, even though his security chiefs had made clear to him that it wasn't the Basque terrorists. In doing so he lost the confidence of the Spanish people, and the election. The day after the election, in a burst of enthusiasm Eguiguren tried to call the new socialist prime minister, Zapatero, to brief him about his conversations with Otegi, but he wasn't put through.

One of the remarkable aspects of the whole negotiation with ETA is that Eguiguren never met Zapatero to discuss the talks in all the years that the process lasted. Nonetheless the replacement of the intransigent Aznar by a socialist government allowed the dialogue in the Basque farmhouse to lead to a full-blown peace process. Eguiguren believes the Madrid massacre also accelerated the end of ETA. They simply could not compete with the terror of Islamic extremists willing to kill unlimited numbers of people. The meetings created a personal bond of trust between Otegi and Eguiguren, who later took the major political risk of appearing in person at Otegi's trial to give evidence in his support.

A similar bond of trust was built by Yair Hirschfeld and Abu Ala in constructing the Oslo process. The day after the Knesset repealed the law forbidding contact with the PLO in January 1993, Hirschfeld met him in Norway to start negotiating. The first meeting was merely a fact-finding session, so Hirschfeld did not need to brief Peres and Rabin about it. He took his academic colleague, Ron Pundak, a historian, with him. The Norwegians had arranged for them to meet secretly in a mansion rented from a businessman in Sarpsborg, a small, ugly industrial town a hundred kilometres south of Oslo (although the meeting nearly didn't happen at all – when Abu Ala arrived at Oslo airport, the border authorities refused him entry because he didn't have a visa; Terje Roed-Larsen and his government colleagues had to scramble to sort it out). When they got to Sarpsborg, both Abu Ala and Hirschfeld were clear that they did not want the Norwegians in the room. This was a bilateral negotiation and it needed to be left to them. For Hirschfeld this was an ideological point, and for Abu Ala a practical one.

The Norwegian organisers never used hotels and public venues or the real names of the participants. After the embarrassment of the visa on the first visit they began to use the VIP suite at Oslo airport. And when they borrowed Heftye House from the city government of Oslo, they told them it was for 'foreign-ministry seminars'. Hirschfeld believes it was crucial that the talks were secret. Each side had to make concessions without knowing what they were going to get in return. If this had been done in public, everyone who thought they knew better would have expressed an opinion, and those who did not want an agreement would have an opportunity to try to kill it off. Uri Savir, who joined the talks later, recalls how they had to dissemble during the Oslo period: 'We lied to colleagues, journalists, and, hardest of all, to friends and families.' But there were benefits to these shared lies, as 'upon reaching Oslo, we regaled the Palestinians with tales of how we had each duped our respective colleagues. We felt like a club of secret agents. And as time went on, outside the negotiating room – at meals, during breaks, and on walks together – we jelled into a group that Terje, master at nourishing the bond, dubbed the "Oslo Club".'

In their first meeting in Norway, Hirschfeld and Abu Ala agreed not to dwell on the past. They were both experts on economics and development, and almost by definition pragmatic. Over dinner on the first day, however, Abu Ala compared Palestinians under Israeli occupation to Norway under the Nazis. Hirschfeld was furious. 'Don't compare us to Nazis,' he insisted. 'If you don't respect my sensitivities I won't continue to talk to you.' He never heard a comment like it again.

Building a close personal relationship is important if the talks are going to work, although that does not necessarily mean becoming friends. In a negotiation you want to persuade others to do things they don't want to do, and if they care about maintaining a good relationship with you it may make them more likely to make an effort to do it for you. Hirschfeld used humour to try to break the ice in Oslo. At the start of the session he told the Palestinians a joke, but a joke that carried a meaning: God agreed to see a group of world leaders. He told them that the world would end in two days. Prime

Minister Shamir came back and told his Cabinet that there was bad news, but he also had two bits of good news. The bad news was that the world was going to end, and the good news was, first, that God exists, and second, and even better, there will never be a Palestinian state. The point he wanted to make, without tabling a formal proposal, was that with the new Labour government in Israel, unlike its predecessor under Shamir, there could be a two-state solution. Hirschfeld tried to keep the mood informal and light, but he did not try to establish a personal friendship with his Palestinian opposite numbers. They had different value systems from him, and he saw no need to become chummy. He did, however, think it was crucial to stick to his word. On one occasion Peres instructed him not to attend a scheduled meeting with Abu Ala, but Hirschfeld had promised he would come and felt he had to attend the meeting if he was to maintain good faith. Peres permitted Hirschfeld to go to Norway and tell Abu Ala that he 'was not coming to a regular meeting' and required some additional goodwill gestures from the PLO.

Uri Savir told Peres about how well the delegates were bonding in their shared isolation from the outside world. Peres, quoting an Indian poet, said: 'I'm alone. You're alone. Let's be alone together.' Savir added, 'The more time I spent with our partners, the more I discovered that we may have known a lot about them but we understood very little.' One of the key purposes of such meetings is to come to understand better the other side's point of view, even if you don't agree with it.

The academic Anthony Wanis-St John argues the Oslo back-channel was of strategic use to both Israel and the PLO: 'One of the first opportunities for such strategic use arose over the issue of East Jerusalem. Was it to be included in an area of eventual Palestinian self-rule during the interim period or not? While the PLO was conceding this point in the Oslo channel, it issued parallel but contrary instructions to the delegation in Washington. The first result was confusion: Which channel was conveying the real PLO position? Was there a single

PLO position? After the confusion, the signal was eventually interpreted correctly – the Israelis concluded they could expect moderation only in the channel in which the PLO was directly present, which was Oslo.' He goes on to quote Abu Ala as saying 'we learned what's serious and what's not, what is true and what is not true with the Israelis'. Savir agreed: 'Part of secret negotiations is really to try and learn . . . what is real, what is fake, where the real sensitivities are, the real issues are.'

The logistics of maintaining a channel with a clandestine armed group are time-consuming and complicated and sometimes involve breaking laws, but they also demonstrate that you can be relied upon. Even the simplest tasks take an inordinate amount of time. It can take two days to get to a meeting that lasts two hours, switching cars and mobile phones and going round and round roundabouts to make sure you are not being tailed. Passing a message can be especially challenging. One HD Centre intermediary was instructed to meet an ETA courier in a truck stop on a French motorway. While he was sitting there, a car drew up. One man stayed in the car and the other came to the table and sat down, coughed into a napkin and pushed it across the table with the instruction 'Open it.' Inside was a microchip the man had been carrying under his tongue, ready to swallow if he were intercepted. When the intermediary returned to Geneva he found the microchip contained a draft ETA statement and a proposal for the next meeting.

The real test of trust comes when things get difficult. Does the intermediary still take the armed group's interests into account? When the talks between ETA and the government broke down in 2007, 'Marc' (Francisco Javier López Peña, the political leader of ETA) asked the HD representative to take him out of Geneva at four in the morning, insisting there was already a police operation in place to arrest him. The representative tried to reason with him, pointing out that as they would be the only car on the road at that time, they would be more suspicious rather than less. But Marc insisted they leave at four. By seven they were near the Jura mountains and Marc said he had to have a coffee, insisting they turn off the road into a small village and stop at a café. There were three locals at the next table and they stared at the unusual visitors with interest. To the representative's horror, Marc started talking loudly about ETA, and one of the locals left the room. The representative decided to go to the toilet and saw the local making a call from the phone box. He came back in and told Marc they had to leave at once. As they drove away they saw in the rear-view mirror the men from the café standing on the street looking after the departing car and writing down its number. Under Marc's instruction, the representative took the mountain road out of the village and as he wound up through the forest above the settlement he saw two police cars entering it. They drove for hours before they finally felt safe.

One of the key ways to build trust is to start treating the members of the armed group like human beings. They are subject to their own traumas, such as torture when captured, and life on the run is tough. Terrorists never see their children, and can't have any sort of normal life. The first time they talk about their family or how hard life is underground they tend to get tearful. During the initial phases of building the channel between ETA and the Spanish government, one of the employees of the HD Centre had to have the two negotiators, 'George' and 'Robert', living in the basement of his house for two months while they worked out what to do with them – even enjoying Christmas with the employee's visiting grandmother. For George and Robert it was heaven. They played with the children, cooked and drank, and talked about their own families and the life they led before they went on the run, even lecturing the parents on the danger of leaving small children at home alone with dogs. As one participant put it, 'Once your children are playing on the knee of a wanted terrorist you know they are thinking that you trust them.'

Of course there is the danger of a form of 'Stockholm syndrome', being sucked in by the terrorist's charm or the excitement of clandestinity, but usually there is a high barrier to be surmounted before trust can even begin to be built. For a rebel leader, the first face-to-face meeting with the government often comes after decades of bloody conflict. A Tajik Islamic rebel leader told me that it was only when he sat down with the government side for the first time in the late 1990s that he saw them as humans, and that after they had met and talked, it was far harder to go back to killing them. Such meetings are not always comfortable for the government representatives either. When ETA representatives met the socialist government delegation in Algeria in 1986, their leader Eugenio 'Antxon' Etxebeste said to Rafael Vera, the secretary of state for security, 'You are on our list.' Vera shrugged it off, regarding the risk as part of his job. The Basque socialist politician who accompanied him, Juan Manuel Eguiagaray, said it was very tough. He had spent all his life in the Basque Country, and his friends and colleagues had been murdered by ETA. It was not easy for him to meet them, especially the two members from the commando in Madrid who had committed 'blood crimes'. Javier Zarzalejos, Aznar's security adviser who met the ETA leaders in Geneva thirteen years later, said 'It was very difficult to talk to these people. They were out of touch with reality, living clandestinely, living in a world of their own.' Ron Pundak says he never forgot Arafat was responsible for Jewish deaths, 'but at the same time I respected the dramatic change that he went through after 1988 and mainly in 1993 – from somebody who was a leader of both a national movement and a terrorist organisation, into somebody who decided to negotiate and sign peace with Israel and compromise on his and his nation's historical demands . . . My attitude towards him was always within this duality.'

The objective of these meetings is in part to put the other side at its ease. Joaquín Villalobos describes a meeting with Violeta Chamorro, the newly elected president of Nicaragua, in April 1990. Nicaragua had been crucial to the rebel war effort because it was where the FMLN had its logistical base, and they had relied on the supply of weapons from the Sandinistas, whom Chamorro had defeated in the elections. The guerrillas therefore approached the meeting with some trepidation. They had decided to tell her that they were ready to commence a ceasefire, something they had been holding back. They dressed in suits and ties rather than the army fatigues they would usually wear when meeting her predecessor, Daniel Ortega. Chamorro decided to use the meeting to demonstrate that she trusted them. Her opening gambit was to use their smartness to tease them, and she said, 'Oh Joaquín, you look as though you've come straight from Paris. But look, there's a problem with the button on your jacket.' Villalobos tried to carry on with the serious subject of the ceasefire, but she interrupted him again to ask him to take his jacket off so she could sew his button back on. He declined and continued with his speech and she asked 'Oh, have you got a pistol in there? Is that why you won't take it off?' She insisted on him removing his jacket and asked her assistant to get her a needle and thread. Villalobos had to explain their position in his shirtsleeves as the president sewed the button back on to his jacket. Chamorro had wanted to demonstrate that she was not their enemy. The first phone call Villalobos made after the final agreement was concluded late in the night in New York on 31 December 1991 was to Chamorro's son-in-law, Antonio Lacayo, who effectively ran the government as the minister for the presidency, to tell him a deal had been reached.

Even when a channel has been established, direct communication is not always easy. David Trimble's Ulster Unionists and Sinn Féin first met in September 1997. Gerry Kelly of Sinn Féin says he was wary. It could be dangerous for Republicans to meet the enemy and they had made a mess of it in the past. The meeting was taking place in Stormont – the Unionists were not used to Republicans being in that bastion of Unionism, and they did not want to be there with them. Kelly's supporters felt the same way. When they got into the conference room the Unionists would not talk directly to Sinn Féin but only to George Mitchell, the American chairman of the talks. This led Gerry Adams to take unusual action to try to engage the Unionists. According to David Trimble, he would lurk in the corridor and when he saw a Unionist going into the Gents he would follow him in and stand at the next urinal trying to engage him in conversation. One young Unionist, Peter Weir, went into the Gents to find Adams already at the urinal, and so rushed into a cubicle, at which Adams shouted after him 'The trouble with you is you still suffer from the siege mentality.'

It can help develop a channel to bring one armed group that has been through a peace process to meet another just starting down the same road, as they have more credibility than diplomats or NGOs. The IRA were much influenced by what the ANC in South Africa had learned, and the IRA in turn influenced ETA. On their first trip to Geneva to meet ETA, two visiting Republicans were picked up at the airport by Martin Griffiths. He drove them into an underground car park beneath the hotel where the meeting was to take place. Griffiths screeched to a halt in the middle of the car park, jumped out and rushed up the stairs. The Republicans got out of the car looking around, convinced they had met their final moment. In fact Griffiths had just left to check all the arrangements were in place. 'Marc' had said before the meeting that he would be able to tell within ten minutes if the people they had brought to see him were 'Uncle Toms' or the real thing. He appeared from the meeting room three hours later saying he was satisfied.

By extension, having a good reference from other armed groups, and a track record of being even-handed, can also help. James LeMoyne was sought out by the FARC in 1997 even though he was an American. He had been recommended by the Cubans, the FMLN in El Salvador, and the Sandinistas. A Sandinista leader called LeMoyne to say that Raul Reyes, one of the FARC leaders, wanted to meet him because he was a

UN official who had been involved in successful peace processes before. They arranged to meet at a café in Mexico City. When they met it was obvious that Reyes had been given a good deal of background information on LeMoyne. The FARC was looking for a backchannel to the American government and wanted the US to see their conflict as a legitimate subject for a negotiated solution and to agree that it could be resolved politically. Above all they wanted the Americans to stop calling them terrorists – armed groups hate being described in this way. If the Americans did so, then they would be willing to have serious conversations. LeMoyne knew the State Department's assistant secretary for the Americas and was able to set up a channel. Shortly thereafter the FARC kidnapped a group of American birdwatchers in the jungle and the channel was used to negotiate their release. The FARC demanded in return there should be an official statement by the Americans. Madeleine Albright duly made a speech at the Summit of the Americas in Santiago and a meeting was agreed between an American envoy and Raul Reyes in Costa Rica. When three Americans working on indigenous peoples' rights in north-east Colombia were kidnapped a few months later, the FARC leadership confirmed they had taken them and undertook to work to get them released. A few days later the bodies of the two women and one man were found, dumped near the Venezuelan border with bullet wounds in the back of their heads. Suspicion fell on 'Granobles', the brother of the key FARC commander Mono Jojoy, widely assumed to be out of control. Raul Reyes claimed the killings had been carried out by a spoiler and said he had tried everything to secure their release. The Americans broke off the channel.

Part of the point of building a channel is educative. Clandestine armed groups have generally lived in their own ghettos, real or metaphorical, for a long time. They mainly talk to people who share their own views. Their leaders are generally those who are prepared to be the most radical. Having contact with them can help open their eyes to how they are perceived by the outside world, to what might be realistically attainable in a negotiation, and to what is out of the question. And it helps the government side to understand better what it is they really want. The Berghof Center in Berlin, an expert body on peace processes, argues 'Pre-negotiation contact and dialogue with an armed group can . . . play a "socialisation" function by helping to build trust and foster the political will essential to making concessions and moderating demands or behaviour . . . Engagement also helps to prepare armed groups for negotiations, encouraging them to think about peace-process requirements and to develop a negotiable political agenda.'

As part of the Caguán peace process in Colombia, a FARC delegation was taken on a tour of Europe in 2000 to gain some exposure to the outside world, to condition their expectations and to allow them to get to know the Colombian government representatives who travelled with them. In four weeks they went from the north of Europe to the south, and from minus 10 to plus 30 degrees. On the first evening in Oslo they were invited to a formal diplomatic dinner, and the organisers had to provide them with suits. Fabien Ramirez, a hardened guerrilla, sat next to LeMoyne. He looked with mystification at the array of silver cutlery and wine glasses, and when LeMoyne explained to him that he had to work through the cutlery from the outside to the inside, he visibly relaxed. (Felipe Rincon, another FARC commander at the meal, was not impressed by the bourgeois excess. He refused to drink wine, insisting that a bottle of Stolichnaya be brought to the table. He turned to LeMoyne and said, 'I am a Communist educated in Moscow. I miss the Soviet Union. Gorbachev is a traitor.' He was later killed by the Colombian army.) During the tour they were taken to a farm in the south of Sweden. They were amazed when the farmer swung through the gates in a huge Mercedes, and even more amazed when he walked into a glass-panelled control room and started pushing buttons to have the cows milked automatically, to have the feed distributed, and so on. They were convinced that it was a set-up, and that the organisers were trying to fool them into thinking that capitalist farms were really like this.

Things did not go well in Switzerland. One FARC participant was seen with a briefcase depositing his money in a Swiss bank. Others went on a shopping spree. At two in the morning one of the guerrillas knocked on LeMoyne's hotel door and insisted he come with him to his room down the corridor. The floor was covered with electronic equipment he had bought, including a GPS device. The guerrilla asked how he could attach it to a mortar so it would be accurate, like the Americans' weapons. LeMoyne had to explain that precision bombing was a bit more complex than simply fixing a GPS to a mortar shell. When the delegation returned to Colombia the FARC required them to hand in all their shopping, which was piled up in the jungle and burned. All the participants in the trip were sent to a special camp for re-education and self-criticism to make sure they were purged of all the vices acquired in capitalist Europe.

Opening and developing a channel to an armed group is much more likely to be successful if the group is united rather than split amongst many factions. The terrorism and radicalisation expert Peter Neumann says a 'factor in deciding whether to negotiate with a terrorist group should be its level of internal cohesion'. According to Muhammad Jusuf Kalla, the Indonesian vice president who negotiated with them, the GAM had a strong vertical structure and the political and armed wings were united. He went to Aceh himself to ask the group's commanders on the ground if they would respect the compromises made by their political leaders in Stockholm. When they confirmed they would, he went ahead with the Helsinki talks. But some armed groups are just so fragmented that it is hard to negotiate with them effectively, and all of them are subject to 'the split'. ETA split a number of times from 1974 onwards, and in Northern Ireland the British government had traditionally tried to divide the Republican movement in every way possible in order to make its defeat easier. The old joke ran that the first item on the agenda at any IRA meeting was the split, as the Provisionals split from the Officials, and the INLA split from the mainstream, and so on. At the end of Tony Blair's first meeting with the Republican leadership in Downing Street in 1997, Gerry Adams took us to one side in the Cabinet Room and said that it was his aim to deliver as much of the Republican movement as he could into a peace process, rather than split it. That would take time, and he appealed to us to give him as much as possible to achieve that aim. Tony Blair's big bet in the peace process was essentially to agree to that proposal so we could make peace once, instead of having to make peace many times with different groups. The policy of divide and rule, such as that employed by the Israelis in building up Hamas at the expense of the PLO, rarely works, and indeed usually backfires on the government by creating new enemies. The aim of the government should be to build up the moderates in the armed group. There are always moderates and hardliners, as in any organisation, and it is important to provide ammunition for the moderates in the form of small successes so they can win the internal argument.

The easiest way to destroy the trust that has been painstakingly built up in constructing a channel is to break your promises. 'Robert', the ETA colleague of 'George' in Geneva, was arrested on 29 March 2007 trying to drive through a French police roadblock near Périgueux. He was armed with a Herstal 9 mm pistol and announced to the police that he was a member of the ETA negotiating team. He gave them the telephone number of a senior official in the interior ministry in Paris, but it cut no ice. There was nothing the Spanish government could do but ETA felt betrayed, having, they believed, been promised safe passage. In Indonesia, the government arrested six GAM negotiators in the hotel in Banda Aceh that served as the headquarters for talks in July 2001. The GAM said it was 'like the Dutch East Indies Company which arrested the Indonesian negotiators' during the independence negotiations. The HDC managed to negotiate their release with the help of the American Embassy, but the government arrested the negotiators again in 2003 and jailed them.

Even if trust can be maintained, before long armed groups get fed up with informal dialogue and want to progress to official talks with the government. Mandela got tired of his conversations with Barnard and Coetsee and said to Barnard that while he was happy to have preliminary discussions with him, 'Botha is the one with the real power. Not you.' In January 1989, Mandela drafted a memo to Botha setting out his views on the way forward, acknowledging white fears of what might happen when there was black majority rule. Thabo Mbeki too chafed at the unofficial dialogue at Mells Park. He demanded to know of Esterhuyse if the talks were official or not, and Esterhuyse had to respond that they were not and he was just a go-between. Mbeki then moved on to the next step of an official meeting with the NIS in Switzerland. Likewise, 'George' and 'Robert' became frustrated by the ambiguity of Eguiguren's non-official status. They had doubts that he was really consulting Madrid at all. Eventually Eguiguren told them that once ETA had issued its statement on a ceasefire and before the planned government declaration on talks, he would be transformed into the government representative and another official would join him. The objective of the secret talks was to agree a road map which would lead to a 'point zero' where a formal process of dialogue would open, which both sides saw as similar to John Major's Downing Street Declaration in 1993 which had kicked off the Northern Ireland peace process.

Hirschfeld was conscious from the very beginning about the asymmetry in the Oslo talks. The Palestinians were officials and he wasn't. His colleague Ron Pundak said that 'The other side will for some time have to live with uncertainty about whether they are negotiating with Rabin's Israel or with two monkeys.' (The Palestinians apparently referred to the two Israelis as 'the bear' and 'the mouse'.) To try to address the problem, Peres invited Faisal Husseini and Hanan Ashrawi for talks at his official residence. Abu Ala would receive the minutes of these meetings and could see that the points raised in Oslo were identical to the points raised by Peres in Jerusalem.

Hirschfeld knew that at some point the government would have to become directly involved; and, as usual, he told an earthy joke to make his point. He said Catherine the Great required her Cossack consort to perform a hundred times a night. One morning they disagreed about how many times it had been the night before – the Cossack said ninety-four, but Catherine insisted it was only eighty-eight. Eventually Catherine said 'Never mind, let's just start again from the beginning.' Hirschfeld wanted to make it clear that once the government became officially involved, much of their work would need to be redone, and that turned out to be right. Yossi Beilin wrote 'the role of those who started the Oslo talks was that of a scout. They had to test the seriousness of those who were sent to talk to them and the seriousness of those who had sent them. Once it became clear that the talks were turning into real negotiations, we had to send official negotiators.'

At the end of April 1993 Arafat ordered the Palestinian delegation from the West Bank and Gaza to restart the official negotiations in Washington and from that moment on Rabin took command of both negotiations. Peres wanted to remain in charge of the Oslo process, which Rabin would not accept but he did agree that Uri Savir, the director general of the foreign ministry, and Joel Singer, a lawyer who had spent twenty years in the Israel Defense Forces legal department, should join Hirschfeld and Pundak on the weekend trips to Oslo. Savir was Peres' man at the negotiation, and Singer was Rabin's man. Since Abu Ala reported directly to Arafat, an indirect line of communication had been established between Jerusalem and the PLO headquarters in Tunis.

Savir recalls his initiation in the process: 'For me, it all began on 14 May 1993, a balmy Saturday afternoon, when my boss . . . Shimon Peres, asked me to his official residence in Jerusalem . . . Peres was relaxed as I entered his living room. Avi Gil, his wise chief of staff, was already seated on one of the comfortable sofas. I sat down opposite him. "A glass of wine?" Peres asked. I nodded, he poured, and as he handed me the glass he asked dryly, "How about a weekend in Oslo?" . . . Peres continued . . . "Be sure to stress that if word of the meeting is leaked, the Oslo channel will come to an end."' The Palestinians accepted the conditions and 'on Peres' orders, I made all my travel arrangements through Beilin's bureau and told my personal staff that I would be holding economic talks in Paris and then would probably join my wife, Aliza, at the Cannes Film Festival'. On their way to the mountains Terje Roed-Larsen indoctrinated Savir into the 'Oslo Spirit': 'He evidently considered me a staid young technocrat, perhaps too stiff for the mission at hand. He explained that humour was an important element in the talks, and that the interchange should be informal, as it had been so far with the two professors. For Terje, the essence of the Oslo channel was to come up with creative solutions by a process of free thinking, not traditional hard-nosed bargaining.' Finally Savir met Abu Ala: 'I was surprised by the man's appearance. Comfortably middle-aged, he wore thick-lensed glasses that failed to hide his penetrating glance. He looked more like a European businessman than the underground leader I had expected . . . The ice thawed a bit as Ron and Yair embraced the three Palestinians, with whom they had been partners for three months.' The channel ceased to be a channel and became a negotiation.

CHAPTER FOUR

How Governments Engage with Terrorists

I have to swallow toads. It's much easier and more popular to make war than to make peace.

President Juan Manuel Santos of Colombia

Democratically elected governments find it very difficult to be seen to talk to armed groups that are killing and maiming innocent citizens. It is politically much less difficult to take a firm security stand. For this reason governments usually start with the conviction that terrorists can be defeated if only they use enough force and introduce enough restrictions – on movement, on freedom of expression, on the formation of groups – to reduce their room for manoeuvre. When the armed group proves more resilient than anticipated, governments sometimes slip into extra-legal measures in the conviction that the end justifies the means.

There is, however, very little evidence that these 'dirty wars' ever help solve the problem in a democracy. In the late 1990s Felipe Gonzalez's socialist government in Spain was found to have co-operated with GAL, the paramilitary group set up by members of the interior ministry to assassinate ETA members in France. The campaign succeeded in killing a number of ETA operatives, and some innocent people too, but it didn't do anything to speed up the resolution of the conflict and merely added to ETA's sense of victimhood. A number of socialist ministers went to jail for their part in the campaign. Apparent collaboration of some elements of the British security forces with Loyalist killers in Northern Ireland was no more successful. Even nowadays there is an invidious argument that creeps into some commentary suggesting that tit-for-tat killings do discourage the terrorists. That is categorically wrong. It may be tempting to wreak revenge on terrorist killers, but all it does is escalate violence. The existence of paramilitary death squads in El Salvador and in Colombia, for instance, prolonged the conflict and made it more difficult to resolve rather than providing a short cut to a solution.

When the security campaign proves longer than expected, military officers argue that if they are just given the resources and if the politicians stand back they will be able to finish the job. This was the argument used in Afghanistan when President Obama was persuaded to surge forces for one last effort against the Taliban in 2009. According to Joshua Lustig of the periodical *Current History*, at the time the decision was made in Washington, American generals 'were reading Lewis Sorley's *A Better War*, a revisionist history arguing that Vietnam was a war that could have been won if not for faltering support at home', while White House staff were passing around *Lessons in Disaster* by McGeorge Bundy, National Security Adviser to JFK and Lyndon Johnson. It is always tempting to believe that with more effort the terrorists can be finished off, but as established in Chapter One, there is little evidence that it ever succeeds (other than in revisionist histories), including in Afghanistan, where the surge was not notably successful.

The next recourse is usually to 'reconciliation' and 'reintegration', also attempted in Afghanistan and Iraq. This is a curious use of the word reconciliation because there is no attempt at reaching an agreement or reconciling two sides, but rather a programme to buy off supporters of the armed group one by one, by offering them a new life and safety, as far as the latter is achievable. In Afghanistan, according to *Guardian* journalist Jason Burke, the programme started with 'Tier Three Taliban', 'simple fighters', who were encouraged by the Afghan government to hand in their weapons and receive a guarantee of immunity from prosecution. Then there were 'the efforts to engage slightly higher-level Taliban, mainly leaders of groups of between a few score and a couple of hundred fighters. These "Tier Two Taliban" had been engaged via a range of intermediaries in a variety of local initiatives. These efforts had also met with mixed success.' While such programmes of reconciliation can reduce the number of fighters, they do not work if the aim is to resolve the underlying problem of the armed conflict.

At this stage governments usually rediscover the lessons of the Malayan campaign, particularly the importance of addressing the grievances on which the conflict feeds. In Northern Ireland it was the army that first saw the need to deal with the sectarian bias in housing and jobs, even before the politicians did. However, addressing the grievances is necessary but not sufficient for resolving the conflict.

Even when governments do come to see the point of talking to the terrorists, they face the argument that they should first get the upper hand militarily to secure a stronger position in the negotiation. F. W. de Klerk remembers the South African security forces saying to him, 'We first need to soften up the enemy before we can talk.' Crocker, Hampson and Aall write that in Israel, Prime Minister Sharon said in March 2002 that 'If the Palestinians are not being beaten, there will be no negotiations . . . Only after they've been beaten will we be able to conduct talks.' A similar argument was put in Afghanistan, where the US military argued that first they needed to secure a victory over the Taliban before it would be right to talk to them from a position of strength. The trouble is that since complete victory is extremely rare and very difficult to achieve, it is hard to know when you have applied sufficient military pressure to give yourself the upper hand. The armed group may not share your view that you are winning. For them, surviving may be enough. Gaining the upper hand is therefore illusory and may in any case have little impact on the outcome of a negotiation, whereas talking earlier may save lives.

Eventually, the government realises a purely security approach will not work and that they have to talk. According to the Italian specialist on conflict resolution Andrea Bartoli, after coming to power in Mozambique, President Chissano held discussions with the military leadership about the direction of the war with the rebel RENAMO movement. They argued that the problem was money, and that they could win if Chissano gave them more, which he did. The military did make some gains initially but budgetary pressures continued due to diminishing support from Soviet bloc allies. This led the military to ask for even more money. They promised to defeat RENAMO and gave a deadline by which they would do so. Chissano granted their request but told them he would seek a political solution if the deadline went unmet. When the deadline passed without military victory, the military's resistance to negotiations diminished and Chissano was able to pursue indirect contacts with the rebels.

There is still, however, the issue of the political opprobrium governments know they will incur if they are seen to be talking. Their engagement with terrorists therefore often begins with 'megaphone diplomacy' rather than direct talks. In the course of 1990 Peter Brooke, the Secretary of State for Northern Ireland, made a series of important speeches in which he first talked about the Cyprus negotiations as a possible model for talks in Northern Ireland and then stated crucially that Britain had no 'selfish strategic or economic interest' in Northern Ireland, effectively declaring the British government neutral in the province. This speech was designed to be heard by the leadership of the IRA and as limited a British audience as possible, and Brooke therefore delivered it to the Association of Canned Food Importers. His speeches were met by matching responses from Gerry Adams and Martin McGuinness indicating their interest in the ideas put forward by the government. Brooke's successor, Patrick Mayhew, carried on the stately minuet, hinting that, given a cessation of violence, a political compromise might be possible. His speeches were partly co-ordinated through the secret channel which had by then been opened up between the government and the IRA.

Speeches like this made right at the beginning of the process can help the government frame the negotiation and thereby gain the upper hand more successfully than by employing any amount of military might. On 2 February 1990 F. W. de Klerk took the world by surprise with his inaugural speech to Parliament. He had been expected to be a conservative successor to P. W. Botha, but instead demonstrated a willingness to set out on an irreversible path of reform. He wrote the speech by hand at the kitchen table in his holiday cottage on the coast, and finished it in the dining room in his official residence (because his wife wanted to watch TV in the study). He didn't tell the ANC, the National Party caucus or even his wife about its content. He believed that 'it would be necessary to identify *all* the remaining obstacles to negotiations and to deal with them in a single statement. I wanted in particular to avoid the impression of making concession after concession under pressure.' He thought 'it was essential that we should leapfrog expectations and put the total package on the table as our opening move. It surpassed expectations; it took the ANC off guard and enabled us to establish ourselves in the eyes of the world as a reasonable and serious partner in the search for a balanced constitutional settlement'.

De Klerk jealously guarded the element of surprise: 'On 2 February 1990, there was a greater concentration of foreign media in South Africa than ever before in our history. However, they had come because they expected the imminent release of Nelson Mandela – not to hear my speech. It was crucially important to delay Mr Mandela's release for a week – during which the communications ball would be in our scrum – and the media would have to concentrate on what we had said.' The journalists were locked in to a briefing room next to Parliament to read the speech half an hour before it was due to be given. As they read through it, a buzz spread across the room, and the South African journalist Allister Sparks murmured to his *Washington Post* colleague, 'My God, he's done it all.' By being bold rather than incremental, committing himself to releasing Nelson Mandela from jail and lifting the ban on the ANC, de Klerk signalled to the other side his willingness to move forward into negotiations and framed the way those negotiations would proceed. De Klerk says 'I realised that we would have little chance of success in the coming negotiations if we did not grasp the initiative right at the beginning and convince the important players that we were not negotiating under pressure but from the strength of our convictions.'

In the end, though, speeches are not enough. The government is subject to a catch-22: if it doesn't talk to the armed group and convince them that a peaceful political way forward exists, then the violence is unlikely to stop. They therefore eventually decide they have to talk, but have to overcome serious obstacles to do so. In some countries it is a criminal offence to have any contact at all with terrorist groups. In 2010 the conservative majority on the US Supreme Court upheld the Patriot Act, making it illegal to provide material support to terrorists, including offering 'expert advice or assistance', 'training' or 'services', even when the aim of such assistance is making peace. Given that the US State Department lists fifty-eight foreign terrorist organisations, and the US Treasury has even more on its own list, this ruling makes it theoretically impossible for any American citizen to sit at a table with representatives of any armed group throughout much of the world. Since US law has extraterritorial effect, it can in fact apply to anyone doing this kind of work anywhere in the world. This has led to a situation in which, as former president Jimmy Carter says, 'Offering training in negotiations or even teaching a course on humanitarian law to a listed terrorist group could land a peace-builder in jail.'

Likewise the proscription of certain armed groups as terrorists by the EU makes it impossible to hold meetings with them in EU countries (increasing the importance of Norway and Switzerland as countries where such work can be conducted legally). The Berghof Center says that 'Though the legal impact of the EU's counter-terrorism legislation on mediation is relatively limited, the political effects of EU proscription are far-reaching. It has increased the political risk for EU envoys and member states and has reduced European mediators' credibility and perceived neutrality with some conflict parties.' Some groups 'believe they are listed for life. This effectively removes any incentive for behavioural change and instead tends to isolate and radicalise groups further, reducing the chances for a negotiated settlement.'

The response of governments to all these difficulties is often to deny they are talking to terrorists, even when they are. John Major said in November 1993, 'to sit down and talk with Mr Adams and the Provisional IRA . . . would turn my stomach. We will not do it', even though he was at the time corresponding secretly with Martin McGuinness. In March 1993, right in the middle of the correspondence, the IRA detonated bombs in Warrington, killing two children. If John Major's contacts with the IRA had been public at the time, the government would have faced irresistible demands to end them immediately after the attack, and it would then have been impossible to persuade the IRA to announce the 1994 ceasefire. Prime Minister Zapatero of Spain and his interior minister Alfredo Rubalcaba both denied that talks with ETA were going on, in response to questions in Parliament. This was part of a long pattern of similar denials going back to Franco's death. In 1980 the conservative prime minister Adolfo Suarez denied there were negotiations with ETA in Parliament, saying 'The government at no time has been meeting to negotiate with ETA.' The leader of the socialist opposition, Felipe Gonzalez, challenged him and said they had discussed the matter personally, but Suarez continued to deny it, even though it was true. In these cases the government uses the distinction between 'talking' and 'negotiating' to be economical with the truth.

Governments go to great lengths to ensure that any contacts with terrorist groups are deniable. Dean Pruitt says that progress in secret using intermediaries 'is easier to achieve, as it is harder for outsiders to follow a chain and easier to deny that the chain exists'. The Zapatero government made its negotiations deniable by deliberately using unofficial channels. They opted for a discreet Swiss-based NGO as the international facilitator and the prime minister delegated the subject not to the interior minister, José Antonio Alonso, responsible for terrorism, but to Alfredo Rubalcaba, the Socialist Party spokesman in Parliament who was technically not a member of the government. This allowed him to maintain the fiction that any contact with ETA was unofficial and to keep it at arm's length as far as possible. Only after the ceasefire announcement in 2006 did Zapatero move Rubalcaba to the interior ministry so that he formally became responsible for the talks he had in fact been conducting for a year already. Face-to-face contact with ETA in Geneva was not with a government representative but with Eguiguren, who was president of the Socialist Party in the Basque Country but had no government position. Eguiguren insists he made it clear at the meetings with ETA that he represented neither the government nor the Socialist Party nationally. Zapatero for his part authorised the discussions but made it clear he would deny them if they ever came out.

The Oslo process was designed to be deniable. Yair Hirschfeld was chosen precisely because he was an academic and not an official, and he chose fellow academic Ron Pundak to accompany him. As Hirschfeld put it, 'it would not even have occurred to an Israeli journalist that what was going on was an official dialogue'. He was close to Yossi Beilin, and Beilin's position as deputy foreign minister meant he could help keep the discussions on the straight and narrow from the Israeli point of view. The relatively junior status of the Palestinian team in Oslo afforded a form of deniability too; the chroniclers of the talks conclude 'it was not Abu Ala's role that made Oslo important but Oslo that made Abu Ala'. He depended on Abu Mazen back in Tunis just as Hirschfeld depended on Beilin. Norwegian involvement was also at arm's length. The talks were organised not by the Norwegian government but by the Institute of Applied Social Sciences, an obscure research institute of the Norwegian trade-union movement which carried out studies on the standard of living in the West Bank and Gaza, providing perfect cover for their activities. Beilin concluded before the 1992 elections that 'if there were no secret talks between us and the Palestinians, nothing would happen'.

Abu Ala agrees, saying 'secrecy was a precondition for the eventual success of the negotiations. Both sides realised this fact from the beginning. Opponents of the talks on both sides would otherwise have been in a position to undermine them at any stage.' Julie Browne and Eric Dickson of New York University give an account of the subterfuge employed: 'In the summer of 1993, Israeli prime minister Yitzhak Rabin went on Israeli television and brushed aside the prospect of negotiations between himself and leaders of the Palestine Liberation Organisation . . . But meanwhile, thousands of miles to the north in a century-old mansion in a forest in Norway, Israeli officials were secretly meeting with PLO leaders . . . Rabin was fully aware of these negotiations when he went on television, yet he continued to condemn the prospect of negotiations with the PLO even as they were being undertaken.' In July 1993, Israeli government spokesmen 'insisted that they had not softened their refusal to negotiate directly with the Tunis-based Palestinian group on the grounds that it is a terrorist group committed to Israel's destruction'. The spokesmen were not lying – it was simply that no one had told them about the Oslo talks. Uri Dromey, Israeli foreign-ministry spokesman at the time, wrote in the *Herald Tribune* twenty years later, 'To say that the Oslo agreement came as a surprise to me would be an understatement. It was a shock. Like all other Israeli officials . . . I had been parroting the mantra that we could never speak to the PLO.'

In South Africa, deniability for the government came in the

form of Niel Barnard's NIS, which set up the secret meetings with the ANC in exile in Switzerland. According to Allister Sparks, the first meeting of 'Operation Flair' took place in the Palace Hotel in Lucerne on 12 September 1989, deliberately timed to fall between de Klerk's election as president and his inauguration. Barnard had chosen Switzerland because South Africans did not need visas to travel there. He sent his deputy Mike Louw and other operatives, all travelling on false passports. Louw checked into a suite at the hotel while another part of the team waited at Geneva airport for the arrival of Thabo Mbeki and Jacob Zuma and tailed them in their car driven by a local ANC member. The two ANC men arrived at the Palace Hotel in the early afternoon. Mbeki recalls saying to Zuma in Zulu as they walked down the corridor, 'It turns my stomach to think that in a few seconds we'll be meeting two arch enemies,' and Zuma confessed later that 'Thabo and I were petrified as we walked towards the hotel rooms of the NIS agents in Lucerne. We kept wondering: What if it is a trap?' As they went through the door Louw had left open, Mbeki said to the NIS representatives, 'Here we are, bloody terrorists, and for all you know, fucking Communists as well.' This broke the ice and the men continued talking till 3 a.m.

Louw reported back to the new president on 17 September. De Klerk was astonished and then annoyed. He demanded to know where they had got the mandate for the talks. Barnard showed him SSC Memo 13. Barnard had put the memo to the State Security Council the day after de Klerk was sworn in, proposing more work on gathering and processing information on the ANC, but not telling him about the proposed meetings. De Klerk had supported the motion which the NIS felt gave them a mandate for contact with Mbeki and Zuma. Barnard later claimed that he needed to force de Klerk's arm in this way but de Klerk says 'Nobody forced my arm . . . It was not necessary to play games regarding meetings between the government and the ANC. I was annoyed that, as acting president, I had not been properly consulted about the meeting in

Switzerland – but I certainly would not have opposed it had I been informed beforehand.'

While using intelligence agencies or neutral organisations and academics can allow governments the deniability they often need for establishing first meetings with illegal groups, and therefore protect the political position of ministers, doing so can also lead to distorted messages and misunderstandings. Pruitt says that 'while intermediaries are often trusted by and intimately familiar with the disputants, which facilitates communication, chains pose problems of distorted messages and intermediary agendas'. Eguiguren agreed a road map for the peace process with ETA with minimal consultation with Madrid, and when the process became serious and the two sides started to implement the package, the vagueness of the understandings and the lack of commitment on the government side led to it unravelling. In Northern Ireland, Martin McGuinness still denies sending the message stating that 'our war is over' which started the correspondence with John Major, and it is pretty clear in retrospect that one of the intermediaries in the chain between the government and the IRA did in fact embellish the message.

Nor do deniable chains of contact protect governments from leaks, whether accidental or deliberate. In May 1993 in the midst of the secret talks in Oslo, as Jan Egeland prepared to leave the foreign ministry for Heftye House where the talks were taking place, the press spokesman rushed into his office with a report from AFP in Washington quoting anonymous State Department sources confirming that there was a secret Norwegian channel between the Israelis and Palestinians. Egeland instructed the spokesman to say the story was a misunderstanding and probably referred to a large, public, multilateral conference on Palestinian refugees which had just taken place in Oslo as part of the US-sponsored peace process. On arrival at Heftye House, Egeland showed the story to the Israeli delegation who said they thought they could deal with it but not to show it to the Palestinians since the talks were at a crucial stage. Ten minutes later he showed it to Abu Ala, who had already been informed about it by Tunis and had issued instructions on how to deal with it, but said not to show it to the Israelis as the negotiations were making good progress. It soon became clear that the source of the story was the deputy to Dan Kurtzer in the State Department. While Kurtzer was fully briefed, his deputy was not indoctrinated into the talks. On a visit to Norway the deputy had gone to see Roed-Larsen, telling him he knew something was going on and if Roed-Larsen didn't tell him what it was, he would do what he could to stop it. Roed-Larsen was frightened and told him. Peres was furious when he discovered and insisted that the Israeli side stop briefing Washington for the next four months.

The bigger danger for a government is a deliberate leak. In 2007 ETA decided to leak its side of the negotiations with the Spanish government to *Gara*, their mouthpiece in the Basque Country. They published their minutes of the meetings in such a way and at such a time to do as much political damage as possible to the socialist government, already reeling from a series of political and economic disasters. Following the leak, Mariano Rajoy, the leader of the opposition, used a debate in the legislative assembly to demand that the government publish the official 'Actas' of the meetings, which they of course refused to do. In Northern Ireland, the IRA decided to leak their correspondence with the Major government to the *Observer* in London when the government stopped the process in 1993. The government responded by publishing their full record of the correspondence, only to have Republicans contradict them and publish their own account. The government had to confess that their version contained a series of errors, and as the Secretary of State Paddy Mayhew prepared to appear before the House of Commons he was convinced he would be called on to resign over the contacts with the IRA which had been explicitly denied in Parliament by the government. Instead he found himself enjoying support from both sides of the House, as MPs understood only too well why the approach and the concomitant secrecy were required.

It is not just the potential political opprobrium that holds governments back; it is also the practical difficulties that such talks create for them. Governments have to carry their militaries with them if they are to succeed, but sometimes the 'securocrats' are determined to undermine the process. In South Africa the South African Defence Force (SADF) and police continued to carry out covert operations behind President de Klerk's back, which helped to stir up the appalling black-on-black violence that nearly derailed the whole peace process and was only eventually uncovered by the Goldstone Commission, leading to the suspension of twenty-three senior officers. De Klerk says that most senior members of the security forces served loyally but 'it was also clear that some small rogue elements were actively involved in efforts to undermine the peace process'.

Sometimes governments have to take a risk on security to move the talks forward at a crucial moment. South Armagh, the hilly area along the border between the North and the Republic of Ireland, had been bandit territory and a centre of smuggling long before the Troubles began. It was the base of the militarily strongest brigade in the IRA. The hills were dotted with towers manned by the army for observation and monitoring what was going on down in the valleys, with some vantage points looking right in the front doors of leading IRA members' houses. Adams and McGuinness urged us to take the towers down, arguing that it was only if the members of the South Armagh brigade could see a real change in their day-to-day lives that they would support the peace process enthusiastically. The military, on the other hand, argued the towers were essential to prevent attacks by the dissident Republicans who had broken away from the IRA. When we relayed this argument to Adams and McGuinness, they countered that the biggest blow we could deal the dissidents was by getting the South Armagh brigade fully on side. Their support would be a far greater deterrent to dissident attacks than any number of towers. It was an argument we accepted, the risk notwithstanding – if a dissident attack had got through as a result, we would have paid a price both in terms of lives and politically, but without taking that kind of risk it is almost impossible to succeed in making peace.

In our pluralistic societies there are a number of groups that can complicate and frustrate governments' ability to open up contact with terrorists publicly, even if they have decided it is the right thing to do. Victims' associations are established to give support to those injured by terrorist attacks and to those whose loved ones have been killed. They do good work in alleviating suffering amongst those who need it most and, remarkably, some victims also put great efforts into trying to help bring about an end to the conflict so that their loved ones have not died in vain, as Colin and Wendy Parry did after their twelve-year-old son Tim was killed by the IRA bomb in Warrington. Sometimes, however, the associations are used for party political purposes and become pressure groups against engaging armed groups in a peace process at all. The Association of Victims of Terrorism (AVT) in Spain became just such a group, organising a series of demonstrations jointly with the conservative PP against the socialist government. The judges can also become an obstacle. The Spanish courts are highly politicised and the battle over the policy towards ETA was fought out as much by the men and women in judicial robes as by those in the corridors of government or the Parliament. At the most crucial moments the judges would knock the process off balance. Jesús Eguiguren says plaintively that he thought the whole world would support the peace process but instead judges affiliated to the conservative PP made it impossible for Batasuna, ETA's political party, to follow the political path by banning the party. Rather than the judiciary becoming more flexible after the ETA ceasefire, things actually got worse.

Despite all these difficulties, when a serious opportunity to talk to terrorists materialises, a government cannot responsibly refuse to seize it. President Santos of Colombia, when announcing talks with the FARC in 2012, said that however difficult the process would be, no responsible government could pass up the possibility of ending the armed conflict. Zapatero justified his approach in Spain saying 'It would have been a crime against the state not to try a negotiation with ETA when it seemed to be served up on a plate.' Responsible governments do therefore in the end opt for talking. Sometimes, as with Aznar, having tried and failed they become completely opposed to talking and hypocritically decry their successors' efforts to do so. This hypocrisy extends to talking to terrorists from other countries even when they refuse to talk to their own. Aznar had no compunction in allowing his ministers to welcome to Spain a FARC delegation, including Raul Reyes, apparently seeing no contradiction with his refusal to speak to ETA. Ironically when Reyes was killed a few years later in Ecuador by a Colombian government air strike, his captured computer showed that FARC had been co-operating closely with ETA.

The aim of the government in initial private contacts is often to persuade the armed group to enter into a ceasefire so that public negotiations can begin. It is difficult to sustain popular support for talks over the time needed for them to succeed against the constant background of violent outrages. Even a ceasefire is not always enough by itself. John Major wanted the IRA to make their ceasefire permanent so it was clear he was not negotiating under the implied threat of renewed violence, but they wouldn't agree. In the 1998 Estella-Lizarra negotiations ETA announced an 'indefinite ceasefire' but then went back to fighting when the talks failed. In the subsequent talks with the socialist government in 2005, Eguiguren would not accept another declaration of 'indefinite ceasefire' and wanted a 'definitive end to violence'. In the end he settled for a 'permanent ceasefire', but not without ETA trying to insert the word 'indefinite' one more time in the last stages of the negotiation.

Even if governments can get armed groups to enter into a ceasefire, they cannot always start negotiations with them straight away, and sometimes a period of 'decontamination' is demanded to demonstrate that the group has ended violence for good. In Spain in 2012 the local PP leader, Antonio Basagoiti, proposed that Batasuna be put 'in quarantine' for four years to test their commitment to democracy. The problem is that if the period of sitting in the 'sin bin' without starting negotiations is too prolonged, the group comes to believe that it is being strung along and returns to violence, as the IRA did with the Canary Wharf bomb in 1996. Tony Blair was prepared to move swiftly to include Sinn Féin in talks after a ceasefire but he demanded they adopt the Mitchell Principles of Non-Violence as a condition for entering talks. These six principles were drawn up by Senator George Mitchell committing parties 'to democratic and exclusively peaceful means of resolving political issues'. The IRA themselves never signed up to them, as doing so would have contradicted their very existence, but their acceptance by Sinn Féin was sufficient to persuade the Unionists to enter talks with them. (Batasuna adopted the same Mitchell Principles in the Guernica declaration of 2011 in the hope of convincing the Spanish government to enter talks, but without success.)

Elections can serve as a means of decontamination by demonstrating that the group has sufficient popular support to merit their inclusion in a negotiation. The threshold needs to be set low to ensure all of the relevant parties are represented at the table. If the armed group wins enough votes to join, however, the government then faces a new conundrum of what to do if they return to violence during the talks themselves. We had to expel both the Republicans and the Loyalists at different moments in the Northern Ireland talks after their respective armed wings committed murders. But having expelled them, the government faces the fresh problem of when to bring them back in – how long is long enough to atone for a human life? Wait too long and you disrupt the talks, perhaps fatally; too short and you appear heartless and perhaps encourage them to kill again. What you shouldn't do is say that a group can join negotiations if they win an election and then change your mind. In 1992 Shimon Peres said the Israelis were 'ready to negotiate with extremists from Hamas if they were freely elected in the Occupied Territories' but in 2006, when they were elected, no one was prepared to negotiate with them, reinforcing their narrative as victims.

Some experts speak as if negotiating with an armed group is somehow separate from normal politics. It is not. The talks are a political process themselves and complaining about politics getting in the way and interfering with the purity of a peace process is to miss the point. It is absolutely crucial to understand that negotiation is a political act which will be impacted on by politics and will in its turn impact on politics. Politicians often pay a heavy political price for talking to terrorists. Ronald Reagan was not known as soft on terrorism but when he allowed contact with Sam Nujoma, the leader of SWAPO in Namibia, he was attacked by right-wing commentators for giving 'de facto recognition to a Communist gangster who, in a civilised society, would be brought to trial for the terrorist murder of hundreds of innocent civilians'. These political tensions over dealing with conflict are always present and tear away at the heart of government.

It is therefore much easier for a democratic government to open contact with an armed group soon after it has been elected, while it still enjoys strong support. Tony Blair used the political momentum of his landslide election in 1997 to push for a rapid ceasefire and the opening of talks with Sinn Féin. Ranil Wickremasinghe's election victory in Sri Lanka in 2001 on an explicit peace agenda made rapid progress with the LTTE possible, and unilateral armistices were in place within a month. The vast majority of the Sri Lankan people were delighted with the ceasefire and the prime minister was hailed a hero, but he failed to use his victory to make progress towards a political agreement, and the negotiations gradually lost public support in 2002–3. Instead of being an asset, the peace process became a liability used by the opposition to attack the government. Conversely when governments have been in office for some time and are weak it is harder to make progress. John Major found it difficult to sustain his Northern Ireland initiative as his parliamentary majority waned in 1996 and he was fighting a desperate battle to survive politically. Looming elections can have a similar impact in freezing negotiations. In the Philippines, as Gloria Arroyo approached the end of her term as president in 2010 and her political difficulties multiplied, the Moro Islamic Liberation Front (MILF) kept their powder dry in the negotiations waiting for a new president. Armed groups ask themselves whether it is worth making concessions to a fatally wounded government rather than waiting for a new one. When Gus Dur came to office in Indonesia in 1999, he and some of his ministers who came from positions in NGOs were keen to seek a negotiated settlement in Aceh, despite the opposition of the military and the elite in Jakarta. He acted while the army was still reeling from the aftermath of its humiliation in East Timor. But by 2001, as he was fighting for his political life and impeachment loomed, he reached out desperately for allies anywhere he could find them, and the military saw an opportunity to regain control. In April he stopped short of reimposing a full state of emergency in Aceh, but signed a decree ordering security forces to restore law and order in an effort to stay in power. A change of government can derail a peace process, particularly if the new leader has no stake in negotiations started under their predecessor. In July 2001 Gus Dur was finally impeached for corruption and incompetence and his successor President Megawati did not have the same interest or sense of ownership in the talks. In fact she made clear her disdain for the process when asked by the press about the negotiations, replying 'I don't know. It's nothing to do with me, ask him,' gesturing to the co-ordinating minister, Yudhoyono, standing next to her. She allowed the military to increase the number of troops and police in Aceh and eventually announced the government had had enough of talks.

Even if leaders remain in office for long periods, their ministers come and go, and each new minister's learning curve causes a hiatus in the negotiations. In the fifteen years of the negotiations with the MILF, the Philippines' government appointed nine negotiating panels, while the MILF's negotiating panel remained virtually unchanged. The MILF had seen hard and soft government negotiators, principled negotiators and pragmatic ones, and took them all in their stride. On the other hand, a change of government can lead to a helpful change of political context. Nothing could have been more different from the traditional, patrician, quasi-military bearing of the last Conservative Northern Ireland Secretaries, Peter Brooke and Paddy Mayhew, than the chaotic charm of their Labour successor, Mo Mowlam, which convinced nationalists that the British government might be open to an acceptable deal.

Peace processes can be frustrated when leaders become distracted by electoral goals, but equally if leaders embark on peace processes for purely electoral motives the outcome can be disastrous. Conservative candidate Andrés Pastrana was badly trailing his Liberal rival, Horacio Serpa, in the first round of the Colombian presidential elections in 1998. He had shown no particular interest in the issue of the FARC but was casting around for a political wheeze when one of his supporters gave him a paper arguing that a strong peace platform would help him win. The paper had arisen from conversations with the FARC political leader Raul Reyes in Mexico City. Pastrana wrote on the paper, 'If one has to go to the mountains to make peace, I am ready to do it.' A few weeks later one of his political allies, Jairo Rojas, met the FARC commanders Manuel Marulanda and El Mono Jojoy in the jungle, where the three of them watched the presidential debates on TV. At the end, Mono Jojoy said of Pastrana, 'That man could be the counterpart we would like to see seated face to face with us.' Marulanda asked if Pastrana would come and see him, and Rojas said he would find out. In response Pastrana sent his campaign manager, Victor Ricardo, to meet the FARC leaders. Ricardo took his life in his hands and flew into a small airstrip in the jungle and was taken to see Marulanda. He agreed that if Pastrana won the election he would meet Marulanda for talks in January 1999. There was no pre-agreement on the structure of negotiations or anything else. It was just a device to win the election. Pastrana subsequently became a prisoner of the peace process. He had bet his presidency on the process and he could not give it up. His place in history would be determined by the success or failure of the negotiations and as a result he kept them going long after they had become discredited with the public. It is crucial that a government maintains the ability to walk away from negotiations, because only by having that option can they force the armed group to negotiate seriously. There always needs to be a convincing Plan B.

The attitudes of political leaders towards talking are of course affected by the impact of terrorism on their personal lives. In 1995 when the leader of the opposition in Spain, Aznar, survived an ETA car bombing, he found it difficult to forgive ETA's attempt on his life. The car's armour plating saved him but one woman died and fifteen people were wounded. In Colombia, President Uribe's father, a landowner, was killed by the FARC during a bungled kidnapping attempt in 1983, and they attempted to kill Uribe himself during the election campaign in 2003 by setting off a bomb under a bridge on a highway as his motorcade passed by. His armour-plated car was wrecked but he escaped unharmed. Three passers-by were killed and fifteen injured. The attacks turned both Aznar and Uribe into hard-line opponents of talks under their successors, although both had tried to open talks with those same armed groups themselves when they were in office. Attacks, however, don't always turn leaders into opponents of talking. John Major survived the IRA mortar attack on 10 Downing Street in 1991 and yet took a major political risk by opening covert contact with the IRA less than a year later. President Kumaratunga survived an attempt by the Tigers to kill her in December 1999, losing an eye, but instead of dropping talks she gave instructions to the security forces to ensure there were no revenge killings of Tamils and went on the BBC to announce she had just approached the people who had tried to kill her and asked the Norwegians to mediate peace with them.

Paradoxically it can be easier for parties on the political extremes to make a lasting peace than for those in the centre, because no one can outflank them and attack them for the concessions they have made. In Northern Ireland we tried to build peace from the centre but the moderate nationalist party, the SDLP, was unwilling to enter into an agreement without the inclusion of Sinn Féin, so we had no choice but to negotiate with the Republicans. On the other side Tony Blair stuck with the moderate Unionist leader David Trimble long after the Unionist voters had given up on him, because he did not believe Trimble's hard-line rival, Ian Paisley, would ever sign up to a peace agreement. In the event we finally concluded a lasting agreement with Ian Paisley's DUP and Sinn Féin, the two extremes. In El Salvador, José Napoleón Duarte, a Christian Democrat, tried a number of times to end the civil war but never managed to convince the guerrillas that he could carry with him the all-powerful military and their ultra-right-wing civilian backers. Alfredo Cristiani, on the other hand, the can-didate of the far-right ARENA party who succeeded him as president, managed to make peace despite coming from the 'oligarchy' of richest families in El Salvador. In the words of the guerrilla leader Joaquín Villalobos, he was 'the real thing'. He could deliver the military and could not easily be outflanked by right-wing political forces inside El Salvador.

It is much easier to make peace if there is a degree of political consensus in the country. In Britain we enjoyed political bi-partisanship in the approach to Northern Ireland. Tony Blair in opposition offered John Major complete support even when he disagreed with what the government was doing. He told me that we could not know what was going on behind the scenes and there was no point in second-guessing the govern-ment. Once we were in government the bipartisanship was more rhetorical than practical, and the Tory opposition tried to make life difficult for us as the negotiations proceeded. In British politics, however, Northern Ireland was not a salient issue. There were no votes on the mainland in pursuing the peace process, but equally there was very little popular opposition to it either.

That is not always the case. In Spain the Basque question is highly divisive. A large majority of Spaniards are against making any concession whatsoever to ETA. Bipartisanship would have given the socialist government a chance of succeeding in their attempt to make peace but that was not on offer from the PP. The Socialist Party in opposition had offered political support to the government throughout the period 1998–9 when Aznar was pursuing talks with ETA. But when in opposition from 2004 to 2011, the PP did not offer the same support to Zapatero's socialist government. Rubalcaba later complained that 'There isn't a country in the democratic world in which a government tries to end a conflict in which you will find the opposition behaving with such complete disloyalty.' At their first meeting after the election, Zapatero briefed the opposition leader Mariano Rajoy confidentially on the meetings with ETA in Geneva that had taken place in the summer of 2005, but the information was immediately leaked to the right-leaning newspaper *El Mundo*. Thereafter Zapatero did not share any more confidential material with Rajoy, and the PP embarked on a campaign of '*crispación*': using the issue to raise the greatest possible political tension. Rajoy's first step was to announce that the PP would formally break 'all relations with the government' to protest the 'ignominy of the government's agreeing to meet Batasuna'. When the government decided to move an ETA prisoner to the Basque region to end his hunger strike and prevent him becoming a martyr, the PP called a massive demonstration in Madrid to 'defend Spain'. Aznar took it to an extreme when he said in 2007 that 'Everyone who does not vote for the PP is supporting ETA.'

The political problem for democratic governments is not just that they are dealing with terrorists but also the nature of the issues around which the conflicts rage. They are often about the very nature of the state, in the case of ideological conflicts like those with the FARC or the Maoists in Nepal, or about the secession of part of the state, like those with the IRA, ETA or the PKK. Self-determination is the most neuralgic issue of all, and it raises a clash of rights. Mindanao in the Philippines provides a classic example. The Muslim Bangsamoro are clearly distinct from the population of the rest of the country but even where they are in the majority on the southern islands there are also Christians and surviving indigenous people living alongside them. How do you decide whether certain areas should be within the new autonomous region or not?

The solution we chose in Northern Ireland was the principle of consent, which meant that it was for the majority in the province to decide on their status. This is not available to all governments. Spain is the country that has perhaps tied itself in the greatest logical knots on the issue. They cannot accept the concept of self-determination for any of the regions because of the delicate constitutional balance reached after Franco's death during the transition to democracy. After the country's troubled history, the army saw itself as the guardian of Spanish unity. They would not accept the notion that parts of the state could split off. So now the Spanish government has to resist fiercely proposals for referenda in Catalonia or the Basque Country even if the majority of people there want one. The Canadian Supreme Court came up with perhaps the best judgement on the issue after Canada had wrestled with the problem of separatism in French-speaking Quebec in 1995, following the close vote on independence and a terrorist campaign. The court concluded that unilateral secession was not legal under either domestic or international law, but that if a majority responded positively to a clear question asked in a referendum on secession, then negotiations between Quebec and the federal government would have to take place. In other words, whatever the constitutional or legal position, you will not reach a happy equilibrium unless the consent of the people is fully respected.

Problems for governments attempting to resolve conflicts can also stem from vested interests, in two different ways. First, communities can feel they are not getting a fair share of the raw materials being extracted from their territory. In Aceh, for example, the local population had been promised 70 per cent of the revenue from the oil and gas being taken from the region, but never saw it. Secondly, the army often sees the conflict as a key source of revenue for itself. In Indonesia the military only had 30 per cent of its costs provided by the government budget and had to raise the rest from enterprises like illegal logging and illegal road tolls. This leads to vested economic interests in the conflict continuing on both sides, as leaders of armed groups and the military make considerable profits from the war economy. Overcoming these interests and providing greater control of their own resources for the areas concerned are key challenges for any negotiation. The agreement has to provide for revenue-sharing between the centre and the region, to ensure both sides end up content with the economic outcome of the peace, and there has to be short-term compensation for those losing out as a result of peace.

Governments are susceptible to pressure from other governments, particularly the US or large neighbours, over the resolution of their internal conflicts. In 1987–90 the Indian government intervened directly – and disastrously – in Sri Lanka with a large peacekeeping force, but even when it didn't have troops on the ground or a direct role in the peace process, it remained a large presence. The Norwegians made a point of always briefing the Indians first and consulting them before the Americans or any of their European allies. Sri Lankan leaders of every stripe were very conscious of India, and as one negotiator put it, 'If the sun rose in the morning, the Sri Lankans believed the Indians were behind it.' Outside influence can also be positive, of course, as well as problematic. In South Africa, the ANC wanted to keep international sanctions in place until the transition had taken place and they were firmly in government, in order to increase their leverage in the negotiations with the National Party. President de Klerk had to win international support quickly to demonstrate to his supporters that his reformist approach was paying practical dividends.

Even before he became president he put out feelers to see if he could set up a meeting with Mrs Thatcher without P. W. Botha knowing about it. Contrary to the caricature of her, de Klerk recalls Thatcher listening carefully to what he had to say rather than constantly interrupting him. He felt she was assessing him and deciding whether or not she could trust him. When he had finished, she advised him to press ahead with the reforms at full speed and said she would support him to the hilt. President George H. W. Bush also offered full support, and despite the more cautious official advice he received from the State Department, announced at their joint Rose Garden press conference that he believed the changes in South Africa were irreversible, enabling sanctions to be lifted.

The greatest impact a neighbouring government can have is in terms of security co-operation. If an armed group has a safe haven in a neighbouring country from which it can launch attacks and then withdraw, it can continue indefinitely. If the safe haven is removed, the incentive to talk increases. The pressure on ETA to negotiate went up markedly once the French started to co-operate fully with the Spanish authorities in fighting the group. The French had been ambivalent after the end of the Franco regime, still seeing ETA as a liberation movement and not wanting to provoke difficulties with its own Basque citizens. Gradually it changed its view and by the early 2000s was arresting ETA leaders in job lots. The fact that the FARC found refuge in camps in Venezuela made it more or less impossible for the Colombian government to wipe them out. President Uribe says he even considered attacking his neighbour to root out the guerrillas. After President Santos replaced Uribe, however, he reached out to President Chávez in Venezuela, who, having for years actively accommodated the presence of the guerrillas in his country, transformed into a powerful advocate for a settlement.

The White House has long had an interest in what happens in Northern Ireland. As a result of pressure from the large and politically powerful Irish American community in the US, Bill

Clinton took a big risk in giving Gerry Adams a visa to visit the US in 1994 even before the IRA went on ceasefire. In doing so he fractured his relations with the government of John Major, at least temporarily, and if the IRA had gone back to violence he would have paid a domestic political price for making the wrong call. I spent a year in the British Embassy in Washington lobbying against the decision, but in retrospect I can see that it was the right thing to do, because it gave Adams a way of convincing the hardliners in the IRA that if they gave up violence there could be a political way forward. Foreign governments are rarely decisive in either supporting insurgents or in contributing to the success of a peace process in other countries, but they can help or hinder. Bill Clinton did not press Tony Blair to reach a settlement, because he knew he was doing all in his power to bring one about, but he offered help by urging and cajoling both Republicans and Unionists to settle.

Governments facing an internal terrorist threat therefore usually try to eliminate the armed group first rather than negotiate. Having exhausted all the alternatives they turn finally to the idea of talking, but in doing so they face major obstacles, particularly public opinion. They usually try to start with secret and deniable talks and face a series of hurdles they have to overcome before they move to public or official negotiations. It is entirely understandable that they would want to keep outsiders out of such delicate internal processes. History shows, however, that the successful resolution of a conflict is much easier when a government overcomes its preoccupations with sovereignty and involves a third party in the negotiations.

CHAPTER FIVE

The Third Party

I have made my career by talking to people that have at some point been branded as terrorists. For me, this is the only way to have a successful peace mediation process. Reaching a solution that ends a conflict means talking to all those who are parties to the conflict.

Martti Ahtisaari

Governments go to great lengths to keep foreigners out of their internal conflicts. For some it is a matter of sovereignty, for others it is pride, and for yet others it is because they are not sure of the strength of their case and fear any third party might take the side of the armed group. Armed groups are naturally keener on internationalising their conflict in the hope of attracting global attention.

India has always been extremely robust in keeping any international third party away from the neuralgic issue of Kashmir. Even in the case of neighbouring Nepal, India was determined to keep foreign meddling to a minimum. The 'People's War' had begun in 1996 when the Nepalese government rejected the forty points put forward by the Maoists, and the People's Liberation Army took up arms. The movement spread rapidly from the foothills on the Indian border to the majority of the country. 13,000 people had died by 2002, 8,000 at the hands of government forces. The Maoists had a two-man leadership: the military leader, Pushpa Kamal Dahal known by his *nom de guerre* Prachanda; and the political leader, Dr Baburam Bhattarai, both of whom operated entirely underground.

The HD Centre was the first international organisation to

make contact with the Maoist guerrillas in Nepal in August 2000. Martin Griffiths and his deputy, Andrew Marshall, had flown to Kathmandu and met the chief government negotiator and a local Nepalese facilitator, Padma Ratna Tuladhar, who had been trying to engineer talks between the two sides. Griffiths told him that they wanted to meet the Maoist leadership, but he couldn't help. Griffiths and Marshall resorted to the internet. The Maoists named their website 'shiningpath.com' in homage to the Peruvian Maoist guerrillas. Marshall, a forthright Canadian, fired off an email and, to his surprise, received a reply.

It took them a couple of years before they actually met a member of the politburo. Marshall was directed to make his way to Naroda in India, where he was picked up on a street corner by a rickshaw and driven down tiny alleys to ensure they were not being followed. He assumed this was just for show, since the Indian secret services must certainly have known exactly what the Maoists were up to. Eventually he was taken to an unfinished skyscraper and deposited in an unfinished apartment. The politburo member was brought to meet him there. Marshall's aim was to give the Maoists some sense of the outside world. Their leaders were from the western foothills of Nepal and had little contact with the international community. He offered to bring outsiders to meet them in India and invited three of them to come to Geneva to meet the Swiss government and visit the HD Centre. The Maoists were suspicious. They agreed to come but treated the trip as a vetting visit. It was not that they wanted the intermediary to be on their side, but they did want to be sure of even-handedness, and asked if there were any Americans on the HDC staff.

In 2003, Marshall secured agreement to a series of meetings in Geneva between two Maoist leaders and two representatives from the Nepalese government. The plan was for the Maoists to stay in Geneva for three months and for the Nepalese officials to fly in and out for negotiating sessions. The Swiss put visas in two blank passports produced by the Nepalese government with photos provided by Marshall, and a private chartered plane was on the tarmac prepared for take-off at Kathmandu airport. A helicopter with a senior Nepalese law-enforcement official was ready to land on the Indian–Nepalese border to pick up the two rebel leaders. At the last minute, at a cocktail party in Kathmandu a foreign ambassador made the mistake of mentioning the plan to the Nepalese foreign minister, who was one of the few government officials privy to the secret, and the government, which had made secrecy a condition, cancelled the meeting. That killed off the contact with the Maoist leadership for the time being. The peace process continued to stutter forward, but without the HD Centre.

When talks finally got going, the Maoists wanted the HDC to be a witness at their negotiations with the government, but the Indians persuaded the Nepalese Congress Party to veto the Centre's participation on the grounds that there should be no foreigners at the talks. An anonymous Indian official expressed their view clearly: India was 'against third-party mediation, UN or otherwise . . . Regardless of the irritants, no one under-stands each other better than India and Nepal, everyone else could come and meddle . . . and if it went wrong they could dash off with their first-class tickets. We could not trust anyone else to look after our concerns.'

This objection extended to the UN. Kofi Annan announced in a speech in 2002 that the UN was willing to use its good offices in Nepal if requested. Almost immediately Padma Ratna Tuladhar received a call from the Maoist leader, Prachanda, wanting a copy of the speech and seeing an opportunity to internationalise the conflict. Tuladhar's house in Kathmandu was just down the street from the Indian Embassy, and it wasn't long before he received a visit from the deputy chief of mission to deliver the message that India saw no need for a third party to get involved. The UN approached the Indian ambassador in New York, suggesting they would send a mid-ranking official to Nepal to look at the possibilities. The ambassador interpreted the approach as a request for permission, and turned it down. Notwithstanding this, the UN sent a relatively junior official,

Tamrat Samuel. While there, he managed to make contact with the political leader of the Maoists, Bhattarai, and thereafter, every couple of months, Samuel would get a phone call dragging him out of meetings in New York, to field questions from Bhattarai delivered in his rapid-fire English, distorted by the static on his satellite phone. In the end India had to accept a role for the UN in the demobilisation of the Maoists and monitoring the Nepalese army. The Nepalese prime minister made it clear to the Indian government that unless they agreed to the UN, India itself would have to assume responsibility for the issue of arms in Nepal.

The Indian position was entirely understandable as they watched the proliferation of third parties in Nepal, with at one stage the Carter Center, the Catholic lay association the Community of Sant'Egidio, Martti Ahtisaari, and the Swiss government all trying to operate there, as well as the HD Centre. One Nepalese commentator complained there were so many NGOs that the 'conflict tourism season' seemed to be well under way. India, as the regional superpower, was funda-mentally important to what happened in Nepal and, having watched the process for three years, decided to effectively take it over in 2005 and become the third party themselves – and a very strong one. The Congress Party was back in power in India, and through the Communist Party, their junior partners in coalition, they contacted the Maoist leaders, many of whom had been at Jawaharlal Nehru University at the same time as some of the Indian Communist leaders. Soon there were descrip-tions in the press of the Maoists being 'quietly chaperoned around . . . by Indian intelligence agencies'. The twelve-point understanding reached in November 2005 between the Maoists and the Seven Party Alliance of opposition parties in Nepal was not only concluded in Delhi, but described as 'written in South Block', the centre of Indian government.

It is not just the Indians who are allergic to outside interfer-ence. The British government long resisted any attempts to internationalise Northern Ireland, and regularly saw off UN resolutions on the issue. This attitude only changed in 1991 when John Major first invited Sir Ninian Stephen, a former Australian Governor General, to chair the inter-party talks. Later George Mitchell, the former US senator first dispatched to Northern Ireland by Bill Clinton as an economic envoy, became the long-suffering chair of the talks.

The South Africans were likewise absolutely determined to keep interfering busybodies out of their conflict. In 1986 a seven-member Commonwealth Eminent Persons Group was sent to South Africa under the co-chairmanship of Malcolm Fraser of Australia and Olusegun Obasanjo of Nigeria to begin proximity talks between the two sides, and got as far as drawing up a 'possible negotiating concept' containing very much the same measures as de Klerk was to announce some four years later. On the day the group was to meet P. W. Botha and his Cabinet, however, the South African defence minister ordered pre-dawn bombing raids on ANC bases in Zimbabwe, Zambia and Botswana. The EPG aborted its mission and flew out of Johannesburg the same day. That suited Botha fine.

Once negotiations started the government made sure that all aspiring third parties were repelled. Niel Barnard claims that 'from the very word go I reached an agreement with Mandela, on my own instigation, that we will as South Africans do our own negotiations. We will not involve the Commonwealth, and the British, and the Americans, and the UN, and Africa and the Eminent Persons Group . . . or anyone else.' One of the first agreements reached between the NIS and the ANC when they met face to face in Switzerland was to exclude third parties. Barnard says 'The more the outside world tried to become involved, the more stubborn we became to try not to let them have any kind of involvement. This is why people like myself fought tooth and nail to convince [Botha] that there must be no facilitators and no outside involvement. We will talk to [the ANC] on our own, direct . . . There was no way that we as a government were going to be prescribed to by clerics, academics, and the private sector as to how we should conduct the political business of the country.'

Despite the attitude of governments, and often in the face of overwhelming disapproval, brave individuals are prepared to risk their political credibility to try to open up a channel to an armed group. John Hume agreed to meet Gerry Adams in the midst of the IRA campaign in 1988 and, when Adams was seen entering his house and the meetings became public, Hume was reviled in the media. He had the last laugh when he was awarded the Nobel Peace Prize, but in the meantime paid a high political price. In South Africa, Botha had wanted all the South African participants in a meeting with the ANC in Dakar in 1985 arrested on their return. Theuns Eloff, a Dutch Reformed Church minister, was particularly harshly treated. He was personally ostracised and vilified, not allowed to finish his doctorate at the Orange Free State University, hounded out of his job and, worst of all, his young children were taunted at school. However, he came back later as a participant in the National Peace Accord and at the Convention for a Democratic South Africa (CODESA) peace conferences. Willie Esterhuyse, who led the private dialogue between Afrikaner intellectuals and the ANC, recalls Botha saying to him at one stage, 'I know about your contacts with the ANC. If the news leaks out, I'll have to haul you over the coals in public.'

The problem with these well-meaning initiatives, however, is that they lose most of their value once they are made public because by definition they have then become unsuitable vehicles for confidential backchannel negotiations. Political leaders often find such efforts inconvenient for the reasons highlighted by Michael Ignatieff's comment that 'Peacemakers . . . by their very presence on a demarcation line effectively ratify the conquests of aggressors and impede attempts by victims to recapture lost ground.' Sometimes, though, attacks on intermediaries are purely political, as when Mariano Rajoy expressed his 'embarrassment' at the government's use of external facilitators to talk to ETA, and accused Zapatero of 'naivety' and 'frivolity' for resorting to them.

It is entirely understandable why governments reject third

parties for reasons of sovereignty and, even more importantly, because they fear losing control of a negotiation and facing compromise proposals they do not like. There is also an argument that an agreement forged by the internal parties alone gives them a greater sense of ownership than an agreement manufactured for them by an outsider. F. W. de Klerk said that 'The strength of the South African process was that it did not require – or seek – foreign mediation. One of the sources of its success was that it was entirely "home-grown".'

On the other hand, without a third party it can be far harder to reach an agreement. Studies suggest that mediated conflicts are twice as likely to end in an agreed fashion as cases without mediation. A third-party chair accepted by both sides can be an effective referee but can of course do much more than just ensure the rules of the game are respected. They can drive the process, set the agenda, arrange meetings and put forward compromise proposals, thereby removing roadblocks. There are many different types of third party ranging from a strong mediator, like the US government's role between the Israelis and the Palestinians, to the humblest, most powerless NGO acting as a witness at a negotiation, and this range of possibilities leads to an endless, and rather fruitless, debate about the technical differences between facilitation, mediation and arbitration. In the end all intermediaries are trying to do the same thing: help the parties get to a lasting agreement. Nicholas 'Fink' Haysom, Nelson Mandela's legal adviser who played a key role in the negotiations in South Africa (and in many other talks elsewhere), says of third parties 'different conflicts require different sorts of approach, some require the resources and leverage that only government or multilateral institutions can bring to bear, while in others powerlessness can be an asset, a basis for confidence and trust building'.

The point about a third party is not that they can impose an agreement but that they can make it easier to reach one by removing some of the hurdles. The US academic J. Michael

Greig argues that mediators can help parties escape the 'bargainer's dilemma' by playing a useful role in 'reducing disputants' fears of exploitation and providing the political cover necessary for the parties to make concessions'. Zartman and Faure's view is that 'The mediator's prime function is as a bridge of trust. Neither party trusts the other but both must trust the mediator for the mediator to work.' In their handbook on negotiations with armed groups, Oliver Ramsbotham, Tom Woodhouse and Hugh Miall say third parties 'help the conflicting parties by putting them in contact with one another, gaining their trust and confidence, setting agendas, clarifying issues and formulating agreements. They can facilitate meetings by arranging venues, reducing tensions, exploring the interests of the parties and sometimes guiding the parties to unrealised possibilities. These are tasks that are usually contentious and even dangerous for the protagonists to perform themselves.' Martti Ahtisaari says 'a good mediator is like a harbour pilot, alerting others to the places to avoid so as not to run aground'.

In certain circumstances a government can be a mediator as well as a party to a negotiation. In Northern Ireland, after Peter Brooke's 1990 speech in which he stated that Britain had no selfish strategic or economic interest in the province, the British government was effectively neutral. It could live with any outcome that was acceptable to both the Unionists and the Republicans and nationalists. We found ourselves, together with the Irish government, shuttling between the two sides to broker an agreement and chairing the crucial private sessions of the talks. The governments were of course, by definition, strong mediators in that they could make things happen through executive action and legislation. Likewise the role of the US government in the Middle East peace process, where they can change facts on the ground both economically and in terms of security, is as a strong mediator. In fulfilling this role the US does not need to be completely neutral. Former CIA director George Tenet recalls a Palestinian negotiator saying to him after one session at the Wye River conference in 1998, 'we know you have a close and strategic relationship with the Israelis that we will never be able to recreate with you. All we ask is that you be fair.' The US has enjoyed success as a mediator a number of times but there are, as Ramsbotham, Woodhouse and Miall write, some 'powerful third parties whose entry alters not only the communication structure but also the power balance of the conflict'. In other words, there is a risk that powerful third parties become players in the conflicts into which they are sucked, as India did in Sri Lanka in the 1980s. Chester Crocker says their role as peacekeeper became 'conflated with other roles, and this confusion worsened as Indian forces engaged in serious fighting, becoming essentially parties to the conflict'. The role of strong mediators therefore has its limitations.

In many Catholic countries the two sides turn to the church almost automatically to set up contacts or provide a safe location for meetings. President Cristiani in El Salvador turned first to the Catholic Church to act as a facilitator and only when that failed did he agree to use the UN. In the strongly Catholic Basque Country the church played the role of convener between ETA and the Spanish government a number of times. Bishop Uriarte of Zamora joined Aznar's negotiating team at the meeting with the armed group in Vevey in Switzerland in May 1999. Father Alec Reid, the Irish Redemptorist priest who had arranged the meetings between Gerry Adams and John Hume in Northern Ireland, installed himself in a monastery in Bilbao and tried to help. He met Mikel Antza, the political leader of ETA, and the organisation even went as far as giving him a code name – 'Aurelio' – but in the end they decided against using his services as a mediator. In recent years the church has become increasingly nervous about becoming entangled in political controversy. Jesús Eguiguren approached the church following his talks with Arnaldo Otegi. Aznar was still prime minister and Eguiguren thought the church would have a better chance than any other intermediary of persuading the conservative PP to engage with ETA. He went to Rome to meet Cardinal

Etchegaray, a French Basque and president of the Pontifical Council for Justice and Peace, who had been the Pope's envoy to Saddam Hussein in 2003 trying to persuade the Iraqis to co-operate with the UN to avoid an invasion. The cardinal gave Eguiguren a glass of anisette, which he did not like, and told him that the conflict was a matter for the local church rather than the Vatican. On his return to the Basque Country Eguiguren went to see the local cardinal, who told him that the church could not be involved in such a delicate matter. Eguiguren suspected that they were nervous that it would affect their relations with the governing PP.

The United Nations was created in part to play the role of mediator, although during most of the Cold War it found it almost impossible to do so because every conflict between the Soviet Union and the US was a zero-sum game. A brief window opened at the very end of the 1980s with the advent of perestroika and glasnost in the Soviet Union, and by 1989 the organisation was the only possible mediator in El Salvador. The Contadora Group of Mexican, Colombian, Venezuelan and Panamanian presidents established in 1983 to mediate in conflicts in Central America had faded away, and the Organisation of American States could not take on the role because the Salvadoran government was a member. The church had tried and failed. Cristiani was elected president in March 1989 and soon afterwards came to see UN Secretary General Javier Pérez de Cuéllar, who gave the green light to UN involvement. Álvaro de Soto, a suave Peruvian diplomat and former adviser to Pérez de Cuéllar, flew down to Mexico to see the FMLN the next day. Although the government wanted the UN to play a minimalist role as a facilitator and the rebels wanted it to be a mediator, both sides knew they needed a third party.

The United Nations had been preparing for this invitation for some time. Francesc Vendrell, a patrician Catalan with impeccable English working in the political office of the UN, had taken the initiative to reach out to the guerrillas. He reasoned that if it was acceptable for the UN to talk to the mujahedin fighting the Soviet Union in Afghanistan, it must also be acceptable to talk to guerrilla forces in Latin America. He decided not to ask for permission from his superiors since it would certainly have been declined, but used the opportunity provided by the annual meeting of the Foreign Ministers of the Non-Aligned Movement ('the world's diplomatic super-market', as he describes it), to make contact with Commander Ana María of the FMLN. Fidel Castro was also keen to intro-duce the UN to the FMLN. He took advantage of an official visit by Pérez de Cuéllar to Cuba in 1985 to arrange a quiet, unscheduled meeting between two of the leaders of the FMLM and de Soto and Vendrell. Castro took the official party on a side trip to the 'Island of Youth' where he had been in prison. When they arrived at the island by means of a very old and very slow boat, he took them to a mansion that had belonged to an American tycoon, and said 'I have some representatives of the FMLN here who happen to be in Cuba. Would you mind meeting them?' De Cuéllar shook hands with them and left, but de Soto and Vendrell stayed and spent eight hours talking to Fermán Cienfuegos, leader of the RN group, and Ana Guadalupe Martínez of the ERP faction. Martínez had been kidnapped by the army in the 1976, raped, beaten and tortured, but was later exchanged by the government for a businessman kidnapped by the guerrillas. Finally by November 1988 sufficient trust had been built up and the FMLN political spokesman, Salvador Samayoa, asked Álvaro de Soto to come to Mexico to meet him. De Soto counter-proposed that he come to New York, but the FMLM representative could not get a US visa. Instead they agreed to meet in Montreal on the margins of an international aviation conference where de Soto was presiding, and not long after negotiations began.

Crocker, Hampson and Aall believe the UN brings specific advantages as a mediator: 'The United Nations confers inter-national legitimacy on an intervention, separating the mediation effort from the foreign-policy concerns of any single state and freeing the mediator from the constant task of convincing government colleagues and international allies of the wisdom of banking on this mediation effort.' But it 'is an intergovernmental organisation and as such brings its own set of constraints: dissension among the permanent members of the Security Council, contending agendas between the Security Council and the Secretary General's office, a mammoth bureaucracy, and very limited resources.'

The UN enjoyed its heyday as a mediator in Namibia and Guatemala as well as El Salvador, but it proved a brief dawn. As the 1990s wore on, governments increasingly rejected the UN's presence in their internal affairs as a threat to sovereignty. In such cases governments of small countries proved to be less threatening intermediaries. Certainly the UN would not have been acceptable to Israel when it opened up a backchannel with the PLO in 1992. Norway had a unique position in having both close ties with Israel and direct contact with Yasser Arafat in Tunis. The Norwegians were therefore the perfect matchmaker once a newly elected Labour government in Norway was joined by a Labour government in Israel in June 1992. The PLO had already asked the Norwegians if they would facilitate contacts with the Israelis and when Jan Egeland, the new deputy foreign minister, went to Tel Aviv he used the opportunity of a nightcap in a hotel room after an official dinner to ask his opposite number, Yossi Beilin, if they could help facilitate contacts with the PLO. Terje Roed-Larsen and his wife Mona Juul, a Norwegian official, were in the room as well as Yair Hirschfeld. The Norwegian offer was opportune: the Madrid process was going nowhere and the Israelis had realised they needed to speak directly to the PLO if they were to make progress. The Norwegians became the facilitators for the secret meetings between Yair Hirschfeld and Ron Pundak and their Palestinian opposite numbers, Abu Ala, Hassan Asfour and Maher el-Kurd. They hosted the meetings, arranged the logistics, paid for everything and funded the Palestinian side.

Egeland believes 'A small country like Norway was able to

play the role of third-party facilitator precisely because it was perceived by the parties as neutral and impartial; Norway did not seek to assume the role of fully-fledged "mediator" and did not seek the mandate to do so.' Egeland says 'we were very good in Oslo at mathematically giving them the same kind of treatment: always the same sized rooms, the same kind of cars, we met them at the airport, whether they would be this or that side. But we were not in the negotiation room. We made a point of not being there. We felt it was important not to be involved.'

In July 1993 the Norwegian foreign ministry rented another large country house, this time a hundred and fifty miles north of Oslo, through a colleague of Egeland's wife, and brought in large numbers of Norwegian security policemen to guard it. They told the owners that they needed the place for a group of eccentric Middle Eastern academics who were finishing a book. Roed-Larsen, Juul and Egeland spent the night dozing on sofas outside the room where the negotiations were going on, hoping there would be a breakthrough by morning. Instead the talks broke down at 5.30 a.m. and both sides asked to be taken to the airport immediately. Of the forty-four hours they were at the house, thirty-five had been spent negotiating. When the owners woke the next morning to prepare breakfast they discovered that all their guests had already gone.

In between meetings the Norwegians tried to keep things moving by mobile phone, which the key participants kept with them twenty-four hours a day. They used a rudimentary code that had been agreed at the first meeting in which 'Grandfather' on either side meant Rabin or Arafat, 'Father' meant Peres, while Beilin was 'the Son', Abu Mazen 'the Holy Ghost', Abu Ala 'Number One', and so on. In the hope of applying pressure on the Palestinian side, Hirschfeld deliberately never agreed the date of the next session when he ended a meeting, so that there was no certainty that the process would continue further. He would tell Roed-Larsen privately where the Palestinians could push him to move further and where there was no flexibility. The Norwegians shuttled back and forth between Tunis and Jerusalem carrying messages between the two sides, and helping to fix dates of meetings. The Israeli side doubted the clout of Abu Ala and the Norwegians needed to see Arafat to reassure the Israelis that he was fully behind the deal so that Rabin would agree to continue the talks. The Norwegian role as trustworthy, neutral facilitator was fundamental to the success of the Oslo process.

The Norwegians managed to build on this success in Sri Lanka later in the decade. There, however, unlike in Oslo, the Norwegians were mediators even though they described themselves throughout as facilitators. President Kumaratunga asked the Tigers who they wanted as a third party and they responded with a list of five candidates. The president chose Norway, seeing states like the UK and Canada as too powerful and too high-profile. She surprised everyone, including the Norwegian government, by announcing Norway's role during a live BBC interview at the end of December 1999. Sri Lanka had tried every other option without success. From 1987 to 1990 India had been a strong mediator with troops on the ground trying to keep the peace, but the LTTE had never accepted their presence and they eventually had to withdraw under the weight of the Tiger onslaught. The Sri Lankan government had tried negotiating directly without third-party support in 1994, but that had unravelled within months. They had finally tried the big-bang option of offering political concessions, including devolution, coupled with a renewed military offensive described as the 'war for peace strategy'. None of these approaches had worked.

Little progress was made in the Norwegian-led process at first, until the election of Ranil Wickremasinghe as prime minister in 2001, when things moved fast. The two Norwegian negotiators – Vidar Helgesen, the state secretary for foreign affairs, and Erik Solheim – went first to see Balasingham in London and then on to Colombo to meet the president and the prime minister, and finally to the north of the country to meet Prabhakaran. Bilateral ceasefires were in place by Christmas and negotiations on a mutual ceasefire agreement were under way. The first face-to-face talks took place in Thailand in September 2002 in a relaxed and amicable atmosphere, in part because they were focused on the easiest issues including the implementation of the ceasefire agreement, economic development and normalisation. The difficult political issues were, however, put off, and came back to haunt the process later. Prabhakaran appeared at a press conference for the first time in fifteen years and said he would take part in peace talks once the Tigers had been de-proscribed. President Kumaratunga tried to stop the government lifting the ban but the government went ahead anyway.

In Solheim's view a serious peace process is difficult without a third party because the actors are focused on their narrow political interests. The go-between has to be trustworthy from the beginning. He says 'we never lied to the parties or did anything behind their backs because if we did that we would be finished', while knowing that the parties were lying to them. He firmly believed it was not possible for a small country like Norway to impose an agenda on the two sides.

The LTTE and the Sri Lankan government had very differing views of what the Norwegian role should be. Balasingham said they were in 'the role of neutral advisor and observer' and should 'involve themselves in the negotiating process to prevent misunderstanding between the protagonists and to help to promote the forward movement of the dialogue without imposing "judgmental decisions" on the parties. It is our view that without the presence and participation of an experienced third party the negotiations between the two historical enemies may run into serious difficulties.' The Sri Lankan foreign minister Lakshman Kadirgamar, however, argued: 'When it comes to substantive negotiation, the Norwegians will have no particular role at all.' Norway's role, he said, is 'limited to bringing the two parties together. Shuttling back and forth between the parties. Carrying messages. And laying the groundwork for them to meet. They will have no mandate to impose solutions. They will certainly have no mandate to make any judgmental decisions. In that sense, they're not arbitrators, they're not judges, they're not mediators.' He said Sri Lanka had had sixteen offers from third parties but chose Norway as 'We had in mind the fact Norway is a small country and, therefore, a country which we thought has no agenda of its own, other than in respect of Sri Lanka or in respect to the region, South Asia. Secondly, Norway is very far away and distance has an advantage in a situation of this kind. Thirdly, Norway has no colonial background at all and therefore, there's no baggage that Norway brings to an exercise of this kind. Then, fourthly, that Norway already has some experience in this area – in other disputes of a somewhat similar nature, although they may not be identical.' Governments and armed groups nearly always have this difference of opinion about what the role of the third party should be, with the armed group wanting them to have a greater role than the government would like.

There are differing views on how far mediators should culti- vate relationships with the representatives of the armed groups in order to help make progress in the negotiations. Lakhdar Brahimi, the veteran UN negotiator, says 'You create a rapport, friendship is perhaps a bit strong. You certainly try to ask about how their children are doing, or whether their old mother is still alive. But all in all I don't think you really get that close. These people have interests . . . They will never forget that you are really after taking things away from them.' Solheim also believes it is important to establish a rapport, but that you should never let friendship be bigger than the process. In Sri Lanka he thought it was good if the mediators could get to know the leaders on both sides, drink with them, relax and talk about other interests. Solheim says Balasingham became a friend but Prabhakaran did not. Prabhakaran would not drink and never relaxed.

Of course the leaders of armed groups can try to become

too friendly. Both sides in Sri Lanka gave Vidar Helgesen wedding presents when he was married in June 2004, and the Tigers sent a wreath to the funeral when his mother died. He comments ironically on what she would have made of this. His story has an echo for me. My mother, who was of Anglo-Irish stock, would always say sympathetically when I had to go off to see Adams and McGuinness, 'Oh, I am so sorry, dear.' Martin McGuinness kindly sent a condolence card when she died and I could only imagine what my mother would have thought.

Mediators are caught in a difficult bind. On the one hand they do not want to be accused of being 'useful fools' for the terrorists. On the other hand, terrorists are often better company than those on the opposing side; the leaders of armed groups are more informal and easier to get on with than government bureaucrats, and they want to form relationships with the negotiators. I have seen mediators take imperceptible steps from being a neutral go-between to becoming a champion for the underdog's case. Governments will then legitimately demand to know who gave them a mandate to interfere in the affairs of their country. Some mediators take so much professional pride in building a relationship of trust that they get distracted from their principal objective. Good but cool relations based on as much knowledge as possible, not so much of the conflict but of the parties, are what is required. Most groups do not expect you to agree with them. That is not your role. They simply want a fair hearing and for you to be even-handed. Negotiators sometimes struggle to get the balance right.

Solheim found himself accused unfairly of being caught in this trap. In June 2001 President Kumaratunga issued an urgent invitation to the Norwegian foreign minister, Thorbjørn Jagland, to visit Sri Lanka. Jagland diverted to Colombo but had only fourteen hours to spend on the ground, his only visit to the island. The president invited him to dinner but deliberately excluded Solheim and the Norwegian ambassador. She told Jagland that she was not happy with Solheim and wanted him withdrawn or replaced with someone more senior to get things kick-started. Jagland agreed and said he would sideline Solheim and take on the role himself. The Tigers reacted with fury, issuing a statement on Solheim's 'impeccable neutrality' and complained about his 'shabby, unfair and insulting' treatment and the decision to 'downgrade and marginalise' his role. They said they had not been consulted and broke off all relations with Norway for six months. According to the Norwegian post-mortem on their efforts in Sri Lanka, Jagland's successor was sceptical about the value of the continuing Norwegian role until he visited Washington and discovered that the Americans were far more interested in asking him about Sri Lanka than they were about Norway – one reason small countries are willing to take on these onerous roles.

When things go wrong in a negotiation the mediators often become a magnet for blame. Sinhalese opinion, having initially been supportive of the role played by the Norwegians, turned against them, picking on Solheim in particular and accusing him of being partisan for the Tigers. Sinhalese nationalists called for him to be made *persona non grata*, and President Kumaratunga accused Norway of going 'far beyond the role of facilitator' and said that its role was now 'incompatible with the sovereign status of Sri Lanka'. Solheim's effigy was burned at Sinhalese demonstrations and there was even a suicide attack on the Norwegian Embassy and a threatened bomb attack on Solheim's convoy. In 2004 an enraged crowd marched on the Norwegian Embassy with a coffin containing the body of Velayadun Ravindran, a Tamil opposition activist who had been murdered by the LTTE, and deposited it at the gates.

Governments expect facilitators to be on their side, but the facilitator must remain neutral. They cannot tell the government the details of logistical arrangements, who they have met and where, for fear that if they are given the information they will use it for intelligence purposes. If a facilitator tells them where they are meeting there is the risk they will endeavour to arrest or even kill their interlocutors. On one occasion when a group of facilitators visited the PKK leadership in the Qandil mountains in Northern Iraq, their convoy was traced by aerial reconnaissance. Nothing happened while they were in the camp, but after they left, the site was bombed and six of their hosts killed.

As well as being criticised by the Sri Lankans for being partisan, the Norwegians were also accused by some in the international community of lacking the necessary 'oomph' to get things going again, and others tried to muscle in. In 2003, the Japanese, as Sri Lanka's biggest aid donor, expressed a strong interest in playing a central role and they, the US and EU joined Norway as co-chairs of the process. It is quite commonplace for other mediators to try to hijack negotiations. After some six months Portugal made a pitch for the Mozambican negotiations to be transferred to Lisbon because of the weakness and incapacity of the Italian negotiators, pointing to the rapid – and, as it turned out, temporary – success of the Angolan negotiations which had just concluded in Evora under their chairmanship. The two parties were, however, totally committed to the Italian route and the Sant'Egidio team saw the raid off in part by inviting the US, Portuguese and other states to join the talks in Rome as observers, where they were able to provide expertise, particularly on the military aspects of talks. When the El Salvador negotiations were stuck in early summer 1991, Venezuelan president Carlos Pérez tried to hijack them, quietly summoning the key negotiators to Caracas in an effort to distract attention from his growing problems at home. He submitted to both sides a bare-bones proposal for an agreement. The FMLN rejected it out of hand and refused to meet the government under any auspices other than the chairmanship of the UN. Álvaro de Soto, the UN negotiator in El Salvador, insists that one of the keys to his success in the mediation there was that 'except for one episode of aborted diplomatic hijacking, there was never any question about the unity and integrity of the third-party mediation and who was in charge of it'.

Even small neutral countries can be too threatening to governments as a third party, and Jimmy Carter notes that 'almost invariably in a civil war, the last thing the ruling party in particular wants is for the United States or the United Nations or some highly identifiable mediation group to come in, because that in effect gives the imprimatur of legitimacy to the revolutionary people in the country'. They do not want foreign governments playing the role because they cannot afford to treat them roughly when the negotiations get difficult, because of the consequences for bilateral relations if they do. Individuals can provide a suitable compromise between the aspirations of both sides. For armed groups they provide the internationalisation of the conflict and an independent referee, making it harder for the government to cheat with impunity. For the government they introduce a mediator who can't push them around and one that can operate with 'plausible deniability' so that initial contacts can take place secretly without the opprobrium which otherwise would make the first steps too costly politically.

When the first effort at making peace in Aceh, led by the HD Centre, collapsed in 2003, the Indonesian government first tried to resolve the problem directly themselves. The two ministers most closely involved in the earlier negotiations, Susilo Bambang Yudhoyono and Muhammad Jusuf Kalla, started a new initiative of their own. Using Acehnese businessman Rusli Bintang as a go-between, they made contact with the GAM commanders on the ground. Jusuf Kalla, who was by then vice president, held secret meetings with the GAM in the Netherlands, Britain and Malaysia, without telling the military or the foreign ministry, and even met the brother of the supreme commander of the group in his official residence. They got as far as signing an agreement on economic compensation for GAM fighters, including giving them two Boeing 737s, which Jusuf Kalla called 'the right bride price'. When that initiative ran into the sand, Jusuf Kalla and Yudhoyono, now president, started casting around for a new mediator. The Indonesian government had been clear from the start that they would not accept the UN after the experience of East Timor. GAM favoured a foreign government as mediator and in 2000 the Malaysian faction, MP-GAM, had approached the Finnish president Martti Ahtisaari after they had been cut out of the earlier HD Centre-led negotiations. At the time, Ahtisaari was politically unacceptable to the Indonesian government because he was still president, but when he left office and became a private individual again, Jusuf Kalla called him in late 2004 to ask him to chair the talks. No one had told the HD Centre, which was still working on the issue, and they felt understandably aggrieved when Ahtisaari took over the negotiations in 2005.

In the last decade there has been a small revolution in diplomacy as individuals and NGOs increasingly take on the role of facilitation and mediation in internal armed conflicts instead of the UN or governments. Terje Roed-Larsen calls it 'venture capital for peace. The costs are so low, and the potential rewards so high that even one success in 100 makes it worthwhile.'

One of the early examples of an NGO playing the role of mediator was the Community of Sant'Egidio, based in the bohemian Trastevere district of Rome. In the 1980s they devoted much of their effort to humanitarian assistance for Mozambique, the poorest country on earth at the time, only to see it eaten up by the conflict there. The country had been in the grip of a particularly ugly civil war between the governing FRELIMO and the rebel RENAMO since its independence from Portugal in 1975 in which more than a million died and 4.5 million people were forced to flee their homes. RENAMO had been supported first by the Rhodesian Central Intelligence Organisation and then by the South Africans as a way of paying back the neighbouring country for supporting the ZANU and ANC guerrillas fighting them. In the words of one Westerner involved at the time, the South African military turned RENAMO into 'the biggest killing machine in Africa'. It was notorious for mutilating civilians, including children, by cutting off ears, noses, fingers and sexual organs. Afonso Dhlakama had become the supreme leader of the movement after a bloody succession struggle in which his rival was killed. He was an insecure leader who wore glasses to appear more intellectual, even though he didn't need them.

Sant'Egidio worked closely with the Catholic archbishop of Beira, Jaime Gonçalves, in trying to build a channel to RENAMO. In May 1988 Gonçalves was finally offered a meeting with Dhlakama. He decided to attend in his full arch-bishop's regalia, and took the precaution of going to confession twice before leaving. He took off in a small private plane from Lesotho with two strangers bound for Zaire, only to find it rerouted to Gorongosa, the headquarters of RENAMO in the Mozambican province of Sofala. They landed on a small dirt runway in the bush in the middle of the night. Dhlakama received him in the jungle next to a blazing fire and they talked for two hours. Gonçalves was seeking a ceasefire for Pope John Paul II's visit to Mozambique as a first step. He didn't get it, but he did manage to get a peace process going which eventu-ally produced an agreement. Dhlakama preferred dealing with Gonçalves than with the Catholic archbishop of Maputo, Alexandre dos Santos, whom he regarded as a friend of FRELIMO. Besides, Gonçalves came from the same region of the country as Dhlakama and his deputy, the foreign affairs spokesman Artur da Fonseca, and there was a distant family connection. Dos Santos lamented 'the tribalism of RENAMO'.

The Mozambican government would not meet directly with RENAMO for fear of giving it legitimacy, and so Mozambican churchmen, including Gonçalves, tried shuttling back and forth between the two sides in Kenya. In August 1989 President Chissano asked them to hand over the task to the Kenyan and Zimbabwean governments. When that failed da Fonseca wrote to Cardinal Casaroli, the Vatican Secretary of State, asking the church to act as mediator. The Vatican was concerned about bishops becoming tangled in a political issue and made it clear they wanted governments to handle it rather than the church. In parallel Sant'Egidio started to make plans for a visit to Rome by Dhlakama. The Italian authorities were nervous because they did not want to disrupt their good relations with the government in Maputo, but agreed to the visit so long as it remained unofficial and secret.

At the same time Sant'Egidio received a direct approach from FRELIMO, when Aguiar Mazula, the minister of labour, came to Rome to sound them out on the possibility of a secret meeting between the two sides in Italy without preconditions. He seemed to be convinced that Sant'Egidio could guarantee the necessary climate of impartiality. A first informal meeting took place in July 1990 in the margins of the opening match of the World Cup between Argentina and Cameroon. The tickets came courtesy of the Italian government, which, according to Andrea Bartoli, over the course of the negotiations also paid for 'hospitality [that] also included shopping trips to fashionable Rome stores where RENAMO's delegates were outfitted in designer suits and shoes. When RENAMO ran up $60,000 in telephone bills between January and July 1992 alone, the Italians met the costs . . . By the time of the signing of the Rome accord, the Italian government had spent some $20 million on the peace process.'

The first formal meeting between the two sides took place in secret in Rome on 8 July, with Mario Raffaelli (on behalf of the Italian government), the head of Sant'Egidio Andrea Riccardi, the charismatic priest Matteo Zuppi, and Gonçalves as observers. The Mozambican government did not want mediators, just witnesses to serve as guarantors of the discussions. The Sant'Egidio team were convinced that Mozambique could not be resolved by a 'muscular' negotiator who forced the parties to make peace. Zuppi writes of the 'many prophets of doom' that 'emerged during these long months keen to prove we were wasting our time. Our weakness became our strength.' Bartoli says Sant'Egidio was 'able to succeed as a conduit of negotiation because of the very weakness that made it such an unlikely leader – its lack of international prestige and power, which prevented it from being cast into and constricted by the formalities of traditional efforts'.

The HD Centre was an early mover in the field of international NGOs playing a role in peacemaking, ever since 1999 when Martin Griffiths had the inspired idea of turning what was then a defunct NGO in Geneva into a body that could create a channel between armed groups and governments with the aim of ending conflict and reducing humanitarian suffering. Blessed with a good deal of luck, the HD Centre walked directly into roles in Aceh and Nepal. Inserting themselves into the long-running Basque conflict required skill as well as luck.

Griffiths had taken the initiative to contact ETA but he also had the good fortune to do so just at the moment ETA was looking for a new mediator. ETA had wanted the Swiss government who were reluctant to take on the role after the abortive talks under Aznar. The HD Centre was the next best thing. An internal ETA report, later captured by the police, described the HDC representatives as 'very professional . . . They don't have prejudices, they don't display postures against us, they won't make inappropriate comments about armed actions (except to know whether they have taken place), they won't "sell" a process in advance'. ETA wanted the HDC to undertake the logistical and security arrangements for the meetings, assume a technical role as note taker, and occasionally steer the discussion. Neither the government nor ETA felt it was appropriate for the HDC to take on a political role, and they were forbidden from having contact with other organisations involved, even with Batasuna.

Such international NGOs have advantages, but there are limits to what they can do. The humanitarian expert Antonia Potter says 'the smaller and less formal the institution which backs [a mediator], the more room they have for manoeuvre especially at the early stages of a process, but the less effective the carrots and sticks they have to apply at critical junctures'.

Crocker, Hampson and Aall think 'if the mediator represents an NGO, he or she may have a great deal of freedom of movement but will also have few points of leverage and almost no ability to induce or force the parties to the conflict to change their behaviour'. NGOs lack the analytical capacity of a government or the ability to deal with problems of representation and coherence of the parties or fully to harness the support of the international community. Most of all they lack the weight to cry foul effectively if one side cheats.

The fundamental job of a mediator is to be a referee. Lakhdar Brahimi says 'From my point of view, when you get into [a] situation with people in which they sign something and the next day do the opposite, you have to do something to show displeasure.' It is not easy for a weak NGO to do this effectively. At the end of the Tokyo negotiations on Aceh in 2003, Martin Griffiths was incandescent about the way the Indonesian government had behaved. Their aim appeared to have been simply to go through the motions to demonstrate to domestic and international audiences that they had exhausted all attempts at negotiation, without responding in any way to the three major compromises put forward by the GAM. The Indonesian military went into action at midnight on the last day of the negotiations; their action had clearly been pre-planned. Griffiths wanted to speak out publicly after the collapse to expose what had happened but was prevailed upon by the Americans and Japanese and other backers of the talks to remain silent. In fact by attacking the Indonesians all he would have done was disqualify himself from further participation in the talks.

Sometimes mediators need to be reinforced. Ahtisaari says 'In general, it is important for mediators to remember that they cannot do everything alone and that they need wide support.' In El Salvador, Álvaro de Soto used a 'Group of Friends of the Secretary General' made up of interested governments as a way of bypassing the Security Council. He was determined to keep the friends firmly out of the negotiating process and made it clear there could only be one mediator, while calling on their

help when he needed it, saying 'It is inherent in good mediation that there should be one agent unquestionably and unequiv-
ocally in charge.' If there are several mediators, parties might
be tempted to play off one against the other. He says 'What I
used to do was to say to country governments who were in a
position to help and had some influence with one or more of
the parties, "This is what I need to obtain from them and here
are the arguments I am using – could you please reinforce
them?" I wouldn't ask questions about how they go about it.'

One side effect of the new diplomacy is a swarming of
NGOs when a conflict becomes unfrozen. Tens of willing
volunteers appear offering to broker a deal. The danger of
this is that armed groups are tempted to go 'forum shopping',
looking for the NGO that seems most in their favour. Brahimi
says 'If you have too many players involved and pulling left,
right, and centre, the risk is that a lot of harm will be done
to the process.' The element of competition is not, however,
completely disastrous, as the government is also looking at
different facilitators and the market usually sorts it out in the
end. In fact the blooming of many mediators can help ensure
a dialogue starts, but when the process graduates from building
trust and creating a channel to actually starting a negotiation,
there should be just one clear channel and the others need to
fall away.

International NGOs are not the only answer. There are
regional bodies like the African Union or the West African
ECOWAS that can play the role of mediator. Emmanuel
Bombande of the West Africa Network for Peacebuilding says
'insider mediators truly care about the outcome. Insider mediators remain after the agreement; they will be there a long time
after the conflict.' In the final stage of the negotiations to release
Corporal Gilad Shalit, the Israeli soldier held for five years by
Hamas, the external German mediator was replaced by two
internal facilitators working together. On the Israeli side was
Gershon Baskin, a long-time peace activist with a direct channel
to David Meidan, the Mossad officer appointed by Netanyahu

to secure Shalit's release, and on the other side Dr Ghazi Hamad, a Hamas official with direct access to Ahmed Jabri, the military leader of Hamas (later killed by the Israelis), who was holding Shalit. Baskin and Hamad had built up a relationship of trust over seven years and hundreds of hours of conversations that allowed them, together, to navigate the delicate steps to getting Shalit finally released from his underground captivity.

Whatever its manifestation, the role of a mediator is a difficult balancing act. In his Nobel Prize speech Martti Ahtisaari said 'The task of the mediator is to help the parties to open difficult issues and nudge them forward in the peace process. The mediator's role combines those of a ship's pilot, consulting medical doctor, midwife and teacher.' The mediator has to counsel each side without taking sides.

There is a disagreement amongst mediators about how neutral they should be. While balance between the two sides is essential, it does not necessarily follow that the mediator should have no view of his own about the outcome. Ahtisaari says: 'In mediation, you should not be neutral. If you say you are neutral, you are saying that you will come to the negotiations to listen to the parties and their views. That kind of a process can take many years, if not decades, because no one is taking the process further. My experience and practice have thus made me sensitive towards the terms "impartiality" and "neutrality". I much prefer the term "honest broker". A mediator must know the outcome and, to some extent, explain it to the parties.' He says that in Aceh 'special autonomy was the end goal. I had to tell the GAM representatives that I would walk away if they insisted on independence. I told them: "If I were you, I would not have anything to lose. During the talks, we will come together to determine what this special autonomy means, and then it is up to you to decide if it is attractive enough for you to accept it instead of independence. But we will not talk about independence during the negotiations."'

A mediator should thus not just be a passive listener heading for the lowest common denominator, but needs to be proactive in generating ideas and driving the process forward. Mediators need to be ambitious. Brahimi says 'Of course you aim for the moon. Why not? But don't say you are going to get to the moon today, if it takes several steps to get to the moon . . . Set achievable objectives.' The two extreme examples of the approach are Richard Holbrooke bullying and blustering his way to a successful agreement between the Bosnian parties at the Dayton negotiations in 1995, and George Mitchell's patient attempt to piece together a deal, ultimately unsuccessfully, in the Middle East in 2010. It is usually best if facilitators have a low ego because the last thing you need is additional complications at the negotiating table but just occasionally you need a bully. One National Security Council official says of Holbrooke, 'He was prepared to be seductive when it was appropriate to be seductive, and . . . brutal when it was appropriate to be as brutal as it took.' The danger of such a muscular approach is that it produces an unsustainable agreement. De Soto says 'If a party reaches the signature table with its arm twisted out of its socket – quite apart from the difficulty of actually signing – it will be much more difficult to implement it and stick to it down the road.' And while an activist mediator may be desirable, a mediator desperate for an agreement at all costs, driven by their desire to achieve a success and the credit that goes with it, can be disastrous.

A mediator then needs to be proactive but they cannot bring their own agenda to the table. Michael Young says that 'As a peace negotiator you are obliged to challenge others but not to come littered with your own baggage and subjectivities . . . it's their show, it's their disagreement.' Mediators may, as individuals, strongly support the protection of human rights or the introduction of a democratic system, but they need to leave their values at home. Norway was criticised for failing to insist that human rights should be part of the Sri Lanka agreement. Vidar Helgesen gives an answer that holds for all such negotiations: 'We don't have a blueprint which we feel would be the best solution . . . We were working on the basic assumption that the biggest human-rights violator is war.' At the same time, the mediators' aim is a lasting settlement, whose durability itself depends on it addressing fundamental issues like preventing human-rights abuses and finding a system that rests on the consent of the people.

A successful mediator requires a particular set of skills. Crocker, Hampson and Aall argue that good mediators are both born *and* made: 'The particular characteristics of quick-wittedness, firmness, flexibility, high tolerance for ambiguity, and a grasp of what motivates people are without doubt traits you are born with. A deep knowledge of the conflict and a personal history or standing that draws the trust of the conflict parties, however, is a combination of individual characteristics, education, professional calling, outside circumstances, and blind luck.' Language skills can be crucially important – too often if the mediator does not speak the language of the two sides, political nuances get literally 'lost in translation'. Antonia Potter says great mediators 'may put their arm around one leader while strolling in the garden, or talk family matters with another in the sauna or the Jacuzzi. They can confine the lead negotiators in a room with a deadline to emerge with an agreement. They might relentlessly invite the teams out for dinner after dinner, or despatch them off for supervised woodland walks like an earnest parent. They can encourage them to ventilate their feelings and frustrations like a therapist. They may lose their temper, deliberately or without guile; or refuse ever to be ruffled . . . Cunning as a fox, they will have thought through the angles of how to keep the process secret and deniable where necessary.' Charm is also an essential ingredient in an effective mediator. Martin Griffiths, charm personified, says 'This business about charm is manipulation.' Tony Blair managed to charm the Unionists in Northern Ireland into talks. They regarded it as a form of black magic, but it was just an ability to empathise with their position and persuade them of a way forward.

Another job of a mediator is to act as an interpreter,

faithfully passing messages from one side to the other and explaining what they mean. If they ever lie or are caught out misleading one side, they can no longer play a useful role. But equally I have seen facilitators be so literal as to pass on the graphic insults of one side to the other with evident relish. All that does is wind up the recipient and raise the temperature, rather than aid the search for a solution. An effective facilitator has to temper the message to remove the hard edges and, at the same time as passing on a rejection, suggest alternative compromises which they think might be acceptable. This combination of skill and restraint is unusual and explains why good mediators are so few and far between.

But what is required of a mediator above all else is patience. Potter describes a memorable example of the ability to wait at the Bonn talks on Afghanistan in 2001, when Brahimi at one stage did not leave his seat for seven and a half hours, not even to go to the toilet, in order to pressure delegates into also staying and working on a deal. As the night wore on, people became less pedantic as they wanted to get it over and done with. Jaswant Singh, the Indian foreign minister, wisely asked the two Norwegian envoys in Sri Lanka when they first came to see him, 'Are you patient?' Solheim, thinking of the suffering of the people in Sri Lanka, replied that he was not patient. Singh said in that case they should go to the airport immediately and buy a one-way ticket out of South Asia and never come back. 'If you are not patient, you will only mess this place up,' he said. Solheim says now, 'He was right and I was wrong. But we had to learn the hard way.' George Mitchell is the best example of patience that I have ever come across. He was prepared to sit through the most awful nonsense from all sides in the Northern Ireland talks, and yet remained good-humoured, maintaining warm relations with everyone.

It is natural that governments should be suspicious of inviting outsiders into their internal conflicts, but the evidence suggests third parties can make both reaching an agreement and implementing it easier and more likely to succeed in the long term.

In the end, though, it is not the mediators who should be awarded Nobel Peace Prizes, but the leaders of the governments and the armed groups themselves who take the real risks with their political futures – and sometimes their lives – in agreeing to the difficult compromises that need to be made to arrive at a lasting peace. Ahtisaari says 'there tends to be too much focus on the mediators. With that we are disempowering the parties to the conflict and creating the wrong impression that peace comes from the outside. The only people that can make peace are the parties to the conflict, and just as they are responsible for the conflict and its consequences, so should they be given responsibility and recognition for the peace.'

CHAPTER SIX

Starting a Negotiation

There are those who believe that as long as the violence [in the Middle East] is going on, one should not talk. I personally disagree with that. I think that is one more reason to talk and it underscores the urgency to bring the parties together.

Kofi Annan, April 2001

Although it may always be right to talk to terrorists, it is not always the right time to start a negotiation. Even after a channel has been constructed and confidence built, certain conditions need to be in place if a negotiation is to succeed.

Crocker, Hampson and Aall suggest that 'There are a limited number of entry points . . . at which the clay of a violent conflict is soft enough to work with,' including a geopolitical shift; a shift in the conflict's internal dynamics; a major change in the leadership structure of one or more parties; and the arrival of a new mediator. What you are looking for is a moment when things are changing, whether inside the country or outside.

Taking the first of these entry points, a geopolitical shift, there is a tendency to ascribe too much importance to the influence of outside events in enabling peace settlements. Some commentators say, for instance, that the terrible events of 9/11 made it impossible for the IRA campaign of violence to continue, and that a lasting peace in Northern Ireland was subsequently inevitable. This, however, exaggerates the impact of such outside events on closed communities. If you live on the Falls Road in West Belfast or in the Bogside in Derry, then New York seems a long way away and the events there have much less impact than developments closer to home. That said, the advent of jihadi terrorism certainly did have an impact, both positive and negative, on terrorist groups and peace processes around the world. Many of the existing armed groups simply could not compete with the level of terror deployed by Islamic extremists. Their willingness to kill themselves as well as others was on a different scale to the individual assassinations or car bombs carried out by the IRA or ETA. The public revulsion in Spain after the train bombs in Madrid in 2004 made it difficult for ETA to go back to widespread violence. 'George' told Martin Griffiths that 'it was bad to be a terrorist after what happened'. And when the bombings in London took place on 7/7, Jesús Eguiguren said George was conscious that the Islamic extremist terrorists 'leave without oxygen, opportunity, legitimacy, justification and explanation the European terrorists left over from the past'.

The security response to the attack on the Twin Towers, which briefly united most of the world, and the ensuing 'war on terror', also reduced the space for armed groups as more and more of them were proscribed. It certainly reduced any international support for the Tamil Tigers and made it easier for the Sri Lankan government to deal with them as purely a security problem. The war in Iraq in 2003 took things further and provided cover for the Indonesian government to renew the military offensive against GAM without incurring international opprobrium. Academics Anisseh Van Engeland and Rachael Rudolph argue that since 9/11 'political violence is not "bankable" any more or even "tolerated" as it was before; each terrorist action had become a matter of international security'.

The end of the Cold War was the geopolitical event that had the greatest impact in improving the chances of successful peace negotiations. According to Yair Hirschfeld it was one of the factors that helped make the Oslo Accords possible. F. W. de Klerk thinks that for South Africa, 'the fall of the Berlin Wall and the collapse of the Soviet Union removed our geostrategic concern regarding the threat of communism.' After the end of the Cold War the proportion of civil wars ended by negotiated settlements increased from 10 per cent to 40 per cent, as the US and the Soviet Union urged sides to settle rather than continue fighting. Indeed in the fifteen years after the end of the Cold War, more conflicts ended than had in the preceding half-century. Its impact was therefore undoubtedly significant, but again we should not exaggerate its importance. Yair Hirschfeld believes that Yasser Arafat's disastrous decision to back Saddam Hussein in the First Gulf War, and the subsequent loss of Arab support, was at least as important. In South Africa F. W. de Klerk believes the success of the Namibia peace process was crucial in helping persuade the military that a negotiated solution was possible for South Africa. The guerrilla leader Joaquín Villalobos says he was far more influenced by the success of peace talks in Angola, in Nicaragua and with the M-19 in Colombia than he was by the end of the Cold War.

Natural disasters can also have the effect of expediting peace agreements. On 26 December 2004, an earthquake off the coast of Aceh triggered a ten-metre tsunami that levelled half the capital, Bandar Aceh, and killed 170,000 people. In the aftermath, an armada of ships from the international community were poised off the coast to deliver emergency aid, but could not do so while the island was in the midst of an armed conflict. GAM lost many of its cadres in the tsunami and had already been substantially weakened by the preceding military campaign which had largely pushed them back into the hills. Military posts had been established in many villages and thousands of villagers had been resettled on the model used by the British in the Malayan insurgency in the 1950s. Those guerrillas who had lived in comfort in Malaysia in the preceding decades and had only returned to Aceh after the Cessation of Hostilities Agreement in 2002 found the hardships of a losing campaign not to their taste. Hopes of independence, which GAM had claimed had been 'only a cigarette away' in 2000, had now faded. They really had believed that 'Indonesia-Java' was going to disintegrate like Yugoslavia or the Soviet Union under the weight of its own contradictions after the fall of Suharto and the independence of East Timor. By 2004, however, they had lost all hope of that happening. There had been significant reforms in Indonesia including decentralisation, and President Yudhoyono had won votes in Aceh. The GAM had originally thought time was on their side but now concluded that it was not.

Although preparations for the new talks had started before the end of 2004, the devastation of the tsunami allowed the Indonesian government to present entering into negotiations as a response to a humanitarian disaster rather than a reversal of policy; and it allowed the GAM to present it as a decision to help the Acehnese people rather than arising out of their own weakness. Ahtisaari was extremely tough in the initial demands he made on GAM, in particular insisting on their acceptance of the territorial integrity of Indonesia. Had he tried to be equally firm a year before or a year after the tsunami, his demands would probably have been rejected. In its immediate aftermath they had little choice but to go along with him. Meeri-Maria Jaarva of Ahtisaari's NGO Crisis Management Initiative (CMI) says 'The tsunami was such a big tragedy for Aceh, so it made GAM more willing to begin talks with the government. Also within the government, apart from the president and the vice president, support for the peace talks was not extensive, but the tsunami spread the support within the government. The tsunami also affected the willingness of the international community to get engaged; particularly in the case of the EU, the tsunami made Aceh more of a priority for the EU, even though it normally focuses on its own neighbourhood . . . The tsunami also had an impact on the length of the peace talks. I don't think that without the natural disaster we would have been able to conclude the talks so fast. The tsunami created a sense of urgency among the parties.' Ahtisaari adds that 'The international community donated generous sums of money to the reconstruction of Aceh. Both sides realised that if the fighting did not end, the money could not be used; it helped us and we were able to conclude the talks in less than six months.'

The same tsunami also affected the negotiations on the other side of the Indian Ocean in Sri Lanka, at least temporarily. 30,000 people died in the disaster on the island and 550,000 were displaced. Prabhakaran was, according to the Norwegians, 'devastated' and 'shattered' by the impact of the tragedy on his people and 'at a different level emotionally than previously'. A window of opportunity opened up for progress. In the immediate aftermath, the Sri Lankan army offered assistance to the LTTE, and the Tigers proposed a mechanism to work with the government to deliver aid to the affected areas. It was the first time in the entire process they had shown such flexibility. International aid donors pushed for co-operation so that assistance could get through to the affected population. Within weeks both parties had agreed to develop a 'Joint Mechanism' or Post-Tsunami Operational Management Structure, which could have provided the contours for a wider political solution. President Kumaratunga, however, dragged her feet. She supported the agreement but could not convince the minority JVP party to take steps that might legitimise the LTTE, and they walked out of the government. The Muslim minority, who had been most affected by the destruction, were anxious about a settlement that gave the LTTE any degree of control. The government added demands and blocked the sending of high-level representatives to LTTE areas. What had been possible in February was no longer possible by June, when the government was finally ready to sign. Prabhakaran concluded that the international community would never stand up for the Tamil people. Violence started again and then, as a *coup de grâce*, the Supreme Court found the agreement to be illegal.

External factors therefore clearly have an influence, but they are not determinative. What really makes a negotiation possible is internal developments, particularly a military stalemate. El Salvador is a classic example. In November 1989, the FMLN deployed 7,000 guerrillas to take San Salvador in the 'Final Offensive', under the slogan 'To the finish'. Some of their leaders believed that with one last push they could win the war and defeat the government. Others, however, wanted to demonstrate that the forces were evenly balanced and that the conflict could only be ended by negotiation. Up until then the war had largely been fought in the countryside, and the FMLN wanted to force the army to fight in the cities where the bloodshed would be covered on national TV.

They got their wish. One of the most famous battles took place in the Sheraton Hotel in San Salvador where the army and the guerrillas fought it out floor by floor, live on television. The guerrillas surrounded nine US marines in the hotel and sent a message to the US government offering to return them safely, not wanting to find themselves fighting the Americans as well. They later discovered that the US government had been on the point of deploying the Delta Force to recapture them. Archbishop Emilio Lorenzo Stehle was dispatched in an armoured car marked with a huge red cross to collect them from the hotel. After they had been released, the US sent another message saying the CIA station chief was in his house also surrounded by guerrillas and could not move. The FMLN said they didn't know where he was, so the US gave them his address and the guerrillas removed their forces, allowing him to escape.

When the FMLN guerrillas initially occupied the poor western part of the city they were not greeted by the popular insurrection that some of them had hoped for. The army, however, played into their hands by bombing residential neighbourhoods, inflicting civilian casualties. In response the guerrillas moved to the prosperous east of the city and came within 200 metres of the presidential residence. As he later admitted, it was then that President Cristiani recognised that the army was useless. According to Joaquín Villalobos, Cristiani at that point opened secret contacts with the guerrilla leaders in Managua through Ignacio Ellacuría, a Jesuit priest and rector of the University of Central America. The FMLN announced that they were prepared to agree to a ceasefire. The military, however, considered that while parts of the capital were still occupied a ceasefire would be seen as a defeat, and assassinated Ellacuría and five other Jesuit priests. These murders separated Cristiani from the military and convinced the US government that they should drop their support for a military solution.

The government realised they couldn't defeat the rebels, who withdrew from the city nonetheless, realising they couldn't hold the city or win the war. After the failure of the offensive, both sides were ready for serious negotiations. A meeting of Central American presidents was convened in Costa Rica at which they all agreed to call on the UN to intervene and lead negotiations.

It wasn't known at the time, but the offensive nearly didn't happen at all. The FMLN had already infiltrated their men into the capital and the attack was ready to begin when the rebels sat down with the government for talks under the chairmanship of the Catholic Church in Costa Rica in October 1989. If the government had accepted the draft human-rights agreement on the table at that meeting, the rebels would have been in a quandary about how to switch off the attack at that late stage. The session went on all night and in the end the two sides prepared a paper setting out their differences, agreeing to meet again. The government side had wanted to end the meeting without agreement, for their own reasons. Villalobos, relieved by the failure, flew back to Nicaragua to prepare, but it was still not plain sailing. The Soviet foreign minister, Eduard Shevardnadze, was visiting Managua at the time and asked to meet the FMLN leaders. Villalobos was worried Shevardnadze would ask them to call off the offensive, and the leader of the Communist wing of the FMLN said that if the Soviet Union asked them to stop then they would have to agree to do so. They decided the only option was to hide. At the official reception for Shevardnadze, Daniel Ortega had to confess he couldn't find the FMLN leaders. However Ortega's brother, the Nicaraguan military commander Humberto, found Villalobos and asked him whether, if they stopped supporting the FMLN logistically, that would put an end to the offensive. Villalobos said they would go ahead anyway. Ortega told him in that case to proceed, and promised support. The FMLN started the operation the next morning.

Villalobos had asked the Nicaraguans for surface-to-air missiles to deal with the El Salvador air force. The Nicaraguans were, however, concerned about the potential American response and offered the guerrillas the choice of a handful of missiles or hundreds of AK-47s. Villalobos chose the guns. Later, in the disorder that followed Ortega's electoral defeat, the chief of the air force summoned Villalobos to his headquarters and gave him twelve missiles. On his way out of the office Villalobos was approached by a more junior officer who was about to be thrown out of the military with the change of government, and wanted money to buy a farm. He offered to sell the guerrillas more missiles and Villalobos bought over a hundred Soviet C2Ms from him. The FMLN used the missiles to shoot down an air force Dragonfly A37 in November 1990, and once they had targeted a second plane a few days later, the air force stopped flying. The president told the pilots they should be as brave as the army, but pilots were shooting themselves in the foot so they would not have to fly. Once the air force had been effectively grounded, the military stalemate was absolutely clear to everyone.

Álvaro de Soto, the UN negotiator in El Salvador, says 'The November 1989 offensive made the government and the Salvadoran elites come to the conclusion that they could not defeat the guerrillas militarily . . . That was the mutually hurting stalemate', when 'the opposing parties perceive that the cost of coming to an agreement has become less than the cost of pursuing the conflict'. The idea of a 'mutually hurting stalemate' (MHS) was developed by William Zartman, who defines it as follows: 'The concept is based on the notion that when the parties find themselves locked in a conflict from which they cannot escalate to victory and this deadlock is painful to both of them (although not necessarily in equal degree or for the same reasons), they seek an alternative policy or Way Out.' Zartman and co-author Guy Faure write that 'When a stalemate hurts, it is rational for the parties to come to terms; if both are caught in the impasse, the conditions are set for negotiations to provide a way out that benefits each. This situation does not guarantee a positive result, but it does provide the minimal conditions for one.' They go on to explain that the MHS has to be perceived to be effective. It 'is the perception of the objective condition, not the condition itself, that makes for a MHS. If the parties do not recognise "clear evidence" (in someone else's view) that they are in an impasse, a Mutually Hurting Stalemate has not (yet) occurred, and if they do perceive themselves to be in such a situation, no matter how flimsy the "evidence", the MHS is present.'

Military stalemate lies at the root of nearly every successful negotiation. It was the case in Northern Ireland, and the final report of the Independent International Commission on Decommissioning (IICD) ends with a general conclusion about armed conflicts based on their experience: 'we believe there is likely to be no lasting ceasefire until key leaders and significant numbers of supporters on both sides accept that while the opposition can perhaps be fought to a standstill, it cannot be permanently eradicated – at least, not without measures being taken that are unthinkable in a free and democratic society'. Mozambique by the mid-1980s was in the grip of a classic stalemate. The government controlled the cities and RENAMO controlled the countryside. The army had 50,000 men but only 5,000 of them were equipped for combat. The government had stopped conscription but was still rounding men up in the villages, and those press-ganged were known as '*tira camis*' because they were tied up by their shirtsleeves. RENAMO for their part had 12,000 guerrillas, poorly equipped and living in terrible conditions, with perhaps as much as a third of their force made up of child soldiers. Their leader, Dhlakama, declared in 1990 that 'RENAMO is tired. FRELIMO is tired too.' At that stage, a serious negotiation was possible.

In South Africa, the MK – the armed wing of the ANC – was ineffective. In the words of Chief Buthelezi, the leader of Inkatha, it had not blown up a single bridge or occupied a single acre of soil. Nelson Mandela said that by the 1980s, 'It was clear to me that a military victory was a distant if not impossible dream . . . It was time to talk.' Some radicals in the ANC still argued they could take power by force and that liberation was around the corner, and saw any talk of negotiation as a synonym for betrayal; but by the time of the Harare Declaration in August 1989, the doves had the upper hand and succeeded in committing the ANC to negotiation. In Mbeki's words, the 'ANC's trump card is not the armed struggle. It is the political struggle – internationally and nationally.' On the other side the National Party government came to realise that it could not win militarily either. As Mike Louw put it, South Africa had six nuclear weapons but no military solution to its problems. There was only one way to go, and that was a negotiated settlement.

If there is a military stalemate but the status quo is nonetheless too comfortable for one side or the other, as in the case of the Greek Cypriots following EU accession, then they will not budge in a negotiation. And while a stalemate is an essential prerequisite for successful talks, if during the peace process either side comes to believe it can win after all, there is a good chance that fighting will flare up again. After the agreement on Namibian independence in 1988, the Angolan government wanted another chance to finish off UNITA and launched a military offensive. A surge of US and South African supplies enabled UNITA to hang on in a crucial see-saw battle in Mavinga. By 1990 stalemate had been re-established and in April the Portuguese invited UNITA's charismatic leader, Joshua Savimbi, to Portugal for talks chaired by the foreign minister, supported by the US and the Soviet Union. The Bicesse agreement, reached relatively quickly, looked like an end to the bitter civil war. When Savimbi realised he was not going to win the election, however, UNITA broke out of the assembly areas where its troops had been confined and resumed fighting, capturing about 70 per cent of the country. In response the government built up its forces and fought back to a stalemate. Further negotiations in Lusaka chaired by the UN reached another agreement, but Savimbi declined to come to the signing ceremony citing security concerns, and shortly afterwards decided to return to war. He felt with his diamond mines and the support of the West he could carry on fighting indefinitely. A perceived mutually hurting stalemate is not therefore a permanent state of affairs, and can fade as quickly as it forms.

The concept of a mutually hurting stalemate is helpful to understanding when a negotiation is likely to succeed, but the theory of 'ripeness', also developed by Zartman, is less useful to practitioners. A conflict is not like a pear on the branch of a tree that you can pinch and see if it is ready to pick. Even if it were not ripe, you could not just shrug your shoulders and let the fighting continue without trying to resolve the issue.

Zartman defines 'ripeness' as parties resolving their conflict 'only when they are ready to do so – when alternative, usually unilateral means of achieving a satisfactory result are blocked and the parties feel that they are in an uncomfortable and costly predicament. At that ripe moment, they grab on to proposals that usually have been in the air for a long time and that only now appear attractive'. Other academics, however, criticise the theory as tautological – you can only tell if the time is ripe after the event, if the talks succeed – and Zartman himself concedes that ripeness 'isn't self-fulfilling or self-implementing. It must be seized, either directly by the parties or, if not, through the persuasion of a mediator', in other words it is in the hands of the negotiators rather than some mysterious ripening process.

Even if there were something to the theory it would not mean practitioners could just wait. Crocker says 'The absence of "ripeness" does not tell us to walk away and do nothing. Rather, it helps us to identify obstacles and suggests ways of handling them and managing the problem until resolution becomes possible.' A mediator must determine how best to 'ripen the conflict' and not 'stand on the sidelines waiting for some magic moment to arrive'. Brahimi and his UN colleague Salman Ahmed believe 'Sometimes . . . haste [to conclude talks] is unavoidable simply to stop the fighting and to prevent the slaughter of thousands or tens of thousands.'

In many democracies a ceasefire is a requirement before public talks can start. F. W. de Klerk says that in South Africa 'The suspension of the armed struggle was a *sine qua non* for the commencement of the negotiations.' In Britain it would have been unimaginable to enter into public negotiations with the IRA while they were still killing people. But sometimes, even if the conditions are not present, you have to try to start negotiating and see if you can change them. In the words of President Kennedy, 'It is never too early to try; and it's never too late to talk.' Fighting and talking can often proceed alongside each other. Karl Hack, a lecturer at the Open University, says negotiation 'should not be seen simply as the positive alternative to conflict and eliminating the enemy. Usually, what the military like to call "kinetic" action (physical force) and talking are tightly inter-related.' Thabo Mbeki said at Mells Park, 'We don't need to have peace to talk about peace. One talks about peace precisely because there isn't peace.'

If one side or the other is against negotiations in principle, then a way has to be found round their objections. It was the GAM policy not to negotiate with the Indonesian government, and Martin Griffiths of the HD Centre had to finesse the issue by saying they were sitting down informally to talk about alleviating humanitarian suffering. In El Salvador it was the other way round. The rebel FMLN's position was that they would agree to any meetings that were proposed, but the government was reluctant to negotiate. After his election, President Cristiani proposed 'a dialogue' with the FMLN, but insisted this was not a negotiation. In order to overcome these hesitations it is sometimes necessary to rush the two sides into talks. The metaphor we used in Northern Ireland, and which has been widely used elsewhere since, is 'the settlement train is leaving the station'. If any party doesn't get on the train now they will be left behind. Parties get lost in endless manoeuvring and it is sometimes necessary to tip them into actually starting by urging them to expose the hypocrisy of their opponents. Tony Blair's challenge to Unionists was that they should enter negotiations to expose the fact that Sinn Féin was not genuine, and once that was demonstrated it would be possible to conclude an agreement with the moderate SDLP alone. It is now clear that Gerry Adams was doing much the same by urging Republicans to go ahead in order to expose the British as having no real intention of making peace.

Of all the factors contributing to the possibility of a successful negotiation, perhaps the most important is political leadership. If the two sides have strong and imaginative leaders prepared to take risks, then a settlement is more likely and if there are no strong leaders then an agreement is correspondingly less likely. In Northern Ireland we were lucky to have leaders of the calibre of Gerry Adams and Martin McGuinness on the Republican side. As Tony Blair commented, they would have been perfectly able to play a leading role on the much bigger stage of British politics. They showed remarkable courage in leading their community crab-like towards a settlement, where a wrong step could have cost them not just their jobs but their lives. On the Unionist side David Trimble was an odd sort of political leader, bookish and shy rather than charismatic, but he was brave enough to sacrifice his party, his job and his political future in the effort to secure peace. Tony Blair and Bertie Ahern, the Taoiseach, formed a remarkable partnership and remained in power for a decade, giving them the chance to take the peace process to its ultimate success. Tony accuses me in his autobiography of saying in the context of the negotiations that he succeeded because he had a 'Messiah complex' (in fact it was Mo Mowlam who once said to me that Tony thought he '*was* fucking Jesus', which is not quite the same thing); but if he hadn't possessed the conviction that the conflict could be solved, and the enormous self-belief that he could solve it, then there wouldn't have been a peace agreement. His predecessors had either believed the problem was insoluble, like Margaret Thatcher, or doubted their own capacity to solve it, like John Major.

Conviction on the part of a leader is essential. If they either don't believe there will be an agreement or doubt that they can bring it about, then that becomes a self-fulfilling prophecy. John Kerry was criticised for approaching peacemaking in the Middle East in an 'emotional and messianic manner' by the Israeli defence minister, but as Gerald Steinberg of Bar-Ilan University says, 'peacemaking is, almost by definition, messianic. The idea that in a few months, or even years, it is possible to reverse the flow of human history with its ingrained violence between tribes, nations and religions, and create trust and co-operation, requires deep faith . . . Efforts to convince warring groups to lay down their arms, agree to painful compromises and accept the risk of being caught unprepared by a deceitful enemy are grounded more in religious belief than in political reality.'

Nelson Mandela is the most dramatic example of natural leadership making a negotiation possible. He was a towering figure who united the ANC, which could easily have split into factions in victory, and his willingness to forgive his oppressors, and to understand the concerns of white South Africans, was unprecedented. He took a series of symbolic steps to reassure them, learning Afrikaans in prison, visiting the widow of the founder of apartheid, Dr Voerword, for a cup of tea soon after being released from prison, and wearing a No. 6 South African rugby shirt to support the national team in a sport which is like a religion for white South Africans. He was always courteous but at the same time tough as nails in negotiating. He made a withering attack on F. W. de Klerk at the beginning of the CODESA conferences, but brought him a tie as a birthday present the next day. He clashed harshly again with de Klerk in the TV election debate, but strode across to shake hands with him at end of the programme. Mandela was seventy-one when he was released from prison and no longer had any personal political ambitions, but he was still a canny politician who knew how to make things happen. However, success in South Africa also required leadership from the National Party, and Mandela told his colleagues that de Klerk 'was a man we could do business with' and confessed to friends that 'My worst nightmare is that I wake up one night and that de Klerk isn't there. I need him. Whether I like him or not is irrelevant, I need him.' De Klerk was also clear from the very early days on the need to take risks. While he was still the leader of the National Party in Transvaal, he had told the British ambassador, Robin Renwick, that 'If I have anything to do with it we will not make the mistake they made in Rhodesia' by leaving it much too late to talk to black leaders. Leadership is such an important component of a successful negotiation that it is hard to imagine success without it; but you can't necessarily wait until inspiring and bold leaders materialise. You just have to start and hope that such leaders turn up, or the existing leaders discover a capacity for boldness.

Generational change is a common factor to many successful

peace agreements. Gunnar Heinsohn, a German academic, concludes that a 'youth bulge' is the best predictor of terrorism. If males between fifteen and twenty-nine years old make up more than 30–40 per cent of the population, then terrorism is more likely – in the Kurdish part of Turkey where the PKK fight, for example, they account for more than 60 per cent. Equally as leaders of armed groups get older, peace is more likely. Gerry Adams and Martin McGuinness both joined the Republican movement very young in the 1970s. By the mid-1980s they were well past fighting age and were beginning to see their nephews and nieces getting arrested or killed. Realising that the conflict could go on forever, they took the first tentative steps towards ending it. In the Basque Country, Jesús Eguiguren felt there was a generational aspect to his initiative with Arnaldo Otegi. He noted they were both around fifty, both had been in politics for around twenty years, and both had suffered losses. He asked himself, 'Was it going to be like this for the whole of our lives?' One of the reasons that the FARC may have agreed to enter into talks with the Santos government in Colombia is generational. The secretariat and the Estado Major, or General Command, of the FARC is made up largely of men in their fifties and sixties who have spent most of their adult years in the jungle, where life is much more bearable if you are young. They see that the conflict can go on indefinitely, but they know that if they die the ideological element of the struggle will be severely weakened. They fear they will be replaced by younger people who in many cases are more interested in the profits to be made from the drug trade, not as a way to fund the revolution but as a way to fund their lifestyles. They would therefore like to reach an agreement now so that something will be left of the original motives for their life's struggle, rather than bequeathing to a new generation what is increasingly a large and well-armed drug gang. Uri Savir says that Peres and Rabin told each other at the outset of the Oslo process: 'We are over seventy, let's now make the difficult historical decisions to spare the younger generations from making them one day.'

Life-threatening illness can also have an impact. President Chávez of Venezuela had considerable leverage over the FARC since they depended on him allowing them to maintain their rear bases on Venezuelan territory. Any threat, even implicit, to remove this access was capable of grabbing their attention. His attitude to the FARC changed in part as a result of overtures from President Santos in Colombia but also in part as a reaction to his terminal cancer. He clearly decided he wanted to help settle the conflict as part of his regional 'Bolivarian' legacy, rather than to continue it as an irritant for his neighbour. A similar thing happened to Ian Paisley, the leader of the Democratic Unionist Party in Northern Ireland. He played a major part in starting the sectarian conflict that gave rise to the Troubles in Northern Ireland, but when he went into hospital in 2004 and very nearly died, he came out a changed man. He told Tony Blair later that he had had a near encounter with his maker, and had decided he wanted to end his life as Dr Yes rather than Dr No. Thereafter he made a major contribution to bringing about a final settlement to the conflict, even in the face of opposition from within his own party.

Negotiations can move fast when the right conditions are in place. One of the most dramatic examples of the impact of the combination of a mutually hurting stalemate, of the end of the Cold War, and of remarkable leadership all leading to a peace agreement was the end of the Movimiento 19 de Abril (M-19) in Colombia in 1990. They were a guerrilla movement with about 2,000 fighters at the height of their powers, whose leadership was largely young, urban and educated, formed when General Rojas, a populist left-wing presidential candidate and former military dictator, was (they believed) cheated of his election victory by his Conservative rivals on 19 April 1970. At first the group confined itself largely to symbolic pranks like stealing Simón Bolívar's sword

from a museum in 1974 as a gesture of a civil uprising against
an unjust regime; but the campaign soon became bloodier. In
1978 they dug a tunnel into a Colombian army arms depot
and stole 5,000 weapons, and in 1980 stormed the Dominican
Embassy while the ambassador was holding a cocktail party,
taking fourteen ambassadors (including the American ambassador) hostage. After sixty-one days of negotiations, the
hostages were released and the captors allowed to leave for
Cuba. In 1985 the group attacked the Palace of Justice in
Bogotá, the home of the Supreme Court, and took 300 judges,
lawyers and staff hostage. The Colombian military stormed
the building, setting it on fire, and in the ensuing crossfire a
hundred people died, including eleven of the country's twenty-
one Supreme Court justices. The event shocked the country
and is still highly controversial. The M-19 had had an ambivalent relationship with the drug cartels, having first fought them
and then carried out tasks for them, and while the burning
of the Palace of Justice was most probably the result of the
army's deployment of high-temperature rockets against the
building, some speculate that the M-19 started the fire to
destroy records that might compromise their alleged associate
Pablo Escobar, the principal leader of the Medellin drugs cartel.
It became clear to the guerrillas they were not going to establish revolution by armed force, and it was also clear the army
could not wipe them out.

Attempts at negotiations in the early 1980s foundered when
the group's leader, Jaime Bateman, died in a plane crash. But
with the end of the Cold War in the late 1980s another window
of opportunity appeared. Ricardo Santamaria was part of the
peace commission for President Virgilio Barco in 1989 when
they received the first approach from the M-19. Eight government representatives were to travel in pairs to meet the guerrillas. The instructions told him and a colleague to go to Cali
and wait to be contacted. He was then told to fly to another
town and await further instructions. Eventually he was directed
to a clearing in the jungle where he met Carlos Pizarro, the

general commander of the group, surrounded by forty armed men. Santamaria says he was immediately impressed by Pizarro's bearing, neatly turned out in his guerrilla uniform and looking every bit the son of an admiral, which is what he in fact was. Pizarro said the M-19 wanted talks and proposed that they concentrate their forces in one area so they could consult their cadres and begin negotiations with the government. They chose a spot in the jungle at the Santo Domingo Gap, high in the Cauca mountains in the south-west of the country. Soon 500 men gathered there surrounded by a small demilitarised zone and then a cordon of the Colombian military to protect them. They set up 'working tables' and visits by outsiders were allowed to prepare them for reconciliation. The government negotiators flew in and out by helicopter, and by March had signed the Declaration of Cauca which started talks. By July the government and the guerrillas signed a peace pact. It was only four years after the bloody siege of the Palace of Justice but the public supported the peace agreement strongly.

The plan was put to Congress, including a series of constitutional reforms, but was rejected. Santamaria and his colleagues had to go back to see Pizarro in the Santo Domingo Gap to explain the deal was dead and there was nothing they could do. Instead of returning to violence, Pizarro and his deputy said they would come to Bogotá to persuade Congress. The government granted them a laissez-passer and they moved to the capital with a hundred bodyguards, sixty of them his own men who were granted police licences. He talked to Congress for two months and then went back to the jungle to persuade his fighters to demobilise in return for an amnesty and the creation of a constituent assembly to revise the 1886 constitution. Pizarro himself ran in the 1990 presidential elections and was doing well when he was shot and killed on board a domestic flight while campaigning, supposedly on the order of Pablo Escobar. The group returned Bolivar's sword, became a political party, the Alianza Democrática

M-19, and won a large number of seats in the constituent assembly elections. Pizarro's successor, Antonio Navarro, became one of three co-chairs of the assembly and played a central role in drafting the new constitution. This turned out to be the high point of the group's political success, and nearly 20 per cent of the former guerrillas were subsequently assassinated by right-wing paramilitary gangs. The party continued, however, and one of the former guerrillas, Gustavo Petro, became mayor of Bogotá. When all the conditions come together in this way – with charismatic leadership, a stalemate, and the end of the Cold War removing the conflict from the destructive context of a zero-sum game between the two superpowers – then progress can be rapid.

But the M-19 process was an exception. The most important thing to remember when a negotiation starts is that it will take longer than expected, usually a lot longer. False starts are more common than fast starts. In Sri Lanka there were a number of misfires before the talks proper began. When President Kumaratunga was elected in 1994, ending seventeen years of UNP rule, there was a huge sense of enthusiasm – 90 per cent of Tamils had voted for her and there seemed to be a real chance of peace. She began immediately with conciliatory measures towards the LTTE, allowing a ceasefire and the visit of a civil society delegation to the Tigers' base in Vanni. One of her close advisers, Ram Manikkalingam, feels in retrospect that they were filled with enthusiastic naiveté and should have listened to those with more experience of the Tigers. The president didn't go for direct talks but exchanged twelve letters with Prabhakaran about meetings. She used to say to Manikkalingam when he would come into her office that she had received 'another letter from my boyfriend'. But she never got beyond talks about talks, and the violence resumed.

In her second term, on the back of her fresh mandate, she tried a different approach, combining a strong military push against the Tigers with an unprecedented offer of federalism for the Tamil north and east of the country, described later by

Anton Balasingham as the 'best plan that was ever put forward'. As Manikkalingam puts it, she had the political momentum necessary to make progress but had no process in place, and political will but no way of getting to an understanding with Prabhakaran.

There were several attempts at negotiations in El Salvador before the UN process started. The first meeting under the auspices of the church took place in the incongruous setting of the Institution for Social Security in Mexico City in September 1989, chaired by the archbishop of San Salvador. The meeting was chaos. The two sides hurled rhetorical insults at each other and the guerrillas openly tape recorded the proceedings so there could be no real frank discussion. Outside the door of the meeting room were hundreds and hundreds of civil servants going about their everyday work on medical insurance. There wasn't even anywhere to buy food, and the guerrillas got hungrier as the meeting went on.

The archbishop was clearly not up to the job of mediating a substantive discussion and contented himself with organising the coffee breaks and other administrative matters. Archbishop Emilio Lorenzo Stehle from Ecuador, the German bishop who had been involved in earlier peace efforts and had been sent to the meeting by the Vatican, began to take on the dominant role. At first he was not allowed into the room, but gradually he infiltrated himself by bringing coffee for everyone; then he took a chair near the door; then he moved to a chair at the end of the table; and finally he started taking a full part in the meeting. He was more political and helped to steer the discussion. The two sides disagreed on the most fundamental question: why were they meeting? The government side insisted they were there to start a dialogue, but the guerrillas said they were only interested in a negotiation. The problem for the government was that the right wing in El Salvador would not accept the verb 'to negotiate', which they said smacked of treason and giving in to the guerrillas. In the end, one of the government negotiators, David Escobar Galindo, a poet, came up with a compromise: their objective was an '*entendimiento negociado*', a 'negotiated understanding'. Villalobos recalls that the meeting was difficult and the discussion strident, but it was not an emotional occasion. He thinks that in ethnic and religious conflicts the two sides really hate each other, but in economic and social conflicts like El Salvador, even where so much blood has been spilled, emotions are more likely to be under control. The country has a tiny elite and people on both sides knew all about each other, or had in fact met before.

At the second church-led meeting between the government and the FMLN to discuss a human-rights agreement, there was more of a frisson. In the back row on the government side was General Mauricio Vargas, the commander of the troops responsible for the death of many of Villalobos's comrades. He was known as a hardliner who had been sent to the meetings to represent the army's interests. Vargas was part of a particular '*tanda*', or promotion, from El Salvador's equivalent of Sandhurst, together with a dozen other officers who had risen up in the ranks alongside each other, including the chief of staff, who were known as 'the philharmonic orchestra' and controlled the regime. When the civil war started they were captains and majors and they bore the brunt of the fighting, and one of them had died. They became extreme right-wingers and anti-Communists, but unlike the generation before them, including the minister of the interior, they had suffered and they wanted peace. The previous generation of military officers had been too senior to actually fight. Their experience was formed under the preceding military regime that had started the dirty war against the opposition, and their ideological purity was unsullied by suffering and hands-on experience, and they were therefore less willing to make compromises.

The guerrillas made a point of urging Vargas to leave the back row and come and sit at the table; after all, he wielded the real power. In the coffee break, Villalobos spoke to him.

Vargas rolled up his sleeve to show him a scar where a bullet had hit him in an ambush mounted by Villalobos's men. The general said there had been a meeting of the key figures in the army in 1984 and they had decided there needed to be a negotiated end to the conflict. Villalobos said that was funny, because the guerrillas had made the same decision in Havana in 1982.

The discussion at the table unfortunately degenerated into a highly charged slanging match about the past. In particular the two older men at the talks – Schafik Handal, the commander of the Communist faction, and the minister of the interior, Colonel Agustín Martínez – argued about what happened at the beginning of the twentieth century and in the 1932 'Matanza', in which the army carried out a mass murder of peasants, while everybody else shuffled in their seats in embarrassment. Right at the beginning Martínez used the snobbish term '*chusma*' in reference to the peasants killed in the Matanza. In a dramatic moment Handal replied 'The *chusma* is here, now, right in front of you.' The exchange provided a crucial cathartic moment that allowed the two sides to move on to discussing the future. As so often in such processes, the real negotiation did not happen at the table but in the coffee breaks and in informal side meetings. Villalobos and his colleagues decided the two key people on the government side were General Vargas, and the poet David Escobar Galindo, an independent who was not even part of the government. He was an academic who had the confidence of President Cristiani, and knew that although the president was seen in public as an extreme right-winger, in fact he was looking for a pragmatic deal.

The next meeting took place in a convent in Costa Rica. The mood in the room was relaxed, and the two sides cracked jokes with each other. At the break the nuns took them through into another room where a splendid bar was laid out with wine, vodka and whisky. The guerrillas looked at it with wonder, but one of the government delegation dug Villalobos in the ribs and said 'Don't touch it. It's for the archbishop.' Villalobos believes such friendly relations are important to make a negotiation work. Without social skills on both sides, things will grind to a halt. Whatever the mood, however, these church-led talks did not succeed and it was only when the UN took over that progress was made.

Once the mediator has corralled the parties into the idea of a negotiation there are a number of pre-agreements that need to be reached. Harold Saunders, a former American diplomat, lists the requirements for the pre-negotiation as: achieving a common definition of the problem; producing a shared commitment to a negotiated settlement; and arranging agreed procedures, formats, and terms of reference for the formal negotiations themselves. These details are not always easy to agree. Richard Holbrooke recalls that in the Balkans, arguments over the location and hosting of meetings 'were a constant and time-consuming subplot of negotiations. In fact, disagreements over substance were rarely as intense as those concerning procedure and protocol.' Holbrooke recalled earlier negotiations he was involved in: 'During the 1968 peace talks with the North Vietnamese in Paris, we had famously wasted more than two months arguing over the shape of the table, while the war continued.'

Agreeing where the talks should take place is a vexed process. The location needs to be secure, and Eemeli Isoaho and Suvi Tuuli of CMI, Martti Ahtisaari's NGO, point out that 'Although removing peace talks away from the conflict zone is sometimes necessary for security reasons, mediators need to be careful not to let the peace talks detach themselves from the realities on the ground. In other words, the peace talks must not become an external matter that is completely out of tune with what is happening in the conflict.' Governments often insist that talks should be held outside the country, firstly so that they do not become a spectacle, and secondly because it is the easiest way of overcoming the thorny issue of how to meet people who are still wanted by the police for heinous crimes in their own country. In the case of Aceh, according to CMI's Meeri-Maria Jaarva, 'The fact that the venue was outside Indonesia in Finland was particularly important for GAM as most of their representatives were living in exile without the possibility to travel to Indonesia.' On the government side, Jusuf Kalla wanted the talks in Helsinki not only because it was far away from Indonesia, but also because he hoped that if something went wrong the Europeans would support the government in condemning GAM.

Sometimes it is the other way around. The Sri Lankan government wanted the negotiations with the Tigers to take place inside the country, but the LTTE insisted they should be abroad, and the first face-to-face meeting took place in September 2002 at the Sattahip naval base in Thailand. The officers, from the admiral down, quit their houses to make way for the two delegations. One issue was placement. The Norwegians decided that the government should speak first, and to compensate for that the Tigers would be allowed to sit in the middle. The Thais objected because protocol dictated that representatives of a state should have pride of place. In the end the Thais agreed to look the other way when Solheim moved the nameplates around the table before the talks started.

The mediator needs to agree the rules of the road before the negotiations start and it is hard to alter them once talks are under way. It is often the armed group that is more *protocolaire*. Their teams are made up of barrack-room lawyers who demand agreed minutes and quibble over every word. The danger of accepting the idea of agreed records, however, is that one side or the other will leak them at a crucial moment or they will be lost. ETA insisted from the beginning that their meetings with the government be minuted by the HD Centre and the minutes agreed. (The HDC kept them in their safe in Geneva, and there was consternation when thieves once stole the safe, although by chance a member of staff had taken the papers home that evening.) The other danger is that an inordinate amount of time can be taken up agreeing the minutes rather than focusing on the substance of the negotiation. It is far better to have each side keep their own records and only jointly write down agreements on substance in order to 'bank' them.

When the UN took over the El Salvador negotiations in 1989, Álvaro de Soto's handling of the pre-negotiations was an example of how to do all this successfully. He was determined to avoid the previous mistakes both of the Contadora Group and the church's efforts, which lacked clearly agreed ground rules. Since neither side was willing to meet face to face, he 'shuttled for eight weeks between Mexico City, where I met, seriatim, all five members of the FMLN general command (who carefully sized me up), and San Salvador, where I saw President Cristiani, in order to work out the framework and the basic rules for the negotiations. It was intrinsically difficult to agree since, not surprisingly, their differences on fine points of procedure masked deeply rooted divergences on strategy and substance.' He says his 'powers in scheduling the pace and venue of meetings and shuttling turned out to be considerably less than dictatorial, and in fact such decisions were taken after arduous and time-consuming wrangling on venues, dates, and duration in which Cristiani was sometimes personally involved. As Woody Allen might have said, half of mediation is making sure that the negotiators show up.'

The FMLN for their part wanted an authoritative third party present so that the 'seriousness of the parties could be independently guaranteed'. The government wanted 'a third party with a minimal role'. Cristiani wanted a dialogue and the FMLN wanted negotiations that would give them legitimacy. The FMLN 'insisted on breaks of several weeks between sessions so as to consult their constituents, who were either in the field or under deep cover in the cities in El Salvador' while the government wanted open-ended negotiating sessions with no break. Cristiani refused to countenance the meetings taking place in El Salvador, so they took place outside, and since Cristiani would not participate in the talks himself, de Soto had to make thirty trips to El Salvador to see him, often in the middle of a negotiating session elsewhere, to get agreement on crucial points. The final details of the rules of the game were agreed in a few hours at a secret meeting in Mexico City on 27 March 1990. De Soto, however, wanted the text signed in public to make it binding on the parties, and persuaded the UN Secretary General Pérez de Cuéllar to stop in Geneva for a few hours between visits to two European capitals and sign what became the Geneva Agreement. The two sides agreed that the talks would be confidential and that they would take place on a conditional basis. It is crucial to get clear agreement on the objective of the talks and de Soto managed to manoeuvre the FMLN and the government into agreeing that 'The purpose of the process shall be to end the armed conflict by political means as speedily as possible, promote the democratisation of the country, guarantee unrestricted respect for human rights and reunify Salvadorian society.'

Having agreed where, when and how the negotiations would take place and their objective, de Soto needed to agree the agenda with both sides. He took the parties to the campus of a think tank on the hills above Caracas in May. Before they could get down to negotiations de Soto lamented they had to sit through 'a lengthy exchange of historical recitations and political analysis'. Trying to get both sides to stop looking to the past and concentrate on the future is a huge challenge for mediators. The FMLN proposed that the agenda should cover the armed forces, human rights, the judicial system, the electoral system, constitutional reform, economic and social issues and then UN verification. By putting economic and social issues at the end the FMLN were indicating that they were of less interest to them than security-sector reform. In the course of the talks they never put forward radical economic or social proposals and settled instead for reintegration of the former combatants as the only gain under this heading. They insisted that the future of the army must be addressed first, since that was central and it would be pointless to address anything else until that had been agreed. Although the government still wanted a dialogue rather than a negotiation, surprisingly they did not object to the FMLN's agenda nor insist on a ceasefire, which should have been their main interest in the talks. Instead they agreed to a two-stage approach, first reaching a political agreement and only then a ceasefire followed by the demobilisation of the FMLN. The meeting had taken one week, the longest the two sides had been together under the same roof since the beginning of the war. Armed with these two pre-accords, de Soto was ready to start the negotiations proper.

Far too often either the government or the armed group (or both) insist on preconditions. Other than perhaps insisting on an end to violence before negotiations can take place, such preconditions are almost always a bad idea. Zartman argues that 'Strict preconditions are generally excuses for non-negotiation.' In Mozambique, both sides proposed preconditions that prevented the talks starting. President Chissano accused RENAMO of demanding the reform of the Mozambican constitution as a precondition for talks, but he himself demanded that they accept the existing constitutional framework and the legitimacy of the FRELIMO regime before starting. It was only when both sides abandoned their preconditions that talks actually started.

A similar thing happened in the Middle East. President Obama, in his first term, made a complete freeze of Israeli settlements a precondition for talks. He may have been absolutely right on the substance, but Netanyahu, who in the end agreed to a ten-month freeze, was then under domestic political pressure not to give in on any other issue of substance, however necessary it was to get the negotiation going. On the other side, the West's demand of a precondition that Hamas recognise Israel is equally unwise, rather like the British government asking the IRA to recognise the existence of Northern Ireland at the beginning of the talks rather than accepting it as the outcome of the negotiations. These issues are much better incorporated as a subject for the talks themselves rather than being erected as a blockage to talking at all. Fink Haysom says 'In general, preconditions can be unhelpful to the party advancing them, especially if they are rejected and the negotiations do not get under way. There is no opportunity to develop reformulated preconditions. Parties that insist on preconditions are frequently left with no option but to capitulate and abandon them, if only to allow negotiations to get under way. It is only in face-to-face negotiations that so-called pre-conditions can be addressed.' In his second-term approach to the Middle East, Obama learned the lesson, abandoning preconditions and saying 'if the expectation is . . . that we can only have direct negotiations when everything is settled ahead of time, then there's no point for negotiations'.

If it is possible to evade the snare of preconditions there is then the major challenge of making the transition from secret talks to public negotiations. It is the moment when both sides are most exposed. Zartman says that 'At some point the potential negotiator will have to come out into the open, yet too early a public position will make him vulnerable to his radical rivals, while holding back impedes the process. It is at that moment they are most vulnerable to attack from spoilers and find it hardest to explain what they have done and defend themselves from conspiracy theorists who are always convinced there is a hidden secret agreement.' It was in the transition from the secret pre-negotiations to official, public talks that things collapsed in the peace process between ETA and the Spanish government in 2006. In Oslo they had agreed the agenda and the rules for the formal negotiations: there were to be a maximum of three negotiators per side and four advisers, nothing was to be published, and before breaking off the talks, the party doing so would consult and meet the other side. Any accidents were to be discussed at the table. It was agreed that the security of the delegations was a matter for the competent governments. The Spanish government sent Javier Moscoso, an aristocratic lawyer from Navarre who had been in Felipe Gonzalez's government, to accompany Eguiguren as things got serious. The ETA delegation changed too, with the addition of Francisco Javier López Peña, or 'Marc', the political leader of the organisation. He had just won out in a power struggle inside ETA and voted his rivals out of the leadership, and as a result took a very hard line. Just as the transition was about to happen, ETA detonated the bomb at Madrid airport, killing two Ecuadoreans. The other victim of the bomb was the peace process.

Even without preconditions, direct contact may be impossible or counterproductive, and it is then necessary for the mediator to shuttle between the two sides, particularly at the beginning of a negotiation. When the Mozambican negotiations began in Kenya in 1989 the two delegations would not meet because FRELIMO refused to recognise RENAMO as a political inter-locutor, so first the Mozambican bishops and then the Kenyan and Zimbabwean governments shuttled back and forth across Nairobi taking papers from one side to the other. The two sides talked past each other. The government side put forward a twelve-point plan on normalisation but refused to use the word RENAMO. In response, RENAMO didn't address Chissano's plan at all, and instead counter-proposed a sixteen-point plan for 'national reconciliation without victors or vanquished' followed by constitutional reform. They only agreed to meet face to face once the negotiations started in Rome. In Northern Ireland, Ian Paisley did not meet Gerry Adams until agreement had already been reached. We had to go back and forth between the two sides for four years to negotiate the text of the agreement. They would sometimes agree to proximity talks as long as they were not under the same roof. On one occasion I put the DUP in the Cabinet Office on Whitehall, and Sinn Féin in 10 Downing Street, and began to shuttle between the two sides. Technically they are two distinct buildings although they are joined by the green baize door made famous in *Yes, Prime Minister*. About halfway through the day I looked out of the window of the grand room in the Cabinet Office to see Gerry Adams and Martin

McGuinness playing with the Blair children's skateboard in the No. 10 Rose Garden below. I had to rush downstairs and chase them back inside before Paisley looked out of the window.

Shuttling can work, but the danger is that when the two sides do not meet face to face, issues can remain imprecise and it is hard to be certain how far they really agree. Nor do the two sides build the trust that is necessary for a funct-ioning agreement. Things went well in the first negotiations on Aceh in 2000 precisely because the two sides were meeting in person. Hassan Wirajuda, the Indonesian ambassador in Geneva, brought only one official with him, ignored the foreign minister and kept only the president closely informed of the substance of the negotiations. In face-to-face meetings in the château at Bavois in March and April 2000 he and the GAM leaders rapidly reached agreement on a humanitarian pause in the fighting. The government wouldn't call it a ceasefire as that would imply that GAM were an equal belligerent with the army, but it had the substance of one. Things went wrong, however, in 2001 when the two sides broke off contact. The process got back on track in 2002 but still the sides wouldn't meet. Yudhoyono, the government minister responsible, had presidential ambitions and did not want to be photographed alongside the GAM. Martin Griffiths had to conduct the negotiations on a Cessation of Hostilities Agreement (COHA) by going back and forth between the two sides, seeing the government in Jakarta and seeing GAM leaders in different locations in Europe, on one occasion in the shadow of Versailles Palace.

When everything was nearly agreed, Griffiths went to meet Yudhoyono in the Intercontinental Hotel in Jakarta in the first week of Ramadan to finalise the document. Yudhoyono turned to the others in the room and asked the military and police commanders if they agreed, and things started to go wrong. It was getting towards dusk so Yudhoyono called for a break for prayers, and proposed they resume when they could break the Ramadan fast together. The talks began again in a better frame of mind when they could all eat, and the HD Centre team were sent away to work on the text and come back with a new draft in the morning. The next day both sides signed the agreement and it was met with jubilation in Aceh.

It began to unravel almost at once. David Gorman of the HD Centre cobbled together an implementation plan with the Indonesian military in three hours and had to have it up and functioning on the ground within two weeks, with Thai, Philippine and Norwegian peacekeepers. He met Yudhoyono in Aceh shortly afterwards and was surprised at the minister's attitude. Gorman thought things were going well – on the day of the signing more than ten people had been killed in Aceh, and prior to that there had been an average of eight or nine violent incidents a day, whereas now they were down to two a day. Yudhoyono, though, griped about GAM not following through on the promise to put their forces in cantonments. Gorman replied that the Indonesian military weren't redeploying either, as they had promised to do. Yudhoyono's tone was worrying. What was happening on the ground was very different from what had been agreed in the negotiating room. The GAM were telling everyone in Aceh that the agreement was about independence, while the Indonesian government was demanding that the HD Centre make clear that it was not. Within three months the COHA had crumbled. Jusuf Kalla believes it failed because the two sides, not having met face to face, had not really reached agreement. He says you need to meet to see the body language of the other side. The debates may be more emotional as a result, but they have a cathartic effect that makes a lasting agreement possible.

When the two sides do eventually meet, the make-up of the delegations can make an enormous difference. A small delegation is better than a big one because it reduces the possibility of internal disagreement and leaks, but you need to have enough expertise present to handle technical subjects. Leaders often choose high-level figures from across the political spectrum to ensure that every sector of society is brought into the process, but then you have too many chiefs and not enough Indians, and normally those chosen for their political affiliations are not the best negotiators. Leaders need someone heading the delegation who is absolutely on their wavelength, who can speak with their complete authority and who consults them incessantly, even in the middle of the night. I regularly rang Tony Blair at two in the morning for instructions, and was usually told to get back into the negotiations and stay there until we reached agreement. In the case of the second Aceh negotiations, Vice President Jusuf Kalla – known as the 'Super Mario' of Indonesian politics for his seemingly limitless energy and willingness to involve himself in every possible policy matter – says he was in day-to-day control of the government delegation and in touch with them at least every two hours. President Yudhoyono, who gave Jusuf Kalla complete authority over the talks, says he learned from the failure of the negotiations under his predecessor Megawati that he had to play instead the vital role of providing a 'political umbrella' which protected his negotiators. The two men agreed the parameters of the possible agreement before the talks started, and the president then left Jusuf Kalla to get on with it. During the talks he only needed to consult Yudhoyono twice on compromises, once in the middle of the night on the crucial issue of local political parties. When he was in Jakarta Jusuf Kalla had the delegation put a mobile phone on the negotiating table in Helsinki so he could follow developments, and sent instructions to them by SMS. The head of the delegation says that in the final stages they ran up a $2,000 phone bill. Jusuf Kalla also had a fax machine installed in his bedroom so he could comment on draft negotiating documents in the middle of the night.

Leaders often decide not to attend the negotiations, holding themselves back as a final court of appeal. Yudhoyono says 'I could not always be at the forefront. Sometimes I had to be in the background and let others take the lead, preserving political capital for when it was really needed.' Leaders may choose a hardliner to head their delegation on the grounds that if they conclude an agreement no one will attack it, and the leader can be confident of unanimity of support. The danger, however, is that you never get to an agreement if the hardliner is determined to stop it.

The government and the armed group have to understand they cannot choose the delegation of the other side. Guerrillas always like to have serving generals across the table from them. They feel they are equivalent and they like the assurance it provides that the military will support the agreement; but it is not in their gift. The South African government tried to prevent the inclusion of Joe Slovo in the ANC delegation when talks began. As the white leader of the South African Communist Party he was a hate figure for the National Party, but the ANC absolutely insisted on his participation as a key member of their leadership, and de Klerk had to back down. The Sri Lankan government included a Tamil in their delegation whom the Tigers regarded as a traitor by virtue of his ethnicity. They couldn't prevent his inclusion but he lived under constant threat to his life, having to change house every few months. The Tigers eventually managed to kill the Sri Lankan foreign minister, also a Tamil.

It is surprising how often governments and armed groups embark on negotiations without any proper preparation. Fink Haysom says leaders 'regard political and military engagement as a professional activity yet see negotiations as an intuitive or amateur activity. However, negotiations will be the most important determinate in the outcome of any struggle for democracy and liberty.' Experience suggests that the best-prepared side wins in a negotiation because they have a plan. They have looked at the lessons that can be learned from similar negotiations elsewhere, and at why previous attempts at resolving their own conflict have failed (there nearly always is a previous failure to study). Jusuf Kalla says he took ten days to train his negotiators for the Helsinki talks. He had them study the background of Aceh and the personalities of their negotiating partners in GAM in detail, and coached them on how to speak politely and look into the eyes of their interlocutors. He believes this preparation is what made success at Helsinki possible.

In this type of negotiation you do not want the other side to be ill-prepared either. It may be tempting to think that the government will have an advantage if the armed group is unprepared, but if the other side isn't well informed on the substance of the negotiation, hasn't thought through the consequences of each step, and doesn't even grasp the concept of compromise, the talks will freeze. It is therefore in the interest of government to ensure that the armed group has access to trusted advisers. Haysom says 'It is a questionable blessing to have unskilled and unprepared negotiating partners. It is certainly possible in the short term to exploit confusion, ignorance and inexperience in an adversary. But the problem of negotiating with such opponents is that they tend not to follow the rules of negotiations. They may renege on undertakings or agreements. Most often, however, if your adversaries lack confidence, they will take no risks, be uncomfortable in the negotiating process and will balk at entering serious negotiations.' He says that in South Africa, the ANC was better prepared than the government, in part because the government had no experience of negotiating.

Making the transition from a secret channel to formal negotiations is indeed perilous. If it is to succeed, certain conditions need to be in place, particularly a mutually hurting stalemate and strong political leadership. But it is no good just waiting for a conflict to become 'ripe' for settlement, and negotiators often have to press ahead, however unpropitious the circumstances. Pre-negotiations on the location of talks, the rules of the road and the choice of delegations will make a big difference to the chances of success, while preconditions can kill off the prospect of getting into negotiations in the first place. Sometimes a mediator needs to shuttle between the two sides before they will agree to meet face to face, but then you cannot be certain that the two sides have really reached agreement. If you can manoeuvre the parties into a negotiation, then the negotiators need to think carefully about the architecture of the talks, the techniques of negotiation and above all their strategy. There is an art of negotiation, and there will only be agreement if both sides understand it.

CHAPTER SEVEN

The Art of Negotiation

If a man knows not to which port he sails, no wind is favourable.

Seneca the Younger

I have never had any training in negotiation or theoretical preparation for half a life spent doing it, first as a diplomat and then between governments and armed groups. In fact I only had a single day's training when I joined the British Diplomatic Service in 1979, Mrs Thatcher's first year in government. We were given a copy of Harold Nicolson's book *Diplomacy: A Basic Guide to the Conduct of Contemporary Foreign Affairs*, first published in 1939 and republished in 1949. (Its first line is a great example of British understatement: 'Since this book was first published, many serious events have occurred.') We were also handed a small pamphlet on 'placement' – where people should sit at diplomatic dinner parties – but nothing on negotiation. There is now a whole academic discipline of negotiation in business schools and universities, and a Harvard Negotiation Project which brings together lawyers, psychologists, diplomats and police hostage negotiators to look at what can be learned from the different types of negotiating.

Much of the academic work is impressive, but negotiation remains an art rather than a science. Richard Holbrooke describes his Balkan negotiations as 'simultaneously cerebral and physical, abstract and personal, something like a combination of chess and mountain climbing'. Damien Kingsbury, an Australian adviser to GAM, says 'The primary difference between negotiating and chess is that in a practical sense, negotiating has no rules other than those which are able to be imposed on the game by one of the parties to it.'

Each negotiation is different and they take place between human beings who are notoriously unpredictable. Although there are similarities between classic diplomatic negotiations and negotiating with terrorists, there are also major differences. Guy Faure calls negotiating with terrorists 'a most peculiar form of diplomacy', as it 'refers to methods that are fundamentally alien to classical diplomacy because of the nature of the counterpart, the issues at stake, the context, and the basic paradigm governing that type of situation. The counterpart is not perceived as an equal, an alter ego. An element of psychological asymmetry characterises the relationship, and as a consequence, communication remains of a relatively poor content. The terrorist is viewed as a counterpart imposing upon the relationship, forcing his way, thus not respecting the other.'

In negotiations with terrorists, however, just as in diplomatic negotiations there needs to be a structure. The first rule of that architecture is the importance of process. When I was researching *Great Hatred, Little Room*, my account of the Northern Ireland peace process, the Cabinet Secretary let me read through all the No. 10 confidential files from 1997 to 2007 in a chilly little room below his office looking out over Horse Guards Parade. The one thing that leapt out of the pages above all else was the centrality of having a process. If there is a peace process in place and negotiations are continuing, people can hope that things will get better. If the peace process collapses, a vacuum opens up and is soon filled by violence. Holbrooke wrote that 'In diplomacy process can often be as important as substance. This is especially true early on, when long-time adversaries are prone to maximise differences rather than reach out for agreements.'

Sometimes the government side tries to jump straight to the endgame of a negotiation without establishing or passing through a process. This nearly always fails. Shimon Peres says that everyone knows the outline of an eventual peace settlement in the Middle East in terms of territory, refugees and even Jerusalem, but the problem is that there is no process to get us there. A master of the one-liner, he sums it up like this: 'The good news is there is light at the end of the tunnel; the bad news is there is no tunnel.' What a negotiator is trying to do is construct that tunnel.

Peace is not therefore an event but a process whereby two warring sides come to trust each other over time. It is not the signing of the agreement per se that is important, but how you get there, and whether you have built trust in doing so. That was clearly evident in the negotiations in South Africa. Willie Esterhuyse says that from the very beginning they consciously decided to 'opt for a *process* rather than a sensational *event*'. In 1990, when he had boarded a plane in Cape Town bound for London, he was hauled off and told he was needed urgently in the airport VIP lounge. When he got there Pik Botha, the South African foreign minister, was on the phone. Botha said he was appearing that evening on Ted Koppel's US TV show *Nightline* with Thabo Mbeki, and wanted Esterhuyse to talk to Mbeki and make sure he behaved in a civil manner. Botha told him to call Mbeki, and his aide would hold the plane for him. Mbeki took the point immediately and said he would address Botha as 'Minister', adding with a chuckle, 'Tell him when the ANC takes over the government, I'll make him my deputy.' Esterhuyse relayed the message back and later watched the programme in which Mbeki memorably said 'We are at the beginning of a process' whose goal is 'a political settlement to end apartheid'.

Once you have got the negotiating process started, the key objective is to make it sustainable. I think of it as 'the bicycle theory'. Once the bicycle is moving forward, if it is allowed to stop it will fall over, and it will be hard to get going again. However difficult the talks are, you should not let them falter. Always try to find something new to discuss, some new approach to consider, and make it as hard as possible for either side to walk out without looking as though they are in the wrong and having to bear the opprobrium of putting the chance of peace in jeopardy. Jim Baker, when pulling together the Madrid Conference on the Middle East in 1991, called it the 'dead cat effect' – no one wanted the dead cat of failure resting on their doorstep. Both sides hope if they behave outrageously enough they will provoke the other side into walking out, but a government cannot let that happen. De Klerk describes the balancing act required in South Africa: 'Other parties had the luxury of being able to grandstand and to withdraw from the negotiation process. For obvious reasons the National Party and the government could not. It was essential for us to get the ANC back to the negotiating table in September 1992.'

To keep the bicycle going it is important to avoid breaks in the negotiation. Fink Haysom says that 'There may always be a good reason to suspend negotiations, sometimes to exercise organisational or political muscle but suspension should be undertaken with the knowledge of its consequences. In South Africa the suspension of the negotiations after the CODESA convention came to be seen as a mistake, as the security and political situation in the country deteriorated sharply.' In Caguán the FARC announced on 19 January 1998, only a few days into the process, that it was freezing the negotiations unless the government prevented massacres being carried out by right-wing paramilitaries. It was the first of four times that the FARC froze the talks, and the stop-start approach helped push the process into failure. In Sri Lanka the Tigers froze the negotiations in 2003. Balasingham wrote to Prime Minister Wickremasinghe to say they had done so because of the non-implementation of the terms and conditions in the truce document, and that talks could only proceed if the government addressed these points. These breaks in the process proved to be fatal. Haysom's advice is not to 'underestimate the importance of maintaining the momentum of the negotiations. Progress begets progress in negotiations. One agreement induces another. As some parties go on to successfully participate in the negotiations, other parties will join the process. The contrary is also true. When the negotiations are suspended, the process does not remain static and usually moves backwards.'

Of course if negotiations go on interminably without achieving anything while the situation on the ground gets worse, there is liable to be an outbreak of 'process fatigue'. The process appears to be no more than a manner of managing the conflict. I remember meeting a group of Palestinians a few years ago who said to me they were fed up with peace processes. They wanted no more process, just an agreement. As the *New York Times* journalist Tom Friedman puts it in the Middle East, 'the Israelis want negotiations without a peace agreement and the Palestinians want a peace agreement without negotiations'. But however fed up you get, you have to keep the process going if there is to be an agreement.

The truth is that peace processes are unending. Even when you reach an agreement then you have to implement it. Building trust, or more often rebuilding it, takes generations. Audrey Cronin says 'negotiations with terrorist groups are best approached as long-term, managed processes demanding patience, resilience, extensive intelligence, and steady determination, rather than the kinds of intensive meetings and well-publicised signing ceremonies that follow civil-war ceasefires or the endings of conventional wars'. The one skill required above all else of negotiators as well as mediators, therefore, is patience. It is difficult to put up with years of circular discussions and extraordinary rudeness, negotiations that go on through the night entirely unnecessarily, and participants who do no discernible work themselves while impugning your integrity and ability, but you have to do so. This is not a new observation. François de Callières, a diplomat and a member of Louis XIV's Cabinet, wrote in *On the Manner of Negotiating with Princes* that a negotiator should possess 'self-restraint, a faultless discretion and a patience which no trial can break down'.

It is often necessary to absorb political and personal pain

to keep the bicycle moving. In one of the more fraught sessions of the negotiations with ETA, 'Marc' yelled at Jesús Eguiguren, 'Typical government propaganda. That's why we shot the people we shot. If that's what you want, we will end the meeting and do it again.' Eguiguren responded, 'As you know I have buried several of my close friends who you shot. Before I came here I looked in the mirror and said peace is so important that I will not let what happened or my personal feelings get in the way. I am not going to respond to what you just said. There is blood on your hands and our aim is to try to stop it.' Martin Griffiths had to keep the Aceh process going more or less single-handedly in 2001, flying between Stockholm and Jakarta thirteen times in six months. Sometimes he would arrive in Jakarta after a twelve-hour flight only to find that his meeting with the government had been cancelled. He had regularly met President Wahid to discuss the negotiations in the earlier period but didn't meet his successor, President Megawati, even once. Griffiths' persistence paid off, however, and the following year the negotiations picked up again.

When you are creating a process, it is crucial to establish a structure that will assist rather than impede progress. If the two sides agree that a negotiation should be sequential, working through an agenda point by point and only moving on as each point is agreed, it will be hard to reach a settlement. They will never resolve all the issues in the first item because neither side will want to make unrequited concessions on important issues without seeing what they might be able to secure elsewhere in return. Negotiations therefore need to move in parallel and to be structured in such a way as to allow trade-offs between concessions in different areas. In Northern Ireland the negotiations were conducted in three strands, the first on issues internal to Northern Ireland, the second on issues that involved both north and south, and the last involving east/west issues between the Irish and British governments, such as the redrafting of the Irish constitution and British laws. This enabled progress to be made in parallel on a range of issues. Haysom says 'negotiators should pass over areas where no consensus can be reached, rather than imposing a rigid sequence or order of matters to be agreed. It can be problematic if the agenda for negotiations requires matters to be dealt with sequentially (and separately).' The only way to get a negotiation moving, therefore, is to proceed on a conditional basis. Most negotiations take place under the rubric that 'nothing is agreed until everything is agreed'. This rule allows both sides to explore possible compromises without committing themselves finally until they see the overall picture. Once the negotiation gets serious, the best way to enable parallel progress is to leave detailed discussion to a series of working groups of experts meeting alongside each other, rather than insisting that every subject be discussed at the main negotiating table.

When negotiations go wrong, more often than not it is the result of a lack of structure, which means the negotiations never get on to substance at all but remain bogged down on points of procedure. If the negotiations are purely ad hoc, no progress will be made, staying at the level of exchanging phone calls and not getting down to the serious business of agreeing text. Michael Vatikiotis, the head of the HD Centre in Asia, recalls his attempt to make peace between the Red Shirts and government forces in Bangkok in 2010. The Red Shirts had taken over the city in protest at the treatment of their champion, former president Thaksin, by the military and the political elite. The tense situation threatened to tip into a bloody civil war at any moment. Already lives had been lost. Vatikiotis was ushered through the various layers of security, weaving around roadblocks and encampments, till he got to the stage at the centre of the Red Shirt protest. Behind it sat a refrigerated unit from the back of a truck where the Red Shirt leadership relaxed while everyone else sweltered in the sun. One of the leaders was wearing a red T-shirt with the face of Mahatma Gandhi emblazoned on it, which seemed out of place at the centre of a violent protest, and many of them were wearing Buddhist amulets and strange clothes. There was almost a sense of voodoo about the scene. Vatikiotis sat down and asked them what they were doing. They said they had been talking to government ministers on their mobile phones. He asked if they had put any of their demands on paper. They hadn't. For the first time they sat down and started to formulate their demands, which enabled a real negotiation to begin.

If talks are to succeed it is important that they are inclusive, and that means incorporating all the relevant parties, not just the ones you like. There is little point in trying to make peace while leaving one party out, as Britain discovered in Northern Ireland when, over many decades, it held a series of fruitless negotiations with all the parties except Sinn Féin. If parties exclude themselves, however, that is a different matter, and can actually make things easier. George Mitchell worried how agreement would be possible in Northern Ireland in the talks he chaired if Ian Paisley insisted on being present, and was relieved when the DUP opted out.

Making progress even in organised processes is hard if there are too many people at the table. Leaders won't make concessions in front of crowds, as it makes them look weak and opens them up to attack from their own side. Confidentiality is almost impossible in a large conference and the real negotiations move elsewhere, usually behind closed doors and that leads to discontent. Mo Mowlam used to urge me to include the Women's Coalition and the smaller Loyalist parties in sensitive negotiations between the Republicans and the Unionists in Northern Ireland, but it was just not possible without freezing the process. Essentially the more people in the room, the less successful the negotiation will be. Anyone who turns up with a delegation of more than five is not serious about negotiating.

Multi-party talks are considerably more complex than bilateral ones. The South African CODESA proceedings were set up to include all the parties in the country, however small. There were forty representatives in each of its five working groups, and if every party wanted to speak (and they usually did), it took a whole day. Having presented their views orally, they then became entrenched in their positions. The first attempt at CODESA failed in part because there were too many parties and no effective decision making process. It ended up being a debate rather than a negotiation. For the second attempt the technical teams were allowed to propose drafting solutions to vexed issues to ensure that no side would lose face by having to accept an adversary's proposal and, most importantly, the key decisions were made through bilateral negotiations between the government and the ANC in the conference's executive steering committee, which included both Roelf Meyer and Cyril Ramaphosa, the chief negotiators of the government and the ANC respectively.

The key problem was the decision-making process. If consensus had been required there would never have been an agreement because a veto would have rested in the hands of every party, no matter how tiny. Equally if the decision had been left to the majority it would have been unacceptable to the others, as the ANC could have just decided everything by itself. So the concept of 'sufficient consensus' was introduced, which meant that the ANC and the National Party had to be on board for any item to be considered agreed. Haysom says sufficient consensus in effect 'guarantees for the major players that their consent is a prerequisite before a decision can be made, but it removes the veto from smaller or individual parties'. Meyer illustrates the decision-making process by describing how they reached agreement on South Africa's new flag. The government initially sought proposals from the public and more than 7,000 designs were sent in. The participants in CODESA couldn't decide between them, so the issue was referred to Meyer and Ramaphosa in the steering committee. They decided they didn't like any of the ideas and turned to the State Herald, who proposed a design which the two of them put to CODESA. It was approved under the 'sufficient consensus' mechanism because both the ANC and the National Party accepted it. We later adopted the same rule in Northern Ireland: nothing could be agreed unless a majority on both the Catholic and Protestant sides accepted it.

There are often calls for civil society to be included in negotiations, but armed groups can be surprisingly reluctant to allow them in. In Aceh, GAM complained that the NGOs were too moderate 'because they have been living too much with the Javanese'. In South Africa civil society and business were not allowed into the negotiations themselves but were involved in a separate 'Peace Accord'. The negotiations in Guatemala had perhaps the most elaborate machinery for involving civil society through a broad-based Civil Society Assembly under the leadership of the Catholic Church, which made proposals to the parties on all agenda items, and after discussion of each signed agreement endorsed them as 'national commitments'. Even this complex machinery was not enough for some campaigners, and after the agreement was signed several 'national dialogues' were started by international NGOs duplicating the earlier work, to the great frustration of Jean Arnault, the UN mediator.

It is also important to understand that a negotiation is not a debate. While scoring a point or winning an argument across the table may give a negotiator some personal satisfaction, it won't do anything to advance a settlement. David Bohm, a physicist who has made important contributions to philosophy, sums up the differences between a debate and a dialogue:

A debate is oppositional – two sides oppose each other and attempt to prove each other wrong. A dialogue involves two or more sides working towards a common understanding. In a debate, winning is the goal; in a dialogue, finding common ground is. In a dialogue, one listens to the other side in order to understand, find meaning, and find agreement. In debate one listens to the other to find flaws and counter its arguments. Dialogue can change a viewpoint; debate reinforces it. Dialogue reveals assumptions for re-evaluation; debate defends them as truth. Dialogue creates an open-minded attitude; debate closes the mind.

It is not possible to persuade the other side to change their minds by speeches or to beat them by playing tricks. Niel Barnard says his rule of thumb is that 'cleverness is stupidity'. You can try and outwit the other side but it never lasts; all it does is undermine your trustworthiness. Schafik Handal, the leader of the Communist faction of the FMLN, always liked to debate the past at the negotiating sessions, trying to establish the blame for previous atrocities, rather than concentrating on constructing an agreement. At one UN-chaired session, Joaquín Villalobos had, by backchannel contact, set it up in such a way that the government would propose something at the negotiating table which the FMLN very much wanted. All the FMLN had to do was sit there and keep quiet. Villalobos pushed a paper napkin in front of Handal with the message to keep quiet scrawled across it. Handal couldn't resist, however, and jumped into the discussion to object to the proposal, upsetting Villalobos's carefully laid plan. Villalobos still has the napkin.

The objective of a negotiation is to agree words on paper, not for the government to persuade the armed group to accept a common world view. Even after the agreement is concluded, the two sides will continue to disagree. In Colombia the FARC had long demanded a fundamental change in the nature of the state and of the capitalist system. Bizarrely at Caguán the government agreed an agenda for the negotiations with twelve main points and over one hundred sub-points, including conservation of natural resources, international relations, political reform, reform of the justice system and ownership of the mining industry. The FARC wanted agreement on all of them before they were even prepared to agree to a ceasefire, let alone an end to the armed conflict. The government presented the agreement on this agenda as the success of the first four months of negotiations, but there was no way the two sides were ever going to agree on changing the capitalist system or the economic and social structure of the state. An open-ended agenda like this simply condemns the two sides to endless negotiation. The aim of a peace process is not that the two sides should agree a common attitude to capitalism or anything else, but simply to remove the blockages that the armed group feel have prevented them from pursuing their aims fairly through politics. The conflict of ideas will continue, but it will be pursued through the ballot box rather than down the barrel of a gun.

And yet it is surprisingly hard to get to the point of drafting a text. If a government tables a paper in the negotiations, the chances are the armed group will reject it as tarnished, whatever its substance. Equally a paper tabled by the armed group will be treated with great suspicion by the government. De Soto found in the El Salvador negotiations that any proposal presented by one side was automatically rejected by the other. No give and take ever took place with the negotiators sitting face to face in the room. Most of de Soto's job was shuttling between the two sides with pieces of paper. He used his experience as the G77 co-ordinator in the Law of the Sea Conference, where developing a single text had been the only way to reach a consensus amongst so many different countries with so many different interests. In the El Salvador negotiations he would consult both sides on each topic, produce a draft which he would discuss with them separately and revise in light of their comments, and then take it back to the other side, rather than discussing the text at the negotiating table itself. His Venezuelan legal adviser would sit beside him during negotiating sessions churning out alternative formulae on his laptop and then discuss them with de Soto 'while the negotiations droned on', as he put it. Then they would table the text for approval by the two sides. According to Haysom the most important role of a third party is exactly this, 'generating proposals and propositions in circumstances where the parties themselves could never accept, or be seen to be accepting, proposals emanating from the enemy, or even compromising on their own propositions'.

When there is no third party, the best way to avoid competing texts is for both sides to present their positions orally and then for one of the negotiators to try to note the points on which they both agree, so that the wording can be further refined. In the Northern Ireland negotiations we resorted to 'angel papers', non-papers that could be introduced without either side claiming authorship as if handed down from the heavens. In that way the two sides can arrive at a common text which can be the focus of discussion, and where phrases still in dispute can be bracketed, or gaps left for disputed passages to be added later. It is, however, generally a mistake to allow ideas to which you strongly object to be recorded on paper, because once written down they will always be hard to get rid of, and you will have to pay a price elsewhere to write them out altogether. Putting difficult proposals 'in the freezer' for later consideration can work, particularly if your intention is just to drop them all at the later stage of the negotiation. When you start agreeing text there is an inexorable logic to the process. It is like getting on to an escalator: once you are on it, it is very hard to run back down. Armed groups and governments rarely enter a negotiation intending to arrive at the place they finally end up, but the momentum of the talks can carry them to unexpected destinations.

Words are the currency of a negotiation, and one side or the other may reject a proposal because of the way it is formulated rather than its substance. Two of the GAM negotiators write 'if the words "independence" and "referendum" were taboo to Indonesia, we were allergic to "autonomy", which represents for us an abhorrent system of brutal oppression and impunity for murders, rapes, disappearances, massacres and all sorts of other brutalities'. They were, however, prepared to explore the phrase 'self-government for Aceh', because it was 'terminology that allows our delegation to venture into new ground in relations with Indonesia without accepting the unjust autonomy law. In many ways, self-government was another word for autonomy, but without the same abhorrent connotations.'

It is precisely because of the significance of words in a negotiation that it is crucially important to win control of the pen.

The Communist Party in South Africa made absolutely sure they kept all the secretarial positions in the negotiations so they were the ones who produced the drafts for agreement. A successful negotiator needs to possess a nimble mind that can see immediately the potential trap in an apparently innocuous phrase proposed by the other side, and formulate a counter-proposal that may sound the same but is in substance very different. In a sense a negotiation is a game of speed compre-hension – and it is interesting how good at it terrorists often are. Much of the Northern Ireland negotiations were taken up with the government side proposing wording for IRA state-ments, but the IRA Army Council appeared to be populated by semanticists, and every time we put forward a proposal in clear English we would get back tortured prose into which buckets of conditionality had been inserted. Eguiguren gives an account of his similar debates with 'George' about the wording of ETA communiqués. Eguiguren was looking for phrases that would be seen by the public as big steps forward, and George was trying to keep them out. He describes them fencing around George's proposals on 'the right of the Basque people to decide' and Eguiguren's proposals on 'respecting the decisions' of the Basque people. To a layman these phrases might seem indistinguishable, but one was acceptable under the Spanish constitution and the other wasn't. He had to insist on wording that was in accordance with the existing laws while ETA of course wanted to change the existing law and constitu-tion. Sometimes the battle over words becomes almost totemic, and governments are often as bad about this as armed groups. In Northern Ireland, Sinn Féin insisted on talking about 'demili-tarisation' while the British government insisted on talking about 'security normalisation', even though they were precisely the same thing.

The only way to make progress on a text rapidly is through intensive negotiations rather than lackadaisical meetings with long gaps in between. Cardinal Richelieu observed in his *Political Testament* that 'Important negotiations should never be interrupted for a moment. It is necessary to pursue what one has undertaken with an endless programme of action so ordered that one never ceases to act intelligently and resourcefully, becoming neither indifferent, vacillating, nor irresolute.' Of course armed groups need time to consult their supporters, and that is difficult because they are in the bush or underground, but if that leads to long gaps then there is an increased chance the negotiations will fail.

In order to make real progress you sometimes have to resort to what the parties in Northern Ireland called 'hot-housing' – taking all the negotiators away from home and not letting them out till they have come to an agreement. Michael Young said 'The secret is to take them away from the theatre where it's all happening, where everybody is shouting the odds, where the media pick it all up and every nuance and every twist is dissected.' Richard Holbrooke took all the parties to the conflict in Bosnia to a US Air Force base in Dayton, Ohio in 1995. He described it as the 'Big Bang approach to negotiations: lock everyone up until they reach agreement'. During the negotiations, no side was permitted to leave and the negotiators worked for forty-eight hours without sleep during the closing session. He advises, however, that 'Those considering other Daytons should proceed with caution. It is a high-wire act without a safety net. Much work must precede the plunge into such an all-or-nothing environment. The site must be just right. The goals must be clearly defined. A single host nation must be in firm control, but it is high risk for the host, whose prestige is on the line. The consequences of failure are great. But when the conditions are right, a Dayton can produce dramatic results.'

Nearly every serious negotiation has to have such a phase. The mediator between Sudan and South Sudan was Lazaro Sumbeiywo, a Kenyan general and a devout Christian, appointed by President Moi. He spent years listening to the grievances of both sides and in late 2004 was close to a breakthrough. The Sudanese vice president Ali Osman Taha, however, threatened to walk out of the talks saying there was nothing left to discuss, accusing the South Sudanese leader, John Garang, of being completely unreasonable. Sumbeiywo had seen this kind of brinkmanship before when one side or the other would pack their bags and send them to the hotel lobby, only to return to the table later; but this time, Taha seemed to mean it. His plane had been cleared to land at the airport. Sumbeiywo and his staff were desperate. They started using every channel they could think of, and persuaded US Secretary of State Colin Powell to call both sides. It worked but still he couldn't get to an agreement so he decided to move the negotiators from the comfort of the Intercontinental Hotel in Nairobi to the Commercial Bank's training centre in a rural area outside the city where they were housed in three post-war concrete blocks around a circular courtyard that looked like a military academy. The parties described it as an 'open prison', and that was the idea. The press weren't allowed anywhere near. The move allowed him to make progress and they signed the final agreement the following January, ending a conflict which had cost 2 million lives and created millions more refugees.

Isoaho and Tuuli argue that 'the choice of venue can optimally have a major positive impact on confidence-building. Creating a relaxed atmosphere is often conducive to honest talks. Therefore, in many cases, the more informal the venue is, the more likely the parties are to openly engage in negotiations.' At their first session of talks in September 2002, the Sri Lankan government and Tamil Tiger delegations would eat at separate tables in the restaurant and steer well clear of each other in their free time. This changed over the course of the negotiations. In the words of one participant, 'by the time of the meeting in Berlin [in February 2003] they were at a "buddy level" and even went out for dinner at night. By the sixth round we were having Jacuzzis together.' Informality and socialising are essential if the two sides are to develop a rapport and make progress; but equally if the two sides appear to be enjoying each other's company too much, and the negotiating session looks like a party with banquets and champagne toasts, then the supporters of one or other side can be alienated when they see the talks as a matter of life and death.

By the time the parties get into an official negotiation, the fact that the two sides are talking is, generally, no longer secret, but it is still necessary for the content of the discussions to remain private. There is a tension between the natural demand for transparency and the chances of making progress. President Woodrow Wilson started off as a champion of openness. In his 'Fourteen Points' set out in the closing stages of the First World War he called for 'open covenants openly arrived at'. The American press took his promise literally and when they arrived in Paris for the peace negotiations they demanded access to the meetings of the Supreme Council of leaders negotiating the Versailles Treaty. Georges Clemenceau commented that it would be 'a veritable suicide' to let them in, and Lloyd George said if it happened the peace conference would go on forever. In the end Wilson agreed with his colleagues and the press were kept out. The journalists complained about the secrecy of the proceedings, accused Wilson of being a hypocrite and threatened to leave Paris and return to the US.

Negotiation is like making sausages; it is not an attractive process and it is better done in private. Niel Barnard said 'You cannot negotiate in public because of the risk of losing face.' In South Africa, the CODESA proceedings in their second phase were governed by rules of confidentiality, and Theuns Eloff, one of its secretaries, said 'You can't negotiate the future of a country in the eyes of the media.' Kissinger believes secrecy is vital in a negotiation because it allows you to avoid domestic pressure and frees you from the agenda of the media and your critics. Kissinger's predecessor (in spirit at least), Cardinal Richelieu, agreed that 'secrecy is the first essential in affairs of the state'.

The press, however, cannot be ignored and managing the media is an important part of ensuring the negotiations succeed.

There needs to be an understanding between the two sides that neither will talk publicly about the work of the negotiations, but they also have to agree on what they can say to the media. While the lack of an agreed communiqué can lead to media speculation, a good deal of time and effort can be taken up negotiating the text of a communiqué. Worse than that, a small variation in language between one communiqué and the next can be interpreted as a significant development in the talks. At one session of the talks on Hong Kong in 1984, the Chinese refused to agree to the inclusion of the word 'constructive', which had appeared in all previous communiqués in front of the word 'dialogue'. As a result the Hong Kong stock exchange fell by 5 per cent in the following two hours.

One side or the other will inevitably leak news in an attempt to gain advantage. The FARC repeatedly leaked information during the Caguán negotiations. In July 2000 the two sides exchanged ceasefire proposals in sealed envelopes that were supposed to remain confidential but the FARC immediately leaked theirs, thereby killing off any chance of a ceasefire. One of the remarkable things about the Oslo talks on the Middle East was that there were no leaks until three days before the announcement of the agreement. Yair Hirschfeld believes that the outbreak of leaking in those final few days came about as people involved tried to position themselves to take credit for the success. Ahtisaari says it 'is only possible to succeed if the parties themselves are disciplined. In this case [the Aceh talks in Helsinki] the parties behaved rather well: there was no "leaking" and a measure of seriousness. Such discretion is, after all, an indication of whether negotiations are genuinely a means to an end (the end to violence for a peaceful outcome) or a vehicle for point scoring and more combativeness.'

Occasionally a political leader becomes obsessed with the press coverage, with disastrous consequences. President Pastrana made himself a spokesman on the Caguán talks, giving an hour-by-hour running commentary on developments, even making live statements as he waited to receive proposals from the FARC. The Sri Lankan foreign minister, G. L. Peiris, was described by his colleagues as having an 'almost narcotic relationship' with the press. Although the first meeting between the government and the Tigers in a naval base in Thailand was supposed to be secluded and private, he insisted on travelling to a nearby town to brief the press. If you devote this much attention to the day-to-day handling of the media, it is not possible to be an effective negotiator.

Of course it is necessary to give people some idea of what is happening in the talks through public statements, but even then you need to be aware that you are addressing not only the electorate but also the members of the armed group. If you try to demonstrate how tough you are being with the terrorists, you may satisfy your domestic constituency but you are also sending a message to the armed group that you are not serious about concluding the negotiations and they may give up hope. It is worth explaining in private to the armed group why you are saying what you are saying publicly and what it really means, in order to avoid serious misunderstandings. And you have to be careful to avoid giving hostages to fortune. Prime Minister Zapatero of Spain gave an interview in December 2006 in which he said he believed 'We are at the beginning of the end of ETA.' The next morning ETA exploded the bomb at Madrid airport that wrecked the peace process.

All of these aspects of the architecture of a negotiation are important to get right but the fact is formal talks rarely produce results. Negotiations don't usually happen across the negotiating table at all; even that limited forum is too public for negotiators to show their hands. More usually progress is made in small groups, informal sessions, walks in the wood and coffee breaks, between individuals who trust each other. The crucial idea of a framework agreement between the MILF and the government of the Philippines was not worked out at the negotiating table but between two negotiators on a flight from Manila to Cotabato in Mindanao. Villalobos and his colleagues identified General Vargas and David Escobar Galindo on the back row of the government delegation right at the very beginning as the men they could do business with, and then brokered most of the deal with them. Cristiani said Galindo was 'philosophical, a strong optimist, a person who lifts your spirits', while General Vargas was chosen to 'make the armed forces feel as if they weren't being double-crossed at the table'. In July 1993, Joel Singer, a Washington attorney who had been the Israeli government's lawyer at the original Camp David negotiations with Jimmy Carter in 1978, was added to the Israeli delegation in Oslo. He put twenty questions to Abu Ala about the text agreed with Hirschfeld and, on the basis of his answers, redrafted the agreement. The Palestinian team was at first irritated by the questions and then deeply upset at the redrafted agreement. It was only after Uri Savir, the Israeli diplomat who now led their delegation, proposed a break and took Abu Ala for a long walk in the woods that they managed to rebuild confidence, and Abu Ala agreed to go through the text line by line.

Backchannels are every bit as important once formal negotiations have been initiated as they were in the earlier stages, and their functioning depends on deep personal trust. In South Africa, the bond between Cyril Ramaphosa and Roelf Meyer proved crucial when formal communications broke down between the ANC and the National Party in 1992. The two men first met in the departure lounge at Heathrow Airport in 1989. They had been on opposite sides of the miners' strike in South Africa, Ramaphosa as the General Secretary of the National Union of Mineworkers, and Meyer as the deputy minister of police. In Meyer's words, Ramaphosa had 'run the biggest strike in history. My job was to control it as police minister.' At Heathrow they agreed to talk, but they only came to trust each other later as a result of an accidental encounter in spring 1991. Meyer had accepted an invitation to spend a weekend fishing with his friend Sidney Frankel, a Johannesburg stockbroker, at the Havelock Trout farm, 170 miles from the city. Frankel had also invited Ramaphosa and his wife, although he had not told him that Meyer was coming until just before the minister arrived, to Ramaphosa's irritation. As Meyer and his sons touched down in a helicopter, Frankel's daughter broke her arm doing somersaults in the garden and Frankel and his family took her to hospital straight away. Meyer's sons kept pestering him to take them fishing, but Meyer knew nothing about the sport. Ramaphosa, a keen fisherman, offered to show them how. As Meyer was trying to cast, he got a hook deeply embedded in a finger. They returned to the lodge, where Ramaphosa's wife, a nurse, tried to manoeuvre the hook out. After an hour or so of twisting it this way and that, and as Meyer grew faint, Ramaphosa announced there was only one way to solve the problem. He poured Meyer a glass of whisky, and fetched a pair of pliers. Taking a firm grip on the hook, he pressed it down hard to make room for the barb and then yanked it out with one pull. Ten months later, Meyer took over as minister of constitutional development and head of the government's negotiating team, and he and Ramaphosa, who was already the ANC General Secretary and their chief negotiator, were able to establish a backchannel.

In June 1992, more than forty people (including a nine-month-old baby) were massacred in Boipatong, a black township south of Johannesburg. In response Nelson Mandela announced that the ANC was formally breaking off talks with the government. He listed fourteen demands that had to be met before talks could resume. Meyer was sitting in his office in a state of shock having watched Mandela's announcement on television. Ten minutes later his phone rang. He picked it up and on the other end was Ramaphosa. 'What the hell are you doing?' yelled Meyer. 'When can we talk?' replied Ramaphosa. During the suspension de Klerk and Mandela communicated only by letters whose tone was often counterproductive, and all substantive business was carried out by secret negotiations between Meyer and Ramaphosa, through what became known as 'The Channel'. They did not want people to know they were talking, so they could not meet at the ANC headquarters or in government buildings and they agreed never to meet at the same location twice. Initially they met in safe houses belonging to the NIS, and later in hotel rooms. After more than forty meetings and more or less constant negotiation between June and September, they concluded the 'Record of Understanding' which put the talks back on track. According to Meyer, the trust that developed between him and Ramaphosa was 'essential in reaching an agreement on the way forward, and also during the actual process of constitution-making'.

While the architecture of the negotiations is vital, there are also hard-learned negotiating techniques that can make the difference between success and failure. In Professor Mnookin's assessment, Nelson Mandela was the 'greatest negotiator of the twentieth century'. He had 'patience and tenacity. When negotiating with his adversaries, he was respectful but never fawning or sycophantic. He demanded respect in return.' He was pragmatic and 'willing to make concessions, but not about what was most important to him. With respect to his key political principles, he was unmovable.' Mnookin thinks he was so persuasive because he 'was a negotiator to whom one could make concessions and yet maintain one's self-respect. Mandela worked hard to establish and maintain a personal, human connection with Afrikaner leaders whose life experiences and attitudes were radically different from his own. These leaders came to see that Mandela really believed in racial reconciliation. They saw that his vision for South Africa included them.'

F. W. de Klerk says of Mandela that he 'got to know him as a very good listener, as a man with a legal mind, with analytical thinking patterns taking into account all facts. Coming forth, generally speaking, with reasonable replies and reactions towards requests, towards suggestions. Solution-orientated. When arguing against certain proposals, saying, "But something else could be considered." So he was a good negotiator. I also got to know him quite soon as an astute politician. As somebody who had a wonderful capacity . . . of grabbing the attention. He's a very good marketer. He has wonderful inbuilt public relations capabilities. He has a lot of charisma. The longer we knew each other, I also got to know another side of his character. That he could be, on occasion, extremely stubborn. That he could, from my vantage point, at times, get unreasonable. That he could lose his temper and be quite fierce and quite a different person.' Mandela was such a good negotiator because he was not just a global icon but also a canny politician who was capable of manipulating people, who knew when to hold and when to fold. Those practical skills are indispensable.

It may sound obvious, but at the heart of successful negotiating is compromise. The word compromise has, however, become synonymous with weakness and a lack of principle. In 1998 I had to set up proximity talks between the Orange Order, a particularly rigid unionist grouping, and the nationalist residents of the Garvaghy Road over the intractable issue of the Orange Order's annual march down the exclusively Catholic street which had led to serious violence year after year. I started with the Orange Order and they gave me their position. I took it down the corridor to the room where the Garvaghy residents were based. Predictably they rejected the Orange Order's position and put forward their own. I took their position back down the corridor to the Orange Order, explained the residents' proposal and suggested various compromises which might get the negotiation going. They reacted with horror. 'No,' they said. Didn't I understand, they had already told me what their position was. I tried to explain that the idea was a bit of give and take to arrive at a compromise, but for them the concept of backing down was immoral. They had given me their honest position, so changing it would imply they had been lying.

Compromise does not mean giving away your position; it means working out what the other side's interests are, and seeing if you can meet them without sacrificing your own. Gavin Kennedy, an expert on negotiation, says that 'Negotiating is about trading. This distinguishes it from other forms of decision-making. In negotiation, there is an explicit trade: I get some of what I want and you get some of what you want.' Kissinger believes negotiations are all about 'trading concessions' and you need to get a 'balance of mutual concessions' to succeed.

In their seminal 1981 book *Getting to Yes*, William Ury and Roger Fisher urge negotiators to distinguish between positions and interests. Positions lead to blockage, but if you can get behind positions to the interests that drive them, then you can find solutions. 'Your position is something you have decided upon. Your interests are what caused you to so decide.' Reconciling interests is easier than trading positions, because 'for every interest there usually exist several possible positions that could satisfy it'. They urge negotiators to put themselves in the shoes of the other side: 'It is not enough to know that they see things differently. If you want to influence them, you also need to understand empathetically the power of their point of view and to feel the emotional force with which they believe in it.' It is extraordinary how often people repeat this mantra yet rarely put it into practice. To do so you have to be prepared not just to listen but to hear – to pick up the nuances of what the other side are saying and what they are not saying, the gaps that indicate what they are not ruling out. If they have not now stressed a point that they stressed before, have they perhaps dropped it? What are the political pressures on them? How can they sell a compromise to their own supporters, and what successes do they need to demonstrate to receive praise? If you can answer these questions you can work out what you can do to help them achieve what they want.

Understanding what the other side wants is not the same as agreeing with them, but it can help find solutions that both sides can accept. Haysom argues that 'The most common barrier to effective negotiations is the confusion between interests and positions. Parties frequently lose sight of the interests and objectives informing their positions. They become obsessed with defending the proposals (positions), which are in fact only the means. The problem frequently arises because campaign or struggle slogans often attach to the position or tactic rather than the long-term interests and principles.' When presented with a position in a negotiation, you should always ask 'why' rather than 'what'. Rather than jump to assumptions about why the other side has adopted a position, you should discover the reasons behind it. And when you are thinking about interests it is not just the interests of those at the table but other relevant parties too, including neighbouring states.

You should do everything possible to make it easy for your negotiating partners to reach an agreement, and construct bridges for them to retreat over. Even better, try to make the negotiation a joint project towards solving a common problem rather than an antagonistic clash where one side or the other wins. Jesús Eguiguren felt that, after a time, his meetings with 'George' took on the air of working together or collaboration in the joint search for a viable way forward. Hirschfeld and Abu Ala also say they felt they were working together for a common aim in Oslo, albeit of course in pursuit of their own national interests. At first the instructions on both sides were general and they did not have to follow them to the letter. They set up a wastepaper basket in the negotiating room and agreed anyone could put ideas in there if they didn't work. Ron Pundak says 'we sat around a round table, as opposed to a rectangular table, whenever we could, looking at ourselves as a joint team with a joint objective, representing two interests – but jointly'.

A negotiation with an armed group is, however, oppositional in the end and it requires the participants to strike a difficult balance between being too tough and appearing a pushover. Being tough can make you popular on your own side but can be disastrous for building trust with the other side. Being soft can leave you open to exploitation. The Sri Lankan foreign minister G. L. Peiris accused his prime minister of falling into the latter trap, saying Wickremasinghe 'was willing to appease Prabhakaran. Whenever he transgressed the ceasefire, we never confronted him head-on.' In Colombia, President Pastrana allowed himself to appear to be a pushover. Every time a deadline came around he allowed the huge demilitarised zone he had conceded to be continued unilaterally, without any reciprocal concessions from the FARC. He hoped it would increase goodwill, but all it did was convince the FARC that he was weak. On the eve of the January 2001 deadline for ending the demilitarised zone, however, Pastrana announced that 'if Marulanda wants an extension of the safe haven, he has to sit down at the negotiating table'. On the day of the deadline itself he extended the zone for four more days in return for a face-to-face meeting with Marulanda. This was the first time the government had insisted on FARC concessions before extending the zone. The meeting resulted in the agreement of Los Pozos, in which the two sides pledged to begin dialogue again, and created a commission of national personalities to consider the way ahead, as well as a humanitarian agreement on the freedom of ill soldiers and guerrillas, one of the few successes of the whole negotiation.

On the other hand those who take a uniformly hard line are usually bad negotiators in the end. They are brittle and if they want to get to a deal they have to collapse from their position in the last stages of a negotiation, which makes the other side uncertain what their real bottom line is. They wonder whether if they just push a bit harder the other side will crumble even further. In my experience it is far better to cut to the chase in a negotiation and get to your bottom line quickly, rather than trying to hold back concessions to make later. If you adopt this position clearly and consistently, your interlocutors will understand your signals and be willing to settle on a deal more rapidly.

Persuading the other side that you are not bluffing is always difficult, and it can help to put the blame on those to whom you answer who are not actually in the room. After all in most negotiations you don't have a completely free hand and you are negotiating *ad referendum* to some higher authority. Gerry Adams and Martin McGuinness used to say they could not move further on a particular text because the IRA Army Council would not let them. Mo Mowlam would joke that when Adams and McGuinness said they were going to consult the IRA, they simply left the room, looked in the mirror and came back in again, but actually it was considerably more complicated than that. I think of it as the 'her indoors' gambit, where you blame your inability to do something on the wife, and it was one of the advantages wielded by anyone negotiating on behalf of Mrs Thatcher. Everyone knew she could be unreasonable, so it was possible to explain a lack of flexibility as the result of her instructions. Contrariwise, weakness can be a strength in a negotiation. If your political position is weak, then your interlocutors know that you are in no position to make further concessions without losing office, and they have to accept there is a limit on what you can offer.

The fact that you are negotiating with human beings who have feelings and emotions should be a central consideration in the way you approach the talks. Ury and Fisher say, 'Benjamin Franklin's favorite technique was to ask an adversary if he could borrow a certain book. This would flatter the person and give him the comfortable feeling of knowing that Franklin owed him a favour.' Oddly doing someone else a favour makes you trust them more. Informal encounters and fraternisation between the two sides can help to create an atmosphere conducive to making a deal. Holbrooke describes meals and drinking sessions in the Bosnian talks, saying Milosevic would often drink without being adversely affected, so Holbrooke resolved to drink only when agreement was reached. Negotiators from the armed group will be sensitive to any slights and it is important to show them respect. Zartman writes 'Respect is a personal relation, not a status recognition, and needs to be conveyed through formal gestures and personal politeness. The negotiator needs to be interested and appear understanding in his contacts with the terrorist representative. Respect does not mean sympathising with the terrorists' aims and goals or even recognising their legitimacy . . . it does mean *understanding* where the terrorist comes from, mentally and experientially.'

Although negotiations are often highly charged emotional occasions – Uri Savir recalls the sessions in Oslo had 'great intensity . . . the confrontations were often brutal, the crises close to shattering, sometimes the tension broke in near-hysterical laughter; sometimes we pushed each other almost to the point of rage. The emotional outbursts in those sessions buffeted us between hatred and empathy' – the very act of negotiating can itself help to build trust. Carl Miller of King's College London says that 'whilst of course legitimacy and trust are vital characteristics of any negotiating partner, these are something that can be developed during negotiations itself. Whilst diplomacy relies on certain conventions and values, it also promotes them: it is both a civilised and civilising institution.'

As far as possible you want to keep anger out of a negotiation. Martin Griffiths describes an occasion in June 2001 when he had to struggle to stop himself hitting the Indonesian government negotiator, Hassan Wirajuda. Wirajuda kept finding reasons to refuse to agree an agenda and eventually pulled a ridiculous procedural trick to halt negotiations. Griffiths raised his hand and was about to strike Wirajuda, when his deputy Andrew Marshall, sitting next to him, said 'Don't do that,' and Griffiths let his hand fall to the table. Holbrooke says that at Dayton 'contrary to popular perception emotional exchanges (yelling) were extremely rare, and usually deliberate'. His account reminded me of one particularly fraught session with the Orange Order in Northern Ireland in Mo Mowlam's office in Castle Buildings in Stormont. One of the Orangemen started being particularly offensive to Tony Blair. Quite uncharacteristically I leapt from my seat, grabbed him by his lapels and was about to punch him when Tony pushed me back into my seat and told me not to be so stupid. After the meeting he took me aside and told me never to lose my temper, 'except on purpose'. In this he was agreeing with his hero Gladstone who said 'Anger is not only the prevailing sin of argument, but its greatest stumbling block.'

The one thing to avoid at all costs is lying to the other side, or saying one thing to one group and another to another group. If you do, you will almost certainly be found out and you will have rendered yourself useless as a negotiator. In one particularly tense session in West Belfast, Gerry Adams leant across the table and said to me, 'The thing I like about you, Jonathan, is that you blush when you lie.' My colleague sitting next to me, Bill Jeffrey, responded quick as a flash, 'Unlike you, Gerry.' Henry Kissinger argues that it is essential to cultivate the appearance of reliability in negotiations: 'Amateurs think of great diplomats as crafty; but the wise diplomat understands that he cannot afford to trick his opponent; in the long run a reputation for reliability and fairness is an important asset. The same negotiators meet over and over again; their ability to deal with one another is undermined if a diplomat acquires a reputation for evasion or duplicity.' For that reason secret agreements or secret side letters to one party or the other, although they may seem to offer a way out of an immediate impasse, are a snare and a delusion. In the Northern Ireland negotiations we gave David Trimble a side letter on decommissioning at the last minute to persuade him to sign up, without telling Sinn Féin. It did him little good in the long term and was an embarrassment for us. In the negotiations with ETA, 'George' proposed secret clauses and annexes to solve the problem of how the province of Navarre should be dealt with, but Eguiguren correctly refused on the grounds that it would lead to difficulties later. Instead they opted for ambiguity by referring to the 'Basque citizen', which ETA could interpret as including Navarre and the government could assert meant just the three Basque provinces on the Atlantic.

If side agreements are a mistake, there is a strong case for offering 'confidence-building measures' during a negotiation.

Small steps to demonstrate that the armed group are making gains during the talks help build the standing of their negotiators with their supporters, and encourages them to believe there may be a political answer to their conflict. Reciprocal confidence-building measures from the side of the armed group may also reassure hardliners on the government side that the negotiations are not just a one-way street. Haysom writes that 'In South Africa the measures designed to build confidence in the negotiating strategy involved securing the release of political prisoners, the repeal of racist legislation and the cessation of hostilities. In the absence of visible benefits from the negotiating strategy, critics will increasingly spread scepticism concerning the benefits of the negotiations.'

It is always necessary, as a government or an armed group, to have a 'Plan B' in a negotiation; what you are going to do if the negotiation fails. However Kissinger advises that you should not formulate fallback positions at the outset of negotiations, as that will undermine the tenacity with which your negotiators stick to their official positions, or at least you should not let your negotiators know what the 'Plan B' is, for if they do they will nearly always tack in that direction from the beginning.

Negotiation is clearly an art to which there are certain tricks of the trade, but there are also certain laws of negotiation that seem to govern the process in most cases. Percy Craddock, the distinguished British diplomat who negotiated the Hong Kong Agreement, insisted that the first law of diplomacy was that the hardest negotiations are always on your own side, and he certainly found the discussions with Margaret Thatcher and with the Governor and the Executive Council in Hong Kong tougher than those with the Chinese. Gerry Adams takes the same line, saying the most difficult negotiation is 'always that with your own band'. Roelf Meyer faced the problem of others in the South African Cabinet second-guessing what he was doing in the negotiation. Those outside the cut and thrust of the talks thought the government could just ignore the ANC demands, but he was in the thick of the negotiations and knew what was possible and what was not. He found that if he was completely on top of the detail he could usually win the argument in Cabinet, particularly if his opponents did not have the facts at their fingertips. This challenge has been described by the political scientist Robert Putnam as a 'two-level game in which a leader must, Janus-faced, negotiate in both directions'.

Holbrooke was very conscious of the challenge posed by internal politics and says he was determined to avoid bureaucratic infighting in his delegation by ensuring that his team had complete trust and openness with each other: 'If we could not come up with a single position, each member of the team could make his viewpoint known to Washington directly – provided only that he shared his dissent with the rest of us.' In his view this was a 'key ingredient' for success. Kissinger says that 'The risk of negotiation in a large bureaucracy is that those who are excluded can always claim that they could have done better and the fewer engaged the more are tempted to do so. Uninvolved in the process of mutual adjustment, they can emphasise maximum objectives, unaware of obstacles they can blame every concession on inadequate toughness or negotiating skill.'

The second law is the importance of symbols, which can often be more significant than substance in such a negotiation. The Indonesian government had accepted in the Memorandum of Understanding with GAM that 'Aceh has the right to use regional symbols including a flag, a crest and a hymn', but the memorandum also prohibited GAM from displaying its 'military insignia or symbols'. After the agreement, the police and army threatened to arrest anyone displaying GAM's symbol of a crescent moon and star at public rallies, but the GAM commander insisted the moon and star was the flag of Aceh and should therefore be acceptable. The government negotiator contested this, saying the flag would be decided later by the Aceh legislature and that whatever they chose it certainly would not be the GAM insignia. It sounds like a trivial issue but it contributed to a number of violent incidents in Aceh which eventually brought down the first peace process, and the issue is still not finally resolved more than twenty years later. It is essential to try to understand why symbolic issues are so important for the parties rather than dismissing them as irrational, and to try to find a way of reconciling them.

Perhaps the single most important issue in such negotiations is the sense of identity of a minority group within a majoritarian state. As David Trimble put it in his Nobel Peace Prize acceptance speech, Northern Ireland was a 'cold house' for the minority Catholics living there. They wanted their Irish identity acknowledged even if they had to continue to live in what was part of the United Kingdom. They wanted 'parity of esteem'. We had to find ways in which they could express their identity other than just painting kerbs in tribal colours and the flying of the Irish tricolour in Catholic enclaves. The same problem arises for the Bangsamoro in the Philippines, the Palestinians in Israel and the Acehnese in Indonesia.

The third law is that the substance contained in an agreement is rarely new. The same issues turn up in very different negotiations all over the globe: power-sharing, federalism, protection of minority rights, resource sharing and so on. In Sri Lanka the issue has been for decades, and continues to be, federalism. Ranil Wickremasinghe offered 'asymmetric federalism' with a special form of Tamil entity in the north-east with more powers than a Swiss canton, having himself opposed a federal solution proposed by President Kumaratunga a few years earlier. The issue of federalism, central to the negotiations in South Africa in the 1990s, was first debated in the National Convention on South Africa in 1909. Power-sharing is often an essential provision to end an armed conflict between a minority and a majority. F. W. de Klerk says 'The inclusion of some form of power-sharing in the final constitution was one of the National Party's central goals. In the end we failed because the Inkatha Freedom Party and the Democratic Party refused to support the principle of power-sharing.' In 1996 he led the National Party out of the Government of National Unity precisely because in his view the ANC were refusing to accept power-sharing in reality. 'The complexity of our population composition and of our economy – and the conflict potential that this involved – could best be managed by a consensus-seeking model . . . Instead we have been saddled with a majoritarian model. I said at the time that this was a mistake and continue to believe that it is one of the greatest weaknesses of our new constitutional system.' Paradoxically, given the continuity of the subjects under discussion, negotiations on the key points of substance can be very quick indeed. In the Good Friday negotiations, agreement was reached on the power-sharing provisions in less than twenty-four hours exactly because all parties had been round the course so many times before.

Provisions on power-sharing are essential to securing an agreement but they can have unintended consequences in the longer term. The agreement on power-sharing in Bosnia reached at Dayton led to the creation of an immovable elite permanently in power which is now the cause of mass protests in the country. In Northern Ireland the agreement on the de Hondt system of power-sharing created a 'forced coalition' where all parties are in government and there is no opposition so that people cannot 'throw the rascals out'. In Colombia the M-19 succeeded in securing the creation of a new elected post of inspector general to root out corruption in the governing elite. In a delicious irony, the former M-19 guerrilla who became mayor of Bogotá was expelled from office by the very inspector general whose position they had helped to create.

One of the key issues facing a negotiator is whether to start with the easy issues or the difficult ones. Isoaho and Tuuli argue that 'Helping the parties around the table to quickly reach an agreement on something, even if it is something minor, is a common way to build confidence in the early stages of negotiations. Starting with an "easy" issue and getting the parties to agree on it shows them that the other side can be trusted and that the talks can yield concrete results.' It is indeed tempting to begin in this way, but if you leave the hard issues unaddressed there is a good chance the negotiations will collapse. At Dayton, Holbrooke 'rejected the minimalist theory that we should negotiate only those matters on which implementation would be relatively easy' and experience suggests that those negotiations that go straight to the central political issues are more likely to succeed.

The impact of that choice is starkly illustrated by the two different attempts at solving Aceh. Martti Ahtisaari started in 2005 with the central issue of the territory's status. In his political judgement the Indonesian government would never go beyond 'special autonomy' status, but equally he knew he could not ask GAM for a statement giving up their claim for independence at the very beginning of the negotiation. In order to allow the talks to take off, he asked the two sides to explore the substance of the autonomy plan on a conditional basis, to see if it could be attractive enough to tempt the GAM, without either side giving up its position of principle. In the opening sessions in mid-January the government side gave the GAM negotiators copies of the existing Special Autonomy Law, something they had already rejected. The talks almost broke down at this point and GAM proposed they talk instead about 'a sustainable ceasefire'. The Indonesian government rejected this as a temporary solution and said this time they were only interested in a comprehensive and permanent solution, not just talks about a cessation of hostilities. By contrast the HD Centre-led talks on Aceh in 2000–2 had started with the easier issues of a ceasefire and humanitarian access and had never managed to get on to the central political issues. The negotiations deteriorated into mutual recriminations about the other side's failure to implement the agreement, and violence escalated. GAM boycotted the talks because of increasing violence by government forces and then when they returned the government froze the negotiations because of breaches by GAM.

In Helsinki, Ahtisaari stuck to his plan, which was essentially to turn the approach adopted by the HD Centre on its head. Instead of starting with easier issues, from the start he took head-on the substance of the disagreement. This was high risk and could easily have led to deadlock and failure, but in the end GAM relented and agreed to explore self-government as an interim step, while not setting aside their demand for independence. They demanded maximum authority for an Acehnese government, leaving only minimal powers for the central government such as external defence and foreign affairs. They wanted a different political system with local parties, a judicial system separate from Indonesia with no right of appeal to the Supreme Court in Jakarta, the replacement of the national army and police by a locally recruited police force answerable to the governor and the right to set their own interest rates and to have an Acehnese flag. Although these demands were of course unacceptable to the Indonesian government, at last there were proposals on the table that opened up the possibility of a real negotiation.

The most dangerous trap into which the government side can fall is to make agreement contingent on solving 'the causes of the conflict'. For armed groups it is a fundamental tenet of belief that the causes of the conflict must be resolved before the conflict itself can be brought to an end. Their definition of the causes, however, will be far wider than the government side can ever accept as part of the negotiations. Many of the issues can only be resolved politically once the armed group has put down its weapons and tried to win support democratically for its positions, and not in a negotiation that does not even include representatives of all the different currents within society. In any case the government and society as a whole cannot wait until deep-seated social and economic problems are resolved before the armed group lays down its weapons. Other political parties are not prepared to compete in elections with a party backed by its own private army. Making resolution of the causes of the conflict a condition for disarmament is therefore a dangerous dead end for such negotiations.

Armed groups, however, can be positively theological on the point. The ETA leader 'George' wanted to discuss the causes of the conflict with Eguiguren in Geneva first, and only then the methods to resolve them. Eguiguren was prepared to respond positively but demanded to know that the ceasefire would depend only on the implementation of the road map which ETA and the government were trying to agree, and not on political talks amongst the parties in the Basque Country, the outcome of which was unpredictable. He could not let ETA say that it would only give up its weapons once its political demands had been met, because Zapatero had made it clear there could be 'no political price for peace'. One of the most memorable events during the negotiations in Northern Ireland was when David Ervine, the articulate and charismatic leader of the small Loyalist PUP, confronted Gerry Adams with an unanswerable question at the Weston Park meeting in 2001. He demanded to know whether in Adams's view the conflict was over when the Good Friday Agreement was in place or only when there was a united Ireland. The question was so pointed because Ervine knew that the IRA constitution made it clear they could not destroy their weapons until there was a united Ireland, and yet Adams was trying to get to an end to the conflict before that key cause of the conflict – the division of Ireland – had been resolved. Adams needed the ambiguity which clouded his position to satisfy both sides and he reacted to Ervine's question with fury, refusing to answer it. Ervine and his party walked out of Weston Park.

If a negotiation gets off to a bad start it is very hard to recover. The initial negotiating session is always the focus of huge attention and sends a public message about the way the two sides treat each other and what they say to the press. If the armed group treats the government with contempt then it will be hard to recover. As they prepared for the opening of talks in late 1998, the FARC announced that Marulanda would not attend the meeting with the government after all. Pastrana said that if Marulanda didn't go, then neither would he.

Forty-eight hours later Marulanda said he would go to the meeting in Caguán on 7 January but would only be present for a few minutes and would speak first, before the president. When 7 January dawned, however, Marulanda didn't show up and his deputy Raul Reyes came in his place. He said that Marulanda was nearby but that security reasons meant he could not be there in person. Pastrana tried to make the best of it and said the absence of Marulanda was no reason not to proceed. The government agreed that meetings could be attended by the press and even filmed live on TV while they were going on. This showed a commendable commitment to transparency, but turned the talks into a farce. The government allowed the guerrillas to bring a gun, a rifle and a machete to the negotiating table and sit there with the gun pointing at the other side with the safety catch off.

Leaving aside the disastrous power relationship at the table from the beginning, the substance of the discussions was little better. According to one at the table at the time, when they moved on to discuss socioeconomic issues and asked if the guerrillas had any ideas, Marulanda said that they just had to 'do something about this neo-liberalism'. Reyes added that unemployment 'should be made illegal, prohibited. It was just wrong.' Marulanda asked what the exchange rate was. On being told that the dollar was at 1,500 Colombian pesos, he said it was just too high. They should cut the exchange rate to 1,000. The same negotiator said that when he left the table to pee, Marulanda followed him and told him as they stood at the urinal, 'You ought to go home. It's late and there are too many guerrillas around here.'

The best way to get a negotiation off to a good start is to put a proposal on the table that is so attractive that the other party simply cannot afford to walk away. In Oslo, Hirschfeld indicated at the third meeting with Abu Ala that the Israelis were prepared to allow Yasser Arafat to return to Palestine. Peres had authorised him to make the offer after discussing it with Rabin. Peres had asked the prime minister for permission and when Rabin replied 'I don't have an answer', Peres took that as meaning he wasn't saying no. Hirschfeld explained to Abu Ala that the Palestinians could only secure this offer if they agreed to a number of things the Israelis wanted. He knew that Arafat would be so keen to get this prize that he would be prepared to meet most of the Israeli demands. Hirschfeld had effectively transformed the Palestinians into the *'demandeur'* in the talks and he then started to load his side of the table with the things he needed to secure. The Palestinians too offered two things the Israelis really wanted: 'Gaza first' and a Marshall Plan for the entire region, both particular dreams of Peres which were now being offered by the Palestinians themselves. To the delight of the Israelis, they also proposed that Jerusalem be excluded from the talks as too difficult. The negotiation was destined to succeed almost from the beginning.

A negotiation may not resolve an armed conflict, or at least it may not resolve it this time. But if there is a peace process in place people have reason to hope and violence will be diminished. As Tony Blair used to say to me, even if we could not solve the Northern Ireland conflict, at least we could manage it. One of the intriguing aspects of a peace process is that often when things look at their bleakest from outside there is about to be a breakthrough, and when to the public they look as if they are surging ahead they are in fact about to collapse. Sometimes the public perception is gloomy because negotiators want to play down expectations. Holbrooke says 'I believed it was best to underplay signs of progress and minimise optimism, while simultaneously seeking to establish a sense of new American commitment and engagement. If the glass was filling up, I would prefer that we said it was still almost empty.' Other negotiators play up success to demonstrate progress and maintain public support for the talks. The lesson is to be phlegmatic: don't greet the breakthroughs with euphoria, and don't sink into gloom when things go wrong. The only thing to do in either case is to keep plodding on, while maintaining a watchful eye on public expectations and trying to manage them.

Perhaps the best indicator of whether a negotiation will succeed is if the two sides are approaching the process strategically rather than merely tactically. If they fail to focus on the eventual result they want to achieve, with a clear plan for getting there, and simply try to wing it with a series of short-term tactical manoeuvres, they will fail. As Seneca observes, 'If a man knows not to which port he sails, no wind is favourable.' The Spanish government fell into this trap in its negotiations with ETA. Arnaldo Otegi, the Batasuna leader, says that some thought 'The only thing the government wanted was a ceasefire and once it had got it was prepared to ignore everything else.' As a result the peace process failed. When I asked Joaquín Villalobos, the FMLN leader, about the importance of trust in the negotiations, he said that he put his trust not in the government but in his plan for the negotiation. That is what he remained focused on throughout.

A plan has to be flexible, however, and you have to adapt as the negotiations develop. In *Strategy: A History*, Lawrence Freedman quotes Mike Tyson: 'Everyone has a plan until they get punched in the mouth.' The end product will not look like your original concept. Holbrooke argued that 'Negotiating requires flexibility on tactics but a constant vision of the ultimate goal.' This is certainly the way he approached the Bosnian negotiations. One of his team said 'Don't expect to find a piece of paper with a plan on it; it was not there. It was very much "make it up as you go along".' But Holbrooke was working to an overall strategy. He said 'Negotiation is like jazz. It's improvisation on a theme. You have to know where you want to go, but you don't know how to get here. It's not linear.'

A successful negotiation, then, requires a robust architecture, negotiators with the necessary skills, observation of the eternal laws, a clear but flexible strategy, and a good start which engages the interests of both sides. But even with all of these in place, a peace process can drag on so that the public becomes weary and the negotiators lose all credibility. When that happens, you have to find a way to force the negotiation into the endgame. As Kissinger says, 'Every negotiator must decide at what point marginal gains are no longer worth the loss of confidence caused by the kind of haggling that merges with sharp practice.'

CHAPTER EIGHT

Why do Some Negotiations Succeed and Others Fail?

Peace is a question of will. All conflicts can be settled, and there are no excuses for allowing them to become eternal.

Martti Ahtisaari

It is far easier to start a negotiation than it is to end one successfully. Armed groups may be inclined to open a peace process because of the legitimacy and publicity it bestows, but they generally move by consensus and would rather talk indefinitely than face up to the difficult compromises necessary to reach an agreement. They often prefer the airplane to circle endlessly rather than land. Finding a way to conclude successfully is the holy grail for negotiators.

Why do some talks conclude successfully (like those in South Africa, Mozambique, El Salvador, Northern Ireland and with the M-19 in Colombia) and others fail (like those in Sri Lanka, the first attempt at Aceh and the talks with the FARC at Caguán)? Audrey Cronin argues that the factors that determine success or failure include: 'the nature of the organisation (with hierarchical groups having an advantage over groups that cannot control their members' actions); the nature of the leadership (groups with a strong leader having an advantage over those that are decentralised); and the nature of public support for the cause (where groups with constituencies who tire of violence are more likely to compromise)'.

While all of these have an influence on success or failure, the key factor is the ability to close a deal: can the two sides be pushed into an endgame and into making difficult decisions? One way of forcing a decision is to set a deadline, but establishing one that people really believe in is not always so easy. After his election in May 1997, Tony Blair set a deadline of one year to conclude the negotiations on the future of Northern Ireland. He did so because in our analysis John Major's failure to make rapid progress after the IRA ceasefire in 1994 had tipped them back into violence. Republicans felt they were being 'messed around' and no matter how long they waited they would never be included in the all-party peace talks. We, by contrast, made it clear to the Republicans, through the Irish government, that if they renewed the ceasefire we would rapidly bring them into the talks, and the talks would be rapidly concluded. As the end date approached in 1998 we were told that the deadline was dangerous and it would be far safer just to forget about it. Tony Blair decided to stick to it anyway and after three days and nights of intensive negotiations we secured an agreement on Good Friday. On that occasion the deadline worked as intended.

Subsequently, however, we set a series of deadlines for the full implementation of the Good Friday Agreement, but they were arbitrary and not anchored to any real-world event, and we rolled through them one after another without any immediate consequences for the parties. As a result our deadlines lost credibility with both sides, who increasingly came to ignore them. In fact they became counterproductive because Sinn Féin in particular would ask me when the next deadline was and then withhold any concessions until we approached it, thus slowing down negotiations rather than speeding them up. We only managed to regain credibility for our deadline by legislating to bring the institutions in Northern Ireland crashing down at the end of 2006, and in this way secured a final agreement in November.

Deadlines can thus be both a solution and a problem. Certainly setting deadlines can put the credibility of the mediator on the line. In concluding the pre-agreements for the negotiation in El Salvador, Álvaro de Soto had been worried that President Cristiani would be unable to sustain support without a ceasefire and without some notion of the duration of the process. He therefore proposed an ambitious 'target date' for the conclusion of the first stage of the talks. Unfortunately this was translated into English as a 'deadline', which set a trap. Subsequently Bernie Aronson, the US assistant secretary for Inter-American Affairs, used the promised 'deadline' to browbeat de Soto for failing to make the FMLN live up to the timetable for a ceasefire. De Soto says 'In El Salvador, I was constantly pressured to set deadlines to the parties, but I would always say that "Firstly, I don't have that power and, secondly, if I do that and the deadline is not met, what then? Do we withdraw?" I stressed that I was not prepared to put at risk my credibility, nor the credibility of the United Nations as a mediator. I would never set a deadline that I am not 100 per cent sure I can carry out. That would be a mistake.'

Isoaho and Tuuli argue that 'deadlines can support a mediation process if they are based on real events instead of being artificially created'. They cite an important example from the El Salvador peace process: 'the then Salvadoran legislature came to an end on April 30, 1991, which meant that the parties would have to reach an agreement on constitutional reforms by that date or they would have to wait for another three years to make such reforms (as constitutional reforms required the approval of two consecutive legislatures). As a real, immovable deadline, the change of legislature on April 30 positively expedited the talks.' A second real deadline had an even greater impact. The El Salvador agreement was reached after midnight on 31 December 1991 because that was the day Pérez de Cuéllar ceased to be Secretary General of the UN. His successor Boutros-Ghali had made it clear to the parties that they should reach an agreement before he took office, because although the Salvadoran crisis was a high priority for Pérez de Cuéllar, it would take a new Secretary General some time to get involved in the process. De Soto used this to persuade both sides to sign the substantive provisions of the agreement before the deadline, even though it was necessary to meet again on 13 January to agree on the timetable for implementation, and the final peace agreement was only formally signed at an emotional ceremony on 16 January 1992 in Chapultepec Castle in Mexico City.

In the Oslo process, the Israelis used the planned visit by Shimon Peres to Scandinavia in August 1992 to set a deadline for the talks. On the morning of 17 August, Peres called the Norwegian foreign minister Johan Holst who was visiting Iceland and asked if they could meet discreetly in Stockholm that evening, saying 'It is now or never.' That night Holst sat in a room in Haga Castle in Sweden for eight hours transmitting messages from Peres in the next room to Arafat in Tunis. At 5 a.m. the final wording on security for Israeli settlers and on the location and authority of the future Palestinian Authority had been agreed. On 19 August Peres paid his official visit to Oslo. Just after midnight, when the official dinner had ended, the Norwegian security service escorted the negotiating teams through the back entrance. They brought with them the final agreed Declaration of Principles. At 1 a.m. Abu Ala and Uri Savir initialled the document in front of Peres and Holst. The process had taken eight months.

Sometimes governments that establish artificial deadlines can find themselves trapped. If it is not met by the armed group they face either a humiliating climbdown or are forced to make concessions in order to persuade the other side to meet the deadline. It may therefore sometimes be better to set milestones, various waymarks on the route to an agreement, such as agreeing to certain chapters by certain dates. These can help speed progress and provide reassurance to the public that advances are being made in what would otherwise be an opaque process. It can also help to concentrate minds if you present the chance of an agreement as a 'fading opportunity' – unless the armed group grabs the agreement now it will no longer be on offer in a year's time. Deadlines can then work to secure an agreement if they are anchored in real world events that mean negotiations have to stop by a certain date; but setting an arbitrary deadline can pose a risk to the party setting it, unless they genuinely intend to break off the talks if the deadline is not met.

It is tempting for mediators to try to end a negotiation by 'calling it', i.e. simply setting out what they think is a reasonable outcome and demanding that the two sides accept it. In Cyprus, after years of patient negotiating between the two sides, the UN under Kofi Annan felt it needed to make a decision on the remaining differences between the Greek and Turkish Cypriots. They put the agreement with those final UN drafted clauses to a referendum and the Greek Cypriot leader, Tassos Papadopoulos, used them as an excuse to urge his constituency to vote no. The agreement failed and there has been no progress in Cyprus since. Brinkmanship can sometimes succeed, and did in the second Aceh negotiations. Martti Ahtisaari announced in advance that the meeting starting on 12 July 2005 would be the last session of talks, even though two major issues remained unresolved: whether or not there could be local parties in Aceh, and the number of Indonesian troops that could remain following an agreement. He took a risk in doing so but it worked and both sides kept negotiating for twelve hours continuously on the final day. The Memorandum of Understanding was signed between the two sides a month later. Ultimata, however, almost never work. Yudhoyono tried in the first Aceh peace process, when in April 2003 he gave GAM two weeks to agree to autonomy as the final goal and to warehouse its weapons. GAM responded by saying it could not accept an ultimatum and proposing a meeting in Geneva in May, after Yudhoyono's deadline had already expired. In a desperate attempt to save the talks, Griffiths proposed a meeting in Tokyo on 17 May, but the talks failed and the Indonesian military went into action against the GAM to 'destroy them to their roots'.

It may be necessary to threaten to walk out of the talks to persuade the other side that it is time to reach agreement. The danger of course is that your bluff may be called and you actually have to do so if you want to retain credibility. The bicycle theory dictates you should keep the process going if you possibly can, so the ideal scenario is to make the threat but not actually have to carry it out. And if you *do* walk out, you need to be careful about the circumstances. John Major had a fractious relationship with Ian Paisley, and at one meeting in the Cabinet Room in Downing Street, which Major used as his office, Paisley accused him of lying. Major demanded that he withdraw the smear, Paisley refused to do so, and Major walked out. Unfortunately for Major, Paisley staged a sit-in, leaving Major without an office. You need to remember where you are before you actually walk out.

It is crucial to comprehend that armed groups will under no circumstances agree to surrender, or appear to surrender, when they have not been defeated. In 2004 we nearly had an agreement in Northern Ireland between Paisley's DUP and Sinn Féin. It collapsed at the last minute when Paisley made a speech demanding that Republicans don 'sackcloth and ashes to show penitence for their crimes', and demanded photographic evidence of the decommissioning of their weapons. For the Republicans this smacked of humiliation and defeat and they refused. The deal was off. In Spain, as elsewhere, there have been repeated efforts by governments to do a deal on the basis that the armed group demobilise and disarm in return for an amnesty for their prisoners. This almost never works. It is impossible for the leaders of the armed groups to explain to their members and the communities that support them what all the suffering and death was for if all they secure is the release of their members from jail. There has to be more to it than that. Jesús Eguiguren says the socialist government in Spain understood that there could not be an unconditional surrender and that the conflict had to end with dignity and with the prospect of a political route by which the Basque separatists could pursue their goals.

For the same reasons of pride it is a mistake to appear to

try to buy off an armed group. Aid and development assistance are essential for war-torn areas and it is necessary for the populations to see a peace dividend rapidly if they are going to support an agreement, but if you try to move too quickly on the economic front without having offered a political perspective, there is the danger of that aid being rejected. In Sri Lanka, the international community was accused of 'buying peace'. After the first agreement in Aceh, a Joint Committee on Humanitarian Action was established and the international community channelled substantial funds into the territory in the hope of underpinning the ceasefire. It didn't work because of the lack of a political agreement. In Myanmar, the armed groups have resisted attempts to direct aid and investment into their areas because they think the government's intention is to deflect them from their sixty-year demand for a federal political solution and persuade them to settle merely for economic progress. In Palestine too, attempts to focus exclusively on building the Palestinian economy and making the lives of ordinary Palestinians better in material terms have failed in the absence of political progress. Prosperity is not a substitute for a political settlement.

One way of focusing the negotiations and trying to ensure they come to a successful conclusion is to aim to agree on general principles or a framework agreement. This helps to rule things in and rule things out of an eventual, detailed, agreement. In Northern Ireland the government put forward 'Heads of Agreement' in February 1998 that set out the main subjects of a possible deal. Doing so caused plenty of turbulence, particularly with the Republicans who objected to many of their favourite issues being ruled out. But David Trimble correctly says it helped make the Good Friday Agreement possible by setting out the skeleton for the negotiators to flesh out, and ruling certain issues and demands out of the negotiations.

Somehow you have to propel both sides to their bottom lines. Ury and Fisher set out the invaluable idea of a 'best

alternative to no agreement' (BATNA) in 1981. They argued
that to work out what your real bottom line is you have to
think about what the BATNA would be – in other words, how
bad is it going to be for you if you don't get an agreement –
and on that basis work out what compromises you are prepared
to make. As they point out: 'The reason you negotiate is to
produce something better than the results you can obtain
without negotiating.' In negotiating with armed groups it is
sensible to work out what your BATNA is and go straight
there instead of fiddling around with 'negotiating fat' to be
discarded later and complicated tactical games that simply
serve to confuse. Even more important is to work out what
the BATNA of the other side is. In the case of an armed conflict,
you are not trying to buy a car at the lowest price but to save
lives and bring a sustainable end to a civil war. If you concede
a bit more than you needed to, or take a bit longer than absolutely necessary, that doesn't matter much set against the consequences of holding out for a cheaper price and losing the peace.
It is in any case intrinsically difficult to know what the bottom
line of a covert armed group is. Intelligence may give you some
clues but it may also be misleading, as I discovered to my cost
a number of times in the Northern Ireland negotiations. It is
particularly difficult because armed groups have a tendency to
over-negotiate. They often don't realise when the optimum
moment to settle has arrived, in part because they cannot
persuade their own constituency to accept a deal until they
have pushed and pushed beyond endurance. Yasser Arafat was
perhaps the best example of the phenomenon of permanent
negotiation. Even at Camp David he did not want to settle
because he did not know how to sell the deal to the other
Arab states.

Another common problem in bringing a negotiation to a
successful conclusion is the recurrent difficulty of explaining
to the public why a government should be discussing political
issues with a terrorist group at all. The best approach is to
separate negotiations into discussions of technical issues (such

as disarmament and the release of prisoners) which can appropriately take place with the armed group, and discussions of political issues which can be conducted with their political party. In Spain the government tried to draw a clear line between the two. It would discuss 'the consequences of the conflict' with ETA in secret talks, covering demobilisation, decommissioning of weapons, prisoners and exiles, but not political questions. Political issues were to be discussed at a separate 'table' with ETA's political arm Batasuna, and other Basque parties. Sinn Féin urged ETA to accept this division, just as they themselves had distinguished between political negotiations between the parties in Northern Ireland and negotiations on arms between the IRA and the IICD.

In an attempt to save the talks with ETA in August 2006, Jesús Eguiguren and Arnaldo Otegi decided they needed to reach a political pre-accord to convince ETA that the government was not tricking them. As political leaders of the Socialist Party and Batasuna, they invited the nationalist PNV to join them in talks at the Jesuit Sanctuary of Loyola (St Ignatius de Loyola, the founder of the Jesuits, was Basque). Altogether they held twelve meetings and reached the 'Loyola Agreement'. The three leaders agreed to consult their parties and then return to sign the document, but before the agreed date Otegi summoned Eguiguren back to the remote farmhouse where they used to meet, to tell him that he had been overruled by ETA and could not sign without agreement on a new autonomous entity bringing together the Basque coastal provinces and Navarre. The political talks collapsed. Thereafter the political and technical issues became increasingly intertwined as the negotiations came closer to breakdown. ETA demanded progress on the political track before it was prepared to agree to lay down its weapons, and the process ended in a disastrous meeting in an old inn beneath the Jura mountains near the Swiss village of Satigny at 1 a.m. on 22 May 2007. 'Marc', the ETA representative, insisted on the government agreeing to support a referendum in Navarre to join with the Basque

Country before he would make progress on the arms side of the equation. The government simply would not agree. If the two strands get muddled up in this way, it is hard to succeed.

As in any negotiation you need to be able to deploy carrots and sticks. The most obvious leverage a government can apply is military force, but as previous chapters have made clear, that doesn't always work in the way intended. Other forms of internal and external pressure can have an impact. Neighbouring countries that have provided safe haven for the guerrillas (as Venezuela has for the FARC), or countries that have provided ideological and materiel support (as Cuba did for the FMLN) can bring pressure to bear, although there is a limit to how far they will go in pressuring their own clients. Above all the domestic communities that support the guerrillas can have an impact on the armed groups by demanding an end to the violence, as the nationalist Basque community did on ETA.

When it comes to carrots, it is necessary to think about the personal interests of those you are negotiating with as well as the interests of the group. If the outcome of a settlement is going to be a long spell in jail for the leaders of the armed group, then it is not surprising if they are unenthusiastic about reaching an agreement. There needs to be a plan that gives the leaders a future in politics or in some other way meets their ambitions. You also need to think about the foot soldiers, who have different needs and ambitions from their leaders. They too want to be pardoned for their crimes but they also want a small farm, perhaps, or a chance to be retrained for a new trade, or they may want to carry on under arms as part of the national army or in a paramilitary police force. That future needs to be apparent to them if they are going to support their leaders in reaching an agreement.

Whatever you do, as Kissinger observes, 'every negotiation reaches a critical point where it will come rapidly to a conclusion or lapse into stagnation'. The problem is that it is much easier to recognise the critical moment in hindsight. In Mozambique a breakdown led to a breakthrough in 1991.

In the sweltering heat of the Rome summer that year the two sides spent their time exchanging insults. RENAMO accused the government of playing a double game by talking peace in Rome while launching attacks in Mozambique. When the meeting broke up Dhlakama made it clear they would not come back to Rome unless the government stopped its attacks and the 10,000 Zimbabwean troops in the country were withdrawn. The soldiers were there to protect Zimbabwe's vital access to the sea by rail, road and pipeline via Beira and via the Limpopo River. The Italian mediators travelled to Malawi and managed to persuade Dhlakama to resume the talks in November without insisting on the precondition of the withdrawal of Zimbabwean forces, as long as the issue was the first point on the agenda. By December the two sides had agreed on the 'corridors formula' whereby the Zimbabwean troops would be confined to a small strip of territory alongside the railway tracks rather than fighting RENAMO right across the country. They concluded agreements on a ceasefire within the corridors, which were 170 and 330 miles long respectively, and both two miles wide. An International Commission of Inspection was appointed, presided over by an Italian diplomat, with political and military experts from eight countries. As always there were unintended consequences. Hundreds of thousands of desperate refugees massed on the edge of the railway tracks to avoid the fighting elsewhere in the country and, once concentrated in these small areas, there was the new problem of how to feed them. The agreement had only been reached after vigorous debate between the two sides but in the end both made concessions and the atmosphere when they signed was cheerful. It was the first substantial agreement in the talks and it opened up the way to the eventual peace settlement.

In South Africa, de Klerk thinks the turning point was agreement on the Record of Understanding in September 1992. The ANC had broken off the negotiations not just because of the Boipatong massacre, but also because of the wider issue of the way the National Party were handling the talks. De Klerk

254 Talking to Terrorists

continued to promote group rights, which the ANC had no intention of accepting, and the negotiations were stuck. The ANC wanted to see if by shaking them up they could make a new start and force the National Party to rethink its approach. 'The Channel' between Roelf Meyer and Cyril Ramaphosa boiled the ANC's initial fourteen demands down to a handful of issues. When the Cabinet saw the draft Record of Understanding, the 'Old Guard' of conservatives objected. At the subsequent meeting with the ANC, de Klerk let Kobie Coetsee, the minister of law and order, and other conservatives lead the argument against Mandela on the key question of the release of prisoners convicted of murder, so that the hardliners, rather than he himself, would be forced to make the concessions in order to get agreement. When they got to the issue of fencing in Inkatha hostels, de Klerk said disingenuously he had not had time to study the draft of the agreement properly and asked if he could do so at a later date. Mandela replied that of course he could have the time to study it, 'provided you understand that when we leave here to have a press conference I shall say that the meeting has been a total failure'. De Klerk therefore agreed that a working committee should study the issue during the lunch break, and appointed only younger moderates on the government side to the committee. When they reassembled, de Klerk announced that the working committee had approved the document, thus bypassing the 'Old Guard', who were furious. But the Record of Understanding had settled the major issues and the peace process had become irreversible.

The point of no return in a peace process usually occurs when the leaders of the armed group come to see that violence is an impediment to achieving their goals rather than a means of securing them. This apotheosis does not generally happen before they enter a negotiation – which they often do tactically to see what might turn up – but only once they are engaged and can see a political route forward. The conversion is essential if the two sides are to reach a lasting agreement; it is only then that the peace becomes irreversible.

This transformation usually happens when the balance in the insurgent movement shifts from the military wing to the political. Historically the IRA had always been the dominant body and Sinn Féin subordinate to it, but Republicans discovered during the 1981 hunger strike that they could win parliamentary seats by running as Sinn Féin, and adopted the dual strategy of 'the Armalite in one hand and the ballot box in the other'. Gradually the leadership passed from the IRA to Sinn Féin, even though the same people were involved in both organisations. The same thing happened in the Basque Country. ETA had historically been the dominant force and Batasuna merely a political front, but that began to change when the talks with the Spanish government broke down in 2007. Otegi and the other Batasuna leaders had looked on in despair as 'Marc' mishandled the negotiations and then walked out. In the aftermath they started a labyrinthine consultation with the large base of supporters of Basque separatist parties under the 'Izquierda Abertzale' umbrella, which showed that the vast majority wanted peace and progress through politics rather than arms.

At first ETA resisted this conclusion but by clever footwork Otegi and his colleague Rufi Etxeberria managed to consolidate the consensus in such a way that ETA could not resist. It was this that made possible the crucial breakthroughs that brought about the permanent end of the armed conflict. In an interview in November 2008 Otegi said violence had become an obstacle to the political goals of radical nationalism, and in January 2009 he urged that they should 'confront the state on its weak point, the political terrain'. He gained an ally in Eugenio 'Antxon' Etxebeste, ETA's long-term interlocutor with the government in Algeria and subsequent negotiations, who was released from jail in 2004. He said he saw himself engaged in 'another kind of struggle'. This group was known ironically by the hardliners as '*los Gandhis*'. They started a strategy of building alliances with the smaller nationalist parties which had broken away from Batasuna in previous decades over their opposition to violence and these negotiations forced the hand of ETA. In 2009 the Izquierda Abertzale got its worst electoral result ever on the back of the 2006 bomb at Madrid airport. Otegi said 'we know that with 100,000 we don't win a democratic scenario'. To gain power they needed to grow their political support, and that implied an end to the armed struggle.

When groups do not make that transition from being primarily military to being primarily political, peace is not possible. The Tamil Tigers failed to make the leap: the LTTE were always militaristic, and Prabhakaran was never exposed to the outside world or the political realities. He remained a military chieftain surrounded by yes men. His key political lieutenant Anton Balasingham understood the political realities and was able to argue back, but the two men became distanced from each other after Balasingham signed up for the Oslo Declaration in 2002, committing both sides to a federal solution. When he died in 2006, the LTTE was left without any real political arm.

Once the political wings of armed groups enjoy electoral success then it becomes almost impossible for them to go back to violence. Sometimes such political success is seen by others as a disaster for democracy, but if the groups have won the votes fairly, there are no grounds to object. The Maoists in Nepal were expected to come a poor third in the elections to the constituent assembly in 2008, but surprised everyone by winning 229 out of 601 seats, nearly twice as many as their nearest rivals, and in 2008–9 their military leader became prime minister. In Aceh, Irwandi Yusuf, a former GAM leader, was elected governor of the province in the first regional elections after the agreement. More often the political party that succeeds the armed group is runner-up in subsequent elections, but over time they have the chance of building their position and coming to power. In El Salvador the FMLN became the opposition in the first elections after the peace agreement in 1994; by 2000 they had become the largest party in the National Assembly, and in 2009 their candidate was elected president. (Former guerrillas of course do not always make good administrators, and even if they gain power they often get booted out by the electorate later for incompetence.)

It is exactly because you want armed groups to opt for a political route that it is such a bad idea to put obstacles in their way when they try and move in that direction. While it is entirely understandable that democratic governments find repugnant the sight of apologists appearing on TV justifying the most ghastly terrorist atrocities, the right way to deal with them is to answer them politically rather than ban them. Mrs Thatcher's decision not to allow Gerry Adams and Martin McGuinness to appear on British TV in 1988 did not weaken them, and the broadcasters' decision to show them speaking with voiceovers by actors made a mockery of the ban. The banning of Batasuna and the new political parties they tried to create after its banning made the transition from violence to peaceful politics take longer and gave the hardliners in the movement a justification for continued violence because the political route was blocked. Insurgents love to see themselves as victims, and giving them more opportunities to claim victimhood is not a good idea.

Prime ministers and presidents often become convinced that the only way to resolve a conflict is by meeting the leaders of the armed group in person. They think that someone is getting in the way of the armed group understanding their arguments and if only they could talk directly they could persuade them. This is not always a good idea. Kissinger says 'When presidents become negotiators no escape routes are left for diplomacy.' For ten years Tony Blair kept asking Gerry Adams if he could meet the members of the Provisional Army Council. He was certain if he could just sit down with them he could persuade them to take the last step to peace. Adams kept saying yes, he would look at arranging a meeting, but never did. He eventually told me he thought it would be a very bad idea. The people Tony wanted to meet were not much interested in politics and a meeting would probably make them more suspicious rather than less. President Pastrana in Colombia met the leaders of FARC and although initially he enjoyed public support for having done so, when the meetings failed to deliver and the process lost credibility it looked more and more as if he had made a mistake.

While it is usually best for such meetings to happen at the end of a process to ratify an agreement or make a key break-through, rather than at the beginning, a personal intervention by a leader can sometimes make a crucial difference. President Aquino of the Philippines took a big political risk in holding a meeting with Al-Haj Murad, the chairman of the MILF negotiating panel, in Tokyo in 2011. It was a leap of faith, and in the words of one of the negotiators 'one of the few secrets we managed to keep'. The president used his political capital to take the surprise step and it allowed both sides to get over a crucial blockage in the negotiations. If he had tried too early it wouldn't have worked, but the timing was such that it propelled the talks to an agreement after negotiations lasting more than fifteen years.

Even after progress has been made, spoilers can still bring negotiations crashing down. In the Middle East peace process, every time there is a suicide bombing in Israel or the occupied territories, the Israelis break the talks off. This reaction to unwarranted murder is understandable, but the problem is that it gives the keys to the negotiation to the most extreme elements. Rabin's attitude, as described by a former head of Shin Bet, is the right one: 'We will fight terror as if there is no peace process and continue the peace process as if there is no terror.' The spoilers are of course not only on one side, and need not be violent. As Duyvesteyn and Schuurman point out, 'the ongoing expansion of Israeli settlement construction on the West Bank also proved a key obstacle to achieving a lasting political compromise'.

It is the reaction to spoilers that determines whether or not they succeed. The final report of the IICD in Northern Ireland says 'we feel that political leaders should not walk away from the table when extremists commit atrocities, whose aim is designed to derail negotiations . . . Leaders should warn their supporters in advance that such behaviour is possible and stress the need not to react to it.' Duyvesteyn and Schuurman write that 'when spoilers cannot count on significant popular support, their acts of sabotage may strengthen the very peace process they are attempting to destroy. When dissidents belonging to the "Real IRA" detonated a car bomb in Northern Ireland's Omagh mere months after the Good Friday Agreement had been signed, this act of terrorism was popularly perceived to underline the importance of more dialogue, not less.' The bomb was the worst outrage in the thirty years of the Troubles, killing twenty-nine and injuring hundreds. Historically, Unionist leaders would have failed to distinguish between different Republican groups, seen the dissidents as a surrogate for the IRA and collapsed the peace process. To David Trimble's great credit, he did the opposite and used the outrage as a reason to proceed more rapidly with the peace process. Adams and McGuinness, with a bit of persuasion, were also bold. Irish Republicans had never before condemned an attack by another Republican group, but this time they did so in clear terms. The peace process was strengthened rather than derailed. Likewise, rather than derailing the South African peace process as it was intended to do, the 1993 assassination by a white extremist of Chris Hani, the former leader of the armed wing of the ANC, gave it new momentum. In response to the murder the two sides fixed 27 April 1994 as the deadline for elections and determined to reach a final settlement. De Klerk says 'We always managed to over-come the crises because in the final analysis none of the main parties could afford or contemplate the prospect of failure . . . we could not allow horrendous incidents of violence . . . to deflect us from our goal.' Dean Pruitt says 'There are almost always diehard extremists unwilling to negotiate and who seek to overturn any agreement; there may also be extremists on the government side who have a similar outlook. The trick is to produce an agreement that is endorsed by a large enough central coalition, which embraces as many groups as possible on both sides of the conflict, to isolate the fringes and prevent them from acting as spoilers.' As the IICD suggest, leaders should inoculate the public against spoilers in advance by warning of the probability of increased violence during the negotiations, so that they don't lose hope when it happens.

*

However careful you are at avoiding all the traps, sometimes the gap between the two sides is just too wide to be bridged. In Sri Lanka the furthest the government was prepared to go was to offer a federal solution, but it is not clear that even that would have been enough for Prabhakaran. He had famously told his bodyguard to shoot him the moment he gave up the cause of a separate Tamil Eelam. While it is hard to believe he really thought he could achieve an independent state through negotiation, he may have adopted the tactical approach of starting talks to see what options were thrown up. It is now impossible to know what his view might have been, but Balasingham clearly stretched his mandate when he signed up for the federal solution contained in the Oslo Declaration in November 2002. It may of course have been possible to persuade Prabhakaran to go further if the negotiation had been proceeding smoothly. Ram Manikkalingam, President Kumaratunga's adviser, thinks Prabhakaran might have accepted a deal that deferred the question of self-determination to a future date with a transitional period in which a Tamil entity continued to be a part of Sri Lanka; but the negotiations never really managed to progress to a proper discussion of the political issues, despite the best efforts of the Norwegian mediators, because they were constantly bogged down in mutual recriminations about breaches of the ceasefire. Negotiations quite often get dragged off in the direction of fruitless exchanges about what is happening on the battlefield. It is a mistake to let this happen because it poisons the talks and at the same time resolves nothing on the ground. In the ETA talks, 'George' insisted from the very beginning that the negotiations be hermetically sealed and should not be diverted by external events like future bombings, which he knew would take place.

If the gap is too great to bridge directly then negotiators sometimes resort to constructive ambiguity. Robert Cooper writes that 'The function of diplomacy is often to find a formula – frequently an ambiguous form of words – on which everyone can pretend to agree while they wait for something to change . . . which may make the problem easier to solve.' Cronin believes 'Good negotiated agreements in conflicts that are as complicated as terrorist campaigns often have an element of ambiguity that actors can interpret in ways that suit their constituents. Indeed, clarity in the negotiations is not necessarily a desirable goal, as it can actually undermine long-term prospects for peace if carefully orchestrated, precisely worded agreements spark additional conflict.' In Nepal, for instance, the Maoists wanted a republic but the Congress party would not accept the word 'republic' in the twelve-point agreement in 2005. The Maoist leader Bhattarai says 'we had to compromise with them on this issue. But we understood that if we agreed to a neutral term, we could interpret in our own way.' Ambiguity solved the problem, at least temporarily.

Alfredo Rubalcaba concedes there were 'many ambiguities' in the pre-accords with ETA, and 'everyone interpreted them as they wanted'. Eguiguren argued that 'for me the lack of definition was positive; it is true that ambiguity could generate misunderstandings, but I held the conviction that in the Basque issue the lack of definition was fundamental for arriving at an agreement'. When challenged at the time, Eguiguren even said the agreements he had reached with ETA were 'understandings', not pre-accords. ETA unfortunately didn't share the government's view on ambiguity. They thought the government was failing to implement its undertakings and that helped tip them back into violence. So while ambiguity can help get you out of a jam it is a short-term solution and sooner or later it will become destructive.

This was certainly true in Northern Ireland, where constructive ambiguity made the Good Friday Agreement possible, but it became destructive over time. We could have sat for three years rather than three days and nights if we had insisted on resolving the issue of decommissioning of IRA weapons there and then. The Unionists and the Republicans just weren't ready to reach an agreement on it. Instead we had to reach for language that could be interpreted in different ways by the two sides. For the Unionists it meant that the IRA would have to disarm before Sinn Féin could join the government, and for the Republicans it meant that the Unionists would have to demonstrate they would share power before the IRA would decommission their weapons. The ambiguity got us to an agreement, but by 2003 Unionist support for it had declined dramatically because the IRA had not disarmed as the Unionists had expected, and low-level paramilitary and criminal activity was continuing. We felt that we had to address the ambiguity or lose the agreement, so Tony Blair made a speech in Belfast in which he demanded that Sinn Féin choose between the Armalite and the ballot box. We were nervous about the response but Adams called me a few days later and said, to my relief, it was a good speech. To my surprise he asked me if I would draft his response. I tried to write in Republican-speak and composed a passage that ended with 'So if you ask me do I envisage a future without an IRA? The answer is obvious. The answer is yes.' I turned on the television a few days later to see Adams deliver the speech unchanged. We had made the crucial breakthrough by squeezing the ambiguity out of the process.

Ambiguity is one way of bridging an apparently unbridgeable gap, but given its dangers, negotiators usually have to seek other solutions if they want to reach a lasting agreement. According to Ury and Fisher, 'Skill at inventing options is one of the most useful assets a negotiator can have.' When you run into a blockage someone has to come up with new ideas to move the process forward and it is rarely the armed group that does so. Crocker writes that 'When faced with "an intractable logjam" the options available to a mediator are finite. You can try to engineer a "split-the-difference" compromise; you can seek a procedural solution (e.g. elections or arbitration); you can explore compensatory payments or side deals to alter the position of one or more parties; or, you can modify the agenda and redefine or restructure the issues in dispute.' There are two ways to do the last of these. One, he says, is to 'break the problem down into pieces and go after them systematically – solving some, redefining others, handling the remainder by trade-offs between them. The other way to change the structure of the issues in a conflict is to increase their number and tie them together into a larger agenda. Linking one complex problem to another adds massively to the size and complexity of the negotiating burden. But it also redefines and increases the number of relevant "parties", and increases the long-term odds of building a situation in which everyone wins.' Henry Kissinger argues that 'linkage' can work in negotiations where progress on one issue is linked to progress on another. It is usually too risky because it jams up the negotiation, but Crocker managed it skilfully in the talks on Cuban withdrawal from Angola and Namibian independence in the late 1980s, where the promise of the latter secured the former.

Haysom too argues for package deals: 'In South Africa, in the final hours before the expiry of the deadline for agreeing on a new constitution, a number of emotive issues, including mother-tongue education and the property clause, were outstanding. The parties' mandates had been exhausted on each of them. It would not have been possible to reach a settlement if each issue had been negotiated separately. A final solution became possible only when all these intractable issues were collected together and a package of concessions was agreed in terms of which the parties were able to share a balance of losses and gains.'

If package deals and ambiguity can't solve the problem then

you have to look for other imaginative solutions. Towards the end of the South African negotiations the key dividing issue was between power-sharing, which is what the National Party wanted, and majority rule, which the ANC wanted. The idea to bridge the gap came from an unexpected source: Joe Slovo, chairman of the South African Communist Party and long a bugbear of the National Party. He turned out, in the words of the journalist Allister Sparks, to be 'a sheep in wolf's clothing'. Writing in the *African Communist* in August 1992, Slovo suggested a 'sunset clause' that would provide for compulsory power-sharing between the ANC and the National Party for a number of years and then fall away. He wrote 'we are not dealing with a defeated enemy' and it would not be possible to force an unconditional surrender across the negotiating table. The ANC should distinguish between 'qualitative' and 'quantitative' compromises, strategic retreat versus a surrender of principle. He argued that a temporary commitment to share power would be a strategic retreat, as would a general amnesty and an offer of job security to the white Civil Service to stop it obstructing change. The two provisions would be prices worth paying to ensure a smooth transition. The article caused a storm of controversy within the ANC, but coming as it did from someone with impeccable revolutionary credentials, it was hard to dismiss. On the back of it the ANC offered de Klerk a Government of National Unity for three to five years, and guarantees for white civil servants, police and military personnel that they could keep their jobs or take generous retirement terms. It was an irresistible offer for most of de Klerk's supporters.

Haysom describes the advantages of 'sunset' and 'sunrise' clauses like this when there are issues of fundamental importance to one party that are unacceptable to the other, at least in the short term. A sunset clause allows for 'introducing a provision which will lapse after a period of time (say five to ten years); introducing an expedient provision that provides reassurance to the other side, but will not become an enduring feature of the country's political and economic life . . . A sunrise clause on the other hand allows for enshrining some essential element of a party's political programme in the settlement and as a central feature of the future dispensation; deferring implementation temporarily in the interests of creating the conditions for transition; and letting both sides claim advantage from the measure, the one in the short term and the other in the long term.'

The other way to deal with a blockage is to think laterally and come up with a completely different answer to the two alternatives lying on the table. Robert Cooper cites Jean Monnet, one of the architects of the EEC, saying that 'if you have a problem you can't solve, enlarge the context', which is what we tried to do in Northern Ireland when we were stuck on the issue of decommissioning of IRA weapons. I spoke to a British general who had served in Bosnia and Kosovo who described the system there, where they had put the weapons of the warring sides in dumps, sealed them and then regularly inspected them to ensure the seals had not been tampered with. I went to see Adams and McGuinness in a safe house in West Belfast and suggested the idea to them. They said it was a non-starter and would certainly be unacceptable to the IRA Army Council. A few weeks later they came to a formal negotiating session and proposed the idea to us. We agreed to consider it without indicating we had ever heard the idea before. Sometimes it helps if you can suggest ideas to the other side that they put forward as their own.

There will always be a need for ingenuity in the closing stage of a negotiation. When we reached the end of the Northern Ireland process and Ian Paisley had finally agreed to meet Gerry Adams, we remained blocked on one issue: where they would sit. Paisley wanted to sit opposite the Republicans so they looked like rivals rather than friends, but Adams insisted on sitting next to Paisley so they looked like equals and colleagues. We couldn't find a way through this blockage until a bright Northern Ireland Office official came up with the idea of building a special diamond-shaped table so they could sit at one end with just an apex between them, both next to each other and opposite each other at the same time.

Sometimes however, when you have exhausted all the imaginative alternatives, there is no choice but to concede to the other side's position if you want an agreement. Ahtisaari's Aceh talks were blocked in their final stages on the GAM's insistence that they be able to run in the elections as a local party while Indonesian law required a political party to demonstrate that it had functioning branches in at least half of the provinces in the country, and in at least half of the districts within each of those provinces. This provision was specifically designed to prevent the emergence of local parties which might lead to the disintegration of the country. In July 2005, as the talks were drawing to their close, the Indonesian government started to look for a compromise. President Yudhoyono and Vice President Jusuf Kalla met the leaders of the major parties and agreed that they would all promise to nominate GAM members in the elections in Aceh so that they could run as members of their parties without the law being changed. When this was rejected by GAM, the government then offered to loan members of existing parties to GAM so they could establish branches in other provinces. GAM rejected this too, saying it was 'a sweetheart deal that excludes the possibility of other political parties . . . The peace talks are not about an arrangement that ensures that GAM gain power in Aceh, but about introducing genuine democracy to Aceh.' At the very last moment, having run out of imaginative compromises, the government agreed to allow GAM, exceptionally, to run as a party in the forthcoming local elections and then to change the law to allow the creation of local political parties in Aceh. This concession clinched the deal.

Even when you succeed in bridging the substantive gap between the two sides, there are still barriers that can prevent you arriving at a lasting agreement.

First you need to decide how detailed you want an

agreement to be. Everything needs to be on the table for a negotiation, but not everything needs to be in the agreement. It may be best to aim for a relatively brief framework agreement which can remain at the level of principles. Of course one side may fear that it will be stuck at the stage of principles and never get beyond it. Tom Friedman writes that in the Middle East, 'The Palestinians are terrified an interim deal will become final and the Israelis are terrified a final deal will become interim.' Nonetheless many successful negotiations have ended in a framework agreement, such as Jimmy Carter's Camp David Agreement between Anwar Sadat and Menachem Begin. But if such an agreement is to be successful it needs to be definitive, so that points cannot be reopened later, even if the detail is subject to further negotiation.

There is a case for the agreement being detailed in order to prevent its implementation being snagged by ambiguity about what was agreed, but it is also true that too much detail can bring down agreements. Isoaho and Tuuli describe how the UN reacted to the demand by both sides in Cyprus for consensus on all issues before moving forward with the accord: 'The UN had identified some seventy pieces of federal legislation that should be agreed upon as part of the comprehensive peace agreement, but the newly elected Cypriot leader Tassos Papadopoulos insisted that nothing should be left for negotiation after settlement and unification. Therefore, the mediation team was forced to find agreement on over 190 pieces of federal legislation – a meticulous task that required a lot of external help but was eventually finalised.' It was, however, the very detail of the resulting Annan Plan that brought about its downfall. The Greek Cypriot leadership called for a vote against the UN draft agreement in the referendum in 2004 on the basis of points of detail that had been added by the UN, and it was defeated.

The agreement between the Philippines government of President Gloria Arroyo and the MILF in 2008 failed for similar reasons. The government was politically weak and desperate to secure a success. As a result there was insufficient consultation with the public. The degree of detail in the draft gave opponents something to challenge in the courts and they argued it had not followed the correct procedure for constitutional change. The Supreme Court upheld their challenge and the government walked away from the agreement. When the two sides returned to the table under a new president, they wisely decided against a comprehensive agreement and instead concluded a framework deal in 2013 that left much of the detail to be worked out later by joint commissions, including annexes on police reform and demobilisation and disarmament.

If an agreement is going to stick, both sides need to carry their constituencies with them as the negotiation proceeds. But a negotiation can all too easily become a bubble where those involved are cut off from the outside world. They are deliberating over matters of life and death, after all, and the negotiations can become intense and completely absorbing. If they do become isolated from their supporters, the two sides will find it very hard to win support for the outcome. David Trimble gave the impression that he rarely even told his senior colleagues what he was agreeing to, with the consequence that he often had to walk away from agreements he had reached in the face of subsequent opposition from his own supporters. Ian Paisley's DUP were far more accomplished at keeping everyone marching together, briefing the leadership of the party and their MPs on every major advance. Sinn Féin were even better, with a complex briefing tree to ensure that all the members of Sinn Féin and the IRA knew about each step forward before it became public. They had the advantage of the discipline of a covert group, which helped to avoid leaks.

GAM prepared their constituency insufficiently for the Helsinki agreement and their supporters were shocked when they finally learned of the concessions that had been made. On the other side, Vice President Jusuf Kalla did a better job of selling the agreement aggressively. When former president

Megawati attacked it, saying 'We have surrendered to GAM' and boycotted the Independence Day celebrations, Kalla told members of Megawati's party they should go to Aceh and 'fight the war themselves' if they didn't like the agreement. F. W. de Klerk says he was greatly assisted by the breakaway of the far right wing of the National Party in 1982, and the remaining more liberal National Party MPs felt frustrated by the slow pace of progress under P. W. Botha. 'When I told the caucus soon after my election as party leader in February 1989 that we needed to make a "quantum leap", the overwhelming response was "Jump, FW, jump!"' He also took great care to keep the whole Cabinet fully involved. 'We held bush conferences where we thrashed out the broad lines of the approach we would take, and I regularly reported back to my colleagues on the progress that we had made and the obstacles that we encountered.' When right-wing opposition to the negotiations threatened to derail them in 1992, de Klerk called a referendum to secure a mandate for his negotiating position and energetically campaigned for a 'yes for change' vote. The strong result gave him the support he needed to overcome the objections and adopt a bold approach to reaching an agreement, rather than constantly needing to look over his shoulder. If you decide to go for an agreement there is no point in being apologetic or half-hearted. The only way to sell it is to do so aggressively.

Politics sometimes makes that difficult to do. There was briefly a Sinhalese political consensus for peace but it rapidly evaporated in the 2000s as the country seemed to be marooned in a situation of 'no war and no peace'. The atrocities committed by the Tigers fed Sinhalese nationalism, but more than that, the rivalry between President Kumaratunga and Prime Minister Wickremasinghe led to them treating the peace process as a political football, and both were eventually outflanked by the Rajapaksa family and a more extreme form of Sinhalese nationalism opposed to the peace process altogether. Ironically Wickremasinghe would have won the presidency if it had not been for Prabhakaran's tactics. The Tamil Tigers had never boycotted a vote before, but Prabhakaran decided to enforce a ban on Tamils voting in 2005 because he felt Wickremasinghe would enjoy too much international support and that Rajapaksa would be a weaker opponent. Rajapaksa squeaked to victory by 50.3 per cent to 48.4 per cent. Balasingham had been opposed to the boycott but he was dying of cancer and his relationship with Prabhakaran was fading by that time.

Perhaps even more dangerous for an agreement than changes in domestic politics is a change in what Marxists call 'the correlation of forces'. When the talks began in Sri Lanka there was a mutually hurting military stalemate but by 2004 things had changed. Colonel Karuna, who commanded the LTTE forces in the east of the country and had originally been Prabhakaran's bodyguard, was part of the Tigers' negotiating team, and the first meeting in Thailand had a major impact on him, opening his eyes for the first time to the outside world. At the Oslo meeting he sided with Balasingham on the issue of federalism, and this created a gap between him and Prabhakaran. Probably more important than that ideological difference, however, was Karuna's liking for women and the good life and the fact that the ceasefire gave him an opportunity to break away without being immediately killed. He defected to the government side, the LTTE forces in the east disintegrated, and thousands of their cadres left the ranks. A military option now began to look considerably more attractive for the government. As so often, one incident tipped the country back into full-scale war. On 20 July 2006 the Tigers closed an irrigation sluice at Mavil Aru, south of the crucial port of Trincomalee, cutting water to 15,000 villagers and thousands of hectares of paddy fields. In response government forces launched 'the final war' which didn't end until Prabhakaran and his fellow leaders had been killed and the LTTE comprehensively defeated.

Splits within the armed group can also imperil a negotiation during its final stages. The talks between the Spanish government and ETA failed in 2006 because ETA demanded that Navarre be included in Basque territory, something the Spanish government could not agree to even if it had wanted to, because it depended on the will of the people of Navarre. ETA took such a tough position on the issue relatively late in the process because the organisation was split and hardliners had taken over. 'Marc' joined the talks and displaced the more moderate and more experienced 'George' as the lead negotiator. Marc was the political leader of ETA and had just won a power struggle with two military leaders, Txeroki and Ata, and thrown them out of the collective leadership of the organisation. When he came to Oslo in October he took an increasingly aggressive line, accused the government of non-compliance and attempted to merge the political and technical talks into one so that ETA could negotiate both. He warned the government side that ETA had a judge in their sights for assassination. When they met again in Oslo in mid-December, George had disappeared altogether and, unbeknownst to the government, ETA had already given the order to launch an attack in Spain. At lunch Marc said to Eguiguren that if the talks broke down 'it would be Vietnam' and the government would be responsible for many deaths. The two sides agreed to meet again in January, but on 30 December the bomb went off in the car park of Terminal Four at Madrid airport. The government was caught completely unawares; in the past ETA had always announced it was ending the ceasefire before it resumed attacks. Bizarrely the organisation had clearly seen the bomb simply as a warning and did not regard it as a breach of the ceasefire. They wrote to Zapatero offering to maintain the ceasefire and saying they were ready to continue with the peace process. The government replied saying it was only possible to restart the process if ETA gave up its weapons. There were further intermittent attempts at talks before this phase of the process was finally ended by Marc at the meeting near Geneva in 2007. He was arrested less than a year later in May 2008 and died in a French prison in 2013.

Even if there is a breakdown it is important to stay in contact, to prevent the bicycle hitting the ground. After the breakdown in Spain, Batasuna gradually asserted itself over ETA and built up a new approach. The mediators who had helped before were still engaged and able to get things moving again. When the process resumed, the approach adopted was completely different. This time a solution depended on an appeal to ETA from international figures from outside prepared to take a risk to play a role in ending Europe's last armed conflict. A group led by Kofi Annan and Gro Harlem Brundtland launched an appeal at the Aiete Conference in San Sebastián in October 2011 to ETA to end its armed campaign and to the Spanish and French governments to engage with them to make it a reality. Almost immediately ETA announced the end of its armed struggle, a historic moment.

When negotiations approach what might be their final stage, one side almost always comes up with last-minute demands and it can look as though the process is about to collapse. In August 1993, the Palestinian side abruptly rejected the draft agreement both sides had been working on in Oslo and put forward twenty completely new demands. The two sides met in the flat of the Norwegian foreign minister in Paris, and the Israelis persuaded them to drop most of the twenty points, but when they put forward yet further new proposals the Israelis broke off the negotiations. In response the Palestinians came up with a new, more reasonable draft. The two sides negotiated through the night on 20 August and finally reached a satisfactory settlement. It is important not to lose your nerve in these final stages when the other side appears to be reopening everything you have already agreed. All they are doing is testing the limits of the possible. The best approach is to stay calm, and even offer a few sweeteners so the other side feels that it has won something in the last stages, and signs the agreement with a smile rather than a grimace.

Another problem that can derail an agreement just as it is falling into place is the insistence by the government on the dissolution of the armed group. While it may seem logical enough to demand the disappearance of a terrorist organisation if there is to be a lasting peace, it is not always sensible. Sometimes you want the group to stay in place to protect 'the brand' rather than some new upstart group taking over the name and starting violence all over again. It is also sometimes better that the group remains, at least for a time, in order to control disarmament and demobilisation rather than to allow it to disintegrate into anarchy. Normally in such negotiations you will not be able to bring the entire organisation into a peace deal but only a part of it; some units will break away. That may not matter as long as you bring more than half with you and they bring the brand with them. In that way, even if fighting continues the political impetus will have gone.

The last and perhaps most difficult problem in concluding an agreement is the question of who will go first. Armed groups always worry that once they have given up their arms, their main negotiating leverage, the government side will fail to deliver on the promises they have made. There is often good reason for this fear, built on historical experience. In that case there needs to be some guarantee built into the agreement that fundamental change will not only happen but will also not be reversed by subsequent governments. Neither side wants to go first because it does not trust the other to reciprocate. In order to get through the impasse in Northern Ireland – in which the Unionists did not trust the Republicans to lay down their weapons and insisted they must do so before entering govern- ment, while the Republicans did not trust the Unionists to share power once they had given up their weapons – we broke down what each side had to do into small steps, and designed a complicated ballet in which a step by one side would be followed by a step by the other, so that neither did anything irreversible until they were confident that the other would follow through on their undertakings. This sequencing of alter- nating steps of disarmament and political change is a common feature of most agreements.

In the end, though, it is only possible to get to a lasting agreement when the two sides succeed in escaping the zero-sum game. If one side feels it has been hard done by in the agreement, it will not rest until it can reopen it, just like Germany after the Versailles Treaty. Gabriella Blum and Robert Mnookin warn against falling 'prey to the zero-sum, or fixed-pie fallacy – the assumption that a conflict is purely distributive, and that any gain by one necessarily poses a loss to the other . . . There is more often than we think the possibility of joint gain.' In the Northern Ireland talks the Republicans were much cleverer than the Unionists in handling this problem. Gerry Adams would come out of a negotiating session smiling and the Unionists would be convinced they had lost, regardless of the substance. The most bizarre example of this was the 1994 ceasefire. For three decades the Unionists had been demanding the IRA stop its violence, but when they actually did so it was the Republicans who drove around town honking their car horns and waving their flags in triumph while the Unionists sank into a deep gloom, convinced they had been sold out by the government in a secret deal. Adams only finally realised in 2005 that if the agreement was to stick, he needed to sell it not only to his own community but also to the Unionists. He had to stop trying to win, as if in a game. Once he had grasped this point he did a very effective job at reassuring the Unionists and we finally got to a sustainable agreement. The point seems so self-evident that I was thunderstruck when, after I repeated it at a press conference in the run-up to the Aiete Conference in the Basque Country, I was lambasted in the right-wing Spanish press. They demanded that the government must be the winners and ETA must be the losers. I cannot fathom how that can be the basis for a lasting peace. Even in Nigeria after the Biafran war, in which the Biafrans had been comprehensively defeated by the military, the government was wise enough to put up posters all over the country insisting there were 'no winners and no losers'.

Governments must also be prepared to pre-sell agreements if they are to work. The dilemma is that on the one hand you need to start selling the agreement to the public, and on the other you have to convince the other side in the final stages of the negotiation how difficult it is going to be for you to make any further concessions. Trying to reconcile the two aims is tricky, and in the last phases of a negotiation governments need to change their rhetoric and talk up the chances of agreement and the need to work with the armed group. There need in fact to be two matching narratives, as the armed group needs to convince its supporters that it is not simply surrendering, and to explain why all the suffering and death were worthwhile. The government's narrative needs to be different but not contradict that of the armed group. In practice each side needs to write the other side's victory speech. We spent a good deal of time in the last weeks of the Northern Ireland negotiations agreeing press lines with both Republicans and Unionists to make sure that they were not directly contradicting each other about what had been agreed.

For the government the most difficult task of all is persuading the public why it is necessary to swallow unpalatable compromises with terrorists. The public naturally want peace on their terms. The historian Malcolm Deas says of negotiations with the FARC in Colombia that President Santos's opponent 'Uribe offers the peace that Colombians want and can't have [with no concessions]. Santos offers the peace they don't want, but might have.' It is only possible to make really difficult concessions, like releasing prisoners with blood on their hands, in the context of a larger package where the public weigh the unpopular concessions against the overall gain of peace.

At the last minute there is sometimes an outbreak of 'buyer's remorse'. As they signed the El Salvador agreement, Schafik Handal asked Joaquín Villalobos, 'What have we done? This is the end, but without definition.' The agreement had failed to bring about the social revolution Handal had fought for, and he was terrified of being accused of selling out. He needed a continuing conflict to maintain his support. The FMLN went ahead and signed the deal anyway, despite his misgivings.

The final moment came in Mexico City in January 1992. President Cristiani shook hands with the FMLN commanders. Joaquín Villalobos had his photograph taken with General Vargas, both with big smiles on their faces, and they fought back tears as they embraced. In twelve years of conflict more than 75,000 people had been killed and millions driven from their homes. After the signing ceremony the FMLN commanders flew back to El Salvador on board the Mexican president's plane *Emiliano Zapata*, and asked James LeMoyne, then a *New York Times* journalist, to accompany them as a witness. The commanders started crying as they entered Salvadoran airspace. They had not been back to their home country legally for decades. But nothing had been done to prepare for their arrival and at San Salvador airport there was only a lone, nervous soldier clutching an M16 rifle, staring at them, unsure whether to shoot. He decided not to. They formed a caravan of cars driving into San Salvador where they were put up at the Spanish and French embassies. A huge rally was held in the main square where some of the worst massacres had taken place. The guerrillas came out of the hills to celebrate, even though the amnesty had yet to be agreed. LeMoyne reports one band of rebels leapt into a battered Toyota pickup and drove down the highway singing revolutionary songs and waving at the soldiers at checkpoints. When the soldiers waved back they realised there really was peace. They joined thousands of others celebrating in the city centre. The government took over one plaza, and there was agreement they had the best fireworks. The guerrillas took over another, and all agreed they had the best bands. Conga lines formed where government sharpshooters had picked off demonstrators in the past, and the cathedral was draped with a huge banner with the face of Farabundo Martí, the founder of the Communist Party. Villalobos, who had been the target of a designated CIA team for years, had his photograph taken with the US ambassador at a party at the American Embassy. At the beginning of the party the FMLN leaders stayed at one end of the room and the military at the other. After ten minutes, like teenagers at a dance, their inhibitions fell away and they got together. They had known each other at school and university, and they were able to pick up acquaintance where they had left off.

Sometimes the end is declared when you least expect it. We had not anticipated that the meeting between Ian Paisley and Gerry Adams in May 2007 would be seen as the end of the peace process, but the media decided the picture was irresistible and ran their obituaries of 'the Troubles'. I only realised it was finally over myself when a few months later we attended the opening session of the new Assembly in Stormont. As I came down from the balcony where I had been sitting with Tony Blair and Bertie Ahern, a colleague told me that the top leadership of the IRA had been sitting a few rows away, even though we didn't recognise them. In Nepal, it was the sudden public appearance of the Maoist leader Prachanda in May 2006. The government flew the Maoist leaders to Kathmandu by helicopter from the provincial town where they had been holding a political training session, and their first press conference at the president's official residence after thirty-five years of clandestinity led the media to declare that peace had arrived, even though there were many crises still ahead.

At the end of the Oslo process, the issue was a gun. Mohamed Heikal, an Egyptian journalist, writes that in the preparations for the signing ceremony at the White House, the chief of protocol came to the Palestinian delegation's hotel and asked Arafat to wear civilian clothes at the event. Arafat refused, saying nobody would recognise him in a suit. They then had to decide what they were going to do with the Smith & Wesson revolver that Arafat always carried. He initially suggested he would take it to the White House, as 'the revolution never surrenders its arms'; but he was told he would be frisked by White House security. Another idea was to take the gun but leave the ammunition at the hotel; a third suggestion was to hand the gun to Clinton as part of the event. Arafat was eventually persuaded to leave it at the hotel. The reaction to the ceremony in Israel gave a foretaste of the problems to come. A crowd of tens of thousands gathered in Tel Aviv's central square, with some people crying for joy. The author Amos Oz gave a speech to the crowd ending with 'and death shall rule no more'. Netanyahu, however, addressing Peres in a speech in the Knesset, said 'You are even worse than Chamberlain. He imperilled the safety of other people, but you are doing it to your own people.'

Manoeuvring a negotiation into the endgame and reaching a lasting agreement requires skill and luck. You need to be able to push the parties to their real bottom lines and bridge the gap between the two bottom lines, often by way of constructive ambiguity or by coming up with an imaginative solution that enlarges the context of an intractable stand-off where the two sides are locking horns. The key turning point is when the armed group finally sees the prospect of political success and realises its weapons are an obstacle rather than the key to success. If the two sides can see off the attempts of spoilers to derail the negotiations and escape the trap of the zero-sum game while carrying their constituency with them, then there is the prospect of success; but it is still far from inevitable that a negotiation will end with a successful agreement. Even if it does, an agreement is only the beginning of a peace process, and that is when you have to redouble your efforts. If we thought we had resolved the problem of Northern Ireland when we took off from Stormont in our helicopters on the morning of Good Friday 1998, we were sadly mistaken. It took another nine years to implement the agreement and get to a lasting peace, and it will take many more years than that before the problem of sectarianism is resolved.

CHAPTER NINE

Only Implementation Creates Trust

I have discovered the secret that after climbing a great hill, one only finds that there are many more hills to climb.

Nelson Mandela

Signing an agreement is not the same as making peace. An agreement does not make the two sides trust each other – indeed they have an agreement precisely because they don't trust each other. It is only when they both start delivering on the promises they have made by implementing the agreement that trust begins, gradually, to develop. The hard work therefore starts once you have signed the agreement which, as Martti Ahtisaari says, is simply what 'enables the process to begin. If the mediation process has been successful, it should give the parties the necessary building blocks to start working towards a peaceful society.'

What happened to the Oslo Accords is a salutary warning of what can transpire if a breakthrough agreement is not implemented or sold to the public enthusiastically. When the accords were announced in August 1993 there was a wave of jubilation, especially amongst the Palestinian population, but no one made a serious effort to sell the agreement to the Israeli public. Ron Pundak says 'Peres and Rabin made a big mistake in not communicating to the Israeli and Palestinian parties, immediately upon signing the Oslo Accord, the fact that this new stage manifested a dramatic transformation of Israeli policy.' Support began to ebb following terrorist attacks in the heart of Tel Aviv and elsewhere in the country, and by 2004 only 26 per cent of Israelis supported the Oslo process, and the figure was probably even lower on the Palestinian side.

There were four major reasons why Oslo was not implemented as intended. Firstly, if Rabin had not been assassinated and if Netanyahu's Likud party had not won the elections in 1996, there would have been a better chance of the necessary strong leadership to deliver Oslo. According to the historian Avi Shlaim, the return to power of Likud 'dealt another body blow to the Oslo peace process. From the very beginning the Likud had been bitterly opposed to the Labour government's land-for-peace deal with the PLO. Netanyahu himself repeatedly denounced the accord as a violation of the historic right of the Jewish people to the Land of Israel and as a mortal danger to their security.' Secondly, if Arafat had been able and willing to build a functioning and clean administration, the Palestinian side would have had greater legitimacy with both ordinary Israelis and ordinary Palestinians. Thirdly, if the violence had reduced rather than increased in the aftermath of the agreement as different factions vied to kill it off, ordinary Israelis would have more confidence that this was a permanent peace rather than a tactical truce. And finally, if the Israeli government under Netanyahu had not continued to expand settlements, the Palestinians might have believed the Israelis were serious about a two-state solution.

The easiest way to kill off an agreement straight away is to fail to deliver on promises made, which is what happened to the agreement between ETA and the Spanish government in 2006. As in the case of Oslo the fault lay on both sides. ETA's declaration of a permanent ceasefire in March 2006 was met by celebration in the Basque Country, but instead of acting, Zapatero announced a period of 'verification' of the ceasefire, which had not been discussed with the organisation. On the basis of his experience in Northern Ireland, Gerry Adams wrote to Zapatero urging him not to leave too long a gap between the ceasefire and implementation. If the period between the

declaration of the ceasefire and the beginning of political negotiations is too long, the armed group can lose hope and the
chance of recurring violence increases.

The Spanish government had agreed that in response to the
ETA declaration Zapatero would make a statement to
Parliament, but when he finally did so in June, instead of
delivering it in the parliamentary chamber as ETA had expected,
he made it in a vestibule outside, known as the 'Salon of Lost
Steps'. The statement contained many of the elements that had
been agreed between the two sides, including the commitment
'to respect the decisions that Basque citizens freely adopt', but
instead of referring to 'Euskal Herria', which is what ETA had
expected, Zapatero referred to 'Euskadi'. This was of enormous
significance for the Basques. 'Euskal Herria' incorporates all
the Basque lands, including Navarre, whereas 'Euskadi' refers
only to the three provinces along the Bay of Biscay. When ETA
complained about these unilateral changes, the government's
explanation was that Zapatero had been speaking from memory
rather than from a written text. Understandably ETA dismissed
the excuse as ridiculous. They also complained about Zapatero's
failure to secure agreement with the PP opposition on a 'Pacto
del Estado', which would give them some reassurance that the
agreement would be implemented even if the socialist government fell. For the government's part, they felt that ETA too
had failed to deliver on its promises. The armed group continued
to infiltrate commandos and arms into Spain, and extortion
and *kale borroka* (street violence) persisted. At a ceremony on
the 'Day of the Basque Soldier', three hooded ETA representatives fired guns into the air before disappearing into the crowd.
This initial breach of trust by both sides became mutually
reinforcing.

A similar problem of non-implementation brought down the
first Aceh agreement. The Humanitarian Pause in 2000
depended for its verification on a Joint Committee on Security
Modalities (JSC) and a Security Modalities Monitoring team
(TMMK) made up of appointees from each side approved by

the other and charged with investigating violations. They set up their base in the Kuala Tripa hotel in Bandar Aceh, the only hotel in the Acehnese capital. The HD Centre established its office on the third floor, and put GAM on the floor above and the government on the floor below. There was, however, a lack of clarity in the agreement as to exactly what would happen on the ground. The government believed the security forces could still engage in routine patrols and they refused to withdraw the army to barracks. The JSC committee structure lacked any real authority and relied on the good faith of the belligerents themselves, with the GAM and the Indonesian military investigating breaches by their own forces, which led to vetoes by one side or the other and a rapid loss of credibility. When the monitors confronted military commanders on the ground they were told that the Humanitarian Pause was 'generals' business' and had nothing to do with them. In March 2001 a member of the TMMK was killed along with his driver and an accompanying human-rights lawyer, and the force was withdrawn.

The signing of the subsequent Cessation of Hostilities Agreement in December 2002 was greeted with popular enthusiasm in Aceh but fared no better. The JSC was reinforced with international monitors from Thailand and the Philippines. The impreciseness about what had been agreed bedevilled the implementation process from the beginning, and within a week each side was accusing the other of major violations. The government started arresting GAM speakers at rallies, and GAM began importing weapons. It had agreed to hand over its weapons but didn't want to give up its main bargaining chip and said it would only do so simultaneously with army withdrawal. The army refused. GAM proposed to hand over 20 per cent of their weapons if 20 per cent of the army relocated as a first step. The army reasonably asked how they would know what constituted 20 per cent, given that they did not know how many weapons there were in total. For their part the military said they needed 220 'temporary posts' and had set up fifty new military posts since the beginning of December. Feelings got increasingly heated on both sides. The army thought GAM was using the breathing space to regroup and reposition itself and started organising spontaneous demonstrations at JSC field monitoring centres. In one incident in March the demonstrators beat the GAM representative on the joint team unconscious, burned their vehicles and set fire to their office. Army personnel were seen handing out banners and placards, and thirty army trucks had brought the demonstrators to the site in the first place. In response the JSC withdrew its observers to the capital and Aceh degenerated back into open warfare.

David Gorman was responsible for the implementation of the agreement on the ground and witnessed the peace process falling apart. He had noticed better-equipped and better-organised special police and army special forces in uniform arriving to replace the ill-disciplined soldiers in camouflage pants, rock and roll T-shirts and flip flops who had previously manned the checkpoints. It became harder and harder to conduct meetings with communities around the island as bombs started going off and villages were burned down. When martial law was declared in May 2003, Gorman and his wife were arrested by the police at their headquarters in the Kuala Tripa hotel. The police said they were taking them to the police station to protect them from GAM assassination attempts, but he knew them well and the arrest was sprinkled with jokey exchanges. At the police station they were interrogated. Why did they support the GAM? What did they know about bomb-making equipment? At the end Gorman and his wife were detained. Gorman called his boss Martin Griffiths, who immediately called the American Embassy in Jakarta and begged them to do something to get the couple out of jail. Gorman overheard the police gossiping about the imminent arrival of the chief of the national police, and told his captors he had to go home and change in order to meet him, and the police reluctantly agreed, sending him off with two armed escorts. Back at the hotel Gorman called the co-ordinating minister, Yudhoyono, who gave him an amber light to remain and keep the process going as far as he could. Gorman stayed on the island for a further month, followed everywhere by a plain-clothes policeman with a bad limp who struggled to keep up with him. Gorman used to wait for him, but in the end the man asked him just to tell him where he was going. In May Gorman went on holiday and when he arrived back the authorities turned him around and sent him back on the same plane he had arrived on. He appealed again to Yudhoyono, who this time said it was just too complicated. The agreement was irretrievably broken.

The paradox is that a negotiator sometimes needs ambiguity to get to an agreement, but if the agreement is too ambiguous it may fall apart in implementation, particularly if there is a lack of clarity about practical issues like weapons or the disengagement of forces. On the other hand, the very detail in a lengthy agreement can cause disagreements when it comes to implementation. Canadian academic Fen Osler Hampson says 'A settlement indicates the direction the parties must move if they are to consolidate the peace, but it usually does not tell them how to get there, except in very general terms. There is usually plenty of ambiguity in an agreement because "ambiguity is the mother of compromise".' Details such as arrangements on arms and demobilisation are 'fertile ground for misunderstanding and delays', and there is therefore an argument for keeping it simple: 'A peace agreement has to be as simple as the instructions you get for home appliances. In fact, a peace agreement should be simpler. It is important as a mediator that you prevent the parties from adding too much to the deal. You must also realise that you cannot solve all the problems in a society during peace talks. The [second] Aceh agreement is good in this sense; it focuses only on a few fundamental issues and creates a framework for democratisation that makes it harder for old disputes to re-emerge.' Ahtisaari is clear which option he favours: 'I don't believe in agreements that are full of details. Then you easily find yourself in a situation in which it can always be said that some or other detail has been violated. A sufficiently compact agreement gives responsibility also to those who implement it and leaves enough room to interpretation.'

More often the problem is not a lack of clarity but that neither side believes the other seriously intends to implement the agreement and therefore doesn't do so itself. There are steps that can be taken to offer reassurance that the government will really implement it in practice, one of which is to ensure a democratic endorsement by a referendum. If an overwhelming majority of the people vote for the agreement, then it is much harder for the government to avoid fulfilling their promises, and it gives them the confidence to implement a deal without worrying about their critics. Governments are of course often anxious about risking a referendum that can be swayed by factors other than the agreement itself, particularly the unpopularity of a mid-term government or because of the need to meet a certain threshold of turnout for the referendum to be binding. They may therefore prefer to ratify the agreement through the legislature, although legislation can take years to prepare and pass – and, as the M-19 discovered in Colombia, it is not in any event certain that the government will be able to get legislation through parliament. Armed groups are therefore reluctant to give up their weapons, their prime bargaining card, till that legislation has been passed, while the government and public are unwilling to wait years for guerillas to put down their weapons.

Even having won the referendum doesn't guarantee continued support. As the IRA dragged their feet in decommissioning their weapons, and as the public saw that low-level paramilitary activity was continuing, Unionist support for the agreement slid precipitously to 30 per cent in 2003. We had to find a way to convince the public that implementation was really taking place, and at the suggestion of David Trimble we appointed an Independent Monitoring Commission to report regularly on how far the IRA and other paramilitary groups, as well as the British security forces, had progressed in implementing their promises. The public, particularly the Unionist public, no longer believed the government's assertions that progress was being made, which looked increasingly like wishful thinking on our part, so we appointed a retired head of the British Special Branch, a retired Irish justice official and a former CIA official, chaired by the leader of the cross-community Alliance Party, to the new body. They were able to draw on intelligence and police reports and make unbiased determinations on what was actually happening on the ground. A crucial aspect of establishing the IMC was drawing up a list of activities the IRA could no longer engage in. Some were obvious, like not targeting police officers and no intelligence work, but it was more difficult to decide where to draw the line on criminal activity like cigarette heists or bank robberies. Obviously they were reprehensible, but we did not want the whole agreement to fail over 'ordinary' criminal acts like these. Eguiguren had to draw up a similar list for ETA during the Oslo negotiations. He describes proudly how the ETA representatives thought he had consulted the Guardia Civil and other Spanish intelligence agencies whereas in fact he had cobbled it together in his hotel bedroom in half an hour. A quick glance at his list suggests he based it mainly on the one we drew up for Northern Ireland.

It is because of the uncertainty about a government's commitment to implementing its undertakings that armed groups often demand a constituent assembly to draw up a new constitution, or amendments to the constitution or, as in the case of ETA, demand an agreement between the principal political parties so that they can be certain that implementation will continue even if there is a change of government. Often a constitutional amendment is just too difficult for a government, especially if it requires a two-thirds majority in the parliament. In the Helsinki talks, GAM wanted to secure an amendment to the Indonesian constitution to entrench the political freedoms they had won in the negotiations, or at least to make any change subject to approval by the members of the National Parliament from Aceh, but Jakarta wouldn't agree. Instead they had to settle for a special Law on the Governing of Aceh (a sort of Basic Law), which enshrined the rules they wanted, and even then they had to wait two years for it to be passed. In the Philippines the MILF insisted in 2007 on agreement to a constitutional amendment to underpin the settlement, but it was over the government's promise to make such an amendment that the agreement fell foul of the Supreme Court and was overturned. When the two sides came back to the issue in the framework agreement of 2012, the MILF did not insist on a constitutional amendment but settled instead on a Basic Law which they were able to play a key role in drafting.

In cases where the whole point of the agreement is political transformation to escape an authoritarian or racist past, there are entirely new constitutions as part of the peace settlement, as in South Africa, Nepal and Burundi. In other cases the armed group chooses a different objective because they believe it will be transformational. According to Joaquín Villalobos, the FMLN chose to focus on military rather than political reform because they believed breaking the military's grip on the country would bring about a more fundamental change than just tinkering with the constitution. In September 1991 he was quoted as saying 'Something the army hasn't seemed to understand is that the bell has tolled to end the war . . . They don't want to hear it . . . because they've converted the war into their business, into their reason for being.'

If constitutional change is not immediately attainable then international guarantees can help offer assurances to the armed group that the promised change will actually happen. This role is usually played by the UN, as it was in Mozambique, but it can take the UN a long time to mobilise. The Rome agreement had anticipated just one year from signature of the agreement to elections, but the transition in fact took two years to implement because of the time it took to deploy UN personnel and to get displaced people back to their villages and registered for

288   *Talking to Terrorists*

elections. Slow or not, the UN was able to take the weight of guaranteeing that implementation would happen. Dhlakama's original plan had been to keep his soldiers in the bush for as long as possible to give himself bargaining power during the transition. However, the UN representative Aldo Ajello was able to convince him that the UN troops were his best insurance policy that the government would not cheat. Ajello explained they cost $1 million a day to maintain, and the international community would not pay for them to stay forever. Dhlakama should therefore demobilise his troops and move rapidly to elections before the international forces were withdrawn. RENAMO agreed and demobilised most of their forces (although they did still maintain some bases out in the bush).

It is only when fair elections have taken place and the armed group and the regime have both agreed to abide by the outcome that you can have some confidence that the settlement will hold. The contrasting examples of Angola and Mozambique illustrate the point.

The Bicesse Accords signed in Portugal in 1991 paved the way for elections in Angola supervised by the UN. It was conventional wisdom that the rebel UNITA would win handsomely, but the government mobilised all the assets of the state and in the parliamentary elections the governing MPLA won 54 per cent to UNITA's 34 per cent, and in the presidential elections dos Santos won 49 per cent to Savimbi's 40 per cent. The UN certified the elections as free and fair, but Savimbi immediately claimed they were fraudulent. UNITA had buried its weapons rather than handing them in and the UN did not have the resources to monitor their camps. The war resumed, with even more horrendous results than before. More than 1,000 people died a day out of a population of about 12 million. The failure to commit to a democratic outcome was not entirely one-sided. When the international community demanded a second round in the presidential elections, as required by the rules, the governing MPLA refused.

Nonetheless the international community's patience with

UNITA's Savimbi had worn out. The UN imposed an arms and
oil embargo on UNITA and threatened additional sanctions.
The government, flush with oil money, was able to re-equip
its army and start retaking ground. Eventually, once a stalemate
had been re-established, UNITA agreed to go back into negotiations in Lusaka in 1993. An agreement was signed in 1994
but Savimbi didn't attend the ceremony. This time the international community tried to learn lessons from its previous failure.
There had been insufficient resources for the UN to monitor
the implementation of Bicesse effectively, so at Lusaka they
agreed to 7,000 monitors and required UNITA to quarter all
its troops in designated assembly areas under its supervision,
while the army was required to withdraw to defensive positions
and to barracks. Even so they were unable to prevent both
sides from cheating. As the UN put it, 'UNITA violated the agreement by day, the government by night.' The MPLA tried to
recapture all the provincial capitals before the ceasefire came into
force, while UNITA put in a false declaration of disarmament.
The UN failed to punish either side for their violations, which
had the effect of further fuelling mutual distrust. Elections had
failed under Bicesse, so this time the UN proposed a Government
of National Unity and Reconciliation with UNITA participating
in government at national and local level. UNITA wanted
control of the country's second city Huambo, which the
Portuguese had originally planned as the capital of their African
empire, but the MPLA were not prepared to give it up. In 1992
UNITA had controlled 70 per cent of the country but now the
balance of forces had shifted in the government's favour.
Savimbi declined the offer of a vice-presidential position and
in 1998 restarted the war. He was eventually killed in 2002
fighting government forces on a riverbank in his native province
of Moxico. He was prepared to negotiate but would never
implement what had been agreed or accept the outcome of the
elections or the political process.

By contrast, despite some last-minute hiccups, Afonso
Dhlakama in Mozambique did. As part of the agreement

Dhlakama accepted elections but RENAMO were ill prepared. The international community gave him $17.5 million as a trust fund to build a political force, including $4 million in cash to prevent the splintering of his organisation immediately after the laying down of weapons. On the eve of the elections in October 1994 Dhlakama suddenly announced that RENAMO was boycotting them. A document purporting to be drawn up by advisers to the government had been faxed to RENAMO's office, listing possible frauds the government could use to win. Ajello immediately announced that on behalf of the UN he would invalidate the elections if any of the frauds in the list were identified as happening in practice. Far from reassuring Dhlakama as intended, the effect was to convince him that the UN was covering up for the government. Shortly before, Dhlakama had been invited to the summit of Frontline States in Zimbabwe, but President Chissano had refused to let him attend the summit itself. Instead Dhlakama was kept in his hotel room all day, and at the end of the summit Mugabe came to see him and told him that if he did not respect the outcome of the elections, there would be military intervention by the neighbours, without saying anything about the elections needing to be free and fair. The impact of all of this was to convince Dhlakama that the government had organised massive fraud, the neighbouring countries were willing to cover it up to ensure stability, and the international community would declare the elections free and fair come what may.

As soon as he heard of the threatened boycott, Ajello called Dhlakama, who told him, 'I am not going back to the bush. I am not Savimbi. I am sure the international community will understand my decision.' Ajello immediately asked Western leaders and ambassadors to call Dhlakama to try to change his mind. At two in the morning Ajello received a message that RENAMO was prepared to compete if they were assured that every complaint they made would be investigated and elections invalidated where significant fraud was detected. He agreed. In the elections FRELIMO won with 44 per cent to RENAMO's

37 per cent and Chissano was re-elected president with 53 per cent against 33 per cent for Dhlakama. Some in the international community suggested power-sharing, but this was declined by Chissano, and RENAMO grudgingly accepted the outcome of the elections.

Implementation is not just about politics, however, but also about demobilising armed groups and their weapons, or Disarmament, Demobilisation and Reintegration (DDR) as it is known in the jargon. In Northern Ireland the peace process got stuck when the Major government tried to insist on decommissioning of IRA weapons as a precondition. That has happened elsewhere too. In July 2006, the Nepalese prime minister Girija Prasad Koirala made it clear he would not include the Maoists in the interim government until the weapons of the People's Liberation Army, their armed wing, had been decommissioned. The issue became a major obstacle and the talks went into a hiatus for four months. The Maoist leaders thought the DDR proposed by the international community was putting the cart before the horse, because it proposed dismantling rebel forces before agreeing to the reform of the army. DDR is therefore normally best at the end of the process not at the beginning, and usually only when there is agreement on security sector reform, in other words what should happen to the army and the police. If you have a complete disparity between the military, who are reduced and redirected but stay in place with their weapons, and rebels who, though not defeated, are asked to demobilise and hand in their arms, you are unlikely to have a lasting settlement.

The first priority after an agreement is to stop the fighting, disengage the forces and make sure it doesn't start again. Quite often this happens as a natural outgrowth of talks. As Villalobos puts it, no one wants to be the last man to die in a civil war, and when the El Salvador peace talks started there was a natural tendency to disengage and avoid encounters with the enemy. There needs to be machinery to deal with accidents, however. Immediately after the ceasefire in El Salvador an

FMLN guerrilla was shot. The incident could have threatened the whole peace process but there was an immediate investigation and the tension defused. Happily it turned out to be an isolated incident, and the UN took charge of demobilisation. Marrack Goulding, the British head of peacekeeping at the UN, met the government and the guerrillas and rolled out a map of the country. Both the FMLN and the army claimed they had control of over a hundred points where their troops could assemble. According to Villalobos, both sides were lying. Goulding cut through the nonsense, saying he did not have enough men to monitor that many assembly points, and that the government could have a hundred, and the FMLN fifty. It took nine months to demobilise both sides.

The transitional period from the signing of the agreement until full implementation is fragile. There have to be stabilisation measures and a joint commission or independent body to track implementation. The catchphrase that covered arms control between the West and the former Soviet Union in the 1980s, 'trust but verify', applies every bit as much to the implementation of peace agreements in civil wars. The key challenge is to try to keep the political and military aspects of implementation synchronised. You cannot have one side waiting for the other to do everything before it will start implementing its side of the bargain. The independent body needs to act as the guardian of the agreed timetable and to resolve any disputes. Sometimes the joint commission can also be charged with elaborating the detail of the agreement itself in continuing negotiations, as in the case of the framework agreement between the government of the Philippines and the MILF in 2012, where working groups continued to negotiate the detailed provisions on DDR and the police at the same time as the broad lines of the agreement were being put into practice. The monitoring body needs to have teeth to ensure that both parties honour their promises and the ability to impose penalties if they don't.

It is very difficult, if not impossible, for an NGO to play this monitoring role. The HD Centre didn't want to do so in

Aceh in 2002, but both sides insisted that it did or they would not agree to sign the COHA. It turned out to be a disaster. Martti Ahtisaari says 'An NGO should not take a role like that. I think it is better to have governmental representatives be monitors because it is difficult for the parties to misbehave before representatives of foreign governments. That is why I suggested that the European Union be involved in addition to half a dozen ASEAN [Association of South-East Asian Nations] countries. Getting another regional actor on board was important for GAM, who remained wary of only neighbouring countries monitoring the agreement. The Aceh Monitoring Mission worked very well in this role. In the end, it was important for me to make clear that implementing the agreement was not the mediator's job but that of the parties.' Immediately after the Helsinki agreement in 2005 the Aceh Monitoring Mission was set up, made up of EU and ASEAN forces charged with demobilisation, decommissioning of weapons, and preparations for the election. It was small, quick to deploy and had a clear exit strategy and timetable. Most importantly it enjoyed complete freedom of movement within Aceh and the parties did not have a veto over its actions.

In Mozambique the UN Secretary General chose an Italian to head the implementation force because of the part Italy had played in reaching the agreement. On arrival, Aldo Ajello, the self-deprecating Italian diplomat who insists he was only chosen because of where his name stood in alphabetical order amongst Italian officials at the UN, wanted to meet Dhlakama and persuade him to move to the capital. He flew up to Gorongosa and at the airstrip was picked up by RENAMO's chief negotiator, Raul Domingos, on a motorbike and driven on a bumpy track through the bush. He met Dhlakama in a hut in Maringue surrounded by his staff. Dhlakama said he would not go to Maputo until suitable accommodation had been found and a significant number of UN troops had been deployed. Immediately after the visit RENAMO launched a military offensive and captured four towns. At this stage there were only thirty UN officials in Mozambique and there was not much they could do about the infraction. Ajello went back to Maringue to see Dhlakama again. He tried to convince him that it was time to change his strategy. He had already demonstrated to the Mozambican people that he had military muscle. Now he had to convince them he also had wisdom. Ajello drew two boxes on a piece of paper, one marked RENAMO and the other FRELIMO. He said FRELIMO had been the ruling party for many years and all the seats in their box were fully booked while the RENAMO box was empty and many bright young people would join them as long as they were not seen as an organisation of bandits. As he left, Dhlakama folded the piece of paper and put it in his pocket and repeated 'wisdom not muscle'. He promised 'No more attacks. Even if I am provoked, and I know I will be, I will not react.'

After seven months the UN started to demobilise the forces on both sides. RENAMO had chosen twenty assembly points and the army twenty-nine. Unfortunately they had selected the sites so as to maintain strategic control of territory rather than suitable places to base troops, with water or access to roads. UN officials had decided in their wisdom that the guerrillas should be given tools to build their own shelters when they arrived at the locations. After many days of strenuous march the fighters were not amused when they were told this. The same officials had also decided that the fighters should only be given the same rations they were providing for refugees. While this might be a fair rule, Ajello concluded it was not a good idea to let a man with an AK-47 get too hungry. As he put it, he needed to 'put enough food into their stomachs to keep them peace-loving'. Lastly it had been agreed that each soldier should be given six months' salary. Given how long reintegration was likely to take, Ajello decided to supplement this with an extra eighteen months' salary. Both sides had intended secretly to leave reserve troops in the bush in case fighting restarted, but as soon as they heard about the eighteen months' salary available for those reintegrating, the reserve troops became the first to turn up for demobilisation. Indeed one battalion of government soldiers in Matola nearly mutinied so as not to lose their benefits and demanded demobilisation within twenty-four hours. After negotiation they agreed to wait for three days.

The extra money had the side effect of reducing the number of soldiers interested in joining the new army. In the negotiations in Rome the two sides had agreed that the army should be 30,000 strong with 15,000 each from FRELIMO and RENAMO. In the end only 12,000, mostly officers and NCOs, put themselves forward for positions, while the majority of the foot soldiers on both sides preferred the generous civilian reintegration offer. Parity was impossible since only a third of those volunteering came from RENAMO. The defence minister thanked Ajello afterwards. There was no way a poor country like Mozambique could afford an army of 30,000 men. In all, 80,000 combatants were successfully demobilised and reintegrated into civilian life.

Demobilisation and reintegration need to take place gradually. Armed groups can't just be collapsed suddenly. In Nepal the two sides agreed that both the Royal Nepalese Army and the Maoist People's Liberation Army should be disbanded and a new force created. It would be made up proportionally of one each drawn from the army and the guerrillas, plus a civilian who had been in neither. In the words of one Maoist leader, the aim was 'to professionalise our Maoist fighters and democratise our national army'. The People's Liberation Army agreed to go into military cantonments, and as the UN couldn't get there in time, their leader Prachanda accepted that they be supervised in the intervening period by ex-Ghurkha soldiers. Two-thirds of the 19,000 combatants volunteered for the 6,500 available places in the army rather than the generous civilian rehabilitation package on offer. In South Africa, integration of the army and the ANC's armed wing, the MK, started in 1991–2, even before the political agreement had been finalised. The minister of defence brought together military and guerrilla leaders to discuss how to do it, and a Joint Military Co-ordinating Council was established. On the MK side formal rank structures were introduced and thousands of cadres were sent abroad for training, particularly to India. The military was reduced in size and a sunset clause introduced to allow members of the previous army to retire early with generous pensions. The result was a new, successfully integrated army.

The first D in DDR, dealing with weapons, is a particularly sensitive issue for armed groups. They do not want to appear to surrender, not least because of the asymmetry between their position and that of the army which usually gets to keep its weapons, so the armed group is unlikely to give up control of its weapons straight away, and nor do they want to hand them over to the government. In Nepal from 2006 to 2011 the People's Liberation Army put their arms in storage under a single lock system where they kept the key. The UN registered the weapons and checked the stores on a regular basis with alarms on the doors of the containers and CCTV monitoring them. The national army's weapons were put under similar supervision. The Maoist weapons were only finally handed over to a mixed security panel (including People's Liberation Army commanders) in August 2011, and were then passed to the new integrated army. In El Salvador the FMLN put their weapons into a UN-run warehouse, while the GAM insisted on destroying their weapons themselves. The leaders of the M-19 in Colombia decided to disarm unilaterally and put the issue to a vote of the guerrillas. They employed their own agency to melt the weapons in front of an international commission rather than hand them over to the state. The IRA would only give their weapons to the IICD. Its final report concluded 'the decommissioning process should suggest neither victory nor defeat, and we believe this principle applies to other negotiations'. Even the terminology can be sensitive, because disarmament smacks of surrender. In Northern Ireland and Aceh it was described as 'decommissioning weapons', in Nepal as 'management of arms and armaments', and in Colombia as 'leaving weapons behind'. Armed groups will not always agree to destroy their weapons, and in Northern Ireland the phrase used was 'put weapons beyond use'.

Then there is of course the question of how you know whether the armed group has got rid of all of its weapons, particularly if you don't know how many they had in the first place. There is naturally an incentive for the armed group to understate the number of its fighters and weapons in the hope of holding some in reserve, in case things go wrong. In Mozambique, where everyone had a gun and an AK-47 cost just $15 on the black market, it was impossible to take all the arms out of circulation. In any case removing weapons guarantees nothing, because armed groups can always acquire more. But it is symbolically important, and you don't want the arms to fall into the wrong hands.

If one side or the other cheats on weapons and is discovered doing so, it delivers a major knock to confidence. The ANC had a secret plan known as Operation Vula, importing and storing arms in South Africa to keep the armed struggle viable. The leadership authorised its continuation even after the ANC was legalised and engaged in negotiations with the government. When the plan was exposed in July 1990 and forty ANC members were arrested, it nearly brought the whole process down because, as F. W. de Klerk says, 'it raised doubts regarding the bona fides and real intentions of the ANC'. Cheating happened elsewhere too. The FPL wing of the FMLN demobilised only older fighters and handed in useless weapons, keeping back substantial amounts of new weaponry, including missiles, new passports and a list of targets. These were kept in a secret arsenal in Managua guarded by ETA members. When it accidentally blew up, their plan was exposed and the incident was used by the army in El Salvador as an excuse to stop implementing the agreement temporarily. The group was forced to give a full account of what had happened to all their weapons.

In parallel with DDR there needs to be security sector

reform in order to create an army or police that will be accepted by the communities that have supported the armed group. In Northern Ireland it revolved around reducing the presence of the British army in the province and implementing the 1999 Patten Report to reform the RUC and turn it into a more balanced police force with 50/50 recruitment of Catholics and Protestants. A similar approach in Kosovo boosted the proportion of Serbs in the security forces to 8.2 per cent, even though the Serbs made up only 5 per cent of the country's population. In Burundi a rule was introduced that no ethnic group could make up more than 50 per cent of the army and police.

Restructuring the army after a conflict is particularly challenging. In the El Salvador agreement, the two sides agreed to appoint a commission to purify the armed forces under Abraham Rodriguez, one of the founders of the Christian Democratic Party. His report recommended purging 103 officers. In a small army this was a huge step, accounting for 85 per cent of those with the rank of colonel or above, which was not taken well by the army. James LeMoyne went to Rodriguez's house and found the gardener sitting by the front door with a shotgun. The head of military intelligence had phoned saying he was going to kill Rodriguez, who was barricaded in his bedroom. Rodriguez told LeMoyne 'Well, I did it. No one believed I would do it, but I did.' LeMoyne asked if he could use his phone and dialled Bernie Aronson in the State Department. He went direct to President George H. W. Bush who called Colin Powell, then head of the US military. Powell got on a plane to San Salvador the next day to give the military leadership a three-hour pep talk. That may have saved Rodriguez's life but it did not resolve the crisis. The head of military intelligence told President Cristiani that the army was not happy and that if Cristiani did not protect the army interest, there would be a coup.

After the agreement the army and the FMLN initially had not talked to each other. LeMoyne arranged for military officers to meet the former guerrillas privately at his home. He would take the officers in the boot of his car and drive into the underground car park below his apartment. One commented that it 'might be the most important thing that happened in the process but also the most dangerous'. Villalobos decided at this stage that the proposed purge was too radical, too sudden, and would destabilise the peace just as it was beginning to be implemented. He negotiated a supplementary deal with Cristiani in October 1992 to make better provision for the ex-guerrillas in return for a smaller purge of the army, but was accused of betrayal by his own side and by the human-rights lobby, and in the process sacrificed his own political career. He was convinced that it was not sensible to humiliate the army if there was to be a lasting peace. Eventually he even surrendered his precious remaining surface-to-air missiles in return for the reintegration of 600 guerrillas, who were offered scholarships, training and jobs. He said to Cristiani, 'I will help you avoid a *coup d'état* and you can help me stop the guerrillas going back to war.'

Although seemingly paradoxical, it is important to keep the structure of the armed group in place for at least a while after the peace agreement is signed, as its command and control system is necessary to ensure implementation of its side of the bargain. Too early a disbandment can lead to a perilous security vacuum and there is always the danger of splintering. In the Philippines the near-agreement between the government and the Islamic rebels in 2008 was undermined by the breakaway of Commander Kato who took with him 1,000 fighting men from the main force of MILF and returned to fighting under the name Bangsamoro Islamic Freedom Fighters. The split made the Philippines government question whether it was possible to make a lasting peace with the MILF as one coherent movement. After the Helsinki agreement, GAM transformed itself from an armed group into a civilian Transitional Committee (KPA) in order to keep the movement's cohesion until a political party could be formed.

On the other hand you need to wrap up the structures and remove the arms of rebel groups before they are appropriated by criminal gangs. In both El Salvador and Guatemala the peace agreements were followed by a substantial rise in violent crime. In El Salvador the number of murder victims after the agreement actually surpassed the wartime death toll. Those who had once feared the police and the state now became frustrated by their failure to act. People began saying to each other, 'It's worse than the war.' It is an awkward and unpalatable truth that most peace agreements are followed by an upsurge in crime as repression is removed.

Many combatants will not want to join the army or police and there needs to be a programme to reintegrate them into civilian society. Sometimes the schemes to do so can be over-generous. In Aceh the reintegration agency asked for bids and received applications from 400,000 people, some 10 per cent of the population. The agency simply didn't have the capacity to process the claims and the scheme was cancelled. The governor tried to address the issue of compensation by giving individual villages fixed sums, and attempted to introduce the '*diyat*' system from classical Islam, under which the traditional payment was a hundred camels for the heirs of a murder victim. The governor proposed $6,500 per murder but lacked the resources to deliver that scheme too.

It is difficult to reintegrate fighters into war-ravaged economies where there are no jobs. Although it is a mistake to try to buy peace with economic aid without the corollary of political progress, it is an even bigger mistake not to provide an adequate peace dividend once the war is over. One of the reasons the ceasefire in Sri Lanka collapsed was because the LTTE did not see tangible economic benefits from the talks. Prabhakaran felt the government got all the aid and investment and the LTTE got nothing. He realised that if the LTTE laid down their weapons he could only draw legitimacy from delivering tangible benefits for his people. The international community needs to be ready to put huge sums to work to underpin a peace process. In Mozambique over $1 billion was invested in supporting peacekeeping and elections in 1993–4, a large amount but a tiny fraction of the $1.283 trillion that the US Congress voted for military operations in Iraq and Afghanistan between 2001 and 2011.

Sometimes the individual fighters' lives have been transformed by the conflict. The young men of MEND (the Movement to Emancipation of the Niger Delta) in Southern Nigeria went from subsistence, living on less than a dollar a day, to unparalleled riches once they joined the movement. Having been at the bottom of the pecking order in a traditional society, the possession of a gun gave them respect and allowed them to defy the elders of their villages. Persuading them to revert to their lower status and give up the wealth to which they had become accustomed was difficult; but unless there is an answer to this challenge – and often it is an answer the rest of society would rather not contemplate – then they will not sign up to an agreement. In Nigeria the government subsidised the fighters to go abroad for training and education, which at least provided a temporary solution.

If nothing else, the government needs to guarantee security for the guerrillas being demobilised and ensure retribution is not visited upon them. In Colombia ex-M-19 guerrillas were moved to regions considered to be safer and less affected by violence. The government constructed a hierarchy of risk with four levels and distributed bodyguards and armoured vehicles, but even that didn't prevent 160 of them being killed. The UP, a party set up by the FARC in Colombia in 1988, lost between 3,000 and 4,000 members to assassination in a few years. Unless the security of ex-combatants can be guaranteed by the government, the guerrilla movement will not risk moving into politics.

One of the central tenets of many armed groups is that 'no one should be left behind' and one of their core demands in a negotiation is therefore the release of their comrades from jail. Granting amnesty to the terrorists used to be the solution, but it was always a fraught route for governments. In Spain, Rubalcaba discovered that an amnesty for all prisoners was not possible under Article 62 of the constitution, and he had to deal with ETA prisoners individually. F. W. de Klerk says 'Amnesty was, from the outset, a *sine qua non* for the negotiations between the ANC and the former government that led to the creation of the new South Africa . . . In fact the question of amnesty was raised at the very first meeting between the ANC and the government in May 1990.' But letting prisoners out who have blood on their hands makes it difficult for democratically elected governments to maintain support for the agreement amongst ordinary law-abiding citizens. De Klerk says of South Africa:

> The government originally proposed that the Norgaard principles [defining a political offence] should be used to determine who should reasonably be granted indemnity or amnesty. The principles had been used successfully in Namibia and, in general, allowed amnesty for all those who had committed offences in the pursuit of political objectives unless they had made use of egregious or disproportionate violence. However the government was forced to abandon the Norgaard principles as the ANC's price for returning to negotiations after 26 September 1992. The ANC insisted that political motive should be the only test and on this basis demanded the release of more than 2,000 of its followers, many of whom had been involved in acts of disproportionate violence, including the Mango Bar killings and the 'necklace' murders. Acceptance of the Further Indemnity Act was one of the most difficult and distasteful decisions I had to take during my presidency.

It is often problematic to agree on exactly who should be released. Two weeks after the agreement in Aceh was signed, 500 prisoners were freed and a further 900 were let out later. That left a hundred disputed cases which had to be ruled on by the international monitors. They brought in a Swedish judge,

Christer Karphammar, who used his remarkable powers of persuasion to convince the Indonesian minister of justice to broaden the amnesty beyond cases of treason to incorporate other crimes. The government offered accelerated remission rather than amnesty in some cases, and only ten individuals were left in prison when the amnesty issue was declared closed in August 2006. Even then, leaving the bombers of the Jakarta stock exchange and the murderers of a respected university rector in jail led to bitterness on the GAM side, with critics claiming that the comrades left behind in prison had been sacrificed to absolve the guilt of the leadership.

A one-sided amnesty for the terrorists is unlikely to survive uncontested. The police and military will demand the same treatment. The retired Indonesian general Kiki Syahnakri complained 'GAM, who have opposed the republic, get a pension. The TNI soldiers who fell in battle, or whose legs had to be amputated, what do they get? They get threatened with a Human Rights Court.' In Colombia, ex-President Uribe has tried to attack the negotiations with the FARC claiming that 'the generals will end up going to jail while the guerrillas will end up elected to the senate'. The security forces, which the government has to continue to rely on, object to the guerrillas being let off while they still have to answer for their crimes. And yet if you offer an equivalent pardon to the security forces as you offer to the guerrillas, you will be assailed by human-rights organisations.

The world has moved on, however, with the creation of the International Criminal Court (ICC) and new international legal norms so that general amnesties are impossible. In fact even the sort of device we used in Northern Ireland, which provided a judicial process to release terrorist prisoners on licence after only two years in jail, would now be open to challenge. Those most responsible have to be held to account if the foot soldiers are to escape prosecution. It is absolutely right that victims' rights should be given greater salience in this way, but as Larry May of Vanderbilt University says, 'the difficulty in achieving a lasting peace is to show respect for those whose rights have been violated but not to insist that compensation be set so high, either monetarily or politically, that peace cannot occur'. It is also right that we should use the threat of prosecution by the ICC to deter future human-rights abusers, and that can only be done if we deal firmly with those who have already carried out such heinous crimes. But it is possible to go too far, as we would if we followed the argument of the ICC adviser Claus Kress, who says that 'Political decision-makers must work according to the assumption that international criminal law takes priority.'

Automatic amnesties are clearly a thing of the past, but should international law really take priority at the cost of more human lives lost unnecessarily by continuing a conflict? The new ICC chief prosecutor, Fatou Bensouda, writes: 'Peace or justice? Shall we strive for peace at all costs, sacrificing justice on the way, or shall we soldier on in the pursuit for justice to end impunity? Past negotiations have done just that: sacrificed justice for peace. Yet history has taught us that the peace achieved by ignoring justice has mostly been short-lived, and the cycle of violence has continued unabated.' Would that it were so easy. In the context of Mozambique, even before the advent of the ICC, Andrea Bartoli says that 'The text of the agreement represented the reality that Mozambicans wanted peace more than they wanted retributive justice.' In the case of the Lord's Resistance Army operating on the borders of Uganda, the ICC indictment of its leader Joseph Kony made it impossible to bring the group into a peace deal. Morris Ogenga-Latigo of the Ugandan political opposition complained that 'The ICC has become an impediment to our efforts. Should we sacrifice our peacemaking process here so they can test and develop their criminal-justice procedures there at the ICC? Punishment has to be quite secondary to the goal of resolving this conflict.'

So far the new ICC rules have not been fully tested by a peace agreement. The next government and armed group to reach a settlement will be guinea pigs for its processes. It is hard to believe that governments will be able to persuade the leaders of undefeated armed groups to sign up to a peace agreement that involves them going to jail for a lengthy period. Few leaders are so altruistic as to be prepared to sacrifice themselves for the greater good. And if that prevents us getting to an agreement, are we really prepared to sacrifice lives for an abstract legal point? Whatever the new legal norms, the balance of benefits in my view clearly points towards favouring peace and the lives that will be spared by ending conflict rather than too doctrinaire an approach to justice.

Even if the perpetrators do not go to jail for lengthy sentences, the past cannot simply be forgotten. Andrew Rigby, an expert on restorative justice, contrasts the 'amnesia' approach – the forgive-and-forget option – with the alternative of 'trials, purges and the pursuit of justice', and suggests that truth commissions and compensatory reparations lie in the middle. 'There needs to be compensation and support and above all remorse and forgiveness if it is to be a lasting peace.' A cathartic moment is necessary for society to move on. In South Africa the peace process ended with the Truth and Reconciliation Commission, designed to bring closure to the past. There is, however, now some debate as to whether it was the right thing to do: it is seen as inadequate in the way it dealt with historical crimes, particularly those committed by the apartheid regime, and the outcome of the process was seen as very one-sided by some white South Africans. F. W. de Klerk says 'I supported the idea of the Truth and Reconciliation Commission because I truly believed that there was a need for some forum where we could deal with our troubled, divisive and often traumatic history', but there was no one on the commission from the National Party or anyone representing the Inkatha point of view, and 'as a result, the TRC left the country more un-reconciled than ever'. He believes that 'The truth is that in divided societies it may be just as important to reach a negotiated agreement on the past as it is to reach a negotiated agreement on the future.

306 Talking to Terrorists

However, it is usually much easier to reach agreement on the future than it is to reach agreement on the past.'

Ramsbotham, Woodhouse and Miall say the ANC used the TRC mainly as a truth commission, focusing less on reconciliation, and they believe there is 'little evidence that the TRC made much impact on reconciliation at the individual level'. They add that 'a public opinion survey published in July 1998 suggested that two-thirds of South Africans at that time thought the TRC had led to a deterioration in race relations rather than to societal reconciliation', but they conclude nonetheless that the TRC, 'no doubt in its details unique to conditions in South Africa at that time, offers a magnificent and hopeful example of a creative attempt to handle the past in a way that furthers societal reconciliation in the present and promotes conflict resolution into the future'. Pumla Gobodo-Madikizela, a former member of the TRC, writes 'reconciliation has become a dirty word, and some people see it as a masquerade for impunity. The value of reconciliation politics, however, is that it shifts from an exclusive focus on prosecutions to allow the emergence of a profoundly new politics of engagement with the past, not in order to rekindle old hatreds, but to learn from it.'

The South African model, even if a success there, is clearly not appropriate for application everywhere. More often it is agreed in principle that there should be a truth and reconciliation commission at the end of the peace process, but they don't in the end get established in practice. In Aceh the agreement included a Human Rights Court. Legislation was passed but the president delayed appointing its members for two more years and it was then revoked by the Supreme Court. There was a debate about establishing a local TRC, but GAM was as ambivalent as the government about the idea and it was never established. One GAM negotiator is recorded as saying his side's 'advocacy of a human rights court was just for "academic purposes" . . . Requesting such a court was simply a matter of underlining that GAM did not agree to "forgive and forget".' A religious leader commented that 'We have all agreed to no longer discuss the old wounds and the parties have resolved to build a new Aceh.' Equally, failure to deal with the past can threaten to derail a peace process, as demonstrated by the arrest of Gerry Adams in 2014 in connection with the murder of Jean McConville. When we left government we established a commission headed by the Protestant archbishop Robin Eames and former Catholic priest Denis Bradley to consult on how to draw a line under the past. After two years they found that neither Republicans nor Unionists had any appetite for a truth and reconciliation process, or any other mechanism that involved digging up their uncomfortable histories. But the disagreeable truths do not just disappear, and when the past comes back to haunt the present, there will be more arrests and further disruptions of the peace-building process unless a way of dealing with the past is agreed.

Asking armed groups to apologise for what they have done and make reparations to their victims helps to heal the wounds caused by conflict, but if that is extended to demanding that they admit that what they did was wrong and express their repentance, they will refuse. And there is the issue of who the victims are: the armed group will almost always insist that there should be a parity of victims, including their fighters and supporters as well as those they have killed, which is difficult for the public to swallow.

We should recognise that as welcome as peace processes are, we are not in a fairy tale where, once the agreement is reached, everyone lives happily ever after. Bringing about reconciliation takes a huge amount of effort and the bitterness brought about by war remains for generations. P. W. Botha continued to be resentful long after he had left office. He refused to testify to the TRC, and when Thabo Mbeki's wife Zanele came to speak at a conference of the Dutch Reformed Church, he called his successor from his retirement home in Wilderness to complain that 'the Mbekis are Communists. Now they have taken over my church too.' There will continue to be political rows and unresolved issues, and some violence is likely to persist, as in Mozambique between RENAMO and FRELIMO more than twenty years after the agreement. Most troubling is sectarianism of the sort that still plagues Northern Ireland. Sectarian divides can open up in a matter of days, as they did after the ethnic-cleansing riots on Bombay Street in Belfast in 1969, or Black July in Sri Lanka in 1983, and they take generations to heal. There were only eighteen peace walls in Belfast separating the two communities when we signed the Good Friday Agreement in 1998, and there are now eighty-eight. As Peter Sheridan, the Catholic policeman from Derry, concludes, peace-building, which follows peacemaking, is an unending process.

We should not, however, let these continuing problems hide what peace processes have achieved. Apartheid will not return to South Africa, the Troubles will not come back to Northern Ireland, and civil war will not recur in El Salvador. The people in all these countries are now focused on new problems and opportunities, and their lives are immeasurably better. Above all we should bear in mind the many lives that have been spared as a result of these and other peace agreements. If we are able to learn the lessons of history, then the challenges of making peace in the future may become easier, and many more lives may be spared.

CHAPTER TEN

The Lessons of History

What experience and history teach is this – that people and governments never have learned anything from history or acted on principles deduced from it.

Hegel, *Philosophy of History*

The principles set out in this book on how to make contact with terrorists, how to start a negotiation, how to build trust, and the importance of implementation are derived from peace processes over the last twenty years. Are they a new phenomenon specific to the post-Cold War world, or do they also apply to earlier engagements with terrorist groups? A brief review of negotiations over the last century suggests the same lessons can be drawn, right back from the early days of terrorism.

One of the first conflicts between a government and a terrorist group to end in a peace settlement was that between the IRA and the British government from 1919 to 1921. The parallels between events then and today are almost eerie.

As so often since, the British government responded to the IRA campaign in a way guaranteed to add fuel to the conflict, meeting each terrorist outrage with a reprisal which was in turn met by an IRA counter-reprisal, constantly escalating the violence. The British deployed irregular forces including the Black and Tans, named after a pack of hounds belonging to the Limerick Hunt, with its uniform of khaki tunic, tam-o'-shanter berets and black leather belts and holsters, who set out to 'terrorise the terrorists', burning shops and houses and dispensing summary justice and executions. Even

Henry Wilson, the chief of the Imperial General Staff, disapproved of the way in which they marked down certain members of Sinn Féin as murderers and 'coolly went out and shot them without question or trial'. How the government hoped 'to solve the Irish question by counter-terrorism, I cannot imagine,' he said. The Black and Tan campaign was the first 'dirty war', and like subsequent dirty wars, it made things worse.

As in succeeding conflicts there were a group of 'securocrats', known at the time as the 'Diehards', including General H. H. Tudor who commanded the irregulars, and Brigadier General Ormonde Winter, or 'O', the enigmatic figure in charge of the intelligence service. In the diaries of Mark Sturgis, the Sir Humphrey Appleby of Dublin Castle, 'O' was described as 'a marvel – he looks like a little white snake and can do everything! . . . He is clever as paint, probably entirely non-moral, a first-class horseman, a card genius, knows several languages, is a super sleuth, and a most amazing original. When a soldier who knew him in India heard he was coming to Ireland he said "God help Sinn Féin, they don't know what they're up against."' Tory Diehards back in London demanded that the IRA lay down its weapons and surrender, and Hugh Cecil, the brother of Lord Salisbury, declared the Irish question to be a 'moral question, not a political question'. The British military thought they were winning in 1920 and pushed for 'one last heave', but in November 1920 Michael Collins's 'Squad' assassinated fourteen suspected British intelligence agents in Dublin and shortly afterwards the IRA ambushed an Auxiliary patrol at Kilmichael and killed all seventeen men. This was a military operation on a different scale to anything they had attempted before. For the government the prospect of winning began to look remote, and they started to consider the possibility of negotiating.

A mutually hurting stalemate made a settlement possible, as in the conflicts of the last twenty years. By 1921 the IRA was running out of men, weapons and ammunition. 5,500 of its 7,500 active combatants were interned or in prison. Michael

Collins, in effect their commander, believed they only had three weeks left to fight, with just 3,000 rifles plus shotguns and about fifty machine guns remaining. He said later 'We had an average of one round of ammunition for each weapon held.' He was so conscious of the danger of the British discovering their weakness as their searches yielded fewer and fewer arms that he deliberately buried weapons for government forces to find. His intelligence system had been broken up and British intelligence had badly penetrated his organisation. Collins admitted 'We had prevented the enemy so far from defeating us . . . [But] we had recognised our inability to beat the British out of Ireland.'

If the IRA had no prospect of winning, the British government, for their part, 'recognised that they could not defeat the IRA without a politically unacceptable escalation of the war of 1919–21', in the words of the leading Irish historian Ronan Fanning. For the British the problem was not the number of their troops killed – as the Liberal minister H. A. L. Fisher remarked, in total only 500 died, 'less than the quietest day on the Western Front during the First World War'. The problem was that they could not suppress the rebellion without bringing in a further 400,000 men and laying waste to the country.

General Nevil Macready, the supremely rational military commander in Ireland, briefed the Cabinet in June 1921 that they could win in Ireland but only at great cost. 'It must be all out or another policy', he told them. In reporting to Lloyd George, he asked rhetorically 'Will they go through with it? Will they begin to howl when they hear of our shooting a hundred men in one week?' The Cabinet decided it was not prepared to dip its hands so far in blood. Once they had made that decision, there was no other choice but a political settlement. As Macready put it, 'the more people that are killed, the more difficult will be the final solution . . . no amount of coercion will settle the Irish question'.

Nor would a solution have been possible any more than in recent decades without strong political leadership on both sides.

Éamon de Valera and Michael Collins were remarkably tough leaders, and progress only really started to be made when de Valera returned to Ireland at the end of 1920 from his extended sojourn in the United States. On the British side Lloyd George had fully earned the sobriquet of the 'Welsh Wizard' by winning the First World War. He clearly had a 'Messiah complex', believing that only he could solve the Irish question. 'If I pull it off, it will be a big thing,' he told his close friend, Lord Riddell. 'You know I am that kind of beggar. I always do think beforehand that I am going to bring things off.' C. P. Scott, the publisher of the *Manchester Guardian*, told Michael Collins that 'Lloyd George was fighting their battle hard under great difficulties and had done wonders in bringing over the Tories . . . Alone of all the statesmen . . . who had taken the Irish question in hand [he] was in a position "to deliver the goods". He surely had a right to expect some help from those he was helping.' Collins replied, 'I know nothing about your politics. I have only to think of Ireland,' to which Scott said, 'You have to think of our politics if you want to get anything done.'

Like all other peace processes before and since, the Irish conflict and the settlement was all about politics. Following the post-war elections, Lloyd George was, in the words of Lord Beaverbrook, 'a prime minister without a party' who depended on the support of a large Conservative majority in the House of Commons. 'The party arithmetic in the House of Commons was the key determinant of policy', according to Fanning. Lloyd George was therefore determined to be as hard line on Ireland as the most hard-line Tory until they were ready to consider peace, in order to preserve his majority. In particular he had to wait for the departure of Andrew Bonar Law, the leader of the Conservatives who came from an Ulster family and was a staunch defender of Unionism. When Bonar Law retired to France to recuperate from an imaginary illness in March 1921 and was replaced as leader of the Tory Party by the more malleable Austen Chamberlain, Lloyd George finally had the room to manoeuvre. He desperately needed a success to keep his coalition government going and a settlement in Ireland was the only obvious option. As he explained to Arthur Griffith, the founder of Sinn Féin and the lead Irish negotiator, 'The politician who thinks he can deal out abstract justice without reference to forces around him cannot govern.'

As in more recent conflicts, external influences had an important impact but were not decisive. Lloyd George was constantly worried about the American attitude. In April 1917 President Woodrow Wilson personally typed a confidential message to his Secretary of State instructing the US ambassador in London to tell the prime minister unofficially and most confidentially that 'the failure so far to find a satisfactory method of self-government for Ireland' was the only thing that stood in the way of 'absolutely cordial' Anglo-American co-operation. In 1920 Lloyd George told Henry Wilson he was ready to authorise reprisals on the IRA but he 'wanted to wait till the American [presidential] elections are over'. Later, during the negotiations with the Irish in November 1922, he worried that the Americans would pull out of the crucial Naval Conference if he pushed the Irish too hard. He was also concerned about the attitude of the empire. General Jan Smuts, who represented the empire in the British Cabinet, told them the situation in Ireland was 'an unmeasured calamity' which poisoned 'both our empire relations and our foreign relations'.

Just like modern leaders, Lloyd George insisted at the beginning that the government would never talk to terrorists, describing the IRA as 'a real murder gang, dominating the country and terrorising it'. But also like subsequent leaders, he came to realise he had to talk to them. In an equally familiar vein, the government worried whether engaging with the IRA would give them legitimacy. Basil Thomson, the head of Special Branch, said 'that even the extremists would welcome peace but would take as a Victory any recognition of themselves implied by negotiating with them. Of course they would say so, a puff to vanity, but would that matter?' So the government overcame their concern about legitimising the IRA.

Lloyd George said in Parliament in August 1920 that he would engage Sinn Féin if they accepted three preconditions: '1) the 6 counties of Northern Ireland must get special treatment; 2) he would not accept any proposal that led to the secession of Ireland; and 3) he wouldn't agree to anything that would harm the security of "these islands" during war.' The preconditions were not accepted by the IRA and he had to go ahead and engage anyway. Like many later leaders, Lloyd George therefore opted for fighting and talking at the same time.

Having decided to engage, the British had the classic problem of finding the right interlocutor in a clandestine group and were unsure who they should be talking to. Sturgis wrote in his diary, 'If we want to talk to Ulster there's Craig or Carson [the Unionist leaders], but when we want to talk to Sinn Féin it's a heterogeneous "collection" of individuals who thanks largely to our own activities are not even collected.' In April 1920 Basil Thomson opened up a relationship with a senior American correspondent, Carl Ackerman, who then acted as one of the backchannels with Sinn Féin. In June he told Ackerman that 'the government was very anxious to make peace in Ireland, but could find no one with authority to speak for Sinn Féin'.

Lloyd George set about trying to find an authoritative channel to the IRA from 1920 onwards but it proved elusive. As in recent peace processes there were a multiplicity of approaches, but the two sides had difficulty developing any of them into a sustainable backchannel.

The 1919–21 process even had its own version of Brendan Duddy, the man who served as the secret channel to the IRA from 1974 to 1992, in the form of Patrick Moylett, an Irish businessman and Republican. Moylett's participation has only recently come to light through the declassification and release of his witness statement given in the 1950s to the Irish Bureau of Military History.

Moylett says he was sent to London by Arthur Griffith in

October 1920 to meet John Steele, the correspondent of the *Chicago Tribune*. Steele offered to introduce him to Philip Kerr, the prime minister's principal private secretary. Moylett worried about being seen going into Downing Street and suspected by his own side of being a spy, but he accompanied Steele to the meeting anyway. Instead of Kerr he saw C. J. Phillips, a former private secretary to Lloyd George and now secretary to H. A. L. Fisher, the chair of the Cabinet Committee on Ireland. Moylett spent three and a quarter hours with Fisher that day. The minister talked of 'the murder gang in Ireland' and Moylett talked about the British murder gang. Moylett insisted he was not there to represent anybody, but he immediately returned to Dublin to brief Griffith who told him to go straight back and get the British to recognise the Dáil Éireann. He should push for a truce, an amnesty and a conference without preliminary conditions.

On 25 October, Moylett attended the funeral procession of Terence McSwiney, the Sinn Féin lord mayor of Cork who had died on hunger strike in prison, and took with him in his taxi from the hotel the four men who formed the IRA guard of honour. At Euston he found a telephone message from Downing Street asking him not to accompany the funeral cortège to Dublin as he had intended, but instead to come that evening to meet C. J. Phillips. When he went in, he was asked if it was possible to arrange a conference between the leaders of republican forces in Ireland and the British authorities, and could the IRA be persuaded to call off its campaign. He said for that they would need to recognise the Dáil.

Four days later Phillips told him that Lloyd George was interested in what he had said. He asked if the Dáil would be prepared to nominate men to meet three or four from England to discuss the basis of a formal conference. He wrote the proposal on a piece of paper which Moylett agreed to take to Griffith that night. Griffith broke down in emotion when he read it, and instructed Desmond FitzGerald, one of his aides (and the father of Garret FitzGerald, the Irish prime minister who negotiated the Anglo-Irish Agreement of 1985 with Margaret Thatcher), to establish a line of communication.

Griffith told Moylett that an IRA man had just escaped capture but his attaché case had been left behind, containing plans for the burning of Liverpool and London docks. Moylett should use this information in Downing Street to establish his credibility, as the contents of the plans would not be known for another three to four days. On arriving at No. 10 Moylett told them of the plans and handed over Griffith's letter. Phillips summoned him back a few days later and asked 'In the event of Dáil Éireann arranging to meet under a guarantee with a view to receiving proposals from the British government, would the first act of the Dáil be to stop the police and soldiers being murdered; we, on our side, ceasing reprisals?' Moylett took the proposal back to Dublin and returned with another letter from Griffith. When he saw this letter Lloyd George reportedly said 'You can start with this man; he has credentials', and even took the letter with him to the country to digest. That was the weekend of 21 November 1920, Bloody Sunday, when the fourteen British agents were assassinated.

The next day Moylett received a message to call at Downing Street as soon as possible. He was given a message from Lloyd George to Griffith, saying 'For God's sake to keep his head and not to break off the slender link that had been established', adding that those killed were soldiers and took a soldier's risk: 'They got what they deserved, beaten by counterjumpers.' Phillips asked Moylett if anything could be done to get a week without violence, in order to produce a better atmosphere in Ireland so that Lloyd George could face the House of Commons and the English people with a move toward settlement. Moylett told them they would have to 'call off their dog' too. He returned to Dublin for new instructions from Griffith and Michael Collins, and came back to London to spend the week in conference with Phillips trying to agree on the location and nature of the talks between the two sides. He suggested Chester as a halfway point and Lloyd George agreed on the danger of meeting in London, where the negotiations would leak to the press every day and wreck the chance of any agreement. Phillips told him they would have a settlement by the end of the week. Lloyd George said that if the conference was not held while the coalition government existed a settlement would never be effected, as one of the English parties would not allow the other party to make a settlement by itself.

Spoilers are nothing new either. At that point Arthur Griffith was arrested in Dublin. Phillips assured Moylett that a statement would be made in the House of Commons that he was being released, and Lloyd George called Phillips while Moylett was in his office, demanding to know who had ordered Griffith's arrest. Phillips replied it was certainly not the Ireland Office in London. On the Monday, however, Phillips again summoned Moylett to say that Lloyd George had decided he could not go forward with the plan. The Irish administration had threatened to resign. These events are echoed in Sturgis's diary. John Anderson, the joint under-secretary at Dublin Castle, told Sturgis that Griffith was arrested without reference to him or anyone else. He added, 'There is some justification for the belief that Lloyd George has been in touch with Griffith behind all our backs so he [the chief secretary at Dublin Castle] is not a little peeved I believe.'

In fact Lloyd George had found another channel to Sinn Féin, and decided to use that instead in the hope of getting a better deal. Phillips told Moylett this Dublin Castle plan would never work, but they had to try it. Although none of the initial secret efforts succeeded, leaders hoped then, as today, that they would get credit for trying. Sturgis writes that 'Even if the inconceivably worst came about and the PM made a definite step forward and was turned down by the lot he would have strengthened his position enormously in the eyes of all the world as having for the sake of Peace made a definite offer over and above his own Act and that the onus for further strife would lie clearly at the door of those who had denied him.'

Lloyd George's next step was to deploy his own version of Michael Oatley to seek out a channel to the IRA, in the form of Alfred 'Andy' Cope, the second secretary at the ministry of pensions. Cope came from a poor family, one of eleven children, and started his career as a boy clerk, working his way up to become a detective in Customs. His real ambition was to be posted to Constantinople as the director of customs investigations there but he was sent to Dublin instead to establish secret contacts with Sinn Féin, despite the explicit ban by the Cabinet on any such contact.

According to Paul Bew, the premier Unionist historian, as early as 16 June 1920 Cope reported to Lloyd George that he had made contact with prominent Sinn Féiners. When the British security authorities raided the home of one senior Sinn Féin figure they found a note on Dublin Castle headed notepaper reading 'I am having the papers you require sent to you', signed by Cope. In December he managed to open a channel through Martin FitzGerald, editor of the *Freeman's Journal*, a leading nationalist newspaper. At one point he was blindfolded and taken to a secret location to meet with Sinn Féin leaders. Cope made strenuous efforts to keep those leaders out of jail, issuing orders that de Valera was not to be arrested. When a patrol arrested de Valera by mistake, the head of the patrol called Dublin Castle and was told by Cope to release him at once. He secured the release of Erskine Childers, the novelist and Sinn Féin activist, and even carried his bag for him out of prison chatting about politics. Childers had been terrified that he had been caught with incriminating material and was going to be executed. And Cope also secured the release of Arthur Griffith, a key demand for Sinn Féin. Cope's activities made him unpopular both with the 'securocrats', who called him a 'buck Shinn advocate', and with the Unionists, who accused him of hobbling Crown forces. Tory MPs even suggested in Parliament that he was working for Sinn Féin.

Michael Collins subsequently denied he had met Cope until after the Truce was signed, but that is clearly not true. An account by Tim Kennedy confirms that they had met. Kennedy was intelligence officer for Kerry No. 1 Brigade of the IRA, and came to Dublin to meet Collins in 1921. He went to Vaughan's Hotel in Parnell Square and told the porter to call Collins out of a meeting to see him. 'When we got inside the door in the hall he told me that the war was over and Sir Alfred Cope of the Castle was in the room to which he was taking me and I wasn't to disclose anything to him and his two bodyguards.' Collins introduced Kennedy to Cope and the two RIC head constables accompanying him under an assumed name. 'Mick again announced about the Truce, and they drank brandy and champagne to celebrate it . . . Both Cope and I and Mick kept drinking glass after glass and Mick pretended to be drunk but I discovered afterwards he was drinking some coloured liquid.' Kennedy and Cope passed out.

It was Cope who set up the 'theatrically clandestine' meeting between James Craig, the Northern Ireland Unionist leader, with whom he had earlier worked at the Ministry of Pensions, and who was visiting the viceroy in Dublin, and de Valera on 5 May 1921. Cope had told both of them that the other wanted to meet. Craig was met off the train from Belfast, blindfolded and driven from the station to a safe house. When his blindfold was taken off he noticed the garden full of Michael Collins's men supposedly working, but in fact on guard. According to Craig, de Valera did all the talking and he listened to him 'harping on the grievances of . . . the last 700 years'.

At this point, Moylett came back into the frame. On 28 May he was summoned by the US consul, Mr Dumont, who revealed he was also the American political agent. He showed Moylett a letter from John Anderson in Dublin Castle, asking for Dumont's help in bringing the British authorities and de Valera together. Dumont had taken the message to the Sinn Féin minister W. T. Cosgrave, who in turn had taken it to the Irish Cabinet. De Valera denounced it as a trap and said he wouldn't go to any such meeting, but agreed that Moylett could go. De Valera told Cosgrave to send four or five men to escort Moylett to the castle the following morning, and to report him missing if he had not returned by two o'clock.

The next day, Moylett walked alone up to the castle gate, leaving his escort nearby. Cosgrave had reminded him of the necessity of leaving by two, so that they didn't have to report him missing. When Moylett knocked at the gate it was clear he was expected because a policeman promptly opened it and escorted him in, showing him where three IRA men had been murdered. Moylett said he experienced a creepy feeling up the back of his legs as the gates closed behind him. He passed a group of Auxiliaries conducting target practice, and was ushered into an apartment on the ground floor where he met Cope. Cope offered him a cigarette and said he was anxious to meet de Valera. Moylett suggested putting an advertisement in the papers, and asked Cope what the agenda was. He replied 'We are willing to acknowledge that we are defeated. There is nothing else for us to do but draft into this country four hundred thousand men and exterminate the whole population of the country, and we are not willing to do that . . . We are willing to withdraw our whole establishment, from the lowest policeman to the highest judge.' Cope said he was the direct representative of Lloyd George and was here to make peace. After two and a half hours of talks, he asked Moylett to go back and be debriefed by Cosgrave. Moylett managed to get out of the castle just before de Valera's 2 p.m. deadline. Forty-eight hours later, de Valera received a letter from Downing Street proposing a truce, an amnesty and a conference. Finally the channel had worked, the negotiations were set up.

As we have seen in modern times it is often the lack of a process that is the problem rather than a disagreement over substance. Sturgis wrote in March 1921, 'What a nightmare it all is – the conviction grows that there is not any material thing between us if we could only get round the table and get at it.' The problem was a lack of trust. Sturgis thought Sinn Féin 'fear that they will be promised something, even given something, and then have it whipped away'. The challenge, as so often, was one of sequencing. Who would go first? Sturgis said 'The only question is how to get over the first fence. The

PM will not make a definite offer so long as they ask for a Republic. They will not cease to ask for a Republic till the PM makes them a definite offer.'

Formal negotiations were preceded, as in Northern Ireland seventy years later, by a stately dance of speeches, notably the 'Olive branch speech' of King George V. The king was to open the inaugural session of the Stormont Parliament in Northern Ireland and had been given a draft speech by James Craig that was pure Unionism. He didn't like it. General Smuts argued that the speech should be used as an opportunity to reach out with an olive branch to Sinn Féin. He advised that 'The promise of Dominion status by the king would create a new and definite situation which would crystallise opinion favourably in Ireland and elsewhere. Informal negotiations should then be set going with responsible Irish leaders.' The speech was redrafted by officials in London and had the intended effect in Ireland and around the world.

It was followed by a secret correspondence, reminiscent of that between John Major and Martin McGuinness. Cope went to London to argue forcibly for peace in front of the Cabinet and then returned to Dublin to deliver the first confidential letter inviting de Valera and Craig to London to discuss an accommodation on 25 June. De Valera immediately rejected the approach because it denied Ireland's essential unity. Smuts was dispatched to Dublin as an unofficial intermediary. As someone who had played a prominent role fighting the British twenty years before in the Second Boer War, he had an entree with the Republicans, who had studied the Afrikaners' campaign carefully. As so often, both sides got hung up on preconditions. Smuts persuaded the British government to drop its demand that the issue of sovereignty be settled first and to agree to meet de Valera without Craig. He advised de Valera to avoid provoking the British with his reply, and de Valera telegraphed Lloyd George to say they were ready to meet to discuss 'on what basis such a conference as that proposed can reasonably hope to achieve the object desired'. The truce was agreed at a meeting in Dublin's Mansion House between the IRA and General Macready and Cope, and in June 1921 Lloyd George agreed to 'shake hands with murder'. The moral question of talking to terrorists continued to bother the British. Sturgis noted 'The *Morning Post*'s attitude of horror at treating with Murderers is one with which one must have sympathy . . . This view certainly is much held by many in England but the whole question is much bigger than that and we must be ready to swallow a lot if a real settlement can result.'

The first meeting between the prime minister and a Sinn Féin leader in Downing Street on 14 July 1921 was a major event. Frances Stevenson, Lloyd George's mistress and secretary, wrote that she had never seen the prime minister 'so excited as he was before de Valera arrived. He kept walking in and out of my room and I could see he was working out the best way of dealing with Dev . . . He had a big map of the British Empire hung up on the wall in the Cabinet room, with great blotches of red all over it. This was to impress on Dev the greatness of the BE and the King . . . [Lloyd George] said he was very difficult to keep to the point – he kept going off at a tangent and talking in formulas and refusing to face facts.' When I read her account, the similarities with the first meeting between Tony Blair and Gerry Adams and Martin McGuinness in 1997 are striking. The two sides even sat in the same places as they did seventy-six years later, Sinn Féin with their backs to Horse Guards Parade and the government on the Downing Street side of the table. Lloyd George said this was 'the first time we have [had] the physical force party round a table in direct discussion'. At the final meeting in the same room six months later, as the Irish delegates were leaving, Bew says 'Collins walked over to a corner where there was an American rifle . . . presented to Lloyd George by President Wilson. This he picked up, while the Cabinet watched in amazement. Walking over to Lloyd George's chair, he sat down and said to the minister: "Now the prime minister can take a photograph of a gunman."' I remember Gerry Adams's fascination with a ceremonial sword presented to John Major by an Arab potentate, which sat on a table in the Cabinet Room. He used to pick it up, and I would worry about whether I should call security.

Lloyd George met his match in de Valera, and twenty years later he recalled 'I have had some experience of Mr de Valera as a negotiator and frankly I have not seen anything like it. He is perfectly unique and this poor distracted world has a good right to feel profoundly thankful that he is unique.' He described negotiating with de Valera as 'like trying to pick up mercury with a fork'. At their meeting de Valera insisted that Northern Ireland be treated as part of the Republic or, if not, he would demand complete independence. Lloyd George said that if those were his last words then there was nothing left to discuss other than when the truce should end. De Valera asked for time to go back to Dublin and consult. Once there he sent another letter, which Lloyd George dismissed as a silly reply. The Cabinet very nearly took it as a rejection of talks, but a telegram from Cope persuaded them to treat it as an open door. The British wrote back to say the correspondence had gone on long enough and proposed a neutral formula as the basis for talks. De Valera accepted, although even then he tried to insist in his reply that Ireland was already an independent sovereign state. The British had to ignore this and send him the invitation again.

The gap between the declaration of a ceasefire and the beginning of political talks is always a dangerous moment when violence can reappear. Sturgis writes of 'the risk that the longer it draws out the more likely it is that an incident happens that would "blow peace to blazes" – such as the killing of leaders on either side'. Jeremy Smith of the University of Wales writes 'moving from ceasefire to agreement was never going to be easy . . . violence had weaned hard men for whom compromise meant a betrayal of dead comrades and venerated ideals. It was clear that an agreement under such conditions would require a Herculean effort.' He adds, however, that 'with both sides exhausted, demoralised and weary of fighting, the military option had all but driven itself into the sand by 1921, leaving politics as the only course open to either side to achieve its ends'.

Once he had started the negotiation, Lloyd George was trapped, as subsequent leaders have been. He needed a success to keep his coalition together and, as Arthur Balfour said, 'success would be about as big as winning the war'. Ronan Fanning's assessment is 'there could be no turning back. Failure would trigger the end of his premiership and the collapse of his coalition government upon which all the British delegates were also dependent for their political survival'.

Success requires pragmatic negotiators. Jeremy Smith writes 'What was needed to ease the process of bargaining and concession were pragmatic, flexible, even rather "slippery" individuals. Ones who could comfortably retreat from fixed positions, who would settle for the obtainable rather than the desirable, and who would risk a great deal to surmount the initial and most forbidding hurdle of actually making an agreement. Luckily, at this crucial moment such leaders emerged on both sides. Lloyd George, Winston Churchill and Lord Birkenhead for the British, all of whom would have cheerfully sold their grandmothers for political advantage. For the Irish, Arthur Griffith was a known moderate and Michael Collins, the de facto leader of Irish Republicanism, was also, thankfully a hard-headed realist.'

Lloyd George was painfully conscious of the first law of diplomacy: the most difficult negotiations are always with your own side. He allowed the Cabinet to remain in the dark about progress, but kept Austen Chamberlain, as leader of the Tory Party, and Balfour, as the most intransigent Unionist in the Cabinet, fully briefed. He deliberately brought hardliners like Churchill and Birkenhead into the delegation for the negotiations. As Beaverbrook put it, 'they were too dangerous to leave out'. And he sent the very worst potential opponents of a deal, Balfour and Maurice Hankey (the Cabinet Secretary), off to Washington to attend the Naval Conference as soon as he could.

The Irish had the same problem of moderates and hardliners, but failed to deal with it. Michael Collins and Arthur Griffith complained that their main problem was with Dublin rather than with the British. De Valera decided to stay behind in Dublin as a final court of appeal instead of participating in the negotiations, and chose the delegation to reflect the different factions in the Sinn Féin coalition rather than for effectiveness. Michael Collins was a brilliant military leader but admitted himself he had little patience with the constitutional minutiae. He was aware he was being set up as the scapegoat, saying he was doing what his Cabinet colleagues 'knew must be done but lack the moral courage to do themselves'. De Valera appointed Arthur Griffith as the leader of the delegation even though he knew he was far more moderate in his aims than de Valera himself, and selected hardliners like Gavan Duffy to keep an eye on the two leaders. But Duffy complained that he was excluded from secret meetings with Lloyd George, and Erskine Childers, whom de Valera had included to keep an eye on his interests, complained in his diary about being picked on by the British: 'AG [Attorney General] attack me about *Riddle of the Sands* [his famous novel] – says I caused one European war and now want to cause another.' Despite all the problems, de Valera made the leaders of the delegation plenipotentiaries, which meant they could sign an agreement without reference back to him, even though he expected to be consulted.

Asymmetry causes problems in all negotiations, and there was a huge disparity between the Sinn Féin and British government delegations. Lloyd George and his colleagues had a long track record in negotiating, including most recently the Versailles Treaty. The British were prepared, they had thought through their position and had studied the other side, armed with reports from Dublin Castle on each delegate. The Irish side had no experience and no instructions. Lloyd George said on meeting them, they 'are simple; they have none of the skill of the old nationalists; these men are not accustomed to finessing'. What was worse they had not prepared for the negotiation. Sinn Féin had spent years talking only to themselves, and lacked the long educative period in other negotiations where the insurgent side has a chance to gain a sense of how the rest of the world sees them and what might be negotiable.

As so often in later conflicts, the 'battle was won in the framing of negotiations not in the negotiation itself', according to Fanning. The passage of the Government of Ireland Act in 1920 created Northern Ireland as a political fact that the republicans had to negotiate around. In the words of Philip Kerr in 1920, 'the government thought the kindest way out was to settle the fundamental issue beyond question now'. The British managed to set the framework on the content of the Treaty from the very beginning of the negotiations. As talks commenced, Tom Jones, Lloyd George's private secretary, told Bonar Law that 'Dominion status with no navy, no hostile tariffs and no coercion of Ulster would be the core of the agreement', and so it was at the end.

The British approach also underlined the importance of controlling the pen in a negotiation. The Irish historian Nicholas Mansergh says of the process that 'however much amended, the basic paper at any conference is apt to determine the parameters of subsequent discussion. This was to prove no exception.' Tom Jones circulated the British proposals on 20 July and the draft treaty in November. The Irish had no paper setting out an alternative position in either case, and found themselves negotiating throughout on the basis of British texts. Arthur Griffith resorted to trying to turn the negotiation into a debate, in Lloyd George's words with 'an elaborate, not to say prolix, exposition on the unnaturalness of Partition'.

Lloyd George demonstrated all the attributes required of a great negotiator. He had honed his skills in settling labour disputes, inviting both sides to sit down with him, in the historian Margaret MacMillan's words 'a normal enough procedure today but highly unusual then'. One witness of his settlement of a rail dispute said 'He plays upon men round a table like the chords of a musical instrument, now pleading, now persuasive, stern, playful and minatory in quick succession.' He was an extraordinarily quick study, as John Maynard Keynes discovered during the negotiations on the Versailles Treaty, when Keynes revised a position paper and rushed to a meeting to find Lloyd George already on his feet. Keynes handed over the paper, the prime minister glanced at it and, without a pause, gradually modified his arguments 'until he ended up with the opposite position to the one he had started out with'. On his own side in the Irish negotiations, Frances Stevenson said he 'successfully wangled Churchill and Birkenhead' to the point where they were 'all out' for a settlement. His flexibility was not an altogether attractive attribute. Lord Riddell, his confidant, said 'You cannot rely on what Lloyd George says . . . He may not actually tell a lie, but he will lead you to believe what he concludes will induce you to do what he wants.' He successfully used secret meetings with Collins and Griffith to flatter them and win their trust, either alone or with Chamberlain. Lionel Curtis, Secretary to the British delegation, described 'Lloyd George negotiating with the Irish [as] like Augustus John drawing. Every stroke was made with precision and mastery, and never needed correction.'

Just like Tony Blair, Lloyd George used his own personal staff to run the negotiations, employing Jones, his trusted Welsh-speaking private secretary, as the secretary of the peace conference and the key go-between with the Irish. Hankey, the Cabinet Secretary, said it was because he 'did not want an Anglo-Saxon to run the show!' and their common language allowed them to keep certain things from his Cabinet colleagues. On one crucial occasion, Lloyd George was at dinner at Churchill's house along with Birkenhead, and had invited Michael Collins and Arthur Griffith to meet them there later. Jones phoned to tell him in Welsh that Collins and Griffith distrusted Churchill and Birkenhead, and instead they wanted to meet the prime minister alone. Lloyd George accordingly set up a separate meeting without telling his dinner companions.

Jones played a role familiar to me, of becoming the friend of the other side and floating ideas with them that they could then present as their own. On 27 October he took the British draft privately to Erskine Childers and assured him it was not to be taken at face value. It was simply designed to placate the Unionist ministers who were threatening to resign from the Cabinet. At another stage Jones proposed a private side letter to the Irish, a device we resorted to more than seventy years later with David Trimble.

Like all such negotiations the talks nearly broke down more than once, and in the words of Sturgis 'whenever one sees daylight in this cursed business something goes wrong'. The Irish response to the draft treaty delivered in November was, according to Fanning, 'drafted mainly by Childers and took the form of a typed two-paged memorandum prefaced by a note stating that the proposals were contingent upon the essential unity of Ireland being maintained. It effectively ignored the British reservations and made no mention of Northern Ireland until the final clause.' Lloyd George said 'This time it is the Sinn Féiners. Last week it was the Ulsterites. They are both the sons of Belial!' He instructed Tom Jones to 'tell the Sinn Féiners the document filled him with despair. Ministers were busy men, they had spent weeks and weeks on this matter and apparently made no progress whatever.' As a facilitator should, when Jones went to meet Griffith and Collins, he chose to soft-pedal his instructions. Instead of telling the Irish delegation to pack their bags, he said that unless their response could be justified, the prime minister would have to write breaking off the negotiations, and suggested there were explanations the Irish could give which might mollify the government. He went back to Downing Street to find Lloyd George lying on a couch with his eyes closed, in despair. He sat down next to him and explained quietly in Welsh what he had done. The Irish response was couched in masterful ambiguity. Austen Chamberlain said he did not know what it meant and told Jones to 'tell the Irish we were being fooled'.

The next time the negotiation met a blockage, it looked terminal, but Lloyd George saved it by an ingenious bit of lateral thinking. The British had been manoeuvring throughout to avoid breaking the negotiations on an issue which they thought would lose the argument for them inside the empire. They therefore tried to get all the crucial issues from their side agreed first, leaving just the question of sovereignty, on which they thought they enjoyed international support, whereas the Irish wanted to leave the issue of the North to last. Lloyd George thought he could persuade the Unionists to make concessions which would help him get round the problem, but Craig rejected any concession. A depressed Lloyd George told Tom Jones to prepare Collins and Griffith for the break-up of the conference and talked to him about resigning rather than coercing the south by military force. But he then came up with the ingenious idea of a boundary commission to decide the frontier between North and South, which might give the South the majority Catholic counties it particularly wanted. In the way of a skilful negotiator he was not addressing the central issue that was blocking the negotiation but trying to find a completely different answer, and it worked. The trouble with it was that it was a classic case of constructive ambiguity which turned destructive over time. Craig had no intention of giving anything on the border, while Collins was certain he would get Fermanagh, Tyrone and part of County Down. The idea of a boundary commission allowed Lloyd George to get to an agreement, but it left a long-term problem that led to another IRA campaign and, in the end, another peace negotiation.

Lloyd George spent all November trying to bring the negotiation to a head without success, and finally in December said it was time to agree or break off. On 4 December, Tom Jones went to visit Arthur Griffith at midnight at Hans Place. Griffith was very emotional, saying that he and Michael Collins believed in Lloyd George's desire for peace but their Dublin colleagues did not. He begged Lloyd George to help them get to peace.

When Jones told him of the late-night session, Lloyd George

sensed an opportunity and agreed to meet Collins and Griffith secretly in the morning. When they came to Downing Street he said he would see the Cabinet at midday and tell them the negotiations had broken down on the question of whether Ireland remained in the empire. Collins and Griffith proposed continuing with the negotiations. When they met again in the afternoon with their delegations, Lloyd George confronted Griffith with a clause on Ulster he had agreed earlier with the prime minister personally, and which had been captured in a memo by Tom Jones. Lloyd George put on quite a show, becoming 'excited. He shook his papers in the air, declared that were trying deliberately to bring about a break on Ulster.' His theatrical approach reminds me of Tony Blair's advice during the session with the Orange Order never to lose my temper 'except on purpose'. Lloyd George accused Griffith of letting him down and breaking his promise. Griffith was taken aback and protested 'I have never let a man down in my whole life and I never will.' He said that as far as he was concerned he could agree to the position on the North but he could not speak for the rest of the delegation. Given that he was the leader of the delegation this was a ludicrous position, and Lloyd George made the most of it.

Sensing he was in sight of an agreement Lloyd George immediately made a tactical retreat on a whole series of other issues to make the Irish feel they had made a series of gains rather than just lost a central point. Both sides had to be winners if they were going to get an agreement. The British gave ground on the vexed issue of the oath to the Crown, on the defence clause allowing Ireland greater freedom in its foreign policy, and abandoned the insistence on free trade, a particular issue for Griffith who had long championed a form of protectionism for Ireland.

Finally Lloyd George set a deadline and forced the Irish delegation to come to a decision. He produced two letters to Craig, one saying the Irish delegation had recommended the agreement to the Dáil and the other saying there was no agreement. He said he had a special train and a destroyer on standby to take one letter or the other to Belfast. If it was the second, 'It is war, and war within three days. Which letter am I to send?' He said they were plenipotentiaries and needed to decide by 10 p.m. that evening. At two in the morning the Irish delegation returned to Downing Street and signed the treaty. For the first time in the proceedings the British and Irish delegations shook hands.

Of course, as with all breakthrough agreements that was not the end of the matter. Spoilers on both sides tried to derail the agreement. Six months after the treaty was signed, Henry Wilson, the recently retired chief of the Imperial General Staff who had just been elected an Ulster Unionist MP, was shot outside his house in Eaton Place in broad daylight by the London Unit of the IRA. The Tories threatened to leave the government immediately. Horrifying anti-Catholic pogroms were carried out by Protestants in Belfast. Forces loyal to de Valera's wing of Irish Republicanism took over the Four Courts in Dublin. The British were not convinced that Collins would deal with them and Churchill ordered Macready and his remaining forces to take action – but Macready, who was scornful of Churchill's 'feverish impetuosity', delayed, and in the end Free State forces attacked and the civil war commenced.

Implementation, as always, was key. The British started to implement their undertakings straight away, handing over Dublin Castle, releasing all IRA prisoners and making preparations to evacuate the army. But they were conscious that the division in Sinn Féin meant that the Irish side might not deliver on its end of the bargain and they were prepared to fight. Lloyd George, anxious to win the support of the Diehards, had put Churchill in charge of implementation. Churchill tottered on the edge of returning to war for months, provoking Robert Cecil to say 'I don't think Winston takes any interest in public affairs unless they involve the possibility of bloodshed.' Despite his posturing, the agreement remained intact and even survived the transition from one government to another when

Lloyd George's coalition fell in October and was replaced by a Conservative government. Despite misgivings, the new prime minister Bonar Law allowed the Irish Free State Constitution Act to pass the House of Commons with Tory votes.

In Ireland the British government had at first refused to talk to terrorists, had then reached out secretly, opened negotiations and found a compromise solution, in a pattern remarkably similar to the one pursued seventy years later. Lloyd George had demonstrated himself to be a masterful negotiator, with skill and perseverance. According to Roy Hattersley, 'All he wanted was a deal – any deal – which, at least for a time, removed Ireland from the political agenda. He had succeeded . . . where Pitt, Peel and Gladstone had failed.' But he also demonstrated that it is possible to be too clever in pursuit of an agreement at any cost. If you rely too heavily on ambiguity and on trickery, and are too desperate to succeed, you may end up with an agreement that contains the seeds of its own destruction.

The lesson painfully learned in the conflict with Irish Republicans – that in the end you will have to talk to any terrorist movement if it enjoys significant political support – did not, unfortunately, stay learned. Throughout the twentieth century governments said they would never talk to terrorists, believed they could defeat them militarily, and when they discovered they couldn't and stalemate took over, had to relearn how to make contact and conduct negotiations.

The next similar problem encountered by the British was in Palestine when they faced the Arab revolt in 1936. As Rory Miller records, British officials were very conscious of the Irish precedent. Lord Dufferin, the deputy in the Colonial Office, argued that de Valera provided a valuable precedent for dealing with the mufti, Haj Amin al-Husseini. Like de Valera, the mufti was the only figure who could control this rising of 'indigenous nationalism', and it was necessary to 'come to terms with the one man who can, on his side, guarantee peace'. The high commissioner, Harold MacMichael, however, was adamant that

Her Majesty's Government 'cannot treat with the instigators of murder' and said there would be 'wholesale resignations' from the Palestinian administration if the mufti 'was recognised in any capacity as a negotiator'. To which Dufferin's colleague in the Colonial Office, Grattan Bushe, pointed out 'on the contrary, peace in Ireland was made by a treaty between Cabinet ministers and murderers'. The colonial secretary, Malcolm MacDonald (Ramsay MacDonald's son), intervened to say the 'analogy with Ireland . . . is not complete . . . In the Irish case our object has been to instate murderers as the new government of the territory. In Palestine this is not so, as we intend to continue ruling ourselves.' Even if they were aware of the lessons that could be learned from their last encounter with a politically popular terrorist movement, they declined to apply them. Instead they opted for a tough security approach led by the police officer Douglas Duff (whose activities inspired the phrase 'duffing up' an opponent), combined with 'carefully orchestrated concessions' which they hoped 'would further erode Arab unity, isolate the mufti, and permit a re-imposition of order'.

Interestingly those on the other side in the conflict in Palestine also drew comparisons with the Irish example. Yitzhak Shamir, later Israeli prime minister, cited Michael Collins as an influence and used the code name 'Michael' once Stern was killed and he took over as leader of the Stern Gang. Menachem Begin, the leader of Irgun and also later an Israeli prime minister, carefully studied the IRA campaign. His aim was constantly to goad the British into cracking down and alienating the Yishuv (the mainstream representatives of the Jewish community in Palestine). In the historian Bowyer Bell's words, 'he wanted to create a scenario where Britain's options were only between repression and withdrawal'. Irgun's most notable operation was the bombing of the King David Hotel in July 1946, when they smuggled seven milk churns of explosives into the basement and killed ninety-one people, including Jewish and Arab civilians as well as British officials. The British responded in the same way as they had in Ireland in 1916 by arresting thousands of people, mainly the wrong ones, and interning them, thus alienating the population further. Field Marshal Montgomery, in charge of military policy, who wanted to kill the top fifty members of the Yishuv, repeated the usual mantra, 'We must beat terrorism or it will beat us.' Alan Cunningham, the high commissioner, wrote in 1946 'the best method of dealing with terrorists is to kill them'. There was even a ghastly parallel with the later conflict in Northern Ireland when Irgun kidnapped and hanged two British sergeants, leaving their booby-trapped bodies hanging from trees. Irgun succeeded in attracting the attention of the newly formed United Nations, which began to consider self-government for Palestine, and support in the United States with a resolution in Congress condemning Britain's behaviour. By 1947 a British government confronting much bigger problems at home now faced the same choice they had in Ireland between total suppression and getting out, and they chose the latter, announcing in September that they were withdrawing. They left behind a bloodbath and a long-running conflict that still bedevils the world.

In Kenya the British made the same mistake again, saying they wouldn't talk to the terrorists and then, when the repression didn't work, they had to negotiate. The then colonial secretary, Alan Lennox-Boyd, described the Mau Mau as a 'conspiracy based on the total perversion of the human spirit by means of the power of the oath and by witchcraft and intimidation', and as 'sub-humans' with 'death as their only deliverance'. When the campaign of repression made little impact the British banned the Kenyan African Union (KAU), arrested its leader Jomo Kenyatta, whom the governor, Patrick Renison, labelled 'the African leader to darkness and death', together with a hundred of his colleagues. Iain Macleod, Lennox-Boyd's successor as colonial secretary, described the governor's attack as unwise 'for the obvious reason that we would sooner or later have to deal with Jomo Kenyatta and this didn't seem a very promising introduction'. Violence increased. The British managed to alienate the Kikuyu in general by treating them as if they were all members of the Mau Mau, detaining some 150,000 in concentration camps and moving a million more forcibly into guarded villages. A state of emergency was declared and the Mau Mau driven into the forests where they were hunted like animals.

Finally progress was made when one official remembered the lessons from Britain's past experiences. Richard Catling was appointed police commissioner in 1954. He had previously been in Palestine, where he had made secret contact with Irgun and was in the King David Hotel at the time of the explosion but suffered only a minor cut. He decided that if the insurgency was to end, they would need to talk to Kenyatta. He went to the prison near Lake Turkana in northern Kenya where Kenyatta was serving seven years' hard labour and struck up a friendship with him. Kenyatta was the prison cook and they held their discussions walking round the prison compound. Kenyatta complained the ground was infertile and he could not produce fresh vegetables for the prisoners' meals. Catling, who came from a family of Suffolk farmers, suggested spinach. Kenyatta had never heard of it but when Catling was back in Nairobi he sent him spinach seeds. Kenyatta would later joke that it was 'the commissioner's spinach' that kept him and his fellow prisoners going.

In 1961 the British freed Kenyatta and he led the KANU delegation to the first and second Lancaster Conferences in London where independence was negotiated. The governor, Evelyn Baring, who, in the words of the historian Keith Kyle, 'had wished that Kenya should be forever unpolluted with [Kenyatta's] name, came to recognise him as a benign and effective ruler'.

Throughout the twentieth century, the British fell into the trap of calling their opponents 'terrorists', saying they would never talk to them, escalating the violence and then belatedly realising they had to negotiate. Finally they would deal with them as equals and even describe them as 'statesmen'. And it wasn't just the British who kept on making the same mistake during decolonisation. The French did so too, particularly in Algeria.

The nationalist insurrection started on All Saints' Day 1954, with attacks across Algeria targeting the police, army and communications infrastructure. Radio Cairo broadcast the key demands of the FLN (Front de Libération Nationale): 'restoration of the Algerian state, sovereign, democratic, and social, within the framework of the principles of Islam' and 'preservation of all fundamental freedoms, without distinction of race or religion'. The French interior minister, François Mitterrand, declared: 'the only possible negotiation is war', and, as always, the conflict escalated. France saw the conflict in terms of its experience in Indo-China and deployed the counter-terrorist tactics learned there, and even called the FLN guerrillas 'Les Viets'. The government brought in the elite parachute regiment led by General Jacques Massu, who had fought in Vietnam. By 1958–9 the French army had through torture, summary execution and a scorched-earth strategy won the battle and regained control of Algeria, but they had lost the war. They had committed nearly half a million troops to the province and were losing support at home and abroad.

The catastrophe of the Algerian war led to the collapse of the Fourth Republic and the return of de Gaulle as president. De Gaulle realised, in the words of French counter-insurgency expert David Galula, 'The objective is the population. The population is at the same time the real terrain of the war.' He began to address some of the grievances behind the rebellion with social reforms and called elections in Algeria separate from those in France. The French made a number of attempts to talk to the FLN but largely without success. On the night of 10 June 1960, de Gaulle secretly met three FLN leaders in the Élysée Palace. The group had been flown to Paris on the promise they would meet a 'high political personage' and were only informed this was de Gaulle himself on the morning of the day they were to meet. To demonstrate that they were trusted dignitaries, the three were not searched for weapons when they entered the Élysée. There was, however, a marksman hidden behind a tapestry in case things went wrong. De Gaulle told them that he would shortly appeal to the FLN to discuss a ceasefire. At the end of the meeting de Gaulle said: 'Because we are fighting each other, I will not shake your hand, but I salute you.'

One of the lessons that the French experience in Algeria most clearly illustrates is that the important role of third parties long precedes the end of the Cold War. The French government had been clear from the beginning of the conflict that they would not welcome intervention by outside powers in Algeria but after a series of failed bilateral initiatives with the FLN and the distrust that had built up as a result, they needed a third party to get the talks going again. The role was played by a Swiss diplomat, Olivier Long, who recorded his efforts in a remarkable internal note for the Swiss foreign ministry.

In November 1960, only four months after the collapse of bilateral talks at Melun in France, Long was approached by a Geneva lawyer he knew, who said that he believed the Algerians wanted to restart negotiations. The lawyer was a friend of Taieb Boulharouf, the FLN representative in Rome, and wanted to introduce Boulharouf to someone in the Swiss foreign ministry. Long agreed to accompany the lawyer to a private meeting with the Algerian on a personal basis and listen to what he had to say. They met in Geneva for a cup of tea. Boulharouf said the only way to resolve the conflict was through direct negotiations with the French but to avoid another public disaster like Melun they wanted to explore secretly whether new talks were possible. The FLN wanted the Swiss to act as a go-between with the French. Both agreed they would have to await the outcome of the referendum on the future of Algeria, just called by de Gaulle to give himself a mandate to negotiate, before approaching the French.

On 10 January 1961, the day after the referendum result, Long went to Paris to see Louis Joxe, the minister for Algeria, a 'suave historian and diplomat', who also happened to be a personal friend of many years standing. They met at his house and Joxe listened with interest to Long's account. He said he saw a great many people every day who said they could put him in touch with the rebels and he turned them away, anxious not to take the French government into a trap; but he had known Long for twenty-five years and knew him to be a serious man. Joxe said he would consult de Gaulle and commented that previous contacts had collapsed because they were not sufficiently discreet. Within a few days Joxe came back with de Gaulle's reply: 'Say to M. Long that he can continue.'

The Swiss were surprised, given de Gaulle's strong opposition to any foreign interference in Algerian matters, but it was clear to them that this was the only serious route the French had to the rebels. The French intelligence services had been trying to open up channels but de Gaulle asked the prime minister, Michel Debré, to close them all down. He instructed the Swiss to tell the Algerians that Georges Pompidou would be his representative. Pompidou had been de Gaulle's chef de cabinet, and later became his successor as president, but at that stage he was a director of Rothschild Brothers in Paris. The Algerians expressed concern since Pompidou was not an official. The French explained that Joxe could hardly come on a secret mission to Switzerland without being noticed. Pompidou had the complete confidence of de Gaulle.

On the evening of 19 February Pompidou arrived in Switzerland, in Long's words 'with a copy of the "Memoirs of Talleyrand" in his hand and with Bruno de Leusse from the Ministry of Algeria'. The Swiss put the two delegations in different hotels in Lucerne and arranged the meetings in a third, the Schweizerhof, having told the owner they were holding confidential financial discussions between French and Arab delegations. The two sides met for seven hours and agreed to meet again in a fortnight. The Algerian side told the Swiss,

'This is a completely different thing than Melun.' It was the first time the opponents had met to discuss substance after seven years of war.

The Swiss decided to move the next meeting to Neuchâtel to avoid the risk of a leak. This time the meeting went badly, with both sides accusing the other of having hardened their position. The French insisted the negotiations should take place on French territory, while the Algerians wanted them on neutral ground. Évian on the French shore of Lake Geneva was proposed, with the Algerians able to withdraw across the border to Switzerland between sessions so they could express themselves freely on foreign soil. The French wanted a ceasefire during the talks, but the Algerians feared that a ceasefire would sap their will to go back to war if the talks failed. The Algerians wanted two parallel negotiations, one military on the ceasefire and the other political. The French wanted the Sahara to be excluded. Both sides left saying they were waiting for a response from the other.

As we have seen repeatedly, such preconditions can stymie a negotiation. Long rushed to Paris to appeal to de Gaulle and secured a handwritten formula from him in which the president abandoned his preconditions and agreed to discuss the Sahara. Joxe also indicated he was ready to meet the Algerians himself in France but near the border with Switzerland. In response the Algerians asked whether their leader Ben Bella could be released from French prison to join the talks, but the French made it clear that that could only happen when a ceasefire was in place.

After long internal deliberations the Algerians came back saying they agreed with the French proposals and the two sides met to negotiate the logistics of the talks. They would take place in Évian but the Algerian delegation would stay across the border in Switzerland. Having finally shepherded them to agreement, the Swiss diplomats had to drive the participants through the night to avoid any risk of them being seen by the press, in the same way that the HD Centre had to drive the ETA representative out of Geneva fifty years later.

Just as the formal talks were poised to open in Évian, they collapsed when the French announced they were going to have parallel negotiations with the FLN's rival, the MNA (Mouvement National Algérien). The French were not prepared to accept the FLN as the sole legitimate representative of Algeria, and wanted to keep the MNA in play, even though it had become an irrelevance. The Algerians sent a message warning that they were going to pull out and asked that it be transmitted to the French as soon as possible. A Swiss diplomat tried all evening to get through to the French on the phone, and eventually managed to wake a senior official at three in the morning to warn him about what was going to happen. The French official cut the conversation short. Even worse, he failed to pass on the message to Joxe and the president. Once they realised the gravity of the situation, the French wanted a solution but it was not easy to see how to get to it. Long decided his role as the third party was to be a shock absorber and play for time. He kept Boulharouf in Switzerland and briefed Joxe on his increasingly emotional mood through cryptic telephone conversations.

Long was then summoned to Paris by Joxe, and when he arrived discovered the minister had never been made aware of the Algerian warning on the MNA, and had only now begun to understand why they felt betrayed. Joxe said that de Gaulle was irritated by the machinations and it was necessary to soothe him. They had to go and see the prime minister again. Joxe drove to the Matignon in his official car and Long entered through the gate into the garden at the back of the Matignon to avoid being seen. Long put forward a series of alternative compromises and Debré and Joxe took them to the general that night. They returned to report that he was in a bad mood and thought they had already made too many concessions.

Long returned to Geneva and told Boulharouf the Swiss had

done all they could. The moment had come to decide between negotiations and war. He warned of the dangers of over-negotiating. International public opinion would not understand why the Algerians were breaking off talks in these circumstances. In any case the Laos peace conference was about to open in Geneva and the Swiss would need to decide between that and the Évian negotiations on Algeria, since they couldn't practically host both at the same time. Boulharouf went off to consult and two days later gave him the Algerians' negative response. Long decided to make the message less unpalatable to the French when he read it over the phone to Joxe. He had to do the same with the aggressive French reply to the Algerians. Boulharouf returned to Tunis to consult, and when he came back to Geneva to meet with Long, the two of them listened to reports of the attempted putsch in Algiers on a radio as they negotiated texts.

After the failure of the coup attempt, Joxe called Long to say de Gaulle was keen to proceed quickly and proposed 16 May as the opening date for the talks. The Algerians preferred to delay till the end of the month but were persuaded by the Swiss to counter-propose 20 May. De Gaulle insisted that since fighting was still going on it would have to be a very simple, even austere, meeting. The *préfet* in Évian would not shake hands with the Algerian delegation; Krim Belkacem, their leader, accepted the arrangement, saying that the result was the important thing. The delegation was housed in the Emir of Qatar's château and ferried across the lake daily in Swiss military helicopters or fast boats, depending on the weather. De Gaulle had banned the two sides from sharing meals because they were still enemies, so the Swiss supplied food to the Algerians.

At that stage the Swiss bowed out. Long concluded in his memo that they had been acceptable to both sides as a third party because of the country's historic commitment to the search for peaceful settlements to conflicts, and because of their discretion; 'we abstained from asking questions', he said. Secrecy was essential and they had managed to keep the negotiators away from the journalists – 'This monstrous hunting of people, a result of the tabloids' activities, does not simplify our task.' Long believed the intermediary had to be selfless, as 'nothing is impossible if one does not want credit for doing it'. He might have added that the key thing was the right people (who knew both the FLN leadership and Joxe) being in the right place at the right time, when de Gaulle realised he needed an intermediary to get talks going.

As so often the gap between the two sides at Évian was vast, and as an unpromising backdrop to the talks the young mayor of Évian was assassinated by the Organisation de l'Armée Secrète (the OAS) – right-wing paramilitaries who wanted to stop Algerian independence, and who actually killed more French people than the FLN. The talks collapsed in July. De Gaulle was desperate to get to a solution and ordered new secret talks to begin. Finding a site for the new meetings was not easy. It had to be safe from the OAS and journalists and yet within easy reach of Switzerland. The French chose Chalet Yéti, 3,000 feet up in the Jura mountains. The initial meetings, which followed close on the heels of the Évian breakdown, were slow and painful. Joxe seemed to be worn down and irritable, to the extent that on one occasion he looked as if he was going to hurl himself across the table at the Algerians. Joxe returned to Paris to ask de Gaulle for reinforcements and was sent Robert Buron, the minister for works, whose assassination had been ordered by the FLN, but whose humour lightened proceedings. De Gaulle's final instructions to the French had been: 'Do not let the negotiations prolong themselves indefinitely . . . Besides that, do not attach yourselves to details. There is the possible and impossible.'

Joxe was the only member of the French team to have a room of his own in Chalet Yéti. The overcrowding was made worse by the fact that the bodyguards were jammed inside for fear that by hanging around outside they would attract attention. The cramped conditions did, however, help break the ice between the teams. On 18 February de Gaulle gave vital instructions to Joxe by phone: 'The essential thing, is to reach an agreement composed of a ceasefire followed by self-determination . . . It is this result, I repeat, this result that must be realised today . . . there is no comparison between the primary interest, which consists of reaching an agreement, and the secondary interest, which consists of holding a little longer certain things which, anyway, we do not reckon to hold forever.' This led to an all-night negotiating session that ended at 5 a.m. The two sides exchanged brief declarations and for the first time they all shook hands. They agreed to meet once more at Évian on 7 March.

On 18 March 1962, the final ninety-three-page agreement was reached. The French had fallen into the usual trap of beginning by saying they would never talk to terrorists, only belatedly realising they had to do so. When they came to start talking much of their negotiating leverage had evaporated and they made a series of the traditional mistakes in handling an armed group. It was only when they called in a trusted third party that they were able to make progress.

On the day the agreement was signed, Nelson Mandela was visiting an FLN camp on the border between Morocco and Algeria, supposedly for military training. He saw Algeria as an example for South Africa in part because of its large white population and the problems that posed. He met a number of FLN leaders, and studied the lessons of the revolution. On his return to South Africa he was arrested, and from jail eventually began the cycle of negotiation that led to the settlement in South Africa.

Writing about the period 1945–67, the historian David French concludes:

Too much can be made of the apparently contrasting aims of mid-twentieth-century and early twenty-first-century insurgents. The objectives being pursued by modern insurgents appear to some Western observers to be vague and ill-defined. Some insurgents apparently want to re-establish the caliphate. Others appear content to make Iraq and Afghanistan ungovernable by maintaining a high level of violence in the hope that they can persuade the Western powers to leave in despair. The conclusion that some Western observers have drawn is that negotiations with opponents whose objectives appear to be nebulous, negative, and opposed to Western liberal norms is all but impossible. But there is nothing new here. Maintaining such a level of violence that the colonial power would decide that the cost of remaining in place was too high was a tactic common to most insurgents in the era of decolonisation. Those who aspire to restore the caliphate reject Western liberal values. But so did many of the insurgents the British fought in the era of decolonisation and that fact did not, eventually, prove an insuperable barrier to negotiations. The British recognised, albeit reluctantly, that to make peace they eventually had to talk to their enemies.

There seems to be a good deal of continuity in the way governments have dealt with terrorists, and the mistakes they have made, not just in the last twenty years but over the last century. It is probable we will carry on making the same errors whenever we think each new group of terrorists we encounter is different from those that have come before – as the philosopher John Gray puts it, 'The obstacle to coping with the terrorist threat is the belief that it is unlike anything in the past.' We will only ever break down this obstacle and escape the cycle in the future if we prove Hegel wrong, and governments learn the lessons of history.

CHAPTER ELEVEN

The Future

There is no present or future, only the past, happening over
and over again, now.

Eugene O'Neill

When I suggested publicly in 2008 that we should be prepared
to talk to the Taliban, Hamas and even al-Qaeda, I was predictably denounced by a government spokesman. These new groups
are considered beyond the pale, fundamentally different from
previous terrorist movements, and even if it was right to talk
to the IRA and the PLO it would not be moral or right to
engage with the new groups. Donald Steinberg, an American
foreign policy expert, firmly believes that we should distinguish
between those who are 'legitimate interlocutors and others that
. . . have, essentially, given themselves a red card and taken
themselves out of the game entirely'.

But as we have seen, every time in the past we have encountered a new terrorist group we have considered it to be fundamentally different, only to realise in the end that we will have
to deal with it in the same way that we dealt with the groups
that came before. Have we really now reached a stage in the
history of terrorism where we face a quite different threat from
those of the last hundred years, and require a quite different
approach?

It is true that, unlike most recent terrorist movements,
al-Qaeda are willing to kill unlimited numbers of people by
ever more terrifying means. For the American professor of

security affairs Jonathan Stevenson, 'by their sheer scale, the
11 September attacks drew a bright line between the "new
terrorism" practised by al-Qaeda and the "old terrorism" exem-
plified by groups like the Palestine Liberation Organisation
[and the] Provisional Irish Republican Army'. While ETA or
the IRA were content with 'propaganda of the deed' through
killing tens or at the most scores, al-Qaeda aim to kill thousands of people through their attacks. They are more vicious.
Alan Dershowitz argues that 'The nature of terrorism will
continuously change in the future, as it has in the past. Yesterday
we worried about retail acts of terror – assassinations, bombings, and hijackings. Among the most difficult dilemmas was
whether or not to give in to specific demands of the terrorists
– usually the freeing of other terrorists. Today we fear wholesale
acts of terror – such as the use of passenger planes as airborne
missiles directed against densely populated targets. These acts
are rarely accompanied by specific demands. They are not
contingent or conditional threats, or if they are, the conditions
are deliberately set so high as to be unrealistic.' In the end,
though, this is just a difference of degree rather than category.
Killing one innocent civilian in a terrorist attack is as morally
wrong as killing hundreds. The aim of the group is the same
– to shock the public into paying attention to them and their
demands. Terrorism is evil, destructive and its consequences
are heart-rending, but the degree of terror that a group is
prepared to use does not make a significant difference to the
argument about whether or not to talk to it.

Academics and policymakers set out four different but inter-
related practical arguments for why we should not talk to these
new terrorists. The first is that they are religiously inspired and
therefore less susceptible to rational approaches. Dan Meridor,
a former Israeli minister, says 'When you get God into discussions, God never compromises.' Some even claim that it is
impossible to talk because the new terrorists are Islamic and
their religion has not enjoyed a reformation. There are, however,
good reasons for thinking that talking to religious terrorists is

just as possible as talking to Marxists or nationalists. Religious difference was, after all, one of the factors in Northern Ireland. It has proved perfectly possible to negotiate with Islamic states, and peace has already been made with a number of Islamic armed groups, including the MILF in the Philippines and the GAM in Indonesia.

The second argument is that there are two kinds of terrorism: rational terrorism, such as the Palestinians, and apocalyptic terrorism like al-Qaeda. The academics Bruce Hoffman and William Zartman distinguish between nihilistic terrorists who have absolute or apocalyptic goals, and traditional terrorists who are 'instrumental' or 'political' and can become constructive interlocutors. Traditional terrorists use violence as an instrument to attain their goals; absolute terrorists 'are those whose action is non-instrumentalist, a self-contained act that is completed when it has occurred and is not a means to obtain some other goal . . . Suiciders – bombers and hijackers – are absolute terrorists, and so are beyond negotiation. They have nothing to negotiate about, they have nothing to negotiate with.' Stacie Pettyjohn of the RAND Corporation adds that 'conciliatory policies will only strengthen and embolden absolute terrorists'. But until we have tried to talk to them, how on earth can we know whether these groups are merely engaged in destruction for its own sake or are prepared to negotiate? The Provisional IRA and the PLO were considered absolutist groups in their early years, unwilling to compromise, but then negotiated in the end. Stathis Kalyvas of Yale University points out that 'even extreme forms of violence are used strategically . . . instances of extreme violence against civilians in the context of civil wars are not wanton and senseless acts: they have a rational basis'. The aim of the 'new terrorists' is not extermination. Even for them, violence is a means to an end.

Within this 'absolutist' or 'apocalyptic' theory is the idea that there can be no compromise with these groups because their demands are incoherent and unnegotiable. Louise Richardson draws a distinction between those groups with 'temporal goals' which 'could be won or lost without over-throwing the fundamental balance of power', and those with a 'transformational' aim which 'by its nature is not subject to negotiation and its satisfaction would require the complete destruction of the regional state system'. Modern terrorists 'are not interested in participating in the political process, nor even in gaining popular support . . . Dialogue or negotiation in the traditional sense is likely to prove futile, since, to the extent that such a group's demands are coherent at all, they are likely to include the complete destruction of the system itself.' In the words of former CIA chief James Woolsey, the current fanatic terrorists do not want to sit at the negotiating table, 'they want to destroy the table and everyone sitting at it'. While it is true that it is unlikely any existing state is going to agree to a cali-phate covering a large part of the world as demanded by al-Qaeda, it is equally true that the British state wasn't going to agree to force the majority population of Northern Ireland to leave the United Kingdom against their will. The IRA, when it entered talks, had to drop its absolutist demand for a united Ireland. The Spanish government had no intention of recog-nising an independent Basque state, nor the Indonesian govern-ment of recognising an independent Aceh. Armed groups always start with unnegotiable demands. If they didn't, they wouldn't have resorted to violence in the first place. The point about talking to them is to persuade them to moderate their demands so that they abandon their initial claims and settle for some-thing else that can meet their interests. The government offers them certain compromises that persuade them they can pursue their aims politically. Again it is not obvious why this process of persuasion should not help to moderate the demands of the Taliban, Hamas and al-Qaeda over time, so they too are prepared to settle for something we regard as reasonable. We need to engage them in order to force them to think about what they really want and what is actually possible.

It does take some time for armed groups to make this journey. It is much easier for them to shelter behind vague and

undeliverable slogans, like 'Troops Out', which was the demand
of the IRA and is the demand of the Taliban, than to persuade
their followers to accept the difficult compromises that are
necessary for a lasting settlement. Some academics write as if
the goals of these groups were immutable, but in fact they
change with time and circumstance, particularly if they face a
stalemate. In a negotiation their original demands can be
altered. The MILF and the GAM both had to be persuaded to
give up their aim of independence and settle for autonomy.
Experience suggests the stated aims and ideology of the armed
group should not therefore be the decisive factor in determining
whether they are willing to compromise or not. We need to
look at their interests rather than their positions.

Mitchell Reiss draws the dividing line between groups that
are reconcilable and those that will always be irreconcilable,
and 'depending on the circumstances, [engaging with them]
may be a fool's errand'. Audrey Cronin thinks that al-Qaeda
Central are irreconcilable: 'The central core of al-Qaeda is a
small, highly dangerous collection of a couple of hundred
operatives clustered around the group's senior leadership and
probably holed up in the border region of Pakistan. There is
no realistic chance of negotiating with them for three reasons:
first, they have non-negotiable terms; second, they are increasingly defined by their indiscriminate violence; and third, they
are unresponsive to their broader constituency.' But that is of
course what we said about the IRA and the Mau Mau, and
yet we found that in the end they could be reconciled. Both
armed groups and governments have hardliners and moderates,
and talking is a way of empowering the moderates at the
expense of the hardliners on both sides.

Thirdly, there is the argument that because al-Qaeda are a
global terrorist group unconfined by national borders, this
makes it harder to deal with them. It may be true that because
al-Qaeda networks straddle borders, the mechanics of engaging
with them are more difficult, but that is not a reason for thinking
it is impossible to talk to them or even to find an agreement.

Indeed the very fact that they cross borders means that there are local al-Qaedas, in Somalia or in Yemen, who have different, specific interests with which we can engage. In any case, global terrorism that crosses borders is a familiar phenomenon in history, from the anarchists and nihilists onwards. The 'new' terrorists are perhaps not that new after all.

The last argument is that these groups don't want to talk to us. That may be true, although of course many of the 'traditional' groups described in this book started off by refusing to negotiate with governments and yet ended up doing so. And in any event, this argument is not a justification for governments refusing to talk to the groups themselves. We should be willing to talk even if they are not.

One of the striking characteristics of these arguments about why the so-called 'fourth wave' of terrorism (following on from the anarchist wave, the anticolonial wave and the New Left wave) is different, uniquely evil and impossible to engage with, is that they have been deployed about all the terrorist groups we have encountered before in our history. They were wrong then, and the chances are they are wrong now. There is of course a perfectly legitimate discussion to be had about how we should go about engaging these new groups in practice. They are not all the same, even if they appear so when observed from a distance. Zartman and Faure, for example, argue that Hamas is 'engageable'; that al-Qaeda is not; and that the Taliban are somewhere in between.

Hamas is religiously based, it attacks civilians, its demands are maximalist and it clearly falls into the common definition of the 'new terrorists'. Its position is that it is not willing to talk to the Israeli government. The Israelis have always been clear that they will not engage with Hamas directly or overtly, although they have negotiated with them through the Egyptian government, through a German intelligence official and through an Israeli peace activist to ensure the release of Corporal Gilad Shalit. When it comes to political issues, however, Israel and the West have imposed preconditions that Hamas will have to fulfil before there can be talks. They will not engage until Hamas recognises Israel, renounces violence, and accepts all previous Israeli–Palestinian agreements. These preconditions are likely to frustrate talks in exactly the same way that the precondition of decommissioning of IRA weapons did in Northern Ireland. The demand for recognition is a bit like asking Sinn Féin to recognise the existence of Northern Ireland before negotiations start, rather than as an issue to be agreed as part of the negotiations. What is more, the exclusion of Hamas is likely to frustrate any successful talks between the Israeli government and Abu Mazen's Fatah. No Israeli negotiator is going to want to make difficult concessions to secure an agreement with Abu Mazen if he knows that to get to a lasting peace he might later have to make further concessions to secure Hamas's agreement. At the point where both sides are serious about getting to a peace agreement a way will have to be found round these preconditions so that talks can be held with a united Palestinian negotiating team.

The question of whether and how to talk to Hamas therefore doesn't look very different from talking to the 'traditional' groups featured in this book. Perhaps the Taliban are different. They too are religiously based, their very name referring to the young clerics who started the movement. They continue to be allied to al-Qaeda. They are unbending in their demands for foreign forces to leave Afghanistan before talks can even start with the West, and they refused to talk to the Karzai government. They use suicide bombers and attack civilians. Initially the West refused to talk to them and our explicit objective was to destroy them. When that proved impossible, US forces surged into Afghanistan with the aim of getting the upper hand before engaging in talks. For a long time leaders in the UK and US were opposed to negotiations. The US government then tried to talk to the Taliban but the efforts were frustrated by preconditions, both those originally imposed by the US and those imposed by the Taliban for the release of prisoners from Guantanamo.

One could ask why the Taliban would want to talk at the stage when NATO forces announced that they were leaving Afghanistan in 2014. They could simply wait till Western forces depart and take control, and no doubt there are people in the movement who have argued just that. There is no evidence that the surge of US troops made any discernible difference to their inclination to talk. Of course they, like all groups before them, crave recognition and legitimacy, and some of their leaders will have doubts about what happens after NATO's withdrawal. They probably realise they won't be able to take control of the whole country as easily as some may think. There will be significant Western assets, including drones, left in Afghanistan as well as a very large Afghan army and police force. Equally the Tajiks, Hazaras and Uzbeks, in addition to a large proportion of the Pashtun population, are not going to let them regain overall control easily. Many of their fighters will be tired of the constant risk of death and the impossibility of settling down and raising a family. Nor can they depend on their Pakistani backers indefinitely supporting them. So engaging in talks is a rational decision.

The problem for the West is that we have left engaging with the Taliban terribly late. In retrospect it was a mistake to have excluded them from the original Bonn talks on the future of the country in 2001–2. In June 2013 General Nick Carter, deputy commander of Western forces in Afghanistan, said 'Back in 2002, the Taliban were on the run. I think that at that stage, if we had been very prescient, we might have spotted that a final political solution to what started in 2001, from our perspective, would have involved getting all Afghans to sit at the table and talk about their future . . . The problems that we have been encountering over the period since then are essentially political problems, and political problems are only ever solved by people talking to each other.' There is very little time left now for the educative part of the process in which a consensus-based organisation like the Taliban can gradually adapt its demands to the real world. Nonetheless there is already evidence that the Taliban are prepared to discuss power-sharing rather than hegemony, although it is far from clear how an effective power-sharing system can be drawn up for the country. It is equally clear that they will be prepared to abandon their connection with al-Qaeda as part of an agreement, but less clear how that break can be demonstrated to be real rather than merely declaratory. Nor are the Taliban likely to stick to their original hard-line stances on women and education; in fact they have already begun to moderate them publicly. And while for them a traditional, speedy and accessible justice system is central, they may be prepared to relax some of their demands on Sharia and traditional punishments. So it is perfectly possible to imagine a compromise agreement acceptable to all sides.

Just like talks with other armed groups, the initiation of private discussions with the Taliban has made those left out suspicious that a secret deal is being done behind their back which will deleteriously affect their interests. President Karzai was understandably extremely wary of foreign intentions, and indeed demanded the expulsion of two EU aides in 2007, whom he suspected of dealing with the Taliban behind his back. Most of all the Tajiks of the Northern Alliance, who were the last to hold out against the Taliban up to 2001, were fearful that the central government would sell out their interests. Those not included will need reassurance that their interests are being taken into account, as will neighbouring states including Iran, Pakistan and India. The essential point is that even though we have left talking to the Taliban late, the prospect of negotiating with them doesn't look so different from talks we have historically undertaken with other groups.

Perhaps, then, it is just al-Qaeda that is somehow different. It is certainly true that al-Qaeda's ambitions are global rather than national or regional and it is more of a network than an organisation. It is also true that Osama Bin Laden is dead and al-Qaeda Central in the Pakistan/Afghan badlands is on the back foot under the pressure of drone attacks. Some US officials have even suggested that al-Qaeda's defeat could be imminent, so perhaps 'decapitation' will have its desired effect. Norwegian historian Brynjar Lia argues that 'At some point, al-Qaeda's image will inevitably fade; just as all extremist ideologies have a limited life span, so too does al-Qaeda's extremist interpretation of Islam. Sometime in the future, al-Qaeda will lose its attraction among the youth, and to pose as a jihadist will no longer be "cool".'

But al-Qaeda is unlikely to disappear. As Bruce Hoffman has said, 'the long-established nucleus of the al-Qaeda organisation has proven itself to be as resilient as it is formidable. For more than a decade, it has withstood arguably the greatest international onslaught directed against a terrorist organisation in history. Further, it has consistently shown itself capable of adapting and adjusting to even the most consequential countermeasures directed against it, having, despite all odds, survived for nearly a quarter of a century.' Hoffman also points out that a new generation is coming through its ranks, which is 'unnerving . . . because successive generations of the same terrorist organisations have shown themselves to be more lethally violent than their predecessors'. In a similar vein *The Economist* hypothesises that 'al-Qaeda believes America is in retreat not just in Afghanistan but also across the Middle East. The poisoning of the Arab Spring has given it new purpose and ideological momentum. Al-Qaeda itself may be divided and in some places depleted. It may be shunned by some with similar ideologies, and its affiliates may increasingly ignore its ageing leadership. But the Salafi jihadist view of the world that al-Qaeda promotes and fights for has never had greater traction.' Hoffman adds 'Al-Qaeda's obituary has been written many times before, only to have been proven to be presumptuously premature wishful thinking.'

If they are not going to be defeated or fade away, and if we can't kill all of them, perhaps we will have to talk to them just as we have to all previous serious terrorist groups. In response to a question about al-Qaeda during her Reith Lectures, Eliza Manningham-Buller said that 'to say that you're never going to speak to them or never going to try to, I think that's foolish . . . we're obviously a great deal away from anything that you could call a negotiation, even if that were possible, but to think about these questions and to make efforts to try and have those conversations must be a starter'. Terry Waite, speaking in favour of talking to al-Qaeda, said: 'My own experience in Lebanon, in Iran and Libya has actually demonstrated the fact that you can talk to people whose stated position seems to be impossible . . . Terrorism is a symptom. It's not a root issue. You must deal with the root issue. And the only way to deal with the root issue is not to drive people against the wall by bombing and fighting but by entering into dialogue.' Yet it is certainly hard to see how we could engage in a direct dialogue with al-Qaeda Central even if we wanted to, given the military pressure it is under.

But an interesting thing has happened to the group. Although it was never a centralised organisation, it is now better defined as a loose federation, designed to avoid detection by Western intelligence agencies. The centre cannot control what the subordinate groups do, as Zarqawi, the leader of al-Qaeda in Iraq, graphically illustrated in persisting in the slaughter of Shia Iraqis in defiance of appeals from the centre. Increasingly its activity has moved from Afghanistan and Pakistan to a series of regional 'franchises', particularly in the Maghreb, Somalia, Syria and Yemen. 'At its broadest,' a report by the Canadian Security Intelligence Service found, 'the phenomenon includes a central group of senior leaders commonly referred to as AQ Core, regional affiliates which together with that core make up the AQ network, like-minded groups in the network's key operating areas (e.g. fellow travellers), home-grown Islamist extremists in Western countries, sympathisers across the globe and the AQ ideology itself.' In a sense al-Qaeda is like a Domino's Pizza franchise where you take the name and the recipes but you have to rent your own shop and recruit your own delivery drivers.

These developments could make it easier to find a way to

talk to them. Carl Miller says that 'Whilst the complex structure of AQ is often presented as a barrier to negotiation, it is instead an opportunity. A networked organisation offers more points of entry than a traditional pyramidal structure. When these points of entry are explored, it is often clear that AQ franchisees, and individuals within them, hold local and temporal, not international and transformational, demands.' It is far easier to imagine that there will be transactional business to be conducted with such groups about issues affecting the areas where they are operating. They are not, or at least not yet, nationalist insurgencies, but they are far more interested in righting grievances in their homelands than Osama Bin Laden was. Cronin says 'Many associates use the term "al-Qaeda" as a kind of evocative brand name, a way to increase their profile and gain strength. Local affiliates in Indonesia, Morocco, Tunisia, and Turkey, for example, have more in common with the classic ethno nationalist separatist groups of the twentieth century than they do with al-Qaeda's ambitious struggle.' If it is possible to speak to AQAP in Yemen, al-Shabab in Somalia and AQIM in the Sahel about concrete issues and to meet some of their demands, maybe it will be possible to corral even al-Qaeda Central into negotiations in the end, just as we have most previous manifestations of terrorism.

The truth is there is no such thing as a 'traditional' terrorist or a 'new' terrorist. The new terrorists are more like the old terrorists than we think. Groups that employ terrorism are constantly changing and adapting precisely because terror is a tactic, not an end. And in any case they co-exist with plenty of continuing 'third wave' nationalist and ideological terrorists including the FARC and the ELN in Colombia, the Maoists in the Philippines and the Naxalites in India, Kashmiri terrorists in Pakistan, and nationalist/religious terrorists in Chechnya.

Even if we did manage to bring all these remaining third- and fourth-wave groups to an end, we would still not have reached the end of terrorism. We can safely predict that there will be new groups that begin to use terrorism to attract attention and try to force governments and publics to accept their demands. What has happened in recent years demonstrates how quickly these groups can appear out of a clear blue sky, from ISIS in Iraq and Syria to the MUJAO in Mali, and form and reform in different shapes and with different names. It is hard to be sure exactly what the next wave will look like. They may grow out of fighters returning to Western countries from Syria, just as the Taliban and al-Qaeda grew out of the war with the Russians in Afghanistan. They may be manifestations of the new fighters in the north of Mali, like Mokhtar Belmokhtar who specialises in kidnaps, and Boko Haram and Ansaru in northern Nigeria. We could face more lone-wolf terrorists like Breivik in Norway, or the two Nigerian assassins in Woolwich who hacked the British soldier Lee Rigby to death. David Kilcullen, the former soldier who advised General Petraeus, predicts a new wave of urban guerrillas of the type that attacked Mumbai in 2008. President Obama thinks 'we'll face more localised threats like what we saw in Benghazi, or the BP oil facility in Algeria, in which local operatives – perhaps in loose affiliation with regional networks – launch periodic attacks against Western diplomats, companies, and other soft targets, or resort to kidnapping and other criminal enterprises to fund their operations'. New issues, like water and resources, and new ideologies will inspire groups to take up arms. Conflicts that have been frozen for decades will suddenly spring back to life as they have in Nagorno-Karabakh and Chechnya, and there will be more failed states which will serve as safe havens for armed groups, as Mali and Libya have become for neighbouring countries in the region. Afghanistan may sink back into that status once Western forces have withdrawn, and Somalia has never managed to pull itself out of that fate since the collapse of government there in 1991. Andrew Parker, the director general of MI5, says:

Ten years ago, the almost singular focus of the international counter-terrorism effort was al-Qaeda in South Asia. Since that time we have seen violent Islamist groupings in various countries and regions exploiting conflict, revolutions and the opportunity of weakened governance to gain strength and refuge. Some have adopted the al-Qaeda brand, becoming franchised affiliates with what at the same time has been a declining al-Qaeda core in South Asia. A time-lapse sequence of a world map over the past decade would show outbreaks in Iraq, North and West Africa, Yemen, Somalia, and most recently Syria. For the future, there is good reason to be concerned about Syria. The ability of al-Qaeda to launch the centrally directed large-scale attacks of the last decade has been degraded, though not removed. We have seen the threat shift more to increasing numbers of smaller-scale attacks and a growing proportion of groups and individuals taking it upon themselves to commit acts of terrorism. Overall, I do not believe the terrorist threat is worse now than before. But it is more diffuse. More complicated. More unpredictable.

Because new groups will carry on resorting to the tactic of terrorism, we have to escape from our collective amnesia and stop being surprised each time terrorism appears in a new form and be more consistent in how we tackle it, drawing on the lessons we learned last time.

The realisation of the repeat nature of terror leads people to look for easy answers, like technology, to the continuing threat. But new technology makes the challenge of terrorism more difficult to deal with as well as providing new solutions. Just as dynamite changed the character of terrorism in the nineteenth century and Semtex did in the twentieth, so new technologies have transformed the capacity of modern terrorists. The acquisition of shoulder-launched missiles gave the mujahedin a much stronger position in driving the Soviet Union out of Afghanistan, and allowed the FMLN to ground the air force in El Salvador. The technology behind roadside bombs has been revolutionised by mobile phones and other electronic advances. A US Department of Homeland Security report on the future of terrorism states that it 'will depend, in large part, on the use and accessibility of technology. Increasingly destructive weaponry makes terrorism more lethal; advances in transportation increase the reach of terrorists; and cheaper and more secure means of communication make terrorism harder to detect. As these technologies advance, proliferate and become available to a wider range of actors, more and more potential enemies may use terrorism as a strategy and tactic.'

We know that a number of armed groups have been trying to acquire chemical, biological and nuclear weapons and we know there are now more irresponsible regimes that might be prepared to help them get their hands on them. In all probability it is just a matter of time before they do, and then the nature of the threat will change fundamentally. Armed groups will be in a position to kill tens or even hundreds of thousands of people and destabilise regimes, or even pose an existential threat to countries. Counter-terrorism expert David Pinder writes 'The day, long dreaded, will come when some group acquires usable weapons of mass destruction and has the capability and will to use them. On that day negotiation may well be the only alternative. It would be irresponsible not to plan for it now.' Technology has improved the capabilities of governments too. Every self-respecting government aspires to have access to drones that can track and kill terrorists and anyone in their immediate environs, along with foliage-penetrating radar so they cannot hide in the jungle. That new technology can put armed groups on the back foot for sustained periods of time, but they will always develop ways to get round the countermeasures governments introduce.

The ability of technology to make terrorist attacks more devastating and the government response more lethal does not solve the fundamental problem this book addresses, and that is that if a political issue lies at the root of the conflict, and if the armed group enjoys significant political support, then there will in the end have to be a political solution and that will involve talking. Cruise-missile strikes on al-Qaeda bases in

Afghanistan and Sudan in response to the bombing of US embassies in Tanzania and Kenya in 1998 didn't do anything to solve the underlying problem. Indiscriminate retaliation that injures innocent civilians as well as the intended targets is more likely to turn the population against the West, just as the British response to the Easter Uprising in Dublin in 1916 created many more rebels than it put out of action, and the shootings by the Paratroop Regiment in Derry on Bloody Sunday in 1972, together with the internment of hundreds of innocent Catholics, served as recruiting sergeants for the IRA.

Globalisation has also altered the character of terrorism and the response to it. Access to the internet, mobile-phone technology and advanced encryption make indoctrination and organisation much easier to undertake undetected. The Department of Homeland Security report concludes that 'The future of terrorism will be affected in part by the mobility of people. Globalisation entails greater mobility in goods, services, and people, as well as money and information. Expanding markets and cheaper, easier, and faster transportation increasingly blur national borders. Whether this trend accelerates or decelerates will have a major impact on the reach of terrorist groups, and the role of national borders in security thinking.' Twenty-four-hour satellite television gives a ready audience for propaganda of the deed, whether it is a Boko Haram beheading or a suicide bomb in Baghdad, while social media makes it possible for these groups to have a much looser organisation. The cell structure was developed in the IRA and in other groups to stop penetration by intelligence agencies bringing the whole organisation down. Facebook and twitter are the modern equivalent, allowing networks to inspire others to undertake attacks rather than organising them directly. Following an electronic trail is only possible with known radicals, and terrorist groups have always relied on the ability to use 'clean skins', young men and women who have not been identified by the intelligence agencies, to carry out the attacks.

These recent developments, however, don't represent a

fundamental change in the nature of terrorism or how it is dealt with. As Margaret MacMillan has pointed out, globalisation was a phenomenon before the First World War as steamships, railways, the telephone, telegraph and wireless suddenly made the world much smaller. It had the same effect as globalisation today, allowing the rapid spread of radical ideology and connecting fanatics. She says 'anarchists and revolutionary socialists across Europe and North America read the same works and had the same aim: to overthrow the existing social order ... Terrorists from Calcutta to Buffalo imitated one another as they hurled bombs on to the floors of stock exchanges, blew up railway lines and stabbed and shot those they saw as oppressors.'

Terrorism is not therefore going to go away and nor are we going to find a new technological or security answer to it. We are condemned to continue facing the same challenge indefinitely. In a sense terrorism is the ugly twin of democracy. The threat grew up alongside modern democracy, and is a manifestation of the vulnerabilities of a democratic system. If democratic governments resort to extra-legal measures to suppress terrorist movements in the way autocracies can, they risk doing irreparable harm to the very essence of their democracy. While there clearly needs to be a strong security component to the solution, we are fooling ourselves if we think it will provide a complete answer by itself. It is rather a way of applying pressure to enable us to solve the problem by other means. General Rupert Smith, the former UN commander in Bosnia and a former commanding officer in Northern Ireland, argues that the entire point of military force, its utility, is to create conditions for the non-military approach: 'we intervene in ... a conflict in order to establish a condition in which the political objective can be achieved by other means and in other ways. We seek to create a conceptual space for diplomacy, economic incentives, political pressure and other measures.'

We can of course become better at addressing the causes of terrorism earlier rather than allowing them to fester. The implementation of a peace settlement between the Israelis and the Palestinians would not just stop terrorist attacks there but remove a grievance that is used to justify terrorism elsewhere. A more sensitive approach to Islam, so that young men didn't feel humiliated by Western encroachment into their countries and the spread of Western culture, might prevent radicalisation. Learning from the past by giving up the habit of playing into terrorist hands through a constantly escalating cycle of retaliation and punishment for terrorist attacks might stop conflicts metastasising so quickly in future. Even those steps, however, will not be enough. The argument of this book, based on historical experience, is that in order to make the men with the guns, the IEDs and the chemical weapons stop, we will need to talk to them in the end. We always have, and we always will. The only way to get to a lasting end to a terrorist conflict is to reach an agreement which both sides accept as just. The school of academic thought that argued that military victories, if they could be achieved, would provide a more lasting peace than one brought about by negotiation, is contested not only by recent academic work at Uppsala University but also more eloquently by poets and philosophers over the centuries. Milton wrote that 'who overcomes by force, Hath overcome but half his foe', and Friedrich Schiller believed that 'A merely fallen enemy may rise again, but the reconciled one is truly vanquished.' The Prussian military theorist Carl von Clausewitz concluded that 'The ultimate outcome of a war is not always to be regarded as final. The defeated state often considers the outcome merely as a transitory evil, for which a remedy may still be found in political conditions at some later date.'

Academics spend a lot of time debating whether we should *never* talk to terrorists or *always* talk to them and most end up sitting on the fence. Neumann writes 'Assuming the negotiations are appropriate in all cases would be no more valid a theory than one that assumes they never are'. Professor Mnookin says he has a natural aversion to saying categorically you should 'always' or 'never' negotiate. Ury and Fisher, on the other hand, come down clearly in favour of talking, saying 'however unsavoury the other side, unless you have a better BATNA, the question you face is not whether to negotiate but how'. I stand with Ury and Fisher. We should always be prepared to talk to terrorists even if they won't talk to us, and we should always be working to turn those contacts into a negotiation rather than waiting until circumstances become 'ripe', not least because the whole process takes much longer than we think, and the earlier we start the sooner we can bring the conflict to an end.

Talking is not an easy option and it often doesn't succeed the first time. Martti Ahtisaari says of his negotiations on Aceh, 'There had been time to think through earlier failures. History matters and time itself is important for weighing up options and opportunities. There was a certain realism about the political trajectory.' The eventual success of the Good Friday Agreement was built on the failures of the Sunningdale Agreement of 1973, of Margaret Thatcher's Anglo-Irish agreement in 1985, and of John Major's 1993 Downing Street Declaration. Seamus Mallon, the leader of the moderate Catholic SDLP, described the Good Friday Agreement as 'Sunningdale for slow learners' because it contained many of the same provisions on power-sharing as had the Sunningdale agreement twenty-five years earlier; but his joke misses the point that successful peace agreements are built gradually on the back of previous failed efforts.

The story of the Basque conflict, even if it has not yet been finally settled, is another example of how failure builds upon failure till you arrive at success. Within hours of Franco's burial in November 1975 an envoy from the new Spanish king, Juan Carlos, was on his way to Biarritz to try to make contact with ETA. The envoy was Marcelino Oreja (later the foreign minister), who went to a Basque bookshop in the centre of the French town to set out his request, and a few hours later met an ETA representative. Sadly the talks didn't lead anywhere – ETA were sceptical about the approach, and the next day assassinated the mayor of a small Basque town. A few months later the owner of the bookshop who had facilitated the introduction was blown up, a fate that befell a series of individuals who tried to enable discussions in the next ten years.

According to the historian Robert Clark, between 1975 and 1987 there were as many as thirty attempts to negotiate with ETA, all of which failed, and between 1988 and 2005 there were a further three major peace initiatives. The first was the negotiation started by Felipe Gonzalez in Algeria in 1987, when ETA declared a temporary ceasefire. The government offered an amnesty in return for peace but ETA demanded impossible political concessions. The government broke off contact after ETA exploded a bomb in Zaragoza killing eleven, including five children, but soon resumed talks, only to break them off again when ETA kidnapped a businessman in 1988. Even then the government restarted talks and held six sessions from January to March 1989. The talks ranged far and wide over Basque history and culture, but in ETA's view the government wanted 'peace in exchange for nothing'. The talks finally ended in April when ETA alleged the government made unacceptable changes to the draft agreements. Spain plunged back into violence.

The next effort at negotiation, inspired by the Good Friday Agreement in Northern Ireland, was a pan-nationalist approach between ETA and the moderate Basque nationalist PNV party in Estella-Lizarra in Navarre in September 1998. This produced the longest ETA ceasefire up to that point, but the PNV was not the national government and was unable to deliver the undertakings that ETA required. This process collapsed too. The third attempt was Aznar's effort in Geneva. When the PP took power in 1996, the interior minister, Jaime Mayor Oreja, rejected an approach from ETA through Sant'Egidio. He told them to tell ETA 'their message was not received', and said to his socialist predecessor, 'This idea of taking the temperature of ETA. I will never do it.' But when ETA announced a 'permanent and indefinite ceasefire', Aznar promised not to be insensitive to the expectations it raised. The government moved 135 Basque prisoners closer to the region and allowed exiles to return. When ETA's talks with the PNV collapsed, Aznar made contact with Batasuna through a Catholic bishop, and representatives of both sides met outside Geneva in May 1999. The government offered peace in return for the release of prisoners, saying 'We are not here for the defeat of ETA.' There was no second meeting, however, and the ceasefire ended in December. From then on, Aznar was implacably opposed to negotiations.

When Arnaldo Otegi and Jesús Eguiguren started their dialogue a year later, they agreed that the Algeria talks had failed because ETA demanded direct political negotiations with the government, while Estella-Lizarra had failed because the government was not involved and a good part of Basque society had been excluded. They also discussed the Northern Ireland peace process and adopted the fundamental idea of consent which had underpinned the Good Friday Agreement in 1998. This series of failed negotiations over twenty-five years were the essential building blocks for the eventual success in bringing the armed conflict to an end in the Aiete Declaration of 2011. In Spain, then, as in Northern Ireland, just because one attempt at negotiation fails, it does not follow that the peace process as a whole will fail.

Of course all conflicts are different and require different solutions, but there is evidence that those involved in one conflict can learn from the successes and failures of others. The visits by the Northern Ireland parties to South Africa gave them a chance to import specific ideas like 'sufficient consensus' from the process between the ANC and the National Party, but perhaps more importantly it gave them a chance to talk to each other and build trust in a way they couldn't do at home. The groups involved in the Basque conflict have imported ideas from the Northern Ireland peace process, and joint visits by the Philippines government and the MILF to Northern Ireland helped contribute to their successful agreement.

I remember a few years ago visiting the MILF headquarters in Mindanao with Gerry Kelly, a former leader in the IRA. As we turned off the main highway and on to a dusty track into the jungle, we noticed armed guerrillas in black uniforms behind the trees. We pulled up in a small clearing and went into a hut to meet the central committee of the MILF. As we entered, each one of them produced a copy of my book on the Northern Ireland peace process, which they had been given by the British Council. The incongruous sight made me think that there is a way that those engaged in negotiations can learn from those who participated in a successful peace process halfway round the world, however different they may be from each other.

The most important lesson I draw from my work between armed groups and governments over the last two decades, and from the peace processes described in this book, is something I observed at the beginning: there is no such thing as an insoluble conflict, however bloody, difficult or ancient. Archbishop Desmond Tutu said that the settlement in South Africa was a sign to the world that even the most intractable problems can be resolved, and so are the other peace agreements described here. President Kennedy captured the same idea saying: 'Peace need not be impracticable – and war need not be inevitable.' Even the Middle East peace process, which has stuttered on for decades, will in the end result in a lasting agreement. The fact that it has failed so many times before does not mean that it will always fail, and an eventual settlement will be built on the past failures and the lessons learned from these failures, as was the peace in Northern Ireland.

It is remarkable how quickly the shift can be from a conflict being 'insoluble' to its solution being described as 'inevitable' once an agreement is signed. Beforehand, and even up to a very late stage in the process, conventional wisdom states that the conflict can never be resolved; but before the ink is dry on the agreement, people are ready to conclude that it was inevitable. They put it down to outside events like the end of the Cold War, to the effect of 9/11 or to changing economic circumstances. Conventional wisdom is wrong in both cases. Just as no conflict is insoluble, nor is it inevitable that it will be resolved at any particular moment in history. Believing that a solution is inevitable is nearly as dangerous as believing a conflict is insoluble. If people sit around waiting for a conflict to be 'ripe', or for the forces of history to solve it for them, then it won't be resolved. If the negotiations are handled badly, they will fail, which is why it is worth trying to learn from the experience of others. Making peace requires political leadership, patience and a refusal to take no for an answer. What we need are more political leaders prepared to take the necessary risks, and who are capable of remembering what happened last time.

Acknowledgements

When Will Sulkin of Bodley Head heard my BBC Radio Four series in 2011 interviewing a series of mediators about their experiences in making peace and suggested the idea of this book to me, I jumped at it. It would give me the opportunity to explore whether the lessons I had drawn from Northern Ireland also applied in previous negotiations with terrorists. I set off to interview former presidents, leaders of armed groups, intelligence and military officials and mediators about their conflicts and subsequent peace processes. For obvious reasons many of them do not wish to be named, but I would like to thank those that I can, including: President F. W. de Klerk and Roelf Meyer in South Africa; Álvaro de Soto, Francesc Vendrell and Joaquín Villalobos in El Salvador; Yair Hirschfeld, the father of the Oslo process in the Middle East; Ram Manikkalingam and Erik Solheim and Vidar Helgesen, the two Norwegian mediators in Sri Lanka.

I would particularly like to thank my former colleagues from the HDC, including its founder Martin Griffiths, his deputy Andrew Marshall, and James LeMoyne, the most indefatigable of mediators as well as Michael Vatikiotis and David Gorman from its Asia office. I still remember when Martin and his two colleagues popped up in my office in Downing Street in 2006 asking for my help in a negotiation that had become stuck. They have all become good friends and helped me extensively with this book. I have learned most of what I know about negotiating with terrorists from them.

Martin was the person who inspired me to take up this line of work full time, and the person who convinced me that it was always right to talk to terrorists. When I left government I was sure it was sometimes the right thing to do, but he persuaded me that you should never leave a conflict stewing with all the human suffering that involves, and always try to get the two sides to talk even if fighting is still continuing.

Researching the book also gave me an opportunity to read widely about previous negotiations with terrorists, and many of the stories in this book are derived from the memoirs of participants in armed conflicts and their peace processes, as well as other accounts by journalists, experts and historians. This is not supposed to be an academic book and does not therefore contain footnotes or endnotes, but I hope the bibliography shows clearly where the stories come from. It also lists the works on the theory of negotiation and the academic studies on terrorism on which I have drawn. I have not tried to give a comprehensive account of the conflicts and the peace processes referred to – that is not the purpose of the book. Instead I have attempted to derive common lessons from them, and it is extraordinary how often the same patterns crop up.

People who were personally involved have reviewed the sections relating to their particular conflicts, but nonetheless I am certain errors will remain. I know that whenever I read a book about the Northern Ireland negotiations I recoil with horror at the mistakes others make in describing what happened, and I am sure the same will be true for those who were participants in the processes I have written about here. I do not believe these mistakes will undermine the general lessons that I draw, but I apologise in advance for them, and ask readers to send corrections to me via the publisher, so I can revise what I hope will prove a useful guide for negotiators for some time to come.

I am truly grateful to my researcher, Matthew Wright, who should get much of the credit for this book for his wide reading on the subject and inspired suggestions, to my assistant Lorna McCaig who has negotiated my execrable handwriting to produce draft after draft, and to all my colleagues at Inter Mediate who have informed and supported my efforts. I would also like to thank those friends who read and commented on the manuscript, including Bill Ury, Dudley Ankerson, Chester Crocker, Teresa Whitfield and Eliza Manningham-Buller, and a number of others I cannot name. The distinguished historians Ronan Fanning and Paul Bew helped me with the section on negotiations with the IRA in 1919–21.

This book would never have existed if it had not been for the persistence of my publisher Stuart Williams, who succeeded Will Sulkin at Bodley Head, and it would certainly not have taken this form without his clear-eyed advice. My agent Natasha Fairweather has encouraged me throughout and kept my nose to the grindstone to ensure I finally produced a book, and any qualities in its structure and writing are due to the brilliant editing of David Milner, who also helped create my previous book. I am very grateful to all of them.

Finally my job as a mediator requires me to travel from one end of the earth to the other on an almost weekly basis and I am enormously indebted to my wife Sarah and my children Jessica and Rosamund for their support and tolerance in putting up with my continued absences for what I hope they think is a noble cause.

Jonathan Powell
London, 1 June 2014

Bibliography

Sources

1. Terrorism

Alonso, Rogelio, 'Leaving Terrorism Behind in the Northern Ireland and Basque Country: Reassessing Anti-terrorist Policies and "Peace Processes"', in Tore Bjørgo and John Horgan (eds), *Leaving Terrorism Behind: Individual and Collective Disengagement* (Routledge, Abingdon, 2008)

Anderson, Jon Lee, *Guerrillas: Journeys in the Insurgent World* (Penguin, London, 2004; originally published 1992)

Bew, John, Martyn Frampton and Inigo Gurruchaga, *Talking to Terrorists: Making Peace in Northern Ireland and the Basque Country* (Hurst, London, 2009)

Bjørgo, Tore and John Horgan (eds), *Leaving Terrorism Behind: Individual and Collective Disengagement* (Routledge, Oxford, 2009)

Burke, Jason, *The 9/11 Wars* (Allen Lane, London, 2011)

Burleigh, Michael, *Blood & Rage: A Cultural History of Terrorism* (HarperCollins, London, 2009)

Carr, Matthew, *The Infernal Machine: An Alternative History of Terrorism* (Hurst, London, 2011)

Crenshaw, Martha, *Explaining Terrorism: Causes, Processes and Consequences* (Routledge, Abingdon, 2011)

Cronin, Audrey Kurth, *How Terrorism Ends: Understanding the Decline and Demise of Terrorist Campaigns* (Princeton University Press, Princeton, 2009)

Dershowitz, Alan, *Why Terrorism Works: Understanding the Threat, Responding to the Challenge* (Yale University Press, New Haven, 2002)

Freedman, Lawrence (ed.), *Superterrorism: Policy Responses* (Blackwell Publishing, Oxford, 2002)

Gray, John, *Black Mass: Apocalyptic Religion and the Death of Utopia* (Penguin, London, 2007)

Hoffman, Bruce, *Inside Terrorism* (Columbia University Press, New York, 2006)

Horgan, John, *Walking Away from Terrorism: Accounts of Disengagement from Radical and Extremist Movements* (Routledge, Oxford, 2009)

Ignatieff, Michael, *The Lesser Evil: Political Ethics in an Age of Terror* (Princeton University Press, Princeton, 2004)

Jones, Seth G. and Martin C. Libicki, *How Terrorist Groups End: Lessons for Countering al Qa'ida* (RAND Corporation, Santa Monica, 2008)

Kilcullen, David, *Counterinsurgency* (Hurst, London, 2010)

Law, Randall, *Terrorism: A History* (Polity Press, Cambridge, 2009)

Reese, Phil, *Dining with Terrorists: Meetings with the World's Most Wanted Militants* (Pan Macmillan, London, 2005)

Richardson, Louise, *What Terrorists Want: Understanding the Enemy, Containing the Threat* (Random House, London, 2006)

Taylor, Peter, *Talking to Terrorists: A Personal Journey from the IRA to Al Qaeda* (HarperPress, London, 2011)

Wilkinson, Paul, *Terrorism versus Democracy: The Liberal State Response* (Routledge, Abingdon, 2011)

Articles

Abrahms, Max (2006), 'Why Terrorism Does Not Work', *International Security*, Vol. 31, No. 1, pp. 42–78

Abrahms, Max (2012), 'The Political Effectiveness of Terrorism Revisited', *Comparative Political Studies*, Vol. 45, No. 3, pp. 366–93

Cronin, Audrey Kurth (2006), 'How al-Qaida Ends: The Decline and Demise of Terrorist Groups', *International Security*, Vol. 31, No. 1, pp. 7–48

Hoffman, Bruce (2013), 'Al Qaeda's Uncertain Future', *Studies in Conflict & Terrorism*, Vol. 36, No. 8, pp. 635–53

Jones, David Martin and M. L. R. Smith (2009), 'We're All Terrorists Now: Critical – or Hypocritical – Studies "on" Terrorism?', *Studies in Conflict and Terrorism*, Vol. 32, No. 4, pp. 292–302

Kalyvas, Stathis N. (2003), 'The Paradox of Terrorism in Civil War', *Journal of Ethics*, Vol. 8, No. 1, pp. 97–138

Lia, Brynjar (2008), 'Al-Qaida's Appeal: Understanding its Unique Selling Points', *Perspectives on Terrorism*, Vol. 2, No. 8

Stevenson, Jonathan (2001), 'Pragmatic Counter-Terrorism', *Survival*, Vol. 43, No. 4, pp. 35–48

News

'The Unquenchable Fire', *The Economist*, 28 September 2013

Other

Canadian Security Intelligence Service, *The Future of Al Qaeda: Results of a Foresight Project* (2013)

'Director General's Speech at RUSI, 2013', www.mi5.gov.uk, 8 October 2013

Homeland Security Advisory Council (2007), *Report of the Future of Terrorism Task Force*, http://www.dhs.gov/xlibrary/assets/hsac-future-terrorism-010107.pdf

'Remarks by the President at the National Defense University', www.whitehouse.gov, 23 May 2013

2. *Conflict resolution*

Butler, Michael J., *International Conflict Management* (Routledge, Abingdon, 2009)

Dudouet, Veronique, Hans Giessmann and Katrin Planta, *Post-war Security Transitions: Participatory Peacebuilding after Asymmetric Conflicts* (Routledge, Abingdon, 2012)

Hampson, Fen Osler, *Nurturing Peace: Why Peace Settlements Succeed or Fail* (United States Institute of Peace, Washington DC, 2005)

Holbrooke, Richard, *To End a War* (Modern Library, New York, 1999)

Martin, Harriet, *Kings of Peace, Pawns of War: The Untold Story of Peacemaking* (Continuum, London, 2006)

Ramsbotham, Oliver, *Transforming Violent Conflict: Radical Disagreement, Dialgoue and Survival* (Routledge, Abingdon, 2010)

Ramsbotham, Oliver, Tom Woodhouse and Hugh Miall, *Contemporary Conflict Resolution* (Polity Press, Cambridge, 2011)

Van Engeland, Anisseh and Rachael M. Rudolph, *From Terrorism to Politics* (Ashgate Publishing, Aldershot, 2008)

Zartman, I. William and Guy Olivier Faure, *Engaging Extremists: Trade-offs, Timing, and Diplomacy* (United States Institute of Peace, Washington DC, 2011)

Articles

Conciliation Resources, *Choosing to Engage: Armed Groups and Peace Processes*, Accord 16 (Conciliation Resources, London, 2005)

Conciliation Resources, *Powers of Persuasion: Incentives, Sanctions and Conditionality in Peacemaking*, Accord 19 (Conciliation Resources, London, 2008)

Griffiths, Martin, *The Prisoner of Peace: An Interview with Kofi A. Annan* (Centre for Humanitarian Dialogue, Geneva, 2008)

Haspeslagh, Sophie (2013), '"Listing terrorists": The Impact of Proscription on Third-Party Efforts to Engage Armed Groups in Peace Processes – a Practitioner's Perspective', *Critical Studies on Terrorism*, Vol. 6, No. 1, pp. 189–208

Haysom, Nicholas 'Fink', *Reflecting on the IGAD Peace Process*, Accord 18 (Conciliation Resources, London, 2008)

Khattak, Daud (2012), 'Reviewing Pakistan's Peace Deals with the Taliban', *CTC Sentinel*, Vol. 5, No. 9, pp. 11–13

Kristol, Irving, 'Conflicts That Can't Be Resolved', *AEI Online*, 5 September 1997, http://www.aei.org/issue/foreign-and-defense-policy/regional/middle-east-and-north-africa/conflicts-that-cant-be-resolved-issue/

Luttwak, Edward N. (1999), 'Give War a Chance', *Foreign Affairs*, Vol. 78, No. 4, pp. 36–44

Stedman, Stephen John (1997), 'Spoiler Problems in Peace Processes', *International Security*, Vol. 22, No. 2, pp. 5–53

Wither, James K. (2009), 'Selective Engagement with Islamist Terrorists: Exploring the Prospects', *Studies in Conflict & Terrorism*, Vol. 32, No. 1, pp. 18–35

Zartman, I. William (2001), 'The Timing of Peace Initiatives: Hurting Stalemates and Ripe Moments', *The Global Review of Ethnopolitics*, Vol. 1, No. 1, pp. 8–18

News

'How to Stop the Fighting, Sometimes', *The Economist*, 9 November 2013, http://www.economist.com/news/briefing/21589431-bringing-end-conflicts-within-states-vexatious-history-provides-guide

'Norway as Peacemaker', *Christian Science Monitor*, 31 May 2000, http://www.csmonitor.com/2000/0531/p1s4.html

Richardson, Bill, Melanie Greenberg and Derek Brown, 'Why Talking Peace is Essential and why it is Threatened', *Insight on Conflict*, 7 October 2011, http://www.insightonconflict.org/2011/10/talking-peace-essential-threatened/

Steinberg, Gerald, 'Peace, War and Messianism', *Jerusalem Post*, 25 January 2014, http://www.jpost.com/Opinion/Op-Ed-Contributors/Peace-war-and-messianism-339344

Other

Ahtisaari, Martti, *Nobel Lecture*, 10 December 2008, http://www.nobelprize.org/nobel_prizes/peace/laureates/2008/ahtisaari-lecture_en.html

'Secretary of State John F. Kerry: Remove the Barriers to Peacebulding', http://www.charityandsecurity.org/system/files/Peacebuilding%20Petition%202013_0.pdf

'Symposium on the Future of Conflict Prevention, Session 1', *Council on Foreign Relations*, 10 December 2007, http://www.cfr.org/conflict-prevention/symposium-future-conflict-prevention-session-rush-transcript-federal-news-service/p15023

3. Negotiation

Atran, Scott, *Talking to the Enemy: Violent Extremism, Sacred Values, and What it Means to Be Human* (Allen Lane, London, 2010)

de Callières, François, *On the Manner of Negotiating with Princes* (Houghton Mifflin, New York, 2000; originally published 1716)

Faure, Guy Olivier and I. William Zartman, *Negotiating with Terrorists: Strategy, Tactics, and Politics* (Routledge, Abingdon, 2010)

Feste, Karen A., 'Terrorist Negotiation Strategy in Lebanon', in, Guy Olivier Faure and I. William Zartman (eds), *Negotiating with Terrorists: Strategy, Tactics, and Politics* (Routledge, Abingdon, 2010)

Fisher, Roger, William Ury and Bruce Patton, *Getting to Yes: Negotiating Agreement Without Giving In*, second edition (Penguin, New York, 1991; originally published 1981)

Goerzig, Carolin, *Talking to Terrorists: Concessions and the Renunciation of Violence* (Routledge, Abingdon, 2010)

Höglund, Kristine, *Peace Negotiations in the Shadow of Violence* (Martinus Nijhoff Publishers, Leiden, 2008)

Lieberfeld, Daniel, *Talking with the Enemy: Negotiation and Threat Perception in South Africa and Israel/Palestine* (Greenwood Publishing Group, Westport, 1999)

Mnookin, Robert, *Bargaining with the Devil: When to Negotiate, When to Fight* (Simon & Schuster, New York, 2010)

Perry, Mark, *Talking to Terrorists: Why America Must Engage with its Enemies* (Basic Books, New York, 2010)

Pinder, David, 'Supping with the Devil', in Guy Olivier Faure and I. William Zartman (eds), *Negotiating with Terrorists: Strategy, Tactics, and Politics* (Routledge, Abingdon, 2011)

Quinney, Nigel and A. Heather Coyne, *Talking to Groups that Use Terror* (United States Institute of Peace, Washington DC, 2011)

Reiss, Mitchell, *Negotiating with Evil: When to Talk to Terrorists* (Open Road Integrated Media, New York, 2010)

Articles

Byman, Daniel (2006), 'The Decision to Begin Talks with Terrorists: Lessons for Policymakers', *Studies in Conflict & Terrorism*, Vol. 29, No. 5, pp. 403–14

Cronin, Audrey Kurth, *When Should We Talk to Terrorists?*, Special Report 240 (United States Institute of Peace, Washington DC, 2007)

Duyvesteyn, Isabelle and Bart Schuurman (2011), 'The Paradoxes of Negotiating with Terrorist and Insurgent Organisations', *Journal of Imperial and Commonwealth History*, Vol. 39, No. 4, pp. 677–92

Duyvesteyn, Isabelle and Bart Schuurman (2012), 'Beware of High Hopes: Counterterrorism and the Negotiation Paradox', *ICCT Commentaries*, 15 November 2012, http://www.icct.nl/publications/icct–commentaries/ beware-of-high-hopes-counterterrorism-and-the-negotiation-paradox

Faure, Guy Olivier (2008), 'Negotiating with Terrorists: A Discrete Form of Diplomacy', *Hague Journal of Diplomacy*, Vol. 3, pp. 179–200

Faure, Guy Olivier and I. William Zartman, *Negotiating with Terrorists: A Mediator's Guide*, IIASA Policy Brief, No. 6 (International Institute for Applied Systems Analysis, Laxenburg, 2009)

Merari, Ariel (1993), 'Terrorism as a Strategy of Insurgency', *Terrorism and Political Violence*, Vol. 5, No. 4, pp. 213–51

Miller, Carl (2011), 'Is it Possible and Preferable to Negotiate with Terrorists?', *Defence Studies*, Vol. 11, No. 1, pp. 145–85

Neumann, Peter (2007), 'Negotiating with Terrorists', *Foreign Affairs*, Vol. 86, No. 1, pp. 128–38

Pettyjohn, Stacie L. (2009), 'Engagement: A Path to Disarmament or Disaster?', *International Negotiation*, Vol. 14, No. 1, pp. 41–69

Pruitt, Dean G. (2006), 'Negotiation with Terrorists', *International Negotiation*, Vol. 11, No. 2, pp. 371–94

Spector, Bertram I. (2003), 'Negotiating with Villains Revisited: Research Note', *International Negotiation*, Vol. 8, pp. 613–21

Wanis-St John, Anthony (2006), 'Backchannel Negotiation: International Bargaining in the Shadows', *Negotiation Journal*, Vol. 22, pp. 119–44

Wheeler, Michael (2013), 'The Fog of Negotiation: What Negotiators Can Learn from Military Doctrine', *Negotiation Journal*, Vol. 29, No. 1, pp. 23–38

Zartman, I. William (2003), 'Negotiating with Terrorists', *International Negotiation*, Vol. 8, pp. 443–50

News

Arquilla, John (2013), 'Getting to Yes with the Taliban', *Foreign Policy*, http://www.foreignpolicy.com/articles/2013/05/20/getting_to_yes_with_the_taliban

Atran, Scott and Robert Axelrod, 'Why We Talk to Terrorists', *New York Times*, 29 June 2010, http://www.nytimes.com/2010/06/30/opinion/30atran.html?ref=opinion

Cambanis, Thanassis, 'Talk to Terrorists', *Boston Globe*, 12 December 2010, http://www.boston.com/bostonglobe/ideas/articles/2010/12/12/talk_to_terrorists/?page='full

'Egeland urges Negotiation, also with Terrorists', *AftenPosten*, 14 September 2007, http://www.freerepublic.com/focus/f-news/1896975/posts

'Interview with Peace Negotiator Erik Solheim', *SpiegelOnline*, 25 May 2009, http://www.spiegel.de/international/world/interview-with-peace-negotiator-erik-solheim-sri-lanka-s-government-must-show-it-can-also-win-the-peace-a-626735.html

'This House Believes it is Time to Talk to Al Qaeda', *Doha Debates*, 5 September 2007, http://www.dohadebates.com/debates/item/?d=8&mode=transcript

'UK Dismisses Al-Qaeda Talks Call', BBC, 15 March 2008, http://news.bbc.co.uk/1/hi/uk_politics/7297896.stm

'"We Should Have Talked to Taliban" Says Top British Officer in Afghanistan', *Guardian*, 28 June 2013, http://www.theguardian.com/world/2013/jun/28/talks-taliban-british-officer-afghanistan

4. Mediation

Brahimi, Lakhdar and Salman Ahmed, *In Pursuit of Sustainable Peace: The Seven Deadly Sins of Mediation* (Center on International Cooperation, New York University, New York, 2008)

Crocker, Chester A., Fen Osler Hampson and Pamela R. Aall (eds), *Herding Cats: Multiparty Mediation in a Complex World* (United States Institute of Peace, Washington DC, 2001; original edition 1999)

Crocker, Chester A., Fen Osler Hampson and Pamela R. Aall, *Taming Intractable Conflicts: Mediation in the Hardest Cases* (United States Institute of Peace, Washington DC, 2004)

Greenberg, Melanie C., John H. Barton and Margaret E. McGuiness, *Words Over War: Mediation and Arbitration to Prevent Deadly Conflict* (Rowman & Littlefield, Lanham, 2000)

Articles

Berghof Peace Support and Conciliation Resources (2011), *Mediating Peace with Proscribed Armed Groups, A Policy Workshop Report on the Implications of European Union (EU) Counter-Terrorism Legislation for Mediation and Support for Peace Processes*, http://www.berghof-peacesupport.org/publications/RLM_Mediating_Peace_with_Proscribed_Armed_Groups.pdf

Curran, Daniel, James K. Sebenius and Michael Watkins (2004), 'Two Paths to Peace: Contrasting George Mitchell in Northern Ireland with Richard Holbrooke in Bosnia-Herzegovina', *Negotiation Journal*, Vol. 20, No. 4, pp. 513-37

Greig, J. Michael (2005), 'Stepping Into the Fray: When Do Mediators Mediate?', *American Journal of Political Science*, Vol. 49, No. 2, pp. 249-66

Isoaho, Eemeli and Suvi Tuuli, *From Pre-Talks to Implementation: Lessons Learned from Mediation Processes* (Crisis Management Initiative, Helsinki, 2013)

Whitfield, Teresa, *Engaging with Armed Groups: Dilemmas & Options for Mediators, Mediation Practice Series* (Centre for Humanitarian Dialogue, Geneva, 2010)

5. Backchannel talks

Articles

Babbitt, Eileen F. (2013), 'The Price of Secrecy: A Journey through Negotiation's Backchannels', *Negotiation Journal*, Vol. 29, pp. 93-8

Browne, Julie and Eric S. Dickson (2010), '"We Don't Talk to Terrorists": On the Rhetoric and Practice of Secret Negotiations', *Journal of Conflict Resolution*, Vol. 54, No. 3, pp. 379-407

Cowper-Coles, Freddie (2012), 'Anxious for Peace: The Provisional IRA in dialogue with the British Government, 1972–75', *Irish Studies Review*

Pruitt, Dean G. (2008), 'Backchannel Communication in the Settlement of Conflict', *International Negotiation*, Vol. 13, pp. 37–54

6. Diplomacy

Berridge, G. R., Maurice Keens-Soper and T. G. Otte, *Diplomatic Theory from Machiavelli to Kissinger* (Palgrave Macmillan, New York, 2001)

Cooper, Robert, *The Breaking of Nations: Order and Chaos in the Twenty-first Century* (Atlantic Monthly Press, New York, 2003)

du Plessis, Armand Jean (Cardinal Richelieu), *The Political Testament of Cardinal Richelieu: The Significant Chapters and Supporting Selections* (University of Wisconsin Press, Madison, 1961)

Kissinger, Henry, *White House Years, Vol. 1* (Little, Brown, Boston, 1979)

Kissinger, Henry, *Diplomacy* (Simon & Schuster, New York, 1994)

Renwick, Robin, *A Journey with Margaret Thatcher: Foreign Policy Under the Iron Lady* (Biteback Publishing, London, 2013)

Tenet, George, with Bill Harlow, *At the Center of the Storm: My Years at the CIA* (HarperCollins, New York, 2007)

7. Peace versus justice

May, Larry, *After War Ends: A Philosophical Perspective* (Cambridge University Press, Cambridge, 2012)

News

Bensouda, Fatou, 'International Justice and Diplomacy', *New York Times*, 19 March 2013, http://www.nytimes.com/2013/03/20/opinion/global/the-role-of-the-icc-in-international-justice-and-diplomacy.html?ref=internationalcriminalcourt

Godobo-Madikizela, Pumla, 'Towards an Anatomy of Violence', *Mail & Guardian*, 15 January 2010, http://mg.co.za/article/2010-01-15-towards-an-anatomy-of-violence

'Uganda: when international justice and internal peace are at odds', *Christian Science Monitor*, 24 August 2006, http://www.csmonitor.com/2006/0824/p09s01-coop.html

8. Conflict

Boot, Max, *Invisible Armies: An Epic History of Guerrilla Warfare from Ancient Times to the Present* (Liveright Publishing Corporation, New York, 2013)

Callwell, Colonel C. E., *Small Wars: Their Principles and Practice* (University of Nebraska Press, Lincoln, 1996; originally published 1896)

Clausewitz, Carl von, *On War* (Princeton University Press, Princeton, 1976; originally published 1832)

Kilcullen, David, *The Accidental Guerrilla: Fighting Small Wars in the Midst of a Big One* (Oxford University Press, Oxford, 2009)

Kilcullen, David, *Out of the Mountains: The Coming Age of the Urban Guerilla* (Hurst, London, 2013)

Smith, Rupert, *The Utility of Force: The Art of War in the Modern World* (Penguin, London, 2012; originally published 2005)

Van Creveld, Martin, *The Transformation of War* (The Free Press, New York, 1991)

Articles

Kilcullen, David (2005), 'Countering Global Insurgency', *Journal of Strategic Studies*, Vol. 28, No. 4, pp. 597–617

MacMillan, Margaret, 'The Great War's Ominous Echoes', *New York Times*, 13 December 2013, http://www.nytimes.com/2013/12/14/opinion/macmillan-the-great-wars-ominous-echoes.html?_r=0

Petraeus, David H. (2013), 'Reflections on the Counter-Insurgency Era', *RUSI Journal*, Vol. 158, No. 4, pp. 82–7

9. Fiction

Conrad, Joseph, *The Secret Agent* (Penguin Classics, New York, 2007; originally published 1907)

Ledgard, J. M., *Submergence* (Vintage Books, London, 2012)

Soans, Robin, *Talking to Terrorists* (Oberon Books, London, 2005)

Modern case studies

1. Basque conflict

Clark, Robert, *Negotiating with ETA: Obstacles to Peace in the Basque Country, 1975–1988* (University of Nevada Press, Reno, 1990)

Eguiguren, Jesús and Luis Rodríguez Aizpeolea, *ETA – Las Claves de la Paz: Confesiones del Negociador* (Aguillar, Madrid, 2011)

Munarriz, Fermín, *El Tiempo de las Luces: Entrevista con Arnaldo Otegi* (Baigorri Argitaletxe, S.A. Bilbao, 2012)

Whitfield, Teresa, *Endgame for ETA: Elusive Peace in the Basque Country* (Hurst, London, 2014)

Articles

Douglas, William A., 'The Unknown Mediator in the Basque Peace Process of 2006', argia.com, 22 November 2009

2. Colombia

Bouvier, Virginia (ed.), *Colombia: Building Peace in a Time of War* (USIP, Washington DC, 2009)

Dudley, Steve, *Walking Ghosts, Murder and Guerrilla Politics in Colombia* (Routledge, London, 2006)

Kline, Harvey, *Chronicles of a Failure Foretold: The Peace Process of Colombian President Andrés Pastrana* (The University of Alabama Press, Tuscaloosa, 2007)

Pardo, Rafael, *De Primera Mano Colombia 1986–1994: Entre Conflictos y Esperanzas* (Cerec, Bogotá, 1996)

Pizarro, Eduardo, *Las Farc (1949–2011): de Guerrilla Campesina a Máquina de Guerra* (Norma, Bogotá, 2011)

Articles

Conciliation Resources, *Alternatives to War: Colombia's Peace Process*, Accord 14 (Conciliation Resources, London, 2004)

News

'Digging in for peace', *The Economist*, 1 June 2013

3. El Salvador

Álvarez, Martín, *From Revolutionary War to Democratic Revolution* (Berlin, Berghof Conflict Research, 2010)

De Soto, Alvaro, 'Ending Violent Conflict in El Salvador', in Chester A. Crocker, Fen Osler Hampson and Pamela R. Aall (eds), *Herding Cats: Multiparty Mediation in a Complex World* (United States Institute of Peace, Washington DC, 2001; original edition 1999)

Samayoa, Salvador, *El Salvador: La Reforma Pactada* (UCA, San Salvador, 2002)

Villalobos, Joaquín, *Sin Vencedores ni Vencidos* (Instituto para un Nuevo El Salvador, San Salvador, 2000)

4. Indonesia (Aceh)

Aspinall, Edward, *The Helsinki Agreement: A More Promising Basis for Peace in Aceh?*, Policy Studies, No. 20 (East-West Center, Washington DC, 2005)

Articles

Aspinall, Edward and Harold Couch, *The Aceh Peace Process: Why it Failed* (East-West Center, Washington DC, 2003)

Conciliation Resources, *Reconfiguring Politics: The Indonesia–Aceh Peace Process*, Accord 20 (Conciliation Resources, London, 2008)

Huber, Konrad, *The HDC in Aceh: Promises and Pitfalls of NGO Mediation and Implementation* (East-West Center, Washington DC, 2004)

Morfit, Michael (2007), 'The Road to Helsinki: The Aceh Agreement and

Indonesia's Democratic Development', *International Negotiation*, Vol. 12, pp. 111–43

Schulze, Kirsten E. (2007), 'From the Battlefield to the Negotiating Table: GAM and the Indonesian Government 1999–2005', *Asian Security*, Vol. 3, No. 2, pp. 80–98

Sebenius, James K. and Alex Green (2010), 'Everything or Nothing: Martti Ahtisaari and the Aceh Negotiations (A)', Harvard Business School, http://hbr.org/product/Everything-or-Nothing-Ma/an/911040–PDF–ENG

5. Israel / Palestine

Agha, Hussein, Shai Feldman, Ahmad Khalidi and Zeev Schiff, *Track-II Diplomacy: Lessons from the Middle East* (MIT Press, Cambridge MA, 2003)

Baskin, Gershon, *The Negotiator: Freeing Gilad Schalit from Hamas* (The Toby Press, London, 2013)

Egeland, Jan, 'The Oslo Accord: Multiparty Facilitation through the Norwegian Channel', in Chester A. Crocker, Fen Osler Hampson and Pamela R. Aall (eds), *Herding Cats: Multiparty Mediation in a Complex World* (United States Institute of Peace, Washington DC, 2001; original edition 1999)

Heikal, Mohamed, *Secret Channels: The Inside Story of the Arab–Israeli Peace Negotiations* (HarperCollins, New York, 1997)

Jones, Deiniol, *Cosmopolitan Mediation? Conflict Resolution and the Oslo Accords* (Manchester University Press, Manchester, 1999)

Klieman, Aharon, *Compromising Palestine: A Guide to Final Status Negotiations* (Columbia University Press, New York, 2000)

Kurtzer, Daniel, *Pathways to Peace: America and the Arab–Israeli Conflict* (Palgrave Macmillan, New York, 2012)

Qurie, Ahmed, *From Oslo to Jerusalem: The Palestinian Story of the Secret Negotiations* (I. B. Tauris & Co. Ltd, London, 2006)

Savir, Uri, *The Process: 1,100 Days That Changed the Middle East* (Vintage Books, New York, 1998)

Waage, Hilde Henriksen, *'Peacemaking Is a Risky Business': Norway's Role in the Peace Process in the Middle East, 1993–1996* (International Peace Research Institute, Oslo, 2004)

Articles

Lieberfeld, Daniel (2008), 'Secrecy and "Two-Level Games" in the Oslo Accord: What the Primary Sources Tell Us', *International Negotiation*, Vol. 13, pp. 133–46

Shlaim, Avi, 'Chapter 11: The Rise and Fall of the Oslo Peace Process', in Louise Fawcett (ed.), *International Relations of the Middle East* (Oxford University Press, Oxford, 2005)

News

Ahren, Raphael, 'No regrets, many laments, from the architect of Oslo', *Times of Israel*, 15 September 2013, http://www.timesofisrael.com/no-regrets-many-laments-from-the-architect-of-oslo/

Dromi, Uri, 'Remembering Oslo', *International Herald Tribune*, 13 September 2013

'Talks Begin on Mideast, to Doubts on All Sides', *New York Times*, 29 July 2013, http://www.nytimes.com/2013/07/30/world/middleeast/kerry-appoints-veteran-diplomat-to-manage-mideast-talks.html?pagewanted=1&_r=0&smid=tw-share

6. Mozambique / Angola

Ajello, Aldo, 'Mozambique: Implemention of the 1992 Peace Agreement', in Chester A. Crocker, Fen Osler Hampson and Pamela R. Aall (eds), *Herding Cats: Multiparty Mediation in a Complex World* (United States Institute of Peace, Washington DC, 2001; original edition 1999)

Anstee, Margaret J., 'The United Nations in Angola: Post-Bicesse Implementation', in ibid.

Bartoli, Andrea, 'Mediating Peace in Mozambique', in ibid.

Bartoli, Andrea, 'Learning from the Mozambique Peace Process: The Role of the Community of Sant'Egidio', in Ronald J. Fisher (ed.), *Paving the Way: Contributions of Interactive Conflict Resolution to Peacemaking* (Lexington Books, Lanham, 2005)

Hume, Cameron R., *Ending Mozambique's War: The Role of Mediation and Good Offices* (United States Institute of Peace, Washington DC, 1994)

Morozzo della Rocco, Roberto, *Mozambique: Achieving Peace in Africa* (Georgetown University, Washington DC, 2003)

Van den Bergh, Lucia, *Why Peace Worked: Mozambicans Look Back* (Association of European Parliamentarians with Africa, Amsterdam, 2009)

Articles

Conciliation Resources, *The Mozambican Peace Process in Perspective*, Accord 3 (Conciliation Resources, London, 1998)

Messiant, Christine, *Why did Bicesse and Lusaka Fail? A Critical Analysis*, Accord 15 (Conciliation Resources, London, 2004)

7. Nepal

Ogura, Kiyoko, *Seeking State Power: The Communist Party of Nepal (Maoist)* (Berghof Series, Berlin, 2008)

Whitfield, Teresa, *Masala Peacemaking: Nepal's Peace Process and the Contribution of Outsiders* (Conflict Prevention and Peace Forum, Center on International Cooperation, New York University, New York, 2008)

8. Northern Ireland

Cochrane, Feargal, *Northern Ireland: The Reluctant Peace* (Yale University Press, New Haven, 2013)

Articles

Dixon, Paul (2011), 'Guns First, Talks Later: Neoconservatives and the Northern Ireland Peace Process', *Journal of Imperial and Commonwealth History*, Vol. 39, No. 4, pp. 649–76

Other

Final Report of the Independent International Commission on Decommissioning (The Stationery Office, London, 2011)

Twenty-sixth and Final Report of the Independent Monitoring Commission (The Stationery Office, London, 2011)

9. Peru

Gorriti, Gustavo, *The Shining Path: A History of the Millenarian War in Peru* (University of North Carolina Press, Chapel Hill, 1999)

10. South Africa

Crocker, Chester A., *High Noon in Southern Africa: Making Peace in a Rough Neighborhood* (W. W. Norton & Co., London, 1993)

de Klerk, F. W., *The Last Trek: A New Beginning* (Pan Macmillan, London, 2000)

Esterhuyse, Willie, *Endgame: Secret Talks and the End of Apartheid* (Tafelberg, Cape Town, 2012)

Haysom, Nicholas 'Fink', *Forty-one Lessons for the South African Negotiators* (University of Cape Town, Cape Town, 2002)

Heald, Geoffrey, 'Learning Amongst Enemies: A Phenomenological Study of the South African Constitutional Negotiations from 1985–1998' (PhD thesis, University of Witwatersrand, Johannesburg, 2006)

Lieberfeld, Daniel, 'Contributions of a Semi-Official Pre-Negotiation Initiative: Afrikaner–ANC meetings in England, 1987–1990', in Ronald J. Fisher (ed.), *Paving the Way: Contributions of Interactive Conflict Resolution to Peacemaking* (Lexington Books, Lanham, 2005)

Mandela, Nelson, *Long Walk to Freedom* (Abacus, London, 1995; originally published 1994)

Renwick, Robin, *Unconventional Diplomacy in Southern Africa* (Palgrave Macmillan, London, 1997)

Sampson, Anthony, *Mandela: The Authorised Biography* (HarperCollins, London, 1999)

Sparks, Allister, *Tomorrow is Another Country: The Inside Story of South Africa's Road to Change* (University of Chicago Press, Chicago, 1996)

Articles

Interview of Dr Niel Barnard by John Carlin for *Frontline*, PBS, 2012

Lieberfeld, Daniel (2002), 'Evaluating the Contributions of Track-Two Diplomacy to Conflict in South Africa, 1984–90', *Journal of Peace Research*, Vol. 39, pp. 355–72

The Reunion: Nelson Mandela's Release, BBC Radio Four, 2009

Young, Michael (2010), 'Alumnus Michael Young and his Role in Ending Apartheid', *University of York Alumni Magazine*, pp. 16–22

News

'Interview: Anthony Sampson', PBS, http://www.pbs.org/wgbh/pages/frontline/shows/mandela/interviews/sampson.html

'Interview: Dr Neil [*sic*] Barnard', PBS, http://www.pbs.org/wgbh/pages/frontline/shows/mandela/interviews/barnard.html

'Interview: Jack Swart', PBS, http://www.pbs.org/wgbh/pages/frontline/shows/mandela/prison/swart.html

'Mandela and Botha: The Crocodile & the Saint', *Independent*, 2 November 2006

11. Sri Lanka

Höglund, Christine and Isak Svensson, *Mediating between Tigers and Lions: Norwegian peace diplomacy in Sri Lanka's civil war* (Informal Perspectives, 2008)

Moorcraft, Paul, *Total Destruction of the Tamil Tigers* (Pen and Sword Books, Barnsley, 2012)

Sørbø, Gunnar, Jonathan Goodhand, Bart Klem, Ada Elisabeth Nissen and Hilde Selbervik, *Pawns of Peace: Evaluation of Norwegian Peace Efforts in Sri Lanka, 1997–2009*, Report 5/2011 – Evaluation (Norad, Oslo, 2011)

Weiss, Gordon, *The Cage: The Fight for Sri Lanka and the Last Days of the Tamil Tigers* (Bodley Head, London, 2011)

Articles

Bullion, Alan (2001), 'Norway and the Peace Process in Sri Lanka', *Civil Wars*, Vol. 4, No. 3, pp. 70–92

Conciliation Resources, *Demanding Sacrifice: War and Negotiation in Sri Lanka*, Accord 4 (Conciliation Resources, London, 1998)

'Sri Lankan Rebel Leader also Served as a Cult Figure', *New York Times*, 18 May 2009, http://www.nytimes.com/2009/05/19/world/asia/19tamil.html?ref=velupillaiprabhakaran&_r=0

News

'Prabhakaran: The Life and Death of a Tiger', *Time*, 19 May 2009, http://content.time.com/time/world/article/0,8599,1899590,00.html

Colonial and older history

French, David, *The British Way in Counter-Insurgency 1945–1967* (Oxford University Press, Oxford, 2011)

Hastings, Stephen, *Drums of Memory* (Pen & Sword Books Ltd, Barnsley, 2001; originally published 1994)

MacMillan, Margaret, *Peacemakers: Six Months that Changed the World* (John Murray, London, 2001)

Newsinger, John, *British Counterinsurgency: From Palestine to Northern Ireland* (Palgrave Macmillan, London, 2002)

Walton, Calder, *Empire of Secrets: British Intelligence, the Cold War and Twilight of Empire* (HarperPress, London, 2013)

Articles

Hack, Karl (2011), 'Between Terror and Talking, the Place of "Negotiation" in Colonial Conflict', *Journal of Imperial and Commonwealth History*, Vol. 39, No. 4, pp. 539–49

News

'Sir Richard Catling', obituary, *Daily Telegraph*, 5 April 2005, http://www.telegraph.co.uk/news/obituaries/1487117/Sir-Richard-Catling.html

1. Algeria

Horne, Alistair, *A Savage War of Peace: Algeria 1954–1962* (New York Review Books, New York, 2006; originally published 1977)

Long, Olivier, *Le Dossier Secret des Accords d'Evian: Une Mission Suisse pour la Paix en Algérie* (Éditions 24 Heures, Lausanne, 1988)

Ruedy, John D., *Modern Algeria: The Origins and Development of a Nation* (Indiana University Press, Bloomington, 2005)

News

Kaufman, Michael T., 'Jacques Massu, 94, General Who Led Battle of Algiers', *New York Times*, 31 October 2002, http://www.nytimes.com/2002/10/31/world/jacques-massu-general-who-led-battle-of-algiers.html

2. Anarchists

Ulam, Adam, *In the Name of the People: Prophets and Conspirators in Prerevolutionary Russia* (Viking Press, New York, 1977)

Articles

Aydinli, Ersel (2008), 'Before Jihadists There Were Anarchists: A Failed Case of Transnational Violence', *Studies in Conflict & Terrorism*, Vol. 31, No. 10, pp. 903–23

Jensen, Richard Bach (2004), 'Daggers, Rifles and Dynamite: Anarchist Terrorism in Nineteenth-Century Europe', *Terrorism and Political Violence*, Vol. 16, No. 1, pp. 116–53

Jensen, Richard Bach (2008), 'Nineteenth-Century Anarchist Terrorism: How Comparable to the Terrorism of al-Qaeda?', *Terrorism and Political Violence*, Vol. 20, No. 4, pp. 589–96

Jensen, Richard Bach (2009), 'The International Campaign Against Anarchist Terrorism, 1880–1930s', *Terrorism and Political Violence*, Vol. 21, No. 1, pp. 89–109

3. Cyprus

Holland, Robert, *Britain and the Revolt in Cyprus, 1954–59* (Oxford University Press, Oxford, 1998)

Articles

Robbins, Simon (2012), 'The British Counter-Insurgency in Cypus', *Small Wars and Insurgencies*, Vol. 23, Nos. 4–5, pp. 720–43

4. Ireland

Bew, Paul, *Ireland: The Politics of Enmity 1789–2006* (Oxford University Press, Oxford, 2007)

Fanning, Ronan, *Fatal Path: British Government and Irish Revolution* (Faber & Faber, London, 2013)

Hattersley, Roy, *David Lloyd George: The Great Outsider* (Little, Brown, London, 2010)

Hopkinson, Michael, *Green Against Green: The Irish Civil War* (Gill & Macmillan, Dublin, 1998)

Hopkinson, Michael, *The Irish War of Independence* (McGill-Queen's University Press, Montreal, 2012)

Mansergh, Nicholas, *The Unresolved Question: The Anglo–Irish Settlement and its Undoing, 1912–72* (Yale University Press, New Haven, 1991)

McMahon, Paul, *British Spies and Irish Rebels: British Intelligence and Ireland, 1916–1945* (Boydell Press, Woodbridge, 2008)

Smith, Jeremy, *Britain and Ireland: From Home Rule to Independence* (Routledge, Abingdon, 1999)

Sturgis, Mark, *The Last Days of Dublin Castle: The Mark Sturgis Diaries* (Irish Academic Press, Dublin, 1999)

Other

Moylett, Patrick, 'Statement by Witness', Bureau of Military History, 1913–1921, Document No. W.S. 767

5. Israel / Palestine

Bowyer Bell, John, *Terror Out of Zion: The Fight for Israeli Independence* (Academy Press, Dublin, 1977)

Miller, Rory (ed.), *Britain, Palestine and Empire: The Mandate Years* (Ashgate, Aldershot, 2010)

Articles

Charters, David (2007), 'Jewish Terrorism and the Modern Middle East', *Journal of Conflict Studies*, Vol. 27, No. 2, pp. 80–9

6. *Kenya*

Anderson, David, *Histories of the Hanged: The Dirty War in Kenya and the End of Empire* (W. W. Norton & Co., New York, 2005)

Kyle, Keith, *The Politics of the Independence of Kenya* (St Martin's Press, London, 1999)

Articles

Porter, Bernard, 'How Did They Get Away With It?', *London Review of Books*, 3 March 2005

Miscellaneous

Lustig, Joshua, 'Second Glance: Halberstam's Vietnam and The Anxiety of Power', *Open Letters Monthly*, http://www.openlettersmonthly.com/second-glance-halberstams-vietnam-and-the-anxiety-of-power/

Manningham-Buller, Eliza (2011), *The Reith Lectures*, BBC, http://www.bbc.co.uk/programmes/b0126d29

Index